Work and Motivation

Work
and
Motivation

Victor H. Vroom

Jossey-Bass Publishers • San Francisco

Originally published in 1964 by John Wiley & Sons, Inc.

Substantial discounts on bulk quantities of Jossey-Bass books are available to corporations, professional associations, and other organizations. For details and discount information, contact the special sales department at Jossey-Bass Inc., Publishers. (415) 433-1740; Fax (415) 433-0499.

For international orders, please contact your local Paramount Publishing International office.

Library of Congress Cataloging-in-Publication Data

Vroom, Victor Harold, date.
  Work and motivation / Victor H. Vroom.
    p.   cm.—(The Jossey-Bass management series)
  Originally published: New York : Wiley, 1964.
  Includes bibliographical references and index.
  ISBN 0-7879-0030-3
  1. Psychology, Industrial.   2. Work—Psychological aspects.
I. Title.   II. Series.
HF5548.8.V7   1995
158.7—dc20   94-28028
                                                           CIP

FIRST EDITION
HB Printing   10 9 8 7 6 5 4 3 2 1   *Code 94111*

The Jossey-Bass
Management Series

Contents

Part Four: Performance in Work Roles

Part Five: Conclusion

Introduction to the Classic Edition

I was delighted when Jossey-Bass expressed interest in including my book, *Work and Motivation,* in its Classics Series, in part because its publication in this forum would keep it alive and available to scholars interested in organizational behavior. A more important reason for my enthusiasm was that its publication would allow me to write a new introduction commenting on my prior work, saying some things that I wish I had been wise enough to say when it was first published.

In 1964 *Work and Motivation* was an ambitious attempt to develop a theoretical structure that could guide and be guided by empirical research in industrial and organizational psychology. Although the particular form of the theory was not novel in other fields of psychology, its juxtaposition with the empirical findings in job performance, work satisfaction, and occupational choice was unique.

This preface will have two parts. In the first part I will put the book in context, elaborating on the historical and personal circumstances under which it was written. I will talk about some ideas that I could have expressed in 1964 but did not. The reasons for these omissions are complex, probably including both life-cycle issues and changes in the norms of implementing and reporting science. To a newly minted Ph.D. writing three decades ago, personal pronouns and personal meanings had no place. Science was objective and factual, expressing the personal dispositions of the scientist only in the choice of problem and methodology.

Times have changed, particularly in the social sciences. Our disciplines have become more reflective and more personal. We have acknowledged how much our theories and explanations reflect processes that go on inside ourselves. Today students of organizational behavior can learn much more about the personal engagement of researchers "doing science" than was possible thirty years ago. Although I have little data supporting it, I share the view advanced by Dan Levinson that self-reflection increases with one's stage of adult development.

In the second part of this preface I will elaborate on the ideas in the book. I will describe how, with the benefit of hindsight, I view the book's core ideas and how I would formulate them if I were to rewrite the book today. I will not undertake to update the review of the literature in the original work. That has been done very well by others, notably Kanfer (1990). Instead, I will focus on expectancy theory—the theoretical orientation of *Work and Motivation*— which represented the key ingredient that distinguished this work from what had gone before. If the book has a legacy, it resides in the concepts of valence, expectancy, and instrumentality, and the demonstration of their potential for organizing and guiding empirical research on the relationship between people and their work.

On the Origins of Work and Motivation

Jeff Pfeffer (1993) has recently lamented the low level of paradigm development in organizational behavior research. He believes this to be reflected in the lack of consensus on research issues, research methods, and key concepts and processes. Pfeffer argues that the fragmentation of the field restricts its advancement and also relegates it to a lower status, with less claim on societal resources, than fields with greater paradigm development, such as economics, population ecology, and the rational choice model in political science.

Pfeffer's position has generated considerable controversy within the field (Perrow 1994). Reading his paper, I was struck by the similarity between his sentiments and my own prior to writing

Work and Motivation. I was, of course, grappling with the much narrower field of industrial and organizational psychology. But his arguments—that organizational behavior research has no paradigm and that this absence is limiting scientific advancement—were reminiscent of views I expressed in the original introduction to this book:

> Research in industrial psychology is still largely atheoretical, with little use being made of the concepts and models that are an integral part of current theories of motivation. . . . There would appear to be a pressing need for some kind of organization and integration of existing knowledge in the field of work and motivation. A critical and comprehensive examination of existing empirical evidence is required to show us where we now stand in our efforts to find principles and generalizations, and to indicate promising new avenues for research. (Vroom 1964, pp. 4–5).

This excerpt indicates where I believed the necessary paradigm could be found: in the parent discipline of psychology. A brief digression into my educational background might help the reader understand my desire for a paradigm and my belief that a suitable one could be found in the discipline of psychology.

The seeds of my yearning for core organizing concepts and processes were sown during my years as an undergraduate at McGill University, where I received a rigorous training in experimental psychology. One of my mentors, Donald Hebb, had just written *The Organization of Behavior* (1949), which examined the possibility of a science of behavior arising out of concepts of brain structure and function. I was fascinated by his ideas along with issues they raised for me about the philosophy of science. Logical positivism was my *ideology* rather than a convenient working assumption. The more abstract the psychological theory, the more it elicited my interest, and mathematical theories struck me as "by definition" of higher status than those stated only in words.

Upon graduation, I was committed to a career in psychology and I thought seriously about experimental psychology. However, the combination of my worldly interests and encouragement from Ed Webster, then a professor of industrial psychology, led me to pursue graduate work in that field at McGill.

Elsewhere (Vroom, 1993) I have detailed the culture shock that accompanied my transition to industrial psychology. Plunged into tests and measurements, techniques of job analysis, job evaluation, and personnel selection and placement, I could see no connection with my former training and no application of the concepts that I had so heartily embraced.

I recall vividly a graduate seminar taught by Ed Webster devoted to a then-recently published book by Morris Viteles, *Motivation and Morale in Industry* (Viteles, 1953). Although this volume reflected Viteles' characteristic dedication to hard facts rather than to organizing theory, the research it reported—the Tavistock studies and the early work of Michigan's Survey Research Center and Research Center for Group Dynamics—was exciting. Here was a body of research findings in industrial psychology that could potentially be explained in terms of a core set of constructs and processes.

In 1955 exciting Ph.D. programs were at Ohio State, where the program of leadership studies, under the direction of Carroll Shartle, was in full swing; the University of Illinois, where Ross Stagner was pursuing research on psychological issues in labor-management relations; and the University of Michigan, which was launching a new doctoral program in organizational psychology and which had active research programs at the Survey Research Center and the Research Center for Group Dynamics.

I decided on Michigan. While I was there, the basic ideas later incorporated into *Work and Motivation* began to take shape. Seminars with Helen Peak and Jack Atkinson gave me a grounding in the psychology of motivation. Jack French and Dorwin Cartwright exposed me to the thinking of Kurt Lewin and instilled in me a belief that theory and application could be mutually beneficial. And a close work association with Norman Maier helped me to see that experimental psychology and industrial psychology were not disjointed fields of inquiry.

My doctoral dissertation, "Some Personality Determinants of the Effects of Participation" (Vroom, 1959a, 1960), enabled me to follow my interest in the interaction of motivational dispositions (such as needs for independence and power equality) and one element of the work situation, the opportunity to participate in decision making. The interaction that I found gave tangible expression to the thoughts in a recently published article by Lee Cronbach entitled "The Two Disciplines of Psychology" (Cronbach, 1957). This classic paper served as much-needed social validation for my attempts to organize my knowledge of the field and also gave me a language for the disparate elements of my training. Atheoretical industrial psychology, to which I had been exposed at McGill, was largely R-R (response-response psychology). Experimental and social psychology were S-R (stimulus-response). According to Cronbach, neither was sufficient to explain behavior, but the integration of dispositional approaches and the search for situational effects was paramount to the development of the discipline.

In the final chapters of my dissertation, I mused about the concepts necessary to explain my results. The final formulation uses the notions of incentive, expectancy, instrumentality, and motive, combined in multiplicative ways to explain why different people may respond differently to the same set of working conditions. I remember thinking at the time that the concepts were general ones and might have greater predictive and explanatory value than merely accounting for my dissertation results.

After receiving my degree, I became study director at the Survey Research Center, where I had an opportunity to relate my emerging conceptual framework to the recent literature as I coauthored the chapter on industrial social psychology for the *Annual Review of Psychology* (Vroom and Maier, 1961).

Before leaving to accept an assistant professorship in the Department of Psychology at the University of Pennsylvania, I decided that my next venture would be a monograph outlining the further development of expectancy theory and exploring its application to our understanding of work satisfaction and work motivation. The move, of course, delayed the start of my work on the monograph. But by the end of my first year at Penn, I began the project with financial support from the Foundation for Research in Human Behavior and with a fellowship from the Ford Foundation. Although its basic objective—establishing a theoretical structure for the field—remained intact, the project increased in size and in scope and the monograph became a 300-page book. Large bodies of literature, such as occupational choice, could not be ignored in any effort to be systematic about motivation and work. Each reference led to new sources to follow up. My motivation was largely intrinsic. I cared less about whether the book would ever be published than about its completeness. At times it felt like a labor of love, at others like a neurotic compulsion.

In scholarly works it is common to acknowledge the support, encouragement, and intellectual contributions of one's colleagues. At the risk of being impolite I can honestly say that my colleagues at Penn played almost no role in the endeavor. The only industrial psychologist there, Morris Viteles, viewed theory with suspicion and exhorted the field to focus on the collection of facts. My other colleagues reminded me that writing a book was the province of those with tenure and that empirically based articles were a far safer course for an assistant professor on a three-year contract. Although they were not particularly helpful, I must admit that they turned out to be right! When my contract was up for renewal the manuscript was only in draft form and had not yet been submitted to a publisher or subjected to critical review. And while a reappointment as assistant professor was not eliminated, it was recommended that I pursue other options.

Fortunately other options were not lacking. The two most interesting were Yale and Carnegie Tech. Although I eventually chose Carnegie, future colleagues at both of these institutions—Chris Argyris at Yale and Bill Dill at Carnegie—gave me the first feedback on my book and much-needed encouragement that the work would significantly contribute to the field.

I put the finishing touches on the manuscript at Carnegie Tech, where I had accepted a position as associate professor. I sent it off to only one publisher—Wiley—whose psychology series I had long admired and whose editor, Gordon Ierardi, had become a legend in the field of psychology. The book was accepted, and many years later it was recognized by the Institute for Scientific Information as a "Citation Classic" because of the frequency with which it had been cited in scientific books and journals.

Reprise

In this section, I will revisit expectancy theory and its applications to work motivation. I am gratified at the attention that this theory has received and more gratified at the acceptance of the need for general theories to guide research in industrial and organizational psychology. These changes in the field are well documented in the recent *Handbook of Industrial and Organizational Psychology* (Dunnette and Hough, 1990). Chapters on motivation theory, learning theory, and judgment and decision-making theory make up a large part of the first volume. Each chapter makes extensive use of general psychological concepts and processes in an attempt to explain behavior in the workplace. Furthermore, the relevant bodies of theory are described with much greater rigor than in prior works, including the previous edition of the *Handbook* (Dunnette, 1976). No longer is work behavior explained by a different set of processes than behavior in other settings. Industrial and organizational psychology are now integrated into the discipline of psychology.

But what of the impact of expectancy theory? It has arguably become the dominant process theory of work motivation. The essential concepts were incorporated (with minor modifications) by Porter and Lawler (1968), Lawler (1973), and to a lesser degree, Naylor, Pritchard, and Ilgen (1980). Few students of industrial/organizational psychology have escaped the concepts of valence, instrumentality, and expectancy, often popularized as VIE theory.

Frequent citations to my work have been gratifying, but they have also been a mixed blessing. Many researchers have been less cognizant of the limitations of the theory than I was at the time I devised it. Several years after its initial publication, people began to send me, as a referee, manuscripts intended to "test" expectancy theory. Such tests usually multiplied questionnaire measures of expectancy, instrumentality and/or valence, summed over outcomes, and used these aggregates to predict choices, preferences, or work performance. In many cases these were statistical tests between subjects rather than of choices made within subjects, which were the focus of expectancy theory.

In retrospect I can see that I invited efforts to test the theory by the unnecessary formalization with which I presented it. To be sure, the tests were not altogether without merit. In general, the theory predicted job choices better than effort or job performance, and its predictions correlated more highly with actual effort when the more appropriate within-subjects designs were used (Kanfer, 1990).

My reservations about this line of research and my reluctance to jump into the fray stemmed from the fact that I had viewed the model as not testable without questionable assumptions about the content of motivation or the measurement and/or manipulation of the concepts. For me, the model had heuristic value. It provided a language for formulating questions and since that language was shared with behavioral theories of choice, it formed a bridge over which insights and research findings could flow in both directions. There were basic questions about how expectancies and valences were measured and about how they were formed and aroused as well as more context-driven questions about the interplay of such processes in work situations. I saw a synergy between basic and more applied research with the end result being a theory that would be not only sound but also useful.

Expectancy theory asserts that human choice is subjectively rational. People do not always make optimal decisions but they do make decisions that they believe to be optimal at the time they make them. In Chapter Two, which outlines the theory, I acknowledge the limits to the accuracy of this assumption and explicitly eliminate frustated behavior or behavior under the control of strong emotions. Since 1964 developments in cognitive psychology have shown more serious limitations to this kind of theory.

My colleague at Carnegie-Mellon, Herbert Simon, was the first to point out to me the unrealistic cognitive capabilities required by a strict application of expectancy theory. First, individual decision makers must consider all alternatives and be capable of evaluating each on every relevant dimension. The demands that such behavior would place on the human brain are inconsistent with what we have come to believe about how humans process information. People process data serially and at relatively slow speed. In many situations they cannot consider all alternatives or evaluate each on all dimensions. The implications of these cognitive limitations are undoubtedly greater for explaining people's choices among jobs, occupations, or careers than, let us say, among levels of effort in the performance of a given task. In the former the alternatives are almost infinite and are usually generated by search and evaluated sequentially. The task of evaluating every occupation on every relevant dimension is a life's work, precisely the kind of situation, Simon would argue, in which people are likely to "satisfice" rather than optimize. In contrast, levels of effort are finite and do not require search. The former may be likened to ordering a meal in a restaurant without a menu but with a chef with a limitless repertoire, the latter to ordering at the corner fast food restaurant.

It is now apparent that the level of processing of alternatives will vary not only with the complexity of the task but also with the affective state of the actor. Research on persuasive communication (Petty and Caccioppo, 1986; Chaiken, 1980) has identified two levels of information processing. They vary in the degree and care of consideration of alternatives. Systematic or central processing involves relatively detailed analysis and is more consistent with the tenets of expectancy theory. In contrast, heuristic or peripheral processing involves more casual and superficial evaluation of message content. There is evidence (Isen, 1987) that a situationally induced negative mood is more likely to produce systematic information processing.

Beyond the cognitive limits on rationality, further difficulties for the theory are the findings that have led to prospect theory (Kahneman, Slovic, and Tversky, 1982). Human choices are led astray by heuristics, biases, or the manner in which alternatives have been framed. As a result, people make decisions that are far from being normatively optimal.

In sum, events in the scientific community in the last three decades have not disabused me of the basic notion that much behavior can be usefully thought of as intentionally rational or goal directed. I would, however, be much more cautious in stating the theory formally as I did in 1964. The level of processing required by expectancy theory is rarely possible and would represent one extreme, found mainly on relatively simple choice problems where the alternatives are clear and information is readily available. At the other extreme would be behavior under the control of emotions or strong habits where actions are largely independent of goals and information. The theory would then have some of the properties of a contingency theory that attempts to specify the conditions affecting the level of processing of alternatives.

My revised expectancy theory would also devote more attention to the arousal of motives. To put it differently, complex issues surround the question of which goals are attended to at different times. In a recent doctoral dissertation at Yale, Hsee (1993) illustrates my point. His research addressed the question of when people's choices are dominated by monetary consequences as opposed to intrinsic affective properties. The dissertation reports an interesting set of experiments in which decision makers choose between jobs that are intrinsically satisfying but lower in pay or less satisfying but higher in pay. Hsee finds that the introduction of elasticity or uncertainty in either the monetary or the affective dimension results in a dramatic shift in choices in favor of the intrinsically satisfying job. His explanation is that people need to be able to justify their choices to themselves and others and that sacrificing monetary gains for goals that are nonmonetary but otherwise desirable is, in our culture, unjustifiable. However, if ambiguity is introduced into the choice (for example, by the assignment of a range of monetary gains rather than a specific amount) the decision maker is "freed" to do what he or she wants.

A contemporary expectancy theory must recognize that valence does not have the same properties as utility. We should not expect transitivity in choices (Behling and Starke, 1973). Valences of outcomes wax and wane and have corresponding effects on the instigation and cessation of behaviors that produce them. Lewin (1936) noted this property in his linking of valence to a state of tension. Cyert and March (1963) referred to this phenomenon as "sequential attention to goals" and Atkinson (1958b) distinguished between need strength (for example, for achievement and affiliation) and aroused motivation. Adding to expectancy theory, mechanisms to link the valence of outcomes to the immediate situation would enable such a theory to handle a range of phenomena including, but not restricted to, the behavioral consequences of goal setting (Latham and Locke, 1979).

If I were to reformulate VIE today, I would allow more room for what Deci and Ryan (1985) call intrinsic motivation in work performance. In the formula for instrumentality, I expressed the valence of an outcome, such as high performance, as dependent on one's beliefs about the consequences of the outcome for other outcomes (like higher pay or self-esteem) and the valence of these other outcomes. I toyed with distinguishing between means-ends processes that were internally regulated and those that were mediated by external agents. Eventually I decided that the distinction impaired the neatness of the formalization, so I chose not to draw attention to it.

Subsequent events have proven me wrong. The intrinsic/extrinsic distinction has been shown to be very useful, not only for research but also for application. Walton (1985) writes about the gradual evolution of organizational forms from systems of motivation based on extrinsic control to systems based on intrinsic commitment. Participation, job design, self-managing work teams, and the like have fundamentally different properties than incentive compensation and promotional systems. Effectiveness of the former depends on systems of internal control or self-regulation, while effectiveness of the latter depend on mechanisms of organizational control. Deci and Ryan have elaborated the concept of intrinsic motivation to include motives that relate not only to what they describe as growth needs and needs for self-esteem but also to internalized norms and codes of conduct.

In explaining differences in the effort that people give to their jobs, we have tended to emphasize situational effects and ignore individual differences. I believe that this omission introduces substantial inaccuracies, particularly in the prediction of intrinsic motivation. Differences in both actual and ideal self-concepts as well as internalized codes of conduct are likely to be associated with marked differences in the intrinsic sources of affect in the conduct of one's job. We have only limited understanding of such phenomena and our theories do not do them justice.

So far I have addressed only issues surrounding the content of expectancy theory and its modification to fit what is known today. I would like to turn now to the aspects of work motivation to which it has been and could be applied.

In the book I applied expectancy theory to three primary questions: (1) Why do people choose the careers they do (Chapter Four)? (2) What factors cause people to be satisfied with their work? (3) What factors cause people to work effectively? It is the last question—the motivation for effective work performance—that has attracted the greatest attention. This interest undoubtedly comes, at least in part, from the question's normative importance. Increased competition has caused organizations not only to downsize but also to extract the highest levels of productivity from those who remain.

In elaborating on the concept of motivation for effective performance, I focussed on the level of task-related effort to be measured by "amount of time worked, frequency of task-related responses per unit time, and amplitude of task-related responses" (p. 193). Consistent with this focus, those doing research on the performance implications of the model have used behavioral measures of effort. This research has been useful, but it is more appropriate to the world of physical labor than to knowledge work. Effort is normatively important among workers loading pig iron onto rail cars or oarsmen working on a rowing team but it is less appropriate for computer programmers, marketing managers, or university presidents. The latter are exhorted to work "smarter, not harder." In this era of empowerment, people at all levels in organizations are urged to become leaders, to *find* problems, not just solve those thrust at them, and to do the right thing rather than do things right. To use the language of Katz and Kahn (1966), the emphasis is changing from dependable role performance to innovative and spontaneous behavior that exceeds role requirements.

It is unfortunate that expectancy theory became fixated on the amount rather than the direction of effort. Such a practice restricts motivation for effective performance to a directionless behavior reminiscent of Hull's (1951) concept of drive, and it relegates all of the residual to a rather vague concept of ability. I believe the theory can do better than that if given a chance!

On the remaining questions to which expectancy theory has been applied, I have less to say. Job satisfaction and related job attitudes have declined in popularity as dependent variables. The reasons may include the lack of relationship between job satisfaction and job performance, and the realization that much of the knowledge concerning the correlates of job satisfaction has relied on self-reports of organizational conditions, which share the same sources of measurement error. In applying VIE theory to the prediction of job satisfaction, I equated that term with the valence of the job to its occupant. The components of the job—wages, promotional opportunities, work group, and supervisory characteristics—formed the instrumentalities of that job for particular outcomes that might have valence, either positive or negative, as a result of the particular needs or motives possessed by the person.

Although I organized the literature review in terms of situational properties, I contested (pp. 172-73) the usefulness of the concept of a satisfying work role and argued for the inclusion of individual differences. The research of Hackman and Oldham (1980), demonstrating interactions between specific job characteristics and the strength of growth needs, represents the approach that I was championing. Another line of research (Staw, Bell, and Clausen, 1986) has extended even further the role of individual differences. They have found that measures of affective dispositions from as early as adolescence can significantly predict job attitudes over a time span of nearly fifty years. Furthermore, affective dispositions have been shown (Staw and Barsade, 1993) to predict many aspects of managerial performance on simulated tasks. Such findings have reenergized work on the job satisfaction–job performance relationship and provide a healthy correction to the situationalism that I railed against in 1964. It remains to be seen how much variance in job satisfaction can be predicted from situational factors alone, dispositional factors alone, or predicted interactions between disposition and situation.

Very few efforts have been made to apply expectancy theory to career and occupational choice. Many of the reasons should be obvious from the prior discussion of the complexity of this particular decision process, including its serial nature. One's occupation or career is the result of a stream of decisions, each changing the alternatives available for consideration at later stages and providing information both about one's values and about their probability of attainment. Discrete phases of the process, such as the choice among alternative jobs, can be singled out for study as was done in the research by Hsee (1993), previously described, but the entire process would require a much more complex model.

To conclude this preface, let me add that revisiting one's intellectual products after a substantial passage of time is not an easy task, but it can be an instructive one for the author, if not for others. Shortly after the original publication of *Work and Motivation,* I ceased my own research on motivation and began a research program dealing with leadership (Vroom and Yetton, 1973; Vroom and Jago, 1988). Although the two topics are not unrelated and I have tried to keep in touch with major developments in the motivation literature, the task of writing this revised preface has given me a better opportunity and incentive to reflect on the work as a whole.

New Haven, Connecticut　　　　　　　　　　　　　Victor H. Vroom
September 1994

Preface

The basic plan for this book was evolved during the summer of 1959. At that time I was working on a chapter entitled "Industrial Social Psychology" for the *Annual Review of Psychology*. I was impressed by the large amount of research being conducted in the field, but I found the task of integrating that research and of identifying the progress made during the period of the review exceedingly difficult. In part, this difficulty was a result of the great differences among investigators in the phenomena they selected for study and the methods they used to study it. A more troublesome problem, however, was the apparent failure of many investigators to consider the possible theoretical implications of their research. Concepts tended to be highly specific and inadequately defined. There was little standardization of terminology and little consideration for the nature of the processes underlying empirical data.

It seemed to me that a critical integration and appraisal of existing knowledge might be of some value in identifying and promoting future advances. I decided to devote the summer of 1961 to undertaking this task with the thought that the end product might be a 150-page monograph.

At the outset, I made a number of decisions concerning the content and scope of the monograph. The first decision concerned the level of analysis to be employed. I resolved to restrict myself to problems of *individual* behavior. Although research on the behavior of groups and formal organizations was of interest to me, I doubted that meaningful generalizations would emerge that would "cut across" phenomena at different levels of analysis. Since I am a psychologist by training, a focus on the behavior of the single person seemed to be the most logical starting point.

The second decision served to restrict further the class of phenomena to be considered. The individual behaviors that I would deal with would be *work* behaviors, that is, behaviors that affect or are otherwise relevant to the work that people perform. This would include the phenomenon of occupational choice as well as job satisfaction and job performance.

The third decision was to focus on the *explanation* of individual behavior rather than its control. Instead of looking specifically at techniques for assisting individuals to make more rational occupational choices or for making workers happier or more effective, I decided to focus on the variables and processes that determined these phenomena.

The fourth decision was an assumption about the kinds of variables that would be useful in explaining these individual work behaviors. I assumed that much of the behavior could be usefully regarded as *motivated*. Actions on the part of individuals could, at least in part, be accounted for in terms of their preferences among outcomes and their expectations concerning the consequences of their actions for the attainment of these outcomes.

The fifth and final decision concerned the sources of data to be considered. I decided to restrict my examination to evidence based on *objective observation*. Discourses based on personal experience and "clinical" analyses of single cases would be passed over in favor of laboratory experiments, correlational field studies, or field experiments.

Work on the monograph proceeded more slowly than anticipated. The end of the summer of 1961 found the planned 150 pages written, but only a small fraction of the proposed content covered. A literature search unearthed a much greater volume of relevant work than was anticipated, and adequate treatment of this work required drastic alterations in both the length of the monograph and the time schedule for completing it.

During the next two years, the 150-page monograph grew into a 300-page book. In spite of this increase in size, some reduction had to be made in content. A few topics that were originally planned for inclusion were dropped, and discussions of many research investigations of lesser significance had to be eliminated.

The preparation of this book has been greatly aided by the financial assistance provided by several foundations. A grant from The Foundation for Research on Human Behavior enabled me to begin work during the summer of 1961. Further progress was made in the spring and summer of 1962 while the writer held a Ford Foundation Faculty Fellowship for Research in the Behavioral Sciences. Completion of the manuscript was made possible by a grant from the General Electric Foundation during the academic year 1962-63.

Writing a book of this scope proved to be a lengthy process, one which far exceeded my original expectations. It was, however, greatly facilitated by the enthusiastic support and cooperation of a number of persons. My debt to my students is a great one. Dr. Jerald Bachman, Dr. Harry Kaufmann, and Stephen Jones read and astutely criticized earlier drafts of the manuscript and contributed invaluable suggestions.

I am also grateful for the assistance of many colleagues and associates. Professors Chris Argyris of Yale University, L. Richard Hoffman of the University of Michigan, Donald Marquis of the Massachusetts Institute of Technology, Julius Wishner of the University of Pennsylvania, and William Dill of the Carnegie Institute of Technology read portions of the manuscript and suggested useful changes and additions.

A seminar devoted to the subject matter of the book, sponsored by the Foundation for Research on Human Behavior during the fall of 1962, permitted me to obtain the thoughtful reactions of members of the business community and contributed to clarification in my thinking and presentation. Use of portions of the first draft of the manuscript as a text in my undergraduate course in vocational psychology also uncovered many sources of ambiguity and provided the basis for valuable changes.

The following publishers and journals have graciously granted permission to quote from their publications: The American Psychological Association, The American Sociological Association, The Atherton Press, Basic Books, Inc., Charles Scribner's Sons,

George Allen and Unwin, HarperCollins, Harvard University Press, Her Majesty's Stationery Office, Holt, Rinehart and Winston, The Institute for Social Research, John Wiley and Sons, McGraw-Hill Book Company, The Macmillan Company, North-Holland Publishing Company, W. W. Norton and Company, Personnel Psychology Inc., Prentice-Hall, Inc., Princeton University Press, Psychological Services of Pittsburgh, The Psychoanalytic Quarterly, The Ronald Press Company, University of Chicago Press, Viking Penguin, and Williams and Wilkins Company.

Special mention must be made of the assistance of Robert McLean who aided in the preparation of the References and in many other ways.

Finally, I would like to acknowledge my gratitude to my wife, to whom this book is dedicated, for her help in making my ideas meaningful to others and for her understanding and support.

Pittsburgh, Pennsylvania   VICTOR H. VROOM
February 1964

The Author

VICTOR H. VROOM is John G. Searle Professor of organization and management at Yale University. He received his B.Sc. degree (1953) and his M.Ps.Sc. degree (1955) from McGill University and his Ph.D. degree (1958) in psychology from the University of Michigan.

Vroom's research has focused on motivation and leadership in organizations. He has received awards for his research from the American Psychological Association (APA), the McKinsey Foundation, and the Ford Foundation. He has consulted to many government agencies and to over one hundred major corporations in the United States and abroad. He has been elected to fellowships in the APA, the American Psychological Society, the Society for the Psychological Study of Social Issues, and the Academy of Management. Vroom is also past president of the Society for Industrial and Organizational Psychology.

Vroom is author of nine books and over fifty articles. His books include *Motivation in Management* (1971 [revised in 1992], with E. Deci), which sold over 100,000 copies; *Leadership and Decision Making* (1973, with P. Yetton), a seminal work in management scholarship; and *The New Leadership: Managing Participation in Organizations* (1988, with A. G. Jago).

Work and Motivation

Part One

Introduction

1

Introduction and
Historical Perspective

The relationship between man and his work has long attracted the attention of philosophers, scientists, and novelists. The interest of psychologists in this problem dates back to the early part of the twentieth century and is reflected in the emergence and development of such fields of specialization as industrial psychology and vocational guidance.

Much of the early work in these fields dealt with the measurement of aptitudes and abilities, and with the utilization of these measurements in improving the selection of occupations by persons and the selection of persons by organizations. This emphasis on improving the "fit" between the abilities of persons and the demands of their jobs made an important contribution to both organizational functioning and individual adjustment. It did not, however, shed much light on the basic processes affecting the behavior of people in work situations. The concepts of aptitude and ability have always been difficult to deal with in any formal or theoretical fashion and, to this day, have not played an important role in systematic theories of behavior. Few principles or generalizations have emerged from the voluminous literature dealing with the relationships between aptitude or ability tests and performance criteria.

The psychologists' interest in the motivational implications of work has two principal historical antecedents. The first of these was the work on vocational interests by Cowdery (1926), Strong

3

(1929), Kitson (1930), Fryer (1931), and Kuder (1946). From its modest beginnings with Freyd's comparison of the personality characteristics of life insurance salesmen and engineering school students (1924), this work has resulted in the development of a number of interest tests, which are widely used in vocational guidance and in research in occupational psychology.

A somewhat different perspective on the problem of motivation and work stemmed from the writings of Elton Mayo and his followers in the human relations movement, and from the research of Kurt Lewin and his associates in group dynamics. Since publication of the investigations conducted in the Hawthorne plant of the Western Electric Company (Roethlisberger and Dickson, 1939) and in the Harwood Manufacturing Company (Coch and French, 1948), a large amount of research has been carried out on the influence of the social environment on the behavior of workers. The results have stimulated the management of many organizations to reevaluate traditional methods of utilizing the human resources of organizations, and have probably been responsible, at least in part, for the marked changes in the philosophy of personnel administration that have occurred during the last thirty years.

The study of motivation now forms an integral part of both industrial and vocational psychology. Books like Viteles' *Motivation and Morale in Industry* (1953) and Maier's *Psychology in Industry* (1955) reflect the serious attention industrial psychologists are giving to such problems as the effects of supervision, wages, and group norms on performance. Similarly, books like Roe's *The Psychology of Occupations* (1956) and Super's *The Psychology of Careers* (1957) underscore the attention being given to motivational issues in vocational psychology. In both fields, concepts like need, motive, goal, incentive, and attitude are appearing with as much or greater frequency than concepts of aptitude, ability, and skill.

One might expect that this emphasis on motivation would bring the industrial psychologist closer to the problems and issues in general psychology. Motivational concepts play a major role in most serious efforts to analyze and explain behavior. In focusing on the motivational aspects of the relationship between men and their work, the industrial psychologist should be able to make use of and contribute to the development of theories of behavior.

Unfortunately it does not appear that this potential is being realized. Research in industrial psychology is still largely atheoretical, with little use being made of the concepts and models that are an integral part of current theories of motivation. There is a marked tendency for industrial psychologists to take their concepts from "everyday" vocabulary. Terms like morale, consideration, participation, fatigue, and vocational interest are seldom given adequate or consistent conceptual definitions. In some instances the same term is used to designate vastly different referents. One suspects, for example, that the concept of morale is seldom given precisely the same meaning by two different investigators. It has been used to refer to such widely different properties of individuals as their satisfaction with their membership in an organization and their willingness to exert effort to attain organizational goals. It has also been used as a descriptive property of social systems ranging in size from the face-to-face work group to a whole nation. Even here the definitions vary from a "group persistence in the pursuit of collective purposes" (Lasswell, 1948, p. 640) to "a shared feeling of like among group members" (Zeleny, 1939, p. 799).

In other instances, very different terms are used to designate roughly the same referent. Democratic leadership, participation, group decision, and decentralization of decision making are very similar in meaning, as are the terms consideration, employee orientation, and socio-emotional leadership. Further confusion is created by the fact that there is little standardization of operational definitions of concepts. There are many measures of each concept and sometimes they have little or no relationship to one another. Nonetheless, investigators typically treat the measure as though "it were the concept," ignoring what is often an extremely tenuous relationship between the observations they make and the events from which they wish to draw inferences.

To some extent this state of affairs may be due to the birth, during the last fifteen years, of large-scale research programs that seem to "spin in their own orbits," maintaining separate conceptual and methodological orientations and remaining largely uninfluenced by other programs. In any event, firmly established motivational principles in industrial psychology are difficult to discern, and advances in knowledge are hard to identify. Mason Haire noted this situation in his chapter on industrial social psychology in Lindzey's *Handbook of Social Psychology* with the comment that "unless there is a real advance here soon, the very richness of the empirical data threatens to be overwhelming in its systematic unintelligibility" (1954, p. 1120).

There would appear to be a pressing need for some kind of organization and integration of existing knowledge in the field of work and motivation. A critical and comprehensive examination of existing empirical evidence is required to show us where we now stand in our efforts to find principles and generalizations, and to indicate promising new avenues for research. It is this admittedly ambitious task to which we address ourselves in this book.

We approach this task with a bias. We assume that applied as well as basic research should be directed by some kind of systematic model of reality, rather than by isolated "hunches" or by expediency. We also assume that there is a lawfulness in the behavior of individuals that transcends the boundaries of applied fields. It is exceedingly unlikely that the behavior of persons in work situations is governed by processes that are basically different from behavior in other types of situations. Accordingly, we regard as a useful starting point for the development of theory in industrial psychology, theories that have proven useful in organizing empirical knowledge and in guiding research in other fields of psychology.

Since the subject of our inquiry is the interrelationship of work and motivation, it is necessary to give some initial attention to the meaning of these terms. "Work" is a particularly ambiguous term. It is used in physics to refer to the transference of energy by a process involving the motion of an object as a result of the application of a force; in experimental psychology and in physiology to refer to muscular activity; and in everyday language to refer to things as different as artistic productions and unpleasant tasks. In order to avoid confusion with the many other colloquial and scientific meanings, we will substitute for "work" the term "work role." A *work role* is defined as a set of functions to be performed by a role occupant, the performance of which contributes to the production of goods and services. It means roughly the same thing as the term "job," as it is used colloquially and in industrial psychology.

No two work roles are identical in all respects. Important

differences exist in the nature of the functions performed by the work role occupant, the amount and basis of payment for his services, the possibilities for movement to other work roles, and the characteristic pattern of the occupant's social relationships with those in other roles. Our focus in this book will be on work roles in which the functions to be performed are specified by an employer who pays the role occupant a wage or salary for his services. This conforms to what Jaques (1961) has called employment work.

The term "motivation" has been used in almost as many different ways as the term work. Psychologists who use it often disagree about the specific processes to which it applies. We will use the term *motivation* to refer to a process governing choices made by persons or lower organisms among alternative forms of voluntary activity. We specifically exclude from the realm of motivated behavior reflexes or tropisms as well as responses mediated by the autonomic nervous system, such as salivation or heart rate.

In choosing to deal with the interrelationship of work and motivation, we are selecting for examination both the effects of motivational variables on persons' behavior in work roles and the effects of work roles on motivational variables. There are three phenomena within this general field of inquiry that have attracted the attention of psychologists and that we will take up in this book. These are the following:

1. The choices made by persons among work roles.
2. The extent of their satisfaction with their chosen work roles.
3. The level of their performance or effectiveness in their chosen work roles.

Each of these phenomena can be treated, at least in part, as a function of the relationship between the motives of persons and the actual or cognized properties of work roles. We will attempt, in the following pages, to summarize existing evidence concerning each of these phenomena, to account for this evidence with a parsimonious set of concepts and propositions, and to identify fruitful avenues for further research.

This book will be divided into five parts. Part One, consisting of Chapters One through Three, is introductory. It includes a discussion of the scope of our inquiry, a conceptual model of motivation, and a brief treatment of the motivational bases of work. Part Two deals with choice of work role. It consists of only one chapter (Chapter Four) entitled "Occupational Choice."

Part Three, consisting of Chapters Five and Six, examines the problem of satisfaction with work roles. It includes discussions of the determinants of job satisfaction and the relationship between job satisfaction and job behavior. Part Four, which consists of Chapters Seven and Eight, concerns the problem of performance in work roles. It includes discussions of the meaning of level of performance, the role of motivation in performance, and the effects of a number of specific motivational variables on level of performance. Part Five concludes the book with a single chapter (Chapter Nine), which contains some final observations regarding methodology and theory.

2

Motivation—
A Point of View

The Nature of Motivation

There are two somewhat different kinds of questions that are usually dealt with in discussions of motivation. One of these is the question of the arousal or energizing of the organism. Why is the organism active at all? What conditions instigate action, determine its duration or persistence and finally its cessation? The phenomena to be explained include the level of activity of the organism and the vigor or amplitude of its behavior. The second question involves the direction of behavior. What determines the form that activity will take? Under what conditions will an organism choose one response or another or move in one direction or another? The problem is to explain the choices made by an organism among qualitatively different behaviors.

The latter question—concerning direction or choice—is probably the more important of the two to the psychologist. Research on conditions affecting the choices made by organisms among alternative acts or responses constitutes a large part of the psychology of learning and of motivation. Furthermore, there are some psychologists (Estes, 1958; Logan, 1956) who have seriously questioned whether differences in level of activity and response amplitude cannot be explained in the same terms as the direction of activity.

Is all behavior motivated? The answer to this question depends somewhat on the range of processes that are subsumed under the heading of motivation. We will follow the relatively common practice of viewing as motivated only the behaviors that are under central or voluntary control. Accordingly, we would not apply the term in explanations of reflexes or tropisms, where responses are strictly determined by external stimuli. It is not necessary to look to motivation to account for the contraction of the pupils of the eye in response to light, or the jerk of the knee in response to a tap.

It is also questionable to treat as motivated responses mediated by the autonomic nervous system, such as heart rate and adrenalin secretion. As well as being governed by a different neural and muscular system, such responses are not under voluntary control and appear to become attached to new stimuli by a process of classical conditioning rather than by operant conditioning.

Maier (1949) has proposed an even greater restriction on the scope of motivation. He distinguishes between motivated behavior, which is variable, constructive, and goal directed, and frustration-instigated behavior, which is rigid, stereotyped, compulsive, and not goal directed. According to Maier, the processes underlying these two kinds of behavior are basically different. Different principles are needed in explaining, for example, the fixated behavior of rats faced with an unsolvable problem (Maier, Glaser, and Klee, 1940; Maier and Klee, 1941, 1945) and the adaptive behavior observed when the problem has a solution. Space does not permit a consideration of the evidence for and against this position. The issues are complex and beyond the scope of this chapter. For a clear exposition of the current status of Maier's views, the reader is referred to a recent article of his entitled "Frustration Theory: Restatement and Extension" (Maier, 1956). At present, we regard it as a distinct possibility that some so-called abnormal behaviors, including fixated acts, are more appropriately treated as involuntary or compulsive acts rather than as motivated behaviors.

To sum up, we view the central problem of motivation as the explanation of choices made by organisms among different voluntary responses. Although some behaviors, specifically those that are not under voluntary control, are defined as unmotivated, these probably constitute a rather small proportion of the total behavior of adult human beings. It is reasonable to assume that most of the behavior exhibited by individuals on their jobs as well as their behavior in the "job market" is voluntary, and consequently motivated.

Historical Approaches: The Influence of Hedonism

Most contemporary conceptions of motivation have their origins in the principle of hedonism. This principle can be traced back to the Greek philosophers as well as to the writings of the English utilitarians like Jeremy Bentham and John Stuart Mill. Its central assumption is that behavior is directed toward pleasure and away from pain. In every situation people select from alternative possibilities the course of action that they think will maximize their pleasure and minimize their pain.

The influence of hedonism on the writings of early psychologists is clear. In his monumental *Principles of Psychology*, William James wrote

> But as present pleasures are tremendous reinforcers, and present pains tremendous inhibitors of whatever action leads to them, so the thoughts of pleasures and pains take rank amongst the thoughts which have most impulsive and inhibitive power (1890, v. 2, p. 550).

Freud also assumed a hedonistic position in his early writings, and Troland (1928) proposed a theory of human motivation that clearly reflects the influence of the English utilitarians. Despite its simplicity and widespread appeal, the philosophical doctrine of hedonism presented many problems for those who saw in it the foundation for a theory of behavior. There was in the doctrine no clear-cut specification of the types of events that were pleasurable or painful, or even how these events could be determined for a particular individual; nor did it make clear how persons acquired their conceptions of ways of attaining pleasure and pain, or how the sources of pleasure and pain might be modified by experience. In short, the hedonistic assumption had no empirical content and was untestable. Any form of behavior could be explained, after the fact, by postulating particular sources of pleasure or pain, but no form of behavior could be predicted in advance.

The study of motivation by psychologists has largely been directed toward filling in the missing empirical content in hedonism. As in the hedonistic doctrine, people are assumed to behave in ways that maximize certain types of outcomes (rewards, satisfiers, positive reinforcements, and so on) and minimize other outcomes (punishments, dissatisfiers, negative reinforcements, and so on). However, some of the circularity of hedonism has been overcome by the development of more precisely stated models and by the linking of the concepts in these models to empirically observable events.

Contemporary Approaches

Two groups of psychologists, each carrying out important work, have helped to translate the hedonistic doctrine from the realm of philosophical discourse to that of testable psychological theory. These two groups have focused on different problems and have developed different types of models to guide their research and interpret their findings. The first group has focused on the problem of *learning* and has approached this problem with a strong behavioristic emphasis. The theories that they have constructed are *historical* in the sense that they assert lawful relations between the behavior of organisms at one point in time and events that have occurred at earlier points in time. The empirical foundation for much of their work is the law of effect, which Thorndike originally stated as follows:

> Of several responses made to the same situation, those which are accompanied or closely followed by satisfaction to the animal will, other things being equal, be more firmly connected with the situation, so that, when it recurs, they will be more likely to recur; those which are accompanied or closely followed by discomfort to the animal will, other things being equal, have their connections with that situation weakened, so that when it recurs, they will be less likely to occur. The greater the satisfaction or discomfort, the greater

is the strengthening or weakening of the bond (1911, p. 244).

The significance of the law of effect and its modern counterpart, Hull's principle of reinforcement (Hull, 1943, 1951) for the doctrine of hedonism, has been noted by Postman (1947). The experiments on which the law was based provided tangible evidence that behavior was directed *toward* certain outcomes and *away* from other outcomes. Those outcomes increasing the probability of responses that lead to them were often referred to as satisfiers or rewards, terms implying that their attainment was pleasurable. Similarly, outcomes decreasing the probability of responses that lead to them were referred to as dissatisfiers or punishments.

Gordon Allport (1954) has noted that theories based on the law of effect or on the principle of reinforcement imply a "hedonism of the past." They assume that the explanation of the present choices of an organism is to be found in an examination of the consequences of his past choices. Responses to a stimulus that have been rewarded in the past will be repeated in the present, whereas those that have not been rewarded or have been punished in the past will not be repeated.

Although the law of effect helped to answer one of the classical problems of hedonism (that is, how behavior came to be directed toward pleasure and away from pain), it was silent in regard to the question of which outcomes are pleasurable and which are painful. Unless one was willing to rely on the subject's report of his experience of pleasure or pain, there was, in the statement of the law, no mention of an independent criterion by which one could distinguish in advance the class of outcomes that would strengthen responses and those that would weaken them. Without such a criterion the law of effect was difficult to test conclusively and was accused of circularity.

A number of attempts have been made to define more completely the classes of outcomes that act as rewards and as punishments. Hull's conception of need, as a condition in which "any of the commodities or conditions necessary for individual or species survival are lacking" (1943, p. 17), represented an early attempt in this direction. Satisfaction, or reinforcement, to use Hull's term, occurred when a condition of need was reduced. This use of changes in states of physiological needs was justly criticized on a number of grounds, and subsequently Hull (1951) and many of his associates changed their conception of the basis for reinforcement from changes in tissue conditions to changes in aversive states called drives. Reinforcement resulted not from the reduction of a biological need but from drive reduction. Although Hull was never very explicit about the defining properties of a drive, Miller and Dollard (1941) have anchored it in the intensity of stimulation. A drive was "a strong stimulus which impels action" (p. 18) on the part of the organism. Increases in stimulation, for example, from an electric shock or a loud noise, constituted increases in drive and were predicted to decrease the probability of responses preceding them. In contrast, decreases in stimulation constituted drive reduction and were predicted to increase the probability of responses preceding them.

The concept of drive reduction as the basis of reinforcement has achieved greater currency than that of need reduction, but it too has been criticized. There is considerable evidence that organisms, under many conditions, seek not to avoid stimulation but to attain it. The optimal state does not appear to be the absence of stimulation, as drive reduction theory would imply. Sensory deprivation studies indicate that humans find very low levels of stimulation highly unpleasant and disruptive (Bexton, Heron, and Scott, 1954). Work by Harlow on manipulation (1953), by Berlyne on curiosity (1960), and by Montgomery on exploration (1954) indicates that, at least under some circumstances, stimulation is rewarding and can strengthen responses. A similar conclusion is suggested by everyday observations of the frequency with which people engage in highly stimulating activities such as riding roller coasters, driving sports cars, and reading detective stories.

In an attempt to account for such observations, Hebb (1949) and McClelland and others (1953) have suggested that the satisfying and dissatisfying properties of any stimulus are dependent on the size of the discrepancy between the stimulus and a hypothetical neural organization or adaptation level, which has been acquired as a result of past stimulation. If the stimulus is mildly different from the adaptation level, it is pleasant; if it is highly different from the adaptation level or very similar to the adaptation level, it is unpleasant. Since these theories shift the basis for affect from tissue conditions or stimulation to central processes, which are by their nature difficult to observe, it is hard to subject them to a critical test. There is as yet no way of predicting in advance for a particular organism how much pleasure or pain will be generated with a particular event.

Although there are clearly many unsolved problems in explaining behavior in terms of reinforcement principles, definite progress has been made. The empirical validity of the proposition that the probability of occurrence of a wide range of behaviors can be altered by the outcomes of those behaviors has been supported by a wealth of research using both animals and humans as subjects. Without a doubt the law of effect or principle of reinforcement must be included among the most substantiated findings of experimental psychology and it is at the same time among the most useful findings for an applied psychology concerned with the control of human behavior.

A second group of psychologists has accepted the empirical evidence underlying the law of effect but has asserted that the stimulus-response-reinforcement theories of Hull and his followers are not sufficient to account for the more complex aspects of choice behavior. Tolman (1932) and Lewin (1938) were among the early advocates of *cognitive* theories of behavior. Although Tolman's work was mainly with animals and Lewin's was with humans, they both attributed to their subjects internalized representations of their environment. The organism was assumed to have beliefs, opinions, or expectations concerning the world around him. To Tolman, learning consisted not of changes in the strength of habits (that is, stimulus-response connections) but of changes in beliefs (that is, stimulus-stimulus or stimulus-response-stimulus connections). He attributed the results of reinforcement studies to learning, but he did not regard reinforcement as a necessary condition for learning to take place.

Although reinforcement was accorded a much less central role, the models of Lewin and Tolman also reflect the influence of hedonism. Both investigators viewed behavior as purposeful or goal directed, with organisms striving to attain positively valent objects or events and to avoid negatively valent objects or events.

Lewin (1935) distinguished between historical and ahistorical explanations of behavior. He pointed out that the former had its roots in Aristotelian thinking and the latter in Galilean thinking. From an ahistorical point of view behavior at a given time is viewed as depending only on events existing at that time. The problem is one of accounting for the actions of a person from a knowledge of the properties of his life space at the time the actions are occurring. From an historical standpoint, behavior is dependent on events occurring at an earlier time. The historical problem is to determine the way in which the behavior of a person at one point in time is affected by past situations he has experienced and the responses he has made to them. Freud's constant emphasis on the dependence of adult behavior on events that occurred in childhood and Hull's stress on reinforcement of previous responses provide us with good examples of historical explanations.

Lewin's own theorizing was ahistorical, but he noted the complementary nature of ahistorical and historical approaches. Past events can only have an effect on behavior in the present by modifying conditions that exist in the present. If a particular childhood experience is to have any effect on adult behavior, it must do so by changing some property of the person that persists through adulthood. Historical explanations are consequently explanations of the process of change, that is, of the ways in which properties of persons are modified by events. Ahistorical explanations, in contrast, concern the effects on behavior of conditions existing at the time the behavior is occurring, and say nothing about how these conditions were established.

Ahistorical models of choice behavior bypass many of the problems that concern the psychologist interested in learning. The choices made by a person in a given situation are explained in terms of his motives and cognitions at the time he makes the choice. The process by which these motives or cognitions were acquired is not specified nor is it regarded as crucial to a consideration of their present role in behavior.

Although bypassing the problem of the origins of psychological properties, an ahistorical approach to motivation is confronted with another set of problems, that is, problems of operational definition or measurement. In order to test ahistorical models, we must develop methods of measuring or experimentally manipulating these variables. The strategy of the learning theorist, creating carefully controlled training conditions, is supplanted by the use of psychometric assessment devices or the manipulation of situational conditions that are assumed to have some relationship to the constructs in the model.

An Outline of a Cognitive Model

In the remainder of this chapter, we outline a conceptual model that will guide our discussion and interpretation of research in the book. The model to be described is similar to those developed by other investigators including Lewin (1938); Rotter (1955); Peak (1955); Davidson, Suppes, and Siegel (1957); Atkinson (1958b); and Tolman (1959). It is basically ahistorical in form. We assume that the choices made by a person among alternative courses of action are lawfully related to psychological events occurring contemporaneously with the behavior. We turn now to consider the concepts in the model and their interrelations.

The Concept of Valence. We shall begin with the simple assumption that, at any given point in time, a person has preferences among outcomes or states of nature. For any pair of outcomes, x and y, a person prefers x to y, prefers y to x, or is indifferent to whether he receives x or y. Preference, then, refers to a relationship between the strength of a person's desire for, or attraction toward, two outcomes.

Psychologists have used many different terms to refer to preferences. The terms valence (Lewin, 1938; Tolman, 1959), incentive (Atkinson, 1958b), attitude (Peak, 1955), and expected utility (Edwards, 1954; Thrall, Coombs, and Davis, 1954; Davidson, Suppes, and Siegel, 1957) all refer to affective orientations toward outcomes. Other concepts like need (Maslow, 1954), motive (Atkinson, 1958b), value (Allport, Vernon, and Lindzey, 1951), and interest (Strong, 1958) are broader in nature and refer to the strength of desires or aversions for large classes of outcomes.

For the sake of consistency, we use the term valence throughout this book in referring to affective orientations toward particular outcomes. In our system, an outcome is positively valent when the person prefers attaining it to not attaining it (that is, he prefers x to not x). An outcome has a valence of zero when the person is indifferent to attaining or not attaining it (that is, he is indifferent to x or not x), and it is negatively valent when he prefers not attaining it to attaining it (that is, he prefers not x to x). It is assumed that valence can take a wide range of both positive and negative values.

We use the term motive whenever the referent is a preference for a class of outcomes. A positive (or approach) motive signifies that outcomes that are members of the class have positive valence, and a negative (or avoidance) motive signifies that outcomes in the class have negative valence.

It is important to distinguish between the valence of an outcome to a person and its value to that person. An individual may desire an object but derive little satisfaction from its attainment—or he may strive to avoid an object that he later finds to be quite satisfying. At any given time there may be a substantial discrepancy between the anticipated satisfaction from an outcome (that is, its valence) and the actual satisfaction that it provides (that is, its value).

There are many outcomes that are positively or negatively valent to persons but are not in themselves anticipated to be satisfying or dissatisfying. The strength of a person's desire or aversion for them is based not on their intrinsic properties but on the anticipated satisfaction or dissatisfaction associated with other outcomes to which they are expected to lead. People may desire to join groups because they believe that membership will enhance their status in the community, and they may desire to perform their jobs effectively because they expect that it will lead to a promotion.

In effect, we are suggesting that means acquire valence as a consequence of their expected relationship to ends. Peak (1955) has discussed this relationship in some detail. She hypothesizes that attitudes, that is, affective orientations toward objects, are "related to the ends which the object serves" (p. 153). From this general hypothesis it is possible for Peak to distinguish two types of determinants of attitudes: (1) the cognized instrumentality of the object of the attitude for the attainment of various consequences; and (2) the intensity and the nature of the affect expected from these consequences. If an object is believed by a person to lead to desired consequences or to prevent undesired consequences, the person is predicted to have a positive attitude toward it. If, in contrast, it is believed by the person to lead to undesired consequences or to prevent desired consequences, the person is predicted to have a negative attitude toward it.

General support for these predictions is provided by a number of studies and experiments conducted by Peak and her associates. Rosenberg (1956) showed that it is possible to predict subjects' attitudes toward free speech for communists and desegregation in housing from their reported goals and their judgments of the probability that free speech and segregation will aid or block attainment of these goals. In a follow-up experiment, Carlson (1956) changed subjects' attitudes toward desegregation by modifying their beliefs regarding the consequences of desegregation for the attainment of their goals. Peak (1960) has also shown that students' attitudes toward conditions believed to hinder the attainment of good grades are more negative on the day of the quiz, when their motivation for attaining good grades was presumably strongest.

We do not mean to imply that all the variance in the valence of outcomes can be explained by their expected consequences. We must assume that some things are desired and abhorred "for their own sake." Desegregation may be opposed "on principle" not because it leads to other events that are disliked, and people may seek to do well on their jobs even though no externally mediated rewards are believed to be at stake.

Without pretending to have solved all of the knotty theoretical problems involved in the determinants of valence, we can specify the expected functional relationship between the valence of outcomes and their expected consequences in the following proposition.

Proposition 1: The valence of an outcome to a person is a monotonically increasing function of the algebraic sum of the products of the valences of all other outcomes and his conceptions of its instrumentality for the attainment of these other outcomes.

In equation form the same proposition reads as follows:

$$V_j = f_j[\sum_{k=1}^{n} (V_k I_{jk})](j=1...n)$$
$$f_j > 0; iI_{jj} = 0$$

where V_j = the valence of outcome j
    I_{jk} = the cognized instrumentality $(-1 \le I_{jk} \le 1)$ of outcome j for the attainment of outcome k

The Concept of Expectancy. The specific outcomes attained by a person are dependent not only on the choices that he makes but also on events that are beyond his control. For example, a person who elects to buy a ticket in a lottery is not certain of winning the desired prize. Whether he does so is a function of many chance events. Similarly, the student who enrolls in medical school is seldom certain that he will successfully complete the program of study; the person who seeks political office is seldom certain that he will win the election; and the worker who strives for a promotion is seldom certain that he will triumph over other candidates. Most decision-making situations involve some element of risk, and theories of choice behavior must come to grips with the role of these risks in determining the choices that people do make.

Whenever an individual chooses between alternatives that involve uncertain outcomes, it seems clear that his behavior is affected not only by his preferences among these outcomes but also by the degree to which he believes these outcomes to be probable. Psychologists have referred to these beliefs as expectancies (Tolman, 1959; Rotter, 1955; Atkinson, 1958b) or subjective probabilities (Edwards, 1954; Davidson, Suppes, and Siegel, 1957). We use the former term throughout this book. An expectancy is defined as a momentary belief concerning the likelihood that a particular act will be followed by a particular outcome. Expectancies may be described in terms of their strength. Maximal strength is indicated by subjective certainty that the act *will* be followed by the outcome while minimal (or zero) strength is indicated by subjective certainty that the act *will not* be followed by the outcome.

The differences between the concepts of expectancy, discussed in this section, and instrumentality, discussed in the previous section, should be noted.

Expectancy is an action-outcome association. It takes values ranging from zero, indicating no subjective probability that an act will be followed by an outcome, to 1, indicating certainty that the act will be followed by the outcome. Instrumentality, in contrast, is an outcome-outcome association. It can take values ranging from -1, indicating a belief that attainment of the second outcome is certain without the first outcome and impossible with it, to +1, indicating that the first outcome is believed to be a necessary and sufficient condition for the attainment of the second outcome.

The Concept of Force. It remains to be specified how valences and expectancies combine in determining choices. The directional concept in our model is the Lewinian concept of force. Behavior on the part of a person is assumed to be the result of a field of forces each of which has direction and magnitude. The concept of force as used here is similar to Tolman's performance vector (1959), Atkinson's aroused motivation (1958b), Luce's subjective expected utility (1962), and Rotter's behavior potential (1955).

There are many possible ways of combining valences and expectancies mathematically to yield these hypothetical forces. On the assumption that choices made by people are subjectively rational, we would predict the strength of forces to be a monotonically increasing function of the *product* of valences and expectancies. Proposition 2 expresses this functional relationship.

> *Proposition 2:* The force on a person to perform an act is a monotonically increasing function of the algebraic sum of the products of the valences of all outcomes and the strength of his expectancies that the act will be followed by the attainment of these outcomes.

We can express this proposition in the form of the following equation:

$$F_i = f_i[\sum_{j=1}^{n} (E_{ij}V_j)](i=n+1...m)$$

$$fi' > O;\ i \cap j = \Phi,\ \Phi \text{ is the null set}$$

where F_i = the force to perform act i
    E_{ij} = the strength of the expectancy ($O \le E_{ij}\ 1$) that act i will
        be followed by outcome j
    V_j = the valence of outcome j

It is also assumed that people choose from among alternative acts the one corresponding to the strongest positive (or weakest negative) force. This formulation is similar to the notion in decision theory that people choose in a way that maximizes subjective expected utility.

Expressing force as a monotonically increasing function of the product of valence and expectancy has a number of implications that should be noted. An outcome with high positive or negative valence will have no effect on the generation of a force unless there is some expectancy (that is, some subjective probability greater than zero) that the outcome will be attained by some act. As the strength of an expectancy that an act will lead to an outcome increases, the effect of variations in the valence of the outcome on the force to perform the act will also increase. Similarly, if the valence of an outcome is zero (that is, the person is indifferent to the outcome), neither the absolute value nor variations in the strength of expectancies of attaining it will have any effect on forces.

Our two propositions have been stated in separate terms but are in fact highly related to one another. Insofar as the acts and outcomes are described in different terms the separation is a useful one. We have in the first proposition a basis for predicting the valence of outcomes, and in the second proposition a basis for predicting the actions that a person will take with regard to the outcome. The distinction between acts and outcomes is not, however, an absolute one. Actions are frequently described in terms of the particular outcomes which they effect. For example, a person may be described as having chosen a particular occupation only when he successfully attains it, or he may be described as having chosen to perform effectively in that occupation only when he succeeds in doing so. In such cases the derivations from the two propositions become identical. The conditions predicted to affect the valence of the occupation or of effective performance in it are identical to those predicted to affect the relative strength of forces toward and away from these outcomes.

In practice we will find it useful to maintain the separation between the two propositions by defining sets of actions and sets of outcomes independently of one another. We will use the term action to refer to behavior that might reasonably be expected to be within the repertoire of the person, for example, seeking entry into an occupation, while the term outcomes will be reserved for more temporally distant events that are less likely to be under complete behavioral control, for example, attaining membership in an occupation.

Testing the Model

The model, as outlined so far, is untestable, for its concepts have not been related to observable events. In order to derive empirical hypotheses from the model, we must specify operational definitions for the formal concepts. Some further assumptions must be made that will permit the measurement or experimental manipulation of the concepts. It is important to note that a model of the sort that has been proposed is testable only in conjunction with a particular set of empirical interpretations. It is impossible to subject it to a "pure test." Tests of a model are always inextricably bound to tests of the operational definitions of the variables. A given research investigation has implications for a model only if we are prepared to assume the validity of the operations. In contrast, it has implications for the construct validity of the operations only if we are prepared to regard the model as correct.

The only concept in the model that has been directly linked with potentially observable events is the concept of force. We have assumed that the acts performed by a person reflect the relative strength of forces acting upon him. If a person performs act x rather than y the force corresponding to x is assumed to be stronger than y and vice versa.

We have, however, said nothing about observable events that would lead us to infer either that an outcome has a certain valence for a person, or that the strength of a person's expectancy that an act will lead to an outcome has a particular value. It is this kind of problem to which we now turn.

Our approach to this problem is "eclectic." Instead of proposing a single operational definition for each of the concepts, we outline a series of broad approaches to their measurement or experimental manipulation.

The Measurement of Valence. What approaches can be taken to the measurement of valence? What observations of behavior need to be made in order to permit us to conclude that one outcome is positively valent and a second negatively valent, or that one is more positively valent than a second?

One approach is to use *verbal reports.* If an individual states that an event is attractive or desirable, it might be assumed to have positive valence. If he states that a second event is unattractive or undesirable, it might be assumed to have negative valence. This procedure can be extended to provide measures of the relative attractiveness or unattractiveness of a series of events or outcomes by requesting the person to make comparative judgments or by using a standard judgmental scale.

Social psychologists have made extensive use of verbal reports of affective orientations. The concept of attitude, which has been described by Allport (1954) as the most distinctive and indispensable concept in contemporary American social psychology, has traditionally been measured by means of verbal reports, and a large number of different scales have been developed for this purpose.

This approach has also characterized the efforts of most psychologists interested in the measurement of individual differences in motivation. The Allport-Vernon-Lindzey Study of Values, the Strong Vocational Interest Blank, and the Edwards Personal Preference Test are examples of measuring instruments that purport to assess motivation through verbal reports.

Despite the popularity of self-report measures, many have questioned the assumptions on which they are based. Perhaps the severest critics have been the Freudians, who have stressed the pervasiveness of unconscious motivation, which, by definition, is not available to direct verbal report, and the behaviorists, who, from the time of Watson, have seriously questioned the usefulness of intro-spective data in the science of psychology.

The most convincing argument against the use of self-report measures is a theoretical one. If a person's reports of his desires and aversions are voluntary responses, it should be possible to explain them in terms of processes similar to those involved in other kinds of voluntary behavior. A person's statement that he prefers outcome x to outcome y should, therefore, be a more reliable indicator of the expected consequences of making this statement than of the ex-pected consequences of attaining outcomes x and y. Investigators who use self-report measures of motivation are aware of this prob-lem, and they try to minimize or eliminate "faking" by structuring the testing situation in such a way that the subject believes his responses are confidential or anonymous.

A second approach is found in the work of Atkinson, McClel-land, and their associates (McClelland, Atkinson, Clark, and Low-ell, 1953; Atkinson, 1958a). They assume that the motives of a person can be inferred from the *analysis of fantasy*. The thematic apperception method (Murray, 1938) is the principal device used for eliciting this fantasy. Subjects are requested to tell stories about pictures, and the content of their stories is scored according to the frequency with which different kinds of imagery appear. The achievement motive has been most frequently studied by this meth-od, but work has also been carried out on a number of other motives including affiliation, power, and sex.

This method has both strong supporters and detractors. A discussion of the arguments, pro and con, would constitute an un-warranted detour from our present course. A wealth of research using this method has been carried out in the last fifteen years and is aptly described in Atkinson's *Motives in Fantasy, Action, and Society* (1958a). Most impressive is the evidence that motive scores based on this system are affected by the experimental conditions predicted to arouse the motive. In contrast, its relevance to the kind of model that we have proposed is restricted by the gross nature of the motivational variables that are employed. At best, this approach yields information concerning the mean valence of a broad class of outcomes, such as influencing others, or being accepted by others, rather than the valence of single outcomes.

A third approach to the measurement of valence involves the use of outcomes to create new learning. If an outcome strengthens a response tendency, it could be assumed to be positively valent; if it weakens a response tendency, it could be assumed to be negatively valent. The measure of valence is the *amount or rate of change in response probability* when the outcome is made contingent on the response. We would expect such data to be a reliable indicator of whether an outcome is positively valent or negatively valent but not to be especially sensitive to differences in degree of positive or negative valence.

A fourth approach rests on the assumption that the valence of outcomes can be inferred from *the choices that persons make* among alternative courses of action. If a person is given a free choice between two outcomes x and y, under conditions in which his expectancies of attaining them are equal (for example, certain), his choice between them may be assumed to reflect their relative valence. Choice of x is assumed to indicate that x is more positively valent than y, whereas choice of y is assumed to indicate that y is more positively valent than x. This approach will easily permit the ordering of a set of outcomes on an ordinal or relative scale. If we introduce differential risks into the choice situation, interval measurement becomes a possibility. Following ideas originally introduced by Von Neumann and Morgenstern (1947), Mosteller and Nogee (1951) and Davidson, Suppes, and Siegel (1957) have outlined methods for obtaining interval measurements of the utility of different amounts of money.

A fifth approach involves observation of *consummatory behavior*. It is consequently applicable primarily to those outcomes such as food, water, and sexual activity where consummation takes place. We might assume that the hungrier a person is, that is, the greater the valence of food, the more food he will eat. Thus, measures of amount or rate of eating, drinking, or copulation could be used to indicate the extent to which the consumed outcomes were positively valent.

Finally, we might be able to use *decision time* as a behavioral indication of differences in valence of outcomes. If a person is given a "free choice" among two outcomes, x and y, the length of time elapsing before he makes his choice could be assumed to reflect the extent to which the outcomes differ in valence. Instantaneous choice of one over the other would indicate a substantial difference in their valence, whereas a long decision time would indicate much less difference. A theory relating decision time to differences in the strength of forces acting on the person has been advanced by Cartwright (1941). It should be noted that, at best, decision time can be used to indicate the amount of difference in valence among outcomes, not which outcome is more positively valent. However, observations of decision time and of the choice can usually be made concurrently, permitting inferences concerning both the amount and direction of difference in the valence of outcomes.

The Experimental Manipulation of Valence. The preceding section dealt with possible methods for inferring the valence of outcomes from behavior. A remaining question concerns the situations that might be assumed to affect valence. How can we vary experimentally the valence of an outcome for a person?

One possibility rests on the assumption that the valence of outcomes is affected by *communicated information concerning their desirability.* For example, a subject may be told that outcome *x* is more desirable than outcome *y*, or that it possesses more of some property that is usually regarded as desirable. This information may be assumed to induce a preference on the part of the subject for *x* over *y*. Such an assumption seems justifiable when subjects have had no prior experience with the outcomes and when they have little reason to distrust the experimenter. This method has been used primarily for inducing in subjects different amounts of valence for objects with which they have little or no familiarity. For example, attempts have been made to create groups of high and low attractiveness by appropriate instructions to members before they join the group (Back, 1951; Schachter, Ellertson, McBride, and Gregory, 1951; Libo, 1953; Berkowitz, 1954).

If we assume that individuals' desires and aversions are not relatively stable but vary predictably with incoming stimulation, an alternative method is suggested. We should be able to increase or decrease the valence of outcomes by *arousing appropriate motives.* The valence of food can be increased by depriving an experimental subject of food for an extended period of time or even by subjecting him to the sight or smell of food. The valence of sexual intercourse can be increased by showing him photographs of unclothed members of the opposite sex, and the valence of doing well on a task can be increased by telling him that it is a measure of his intelligence. To be sure, these techniques imply somewhat different assumptions about motive arousal, a problem on which psychologists are far from agreeing. Depriving the subject of outcomes necessary for survival, for example, food, has been demonstrated to affect a number of behavioral indicators of the valence of food, including learning rate when food is used as a reinforcement, fantasy about food, choice of food over other outcomes, and amount of food consumed. However, it is not at all clear that deprivation has the same effects on the arousal of more complex motives in which learning has played a greater role.

One of the most difficult problems is to specify the role of learning in determining the valence of outcomes. Psychologists interested in the learning process have shown that outcomes that were previously neutral can acquire rewarding or aversive properties as a result of being *associated contiguously with established rewards and punishments.* A stimulus such as a light or a click can be used to increase the probability of a response after it has been repeatedly paired with receiving food; or it can be used to decrease the probability of a response after it has been repeatedly paired with a shock or a loud noise. The learning process seems to be essentially that of classical conditioning. Evidence is insufficient to permit the conclusion that such a process is involved in all long-term changes in the valence of outcomes. Existing data suggest that it is easier to produce a relatively stable fear of an outcome by this process than it is to produce a desire for it.

The Measurement of Expectancy. How is the strength of expectancy to be measured? What behaviors can be taken as evidence that a person believes that the probability of an outcome following a response is 0, or .50, or 1.00? This problem is by no means simple. A number of different approaches are available, but each presents certain problems.

One possible approach rests on the assumption that expectancies are reflected in *verbal reports* by individuals about the probability of outcomes. Just as verbal reports may be taken as evidence for the valence of outcomes, they may also constitute the main form of evidence for expectancies. If a person states that an outcome is certain to follow an act, we assume an expectancy value of 1.00, whereas if he states that an outcome has a 50-50 chance of following that act, we assume an expectancy value of .50. This approach has not received enthusiastic support from decision theorists (Davidson, Suppes, and Siegel, 1957). The arguments against it are similar to those noted earlier in connection with self-reports of motives. Despite these arguments, verbal reports of probabilities have been found to be meaningfully related to relevant variables in social psychology and personality (Diggory, Riley, and Blumenfeld, 1960; Diggory and Ostroff, 1962; Rotter, Fitzgerald, and Joyce, 1954) and in industrial psychology (Georgopoulos, Mahoney, and Jones, 1957).

Other investigators have assumed that expectancies are best inferred from *actual choices or decisions made by the person*. For example, Preston and Baratta (1948) assumed a linear relationship between psychological probabilities of attaining a given prize and the amount that the subject was willing to wager to get a chance at the prize. If a subject was willing to wager $5 for a possible prize of $50, his psychological probability was assumed to be .10. Psychological probabilities measured by this procedure were generally related to mathematical probabilities. However, they tended to be larger than mathematical probabilities at low values of probability, and smaller than mathematical probabilities at higher values.

The problem with this approach is to disentangle the roles of expectancies and preferences in actual decisions. Davidson, Suppes, and Siegel (1957) have offered a solution to this problem based on a model of the decision process similar to the one proposed here. Since their solution is a fairly complex one and would involve us in a rather lengthy discussion of their experimental procedure, we will not attempt to describe it here. The interested reader should consult the original source.

The Experimental Manipulation of Expectancy. There are a number of different assumptions that might be made about the situational determinants of expectancies. One approach might be to assume that expectancies correspond perfectly with the *objective* *probabilities.* If we know that the actual probability of an outcome following an action is 1.00, we ascribe this identical value to expectancy; if we know that the actual probability is .50, we assume an expectancy of .50, and so on. This assumption shifts the problem of measuring expectancies to one of measuring objective probabilities. Sidestepping the question of how this can be done, let us examine the plausibility of the general assumption. How legitimate is it to assume that people can accurately estimate the actual probabilities of events? Under some conditions, such an assumption may be justified. If a person has had a considerable amount of experience in the situation attempting different courses of action and if he has been provided with prompt feedback following these actions, it might be appropriate to assume that his expectancies approximate actual probabilities. For example, a worker who has worked for the same supervisor for a period of years may accurately assess the probability that his supervisor will approve or disapprove of different behaviors on his part. But it would clearly be incorrect to attribute the same degree of "realism" to a person who had little or no experience in that situation.

Alternatively we might assume that expectancies are identical with *communicated probabilities.* Thus, if a subject is told by an experimenter that a response is certain to be followed by an outcome, his expectancy is assumed to be 1.00. If he is told that the probability is some particular value that is less than certainty, his expectancy is assumed to take this value. Typical of this approach is the experiment of Rosen (1961), who gave subjects information concerning the probability of their being able to enter an occupation. The assumption that expectancies are completely determined by communicated probabilities seems tenable when subjects have little additional basis for judging probabilities and when they have not previously been deceived in experimentation.

Another approach might be to link expectancies directly with *the proportion of times the person has received the outcome following the act.* If, in previous exposures to a situation, a person has received an outcome each time he has performed an act, his expectancy is assumed to be 1.00, if he has received the outcome only 50 percent of the time, he is assumed to have an expectancy of .50, and if he has never received the outcome, he is assumed to have an expectancy of 0. We can modify this assumption by attaching differential weight to the receipt or lack of receipt of outcomes on different trials (for example, primacy or recency effects) or by incorporating variations in the time interval between action and outcome.

This assumption relates the model to experimental work on the learning process. Research on learning using both animal and human subjects has demonstrated quite consistent effects on the probability of response of such variables as the proportion of reinforced responses and delay of reinforcement.

Figure 2.1 summarizes the preceding discussion concerning the empirical coordinates of valence, expectancy, and force. Each arrow in the diagram relates one of these inferred states to observable situations, both past and present, or to observable behaviors. We do not pretend that these are the only assumptions that could be made or that they will ultimately prove to be of equal value. With respect to a number of them, limitations were noted that indicate the need for modifications or elaborations. In some cases, these limitations may eventually prove to be so severe as to warrant a complete rejection of the assumption. Nonetheless, the model, together with its empirical coordinates, is consistent with a great deal of existing data in psychology and suggests a wealth of problems for further research. These characteristics should make it a useful starting point in our efforts to conceptualize the problems of work and motivation and to describe and evaluate existing research. It is these problems to which we turn in the remaining chapters.

Summary

The central problem of a theory of motivation was asserted to be the explanation of choice or direction in behavior. The doctrine of hedonism—that people strive to attain pleasure and to avoid pain—was discussed and related to two contemporary approaches to the study of choice behavior. Both approaches can be regarded as refinements and elaborations of hedonism, although the historical nature of one and the ahistorical nature of the other have led to an emphasis on different problems.

On the assumption that an ahistorical approach represented a more fruitful starting point for an examination of the problem of

Figure 2.1. Empirical Coordinates of the Model.

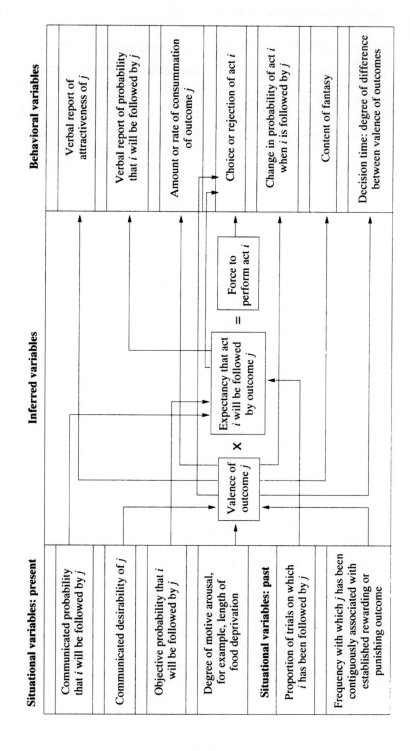

work and motivation, a conceptual model was developed that has drawn heavily on previous theoretical statements by Lewin (1938); Edwards (1954); Rotter (1955); Peak (1955); Davidson, Suppes, and Siegel (1957); Atkinson (1958b); and Tolman (1959). In the model, choices by persons among alternative courses of action are hypothesized to depend on the relative strength of forces. Each force is in turn hypothesized to be equal to the algebraic sum of the products of the valence of outcomes and expectancies that the outcomes will be attained.

3

The Motivational Bases
of Work

Introduction

At some time during their lives virtually every man and about four out of every five women are members of the labor force (Bancroft, 1958). Working by both men and women is so commonplace that the question why people work is seldom asked. We are much more likely to wonder why people climb mountains, drive sports cars, or commit suicide than to question the motivational basis of the decision to work. If asked directly why they work, most individuals would probably give a simple answer. They work because there is work to be done, because they like work, or because they need to earn a living. Although these answers contain a grain of truth, their apparent simplicity obscures what is, on close examination, an extremely complex and basic problem. In this chapter we deal with this problem in more detail, drawing on any research findings that bear on its solution.

When the scientist asks *why* a phenomenon occurs, he usually wants to know *under what conditions* it occurs. Consequently when we ask "Why do people work?" we mean "Under what conditions do people work?" There are two types of conditions that affect the likelihood that people will work. One is economic in nature. In order for people to work there must be some opportunity to work. There must be a demand on the part of members of a society for goods and services and a demand on the part of employers for people to produce these goods and perform these services. The second type of condition is motivational. People must prefer working to not working. Our model leads us to predict that given the opportunity a person will choose to work when the valence of outcomes that he expects to attain from working is more positive than the valence of outcomes that he expects to attain from not working.

These two types of conditions—economic and motivational—may vary independently from one another. There may be a larger number of job vacancies than there are people seeking work, or there may be a larger number of people who prefer to work than there are job vacancies. Both sets of conditions must exist to the same degree in order for there to be full employment.

It is the motivational aspect of this problem that is of interest to us here. In this chapter we will seek an answer to the question "Why do people work?" by looking at the motivational significance of outcomes that are attained through working.

There are two ways in which we can approach this problem. We can start with some conception of the motives or needs of man and then ask in what ways these motives are gratified or frustrated by working; or we can begin with some conception of the consequences of participation in work roles and then ask what motivational implications these consequences have. In view of the difficulty in formulating a meaningful list of motives that are common to all persons, the latter would appear to be the more parsimonious approach and will be used here. In the remainder of this chapter we discuss the motivational implications of the following properties of employment work roles:

1. Work roles provide *wages* to the role occupant in return for his services.
2. They require from the role occupant the *expenditure of mental or physical energy.*
3. They permit the role occupant to contribute to the *production of goods or services.*
4. They permit or require of the role occupant *social interaction* with other persons.

5. They define, at least in part, the *social status* of the role occupant.

Wages

One indisputable source of the desire of people to work is the money they are paid for working. Although we may disagree with the monolithic conception of the classical "economic main," few people would dispute the importance of anticipated economic consequences in the guidance of human conduct. Despite the old saw that money can't buy happiness, money can be exchanged for many commodities that are necessary for survival and comfort.

It would be incorrect to link the importance of money in our society strictly to the satisfaction of biological needs. The goods and services that are purchased with money go far beyond ensuring survival. They serve, among other things as an indicator of social status of the purchaser. The connection between the quantity and quality of goods consumed and the status of the consumer was graphically depicted by Thorstein Veblen in his famous treatise, *The Theory of the Leisure Class*. Veblen wrote

> The quasi-peaceable gentleman of leisure, then, not only consumes of the staff of life beyond the minimum required for subsistence and physical efficiency, but his consumption also undergoes a specialisation as regards the quality of the goods consumed. He consumes freely and of the best, in food, drink, narcotics, shelter, services, ornaments, apparel, weapons and accoutrements, amusements, amulets, and idols or divinities. . . . Since the consumption of these more excellent goods is an evidence of wealth, it becomes honorific; and conversely, the failure to consume in due quantity and quality becomes a mark of inferiority and demerit (1935, pp. 73-74).

The weekly or monthly paycheck by no means represents the only form of financial remuneration. Originally restricted to wages, the economic outcomes derived from the occupancy of work roles now include a wide range of fringe benefits including retirement programs, life and health insurance plans, free meals, and free recreational and educational programs. In this country, costs to the employer of so-called supplementary remunerations average approximately 20 percent of the total payroll, and this figure seems to be on the increase.

Although economic factors undoubtedly play an important part in the decision to work, it is highly improbable that they are the only inducements. The importance of noneconomic factors is suggested by an interview study described by Morse and Weiss (1955). A national sample of employed men was asked the question, "If by some chance you inherited enough money to live comfortably without working, do you think you would work anyway or not?" (p. 191). Eighty percent of the 401 respondents said that they would keep on working. The percentage of those who said that they would keep on working varied with the age of the respondent, from 90 percent of those in the 21- to 34-year-old category to 61 percent in the 55- to 64-year-old category. This percentage also varied with the present occupation of the respondent, as shown in Table 3.1.

In general, the percentage of persons reporting that they would continue working is positively related to the amount of training required by the occupation. However, even among unskilled

Table 3.1. Percentage of Respondents, by Occupation,
Who Say They Would Continue to Work
After Receiving a Large Inheritance.

	N	Percent Who Would Work
Professional	28	86
Manager	22	82
Sales	22	91
Trades	86	79
Operatives	80	78
Unskilled	27	58
Service	18	71
Farmers	43	86

Source: Morse and Weiss, 1955, p. 197.

workers, more than half (58 percent) said they would continue to work after receiving the inheritance.

The evidence concerning noneconomic incentives to work is not restricted to people's reports of their motivations. The existence of "dollar-a-year men," who work with only token economic rewards, and entrepreneurs, who continue to work after having amassed tremendous fortunes, is well known. Furthermore, there is at least anecdotal evidence that people actually do return to work after inheriting large sums of money. Brown (1954) mentioned three workers in London factories who won large sums of money from football pools, which, if suitably invested, would provide enough income to enable the men to live comfortably for the rest of their lives. In each of the cases, after a short period of leisure, the men returned to work—"two on 'routine repetitive work' and one as a fitter" (p. 188).

Obviously, it is impossible to perform the really crucial experiment on the role of financial remuneration in the motivation to work, that is, suspend all economic compensation for work performed and determine what proportion of the population continue to work. Nonetheless, it seems clear that for a large proportion of individuals the decision to seek or to continue work is based partly on anticipated rewards obtained from work that have nothing to do with money or the uses to which money may be put.

The Expenditure of Energy

All work roles require some energy expenditure. This energy may be expended in physical activity, in mental activity or, as is true for most work, in both. Any discussion of "why men work" would be incomplete without some mention of the affective consequences of energy expenditure.

Virtually all general theories of behavior postulate that dissatisfaction results from energy expenditure. Hull (1943), for example, postulated that making any response in the presence of a stimulus results in an increase in a drivelike state called reactive inhibition, which reduces the strength of the response. Reactive inhibition is an increasing function of the amount of work involved in the performance of the response in question and is hypothesized to decrease with the passage of time according to a simple decay or negative growth function.

Similarly, Tolman (1959) hypothesized that the probability of an organism making a particular response (that is, Tolman's performance vector) will be decreased to the degree that he has a drive stimulation against work (a transient state roughly corresponding to fatigue), expects that the response will involve work, and expects the work to be arduous. In terms of the model that we outlined in the preceding chapter, the expenditure of effort that is intrinsic to the performance of any task or job has usually been assumed to be negatively valent, with the amount of the negative valence a function of the recency with which that or some similar task has been performed and of the amount of effort involved in the performance of the task.

This principle of least effort, as it has frequently been called, has received considerable support, primarily in research using animals as subjects. A large number of experiments (Kuo, 1922; Gengerelli, 1931; Tsai, 1932; Waters, 1937; Thompson, 1944) indicate that given two or more paths to the same goal, each involving differing amounts of energy expenditure, an organism will learn to choose the path involving the least effort. Solomon (1948) has shown further that the assumption that the expenditure of effort produces a negative motivational state with cue properties is also consistent with data concerning the avoidance of repetition of responses and massed practice versus distributed practice in learning.

Some writers, however, have suggested exactly the opposite notion. They propose that the expenditure of effort is basically satisfying rather than dissatisfying. DeMan (1927), for example, writes

> Inactivity, were it only for physiological reasons, is a torment to a healthy human being. Every muscle is alive with the impulse to activity. The normal form of this activity is: in the child, play; in the adult, bodily work. The fact that, even in the adult, the urge to activity sometimes finds expression in games and sports, shows that there is an impulse to bodily activ-

ity in virtue of which movement may be an end in
itself (p. 17).

In support of such an idea it has been customary to point to
the reports of many persons concerning the feeling of physical well-
being that they derive from hard physical labor. Some recent experimental evidence with animals provided a stronger empirical basis
for this notion. Hill (1956) reports that rats will run in an activity
wheel in proportion to the amount of time their activity has been
restricted. The confinement cages contained food and water, making it difficult to explain the behavior in terms of these tissue needs
and related drive stimulation. In interpreting these findings, Hill
suggests that there is an activity drive that is related in strength to
the amount of activity deprivation. Kagan and Berkun (1954) have
also found that running in an activity wheel will serve as a reinforcement for a bar-pressing response.

It is not easy to reconcile the idea that activity reduces some
aversive state that is produced by inactivity with the notion that
activity increases some aversive state that is reduced only by inactivity. Each of these assumptions directly controverts the other.
Probably neither is a complete statement of the unlearned affective
consequences of energy expenditure. Conceivably there is some optimal level of activity. Lower amounts are unpleasant and tend to
result in an increase in activity level; and higher amounts, as in
fatigue, are also unpleasant and tend to result in a decrease in activity level. In terms of our model, the valence of energy expenditure
could be positive after prolonged inactivity but negative after prolonged activity.

The preceding discussion has emphasized hypothetical unlearned mechanisms that determine the amount of satisfaction or
dissatisfaction that persons derive from the expenditure of effort. It
is also possible that energy expenditure may acquire rewarding or
punishing properties as a result of learning. Conceivably, people
could be trained to like or dislike expending effort by the continuous association of effort with either rewards or punishments. If the
amount of reward that a person receives is always directly related
to the amount of effort he has expended, this might have the effect
of transferring to the effort or activity some learned affective value.

Similarly, if the person has been rewarded for being inactive and punished for activity, we might expect that activity will acquire some aversive quality.

To this writer's knowledge there is no experimental evidence bearing on the learned value of energy expenditure. It has, however, frequently been proposed that the particular form of energy expenditure in which we are primarily interested, that is, that involved in the performance of work, does have learned affective connotations. These proposals have been based not on experiments conducted in the laboratory but on the analysis of cultures, particularly those existing at an earlier time. Tilgher (1930), for example, has discussed the way in which man's attitude toward work has changed throughout the ages. He points out that work to the Greeks and Romans was aversive in character, merely a necessary evil to which mankind had to submit. This conception was modified appreciably in the Hebrew and early Christian cultures, but it was not until the Reformation that work is said to have acquired positive affective connotations. In his classic work, *The Protestant Ethic and the Spirit of Capitalism,* Max Weber (1930) documents his thesis that conceptions of the value of work have their roots in the teachings of Calvin and his followers. According to Weber, the sixteenth- and seventeenth-century Protestant believed that continuous bodily or mental labor increased the glory of God. Time devoted to leisure and enjoyment was wasted and worthy of moral condemnation. The route to salvation and to escape from eternal damnation was a laborious one and involved conscientious dedication to one's calling. Weber maintains that this system of moral values was the basis for the development of capitalism. As he puts it,

> . . . the religious valuation of restless, continuous, systematic work in a worldly calling, as the highest means to asceticism, and at the same time the surest and most evident proof of rebirth and genuine faith, must have been the most powerful conceivable lever for the expansion of that attitude toward life which we have here called the spirit of capitalism (p. 172).

If we accept Weber's contention that strenuous productive effort carried strong moral connotations for Protestants during the sixteenth and seventeenth centuries, there is still the question of the importance and pervasiveness of this source of motivation in the present day. Is the Protestant ethic a dominant theme in our present American culture or has it been diluted with the passage of time and replaced by different values?

During his lifetime Weber reported the beginning of the decline of the Protestant ethic and its replacement by material values, particularly in the United States. In the first decade of this century he wrote

> Since asceticism undertook to remodel the world and to work out its ideals in the world, material goods have gained an increasing and finally an inexorable power over the lives of men as at no previous period in history. . . . In the field of its highest development, in the United States, the pursuit of wealth, stripped of its religious and ethical meaning, tends to become associated with purely mundane passions, which often actually give it the character of a sport (pp. 181–182).

More recently, other writers (for example, Riesman, 1950; Whyte, 1956) have commented on changes in values in American culture, including the removal from its position of prominence of the Protestant ethic. These ventures into social criticism, although not documented with the quantitative measurements characteristic of the scientific method, seem entirely plausible. They do not dispute the role of learning in affecting the attractiveness or unattractiveness of hard work nor do they rule out the possibility of individual differences. They do, however, seriously question whether the social conditions exist at the present time for developing in large numbers persons who positively value hard productive labor.

Related to the problem of the affective consequences of effort is the effect of effort on the value of outcomes that are attained as a result. Festinger (1961) and Festinger and Aronson (1960) proposed that when individuals receive "insufficient rewards" following an expenditure of energy, there is a tendency to attribute additional value to the consequences of the energy expenditure. An outcome that has been acquired as a result of considerable effort tends to be more positively valent than it would have been if it had been more easily attained.

Festinger views the effects of effort on valence as a specific case of his theory of cognitive dissonance (Festinger, 1957). When a person exerts effort with the expectation of reaching some highly desired goal but does not reach it, dissonance is created between his cognition of the effort he has expended and his cognition that he has been unrewarded. One means of reducing this dissonance is to find something about the situation to which he can attach value.

A number of studies (Wright, 1937; Olds, 1953; Aronson, 1961; Lewis and Cairns, 1961) provide support for the hypothesis that objects acquire increased valence as a consequence of actual or anticipated effort. However, some contradictory data exist (Child and Adelsheim, 1944) and some evidence shows that the effects of effort on valence increase with age and are greater in boys than in girls (Child, 1946).

The problem of the effective consequences of energy expenditure is central to the relationship between work and motivation, but its solution appears rather complex and probably entails both innate and learned mechanisms. It does seem safe to conclude that the physical and mental efforts involved in work are not solely sources of negative affect. There are probably conditions, for example, continued inactivity and certain early socialization conditions, under which people derive satisfaction from energy expenditure. Some industrial studies lend support to such a notion. Friedmann and Havighurst's study of coal miners (1954) and Morse and Weiss's study of a national sample of employed workers (1955) indicate that a large proportion of workers state that they like their work because it keeps them busy and active and would dislike not working because they would have nothing to do with their time and would dislike being idle. There may be important individual differences in the affective consequences of energy expenditure or in the specific forms of energy expenditure that are sources of satisfaction. So far we can only speculate concerning possible answers to these problems. Their solution awaits further research.

The Production of Goods and Services

Work roles involve not only the expenditure of energy but also energy expenditure for some purpose. The mental and physical efforts are directed toward the production of goods or services—the assembly of transistors, or the growing of food, or the curing of the sick. Our interest here is in the motivational implications of these functional properties of work roles. To what extent and in what ways do the particular functions involved in a work role represent a source of satisfaction or dissatisfaction to the worker?

A great deal has been written about the pleasures and frustrations associated with different kinds of jobs. Historians have described the enjoyment that the craftsman during the Middle Ages obtained from plying his trade; novelists have described the dedication of the scientist and the artist; and social critics have assailed the plight of the modern industrial worker. Although such observations lack the objectivity and rigor demanded by the scientist, they do underscore the difficulty of drawing any firm conclusions on this problem without at least specifying the particular form of work being considered, if not the person who carried it out.

Psychoanalytic theorists have speculated about motives that might explain the intrinsic satisfactions derived from work. In *Civilization and Its Discontents*, Freud (1930) stressed the opportunity that work afforded individuals for discharging libidinal impulses. Workers could sublimate their sexual and aggressive impulses and at the same time bind themselves more closely to reality. Hendrick (1943) has proposed a modified psychoanalytic view of motivation with his concept of a "work principle." He suggests that

> . . . work is not primarily motivated by sexual need or associated aggressions, but by the need for efficient use of the muscular and intellectual tools, regardless of what secondary needs—self-preservative, aggressive, or sexual—a work performance may also satisfy. I shall call this thesis the *work principle*, the principle that primary pleasure is sought by efficient use of the central nervous system for the performance of well-

integrated ego functions which enable the individual
to control or alter his environment (p. 311).

Goldstein (1940) proposed a similar motivational mecha-
nism with his discussion of the tendency toward actualization as did
Maslow (1955) with a concept of growth needs. These motivational
conceptions, although intuitively appealing, do not easily lend
themselves to empirical test. The basic problem remains to determine what outcomes associated with jobs or tasks are rewarding
under what conditions.

Beginning about 1950, research in experimental psychology
using animal subjects has contributed a new perspective to the
problem. Since that date there have been numerous references to
rewarding properties of outcomes that are not easily reducible to
physiological needs or drives, suggesting a motivational system
more akin to the self-actualization tendencies proposed by Goldstein and Maslow. In brief, the data suggest that higher organisms
are rewarded by the opportunity to explore and manipulate their
environment. To cite just a few of the many relevant experiments,
Butler (1953) and Butler and Harlow (1957) have shown that monkeys will learn discrimination problems when the sole outcome is
the opportunity to inspect new territory; and Harlow, Harlow, and
Meyer (1950) found that monkeys will repeatedly solve a mechanical
problem even though they are not explicitly rewarded for doing so.

This development, along with parallel trends in psychoanalytic theory and general psychology, has led White (1959) to propose
the concept of effectance motivation:

> Effectance motivation must be conceived to involve
> satisfaction—a feeling of efficacy—in transactions in
> which behavior has an exploratory, varying, experi-
> mental character and produces changes in the stimu-
> lus field. Having this character, the behavior leads the
> organism to find out how the environment can be
> changed and what consequences flow from these
> changes (p. 329).

White argues convincingly that effectance motivation is not
learned through association with primary drive reduction. The feel-

ing of efficacy is innately satisfying. He does suggest, however, that learning results in the differentiation of effectance motivation and makes it profitable in adults "to distinguish various motives such as cognizance, construction, mastery, and achievement" (p. 323).

In spite of the fractionalization of tasks that accompanied the industrial revolution, many work roles in our present society provide opportunities for their occupants to experience a continually changing environment, to play an active part in inducing change in that environment and, in so doing, to use and develop further their skills and capacities. Studies of the unemployed and of the retired, as well as of members of such diverse occupational groups as accountants and engineers (Herzberg, Mausner, and Snyderman, 1959); managers (Porter, 1963); steel workers, salesmen, coalminers, and physicians (Friedmann and Havighurst, 1954); and assemblers (Turner and Miclette, 1962), point to the importance attached to such aspects of work.

Working may also serve a moral purpose for the worker. Many work roles provide their occupants with an opportunity to contribute to the happiness and well-being of their fellow man. The physician reduces the pain and prolongs the life of his patients; the teacher broadens the intellectual horizons of his students; the policeman protects members of the community against those who would break its laws; and the minister enriches the spiritual life of his congregation. Even when the actual value of a worker's contribution to society is more problematical, it may not be so viewed by the worker. People seem to structure their world cognitively so as to provide moral justification for their labors. Members of the armed forces charged with wholesale destruction of the enemy may view themselves as preservers of freedom; lawyers, hired to defend clients whom they believe to be guilty, may view themselves as defenders of the judicial system; and scientists involved in the development of weapon systems of frightening destructive power may stress their role in extending the frontiers of knowledge.

There is no doubt that the magnitude or nature of these satisfactions may vary greatly from one job to another or that the sources of satisfaction from jobs are different for different people. We still have much to learn about the nature of the interaction between the task or functional properties of work roles and the motivational systems of their occupants.

Social Interaction

Social psychologists usually emphasize the fact that work is a social activity. Virtually all work roles require social interaction with other people. The salesman interacts with his customers, the doctor with his patients, the supervisor with his subordinates, and the teacher with his students. Furthermore, most workers are members of one or more work groups, with whom they may interact more frequently than with members of their immediate family.

It has frequently been suggested that the social outcomes provided by the work may constitute an important factor in the decision to work. Miller and Form (1951) state

> The motives for working cannot be assigned only to economic needs, for men may continue to work even though they have no need for material goods. Even when their security and that of their children is assured, they continue to labor. Obviously this is so because the rewards they get from work are social, such as respect and admiration from their fellow men. . . . For all, work activity provides fellowship and social life (p. 115).

The tendency to gain satisfaction from social relationships has long been recognized as a human attribute. Nietzsche (1901) wrote of the *heerdeninstinkte*, or herd instinct, McDougall (1923) included gregariousness in his list of instincts, and contemporary psychologists refer to affiliation motives (Atkinson, 1958a) and needs for affection and inclusion (Schutz, 1958).

The importance of socially derived satisfactions in the motivation to work is suggested by a number of studies. In the Morse and Weiss study described earlier, for example, 31 percent of the respondents who said they would go on working even though it was not necessary economically gave as their reason their relationships with the people with whom they worked. If they did not work they would greatly miss their friends at work.

Herzberg, Mausner, Peterson, and Capwell (1957) have compiled data from fifteen studies of over 28,000 employees that point to the importance of the social satisfactions derived from work. In each of the studies, employees were asked what gave them satisfaction from their jobs. The most frequently mentioned sources of satisfaction were the "social aspects of the job," a term that the authors used to refer to all "on the job" contacts made by the worker with other workers, especially those at the same or nearly the same level within the organization. The second most frequently mentioned factor was the worker's relationship with his immediate supervisor.

The complexity of the relationship between social motivation and work becomes apparent when we attempt to specify the kinds of social outcomes that provide satisfaction. Clearly, it is not social interaction in any general sense that is satisfying to a given person, but specific kinds of socially derived outcomes, for example, having influence over other people, being liked by other people, being cared for by other people, and so on. Undoubtedly, there are extensive individual differences in the amount of satisfaction afforded by these particular kinds of outcomes. One person may derive satisfaction from one type of outcome, whereas a second may derive satisfaction from a very different kind of outcome. Furthermore, there are variations in the degree to which different kinds of social outcomes are provided by different work roles. A complete explanation of the role of social interaction in the motivation to work must be based on both individual differences in the strength of tendencies to derive satisfaction from particular kinds of social interaction as well as differences in the amount and kind of social interaction permitted or required by work roles.

Social Status

Sociologists have emphasized the importance of the work role in determining social status. A person's occupation greatly influences the way in which other people respond to him outside the work situation. Members of a high-status occupation (for example, physicians) are accorded greater respect and have greater freedom in choosing leisure activities than those of lower-status occupations receiving comparable economic rewards. The significance of occupational determinants of status is indicated by Warner, Meeker, and Eells (1949). They report a correlation of .91 between an individual's status and the status of his occupation.

Friedmann and Havighurst (1954) have discussed the effect of the work role on social status as follows:

> The job is a description or a tag which marks the person, both at his place of employment and in the world outside. The tailor is so described in his shop. But he also might be thought of as a tailor by his family, his golf partners, his insurance agent, his minister, and other persons who enter his nonwork life.
>
> As the worker carries the identity of his job, so he also acquires the status which society has assigned to it. This status might be related to his particular type of employment, or it might be based merely on the fact that he holds a job. In either case job status is an important determinant of the individual's status in his family and community (p. 4).

The source of satisfaction represented by social status is very similar to that discussed in the preceding section, that is, rewards derived from interaction with other persons. Here, however, we are concerned not only with persons with whom one interacts within the context of the work role but also with those with whom one interacts in other situations, such as family, friends, neighbors, and relatives.

Undoubtedly work roles vary in the amount of social status they provide. Methods developed for measuring the relative status of occupations have been adequately described elsewhere (Caplow, 1954; Roe, 1956; Reiss, Duncan, Hatt, and North, 1961). Because our focus in this chapter is on factors affecting the decision to participate in the labor force rather than on choice of work role, our interest is in differences in social status between persons who are and persons who are not members of the labor force.

A person may desire to work because he expects that doing so will affect his social status or, to be more precise, because he believes that others will be more likely to accept him if he does so. Working may be perceived to be instrumental to social acceptance and respect, whereas not working may be anticipated to result in social rejection and disapproval.

Bakke (1940a, 1940b) has described the loss of status experienced by the unemployed during the Great Depression. The worker who had lost his job and was "wandering from gate to gate begging for a chance to work" was no longer accorded the respect of "a fellow your mates look to" or "a man who never lets his family down." Although the economic deprivations of unemployment could be somewhat reduced by going on relief, this public declaration of his failure brought with it further disrespect from his associates.

The effects of employment on social status depend on the norms of the culture or subculture of which the person is a member. Conceivably there are some segments of the population in which not working has no detrimental effects on status, or may even enhance one's status.

The difference in the proportion of men and women who occupy work roles in our society may be attributed, at least in part, to cultural definitions of the "proper role" of the two sexes and to differences in the forces induced on members of the two sexes to work. In our society the man is expected to be the breadwinner. With few exceptions, men between the ages of 20 and 65 are expected to attempt to secure gainful employment and to accept such employment if it is offered to them. The man who is not working and who makes no effort to secure work may experience disapproval and rejection.

The situation confronting the woman in our society is somewhat different. Because she alone has the capacity to give birth to and nurse children, her primary function is seen as one of mother and homemaker. It is indeed possible that, for married women with children, social pressure may tend to increase the force on her away from working.

Whatever the cause, it is clear that at the time of this writing, working occupies a more important place in the lives of men than women. In his study of the values of college students, Rosenberg (1957) found that men were much more likely than women to report that their career or occupation would give them the most satisfaction in their lives; women were more likely to report that their primary satisfaction would come from family relationships. A further indication of current differences in the importance of work to men and to women is Brayfield, Wells, and Strate's finding (1957) that job satisfaction is more highly correlated with general satisfaction among employed men than among employed women.

Discussion and Summary

Later sections of this book will deal with the problems of how people choose among different kinds of work roles and with factors affecting their satisfaction with and performance in a given work role. Our concern in this chapter was, "Why do people work at all?" Virtually every man and almost every woman at some point in the course of his or her lifetime engages in remunerated employment. By examining the rather simple-minded and yet seldom-raised question of why people work, we have tried to set the stage for later consideration of the more specific and more easily researched aspects of the work-motivation relationship.

We have assumed that the probability that a person will work is dependent both on the availability of work and on his preference between working and not working. In an attempt to specify what some of the determinants of this preference are, we have examined five properties of work roles:

1. They provide financial remuneration.
2. They require the expenditure of energy.
3. They involve the production of goods and services.
4. They permit or require social interaction.
5. They affect the social status of the worker.

We have no basis for judging the relative influence of these different properties of work roles on the strength of preference for working. To study this question adequately we would have to vary systematically the outcomes provided by work, for example, eliminate economic remuneration and observe the effects on the number of people in the labor force. Such research is obviously impossible, so we have had to rely on other more indirect sources of data. With the possible exception of expenditure of energy, there is reason to believe that each of these properties is satisfying to most persons. The desire to work is not to be explained solely in terms of its instrumental relationship to the attainment of money but also in terms of its consequences for the use and development of skills, the attainment of acceptance and respect by others, and the opportunity to contribute something useful to society.

Although we have said little in this chapter about individual differences, there is no reason to believe that working serves the same purpose for different individuals. People differ in their desires and aversions, and for this reason simple generalizations about why people work are meaningless. We should also not lose sight of the extensive differences existing among work roles. All work roles may provide financial remuneration, but some provide more than others. Similarly, work roles differ in the amount and kind of energy expenditure they require, in the content of the functions performed, in the social interaction they permit or require, and in the social status they afford. These work-role differences are exceedingly important for a consideration of satisfaction and performance, and it is in this context that they will be treated in subsequent chapters. However, they cannot be overlooked in an analysis of the decision to work. Such decisions are probably never made in the abstract on the basis of evaluations of the consequences of *working in general.* On the contrary, it seems very likely that the decisions are always made with respect to relatively specific work possibilities that are accessible to the person. These possibilities are very different for the college graduate than for the high school dropout and are very different for men than for women.

A consideration of the rewards associated with work is of particular importance in a society having serious unemployment problems, which threaten to increase with continued developments in automation. During the last decade a tremendous number of jobs were eliminated by automation. The effects have been most marked in manufacturing, agriculture, and mining. One million fewer workers were employed in manufacturing in 1962 than a scant six years earlier. Agricultural employment has been declining by about 200,000 a year; and in mining, total employment has been reduced by over one-fifth since 1957. To some extent these declines have been offset by increased employment in private and public services. However, the increases in these areas have not been sufficient to offset both the declines and the continual growth of the labor force. Conceivably, opportunities for employment in managerial positions will be reduced as computers are adopted to take over day-to-day decisions.

Doubt is growing that our nation can maintain the level of economic growth necessary to provide employment for those workers who are the victims of automation. Unemployment seems likely to continue at present or even greater levels, and the possibility exists that we may ultimately reach a point where the major portion of the population is deprived of the opportunity to contribute to its economy.

Studies of the unemployed during the depression of the thirties (Lazarsfeld, 1932; Williams, 1933; Hall, 1934; Israeli, 1935; Rundquist and Sletto, 1936; Stouffer and Lazarsfeld, 1937; Bakke, 1940a, 1940b; Komarovsky, 1940) aptly testify to the emotional and social problems created by continued unemployment. If we are correct in assuming that work provides many sources of satisfaction that are not economic in nature, the deprivations of unemployment cannot be eliminated by making up the worker's economic losses through the extension of unemployment insurance or more abundant programs of relief. The problem facing a prosperous society with a high level of unemployment is to find ways of incorporating into leisure activity rewards that are customarily attained through work.

Part Two

Choice of
Work Role

4

Occupational Choice

According to the 1949 edition of the *Dictionary of Occupational Titles,* Americans are employed in 22,028 different jobs. These jobs represent tremendous variations in kinds of work, from bank president to building foreman, from hosiery mender to horse trainer, and from longshoreman to linotype operator. They provide considerable latitude of choice for the typical person entering the labor market. This is not to suggest that all alternatives are open to all persons. Some of them, such as corporation president, usually are not entered from outside the labor market but are attained only after considerable work experience. Still others, because of factors of supply and demand, may be relatively inaccessible at any given time. Nonetheless, the range of actual possibilities is for most persons exceedingly large and presents a problem of occupational choice.

Far from being an inevitable aspect of social life, occupational choice exists only in societies with some division of labor and with some occupational mobility. In some primitive societies there is no occupational choice because virtually all occupations are the same. Even in more complex societies there are sometimes strong sanctions compelling a person to work in the occupation of his father. If the father is a slave the son becomes a slave; if the father is a carpenter the son becomes a carpenter.

Occupational choices have important consequences for the individuals who make them and for the larger society in which

the choices are made. For the individual—particularly the male—
the decision concerning occupation ranks with the choice of mate
in its implications for later satisfaction and adjustment. The forty
or more hours a week spent on the job represent, over the course of
a working lifetime, a tremendous investment that may reap rich
rewards or produce intense dissatisfaction. Furthermore, the effects
of the occupational choice are not restricted to the work situation
but often influence where and how the person will spend his non-
working hours. Super (1957) has indicated the extensive effects of
the occupation on recreation and friendship patterns and family
activities as well as on other aspects of the style of living.

The significance of the occupational choice for the individual stems primarily from the irreversibility of the decision. Although people do change their occupations, the psychological and
economic costs of doing so are great, particularly where the occupations require extensive training or preparation. Consequently,
the majority of vocational choices in our society are lifetime choices
and commit the decision maker to pursuing a kind of work and, in
many cases, a style of life for the remainder of his working years.

From a societal standpoint the process of occupational
choice is no less important. In order to function effectively, any
social system, be it a nation or an industrial organization, must
attract qualified persons to perform its various roles. A shortage of
personnel who are both competent and willing to work in a given
occupation places serious restrictions on the degree to which the
system can attain its goals. The difficulty faced by industry in recruiting enough trained scientists and engineers, as well as the current national problem in staffing our educational institutions with
trained teachers, illustrates the basic dependence of social systems
on the vocational decisions of individuals.

People make choices not only among occupations but also
among organizations in which to practice their occupations. Usually, a person selects his occupation before deciding on an organization. He decides to become a doctor before choosing a hospital
with which to affiliate or decides to become an engineer before
joining a particular corporation. In some instances, however, the
temporal relationship between these two decisions may be reversed.

A person may decide to go into his father's business before deciding on the kind of role he will play in it.

Occupational and organizational choices are not independent of one another. Choice of the occupation of lawyer, for example, limits the organizational choice to those institutions employing lawyers. Similarly, prior choice of an organization limits the person to the occupations that can be practiced in that organization.

Although a great deal of research has been conducted on the occupational choice process, comparatively little attention has been directed to factors affecting peoples' choices among organizations. To be sure, single employers have conducted studies of the effectiveness of their recruitment programs, but this research is seldom broad enough in scope to provide much insight into the organizational choice process. We remain pretty much in the dark concerning the variables affecting peoples' decisions to work for the government, private industry, educational institutions, hospitals, or social agencies.

A treatment of the problem of choice of work role involves both occupational and organizational choices, but we have chosen to focus our attention on the former. The absence of a large body of sound, published empirical research on the organizational choice process makes it impossible for us to give it the attention it justly deserves.

Normative and Empirical Approaches

It is possible to distinguish two somewhat different approaches to the study of any choice process. One approach, often called "normative," is concerned with how choices ought to be made. Traditionally, the development of normative models of choice behavior has fallen within the province of economists and statisticians. The second approach, which has been called "empirical" or "descriptive," is concerned with the explanation of how choices are, in fact, made. Empirical models of choice behavior have primarily been of interest to the psychologist, although this area of inquiry by no means defines the discipline of psychology.

Insofar as psychology is a profession as well as a science, its members are also interested in normative questions. Psychologists are frequently called upon to give advice on how decisions *should* be made. Sometimes their approach has been to construct formal models of the decision-making process that will permit a rational weighting of the expected consequences of alternative courses of action (see, for example, Cronbach and Gleser, 1957). More frequently, however, they have developed methods for dealing with decision makers that are designed to increase the rationality of the choices made.

Applied to the realm of occupational choice, this distinction between normative and empirical approaches helps to clarify the role of vocational guidance in the study of occupational choice. Vocational guidance is essentially normative in nature. It consists of a series of methods, such as interviewing and psychological testing, which are expected to help individuals make better occupational choices. The criterion of decision quality is usually stated in terms of the person's adjustment to the occupation—a criterion that includes both satisfaction and performance.

An empirical approach to occupational choice is concerned with how persons make vocational decisions. The objective is to determine the factors that explain the occupational choices that are made.

A great deal more attention has been directed toward the normative than to the empirical study of occupational choice. Vocational guidance has flourished as a field of knowledge and specialization for over fifty years. Yet the study of the variables affecting vocational decisions is comparatively recent.

It can be argued that ultimately the technology of vocational guidance must be based on a sound conception of occupational choice. If we are to alter effectively the vocational decisions of individuals, we must understand the dynamics of the process by which decisions are made. In a sense, the methods of the vocational counselor represent attempts to modify the values of variables that influence occupational choice. If the nature of the variables and their manner of interaction are clearly understood, the task of the counselor may be appreciably aided.

The Definition of Occupational Choice

A prerequisite to a scientific study of any phenomenon is a definition that will permit the researcher to distinguish it from other phenomena. Before we can examine the determinants of occupational choice we must have a working definition of occupational choice so that we can tell when such a choice has been made and what occupation has been chosen.

Roe (1956) has pointed out different meanings of the term:

> We need first to define what is meant by choice. Do we mean what a person would most like to do, assuming that he had the capacities, training, and opportunity? Do we mean what he will try to do? Or do we mean what he actually does come to do? (p. 251).

In terms of our model we can distinguish three different meanings of the chosen occupation:

1. The occupation with the most positive valence (subsequently called the preferred occupation).
2. The occupation toward which there is the strongest positive force (subsequently called the chosen occupation).
3. The occupation in which the person is a member (subsequently called the attained occupation).

Although in many cases the most positively valent occupation is sought and finally attained, these three meanings of occupational choice can be distinguished both conceptually and operationally. In the balance of this chapter we will refer to them as occupational preferences, occupational choices, and occupational attainments. The term "occupational choice process" will be used in a very broad sense to indicate all three of these referents and their determinants.

Occupational Preferences. For any given person, at a given time, occupations may be assumed to differ in their valence or attractiveness. Some occupations may be positively valent, others negatively valent, and still others the object of indifference. The preferred occupation of a particular individual at a given time is defined as the occupation which at that time has the highest positive valence.

The valence of occupations and preferences among occupations have typically been measured by means of verbal report. Persons are asked to state the degree to which they like various occupations or to state the occupations they most prefer. As we pointed out in Chapter Two, there are other means of measuring preferences but they are difficult to apply to occupations. Although observations of actual choices in situations in which people believe they can have the occupation they choose would be a better indicator, the research investigator is seldom in a position to create such a situation. In one experiment in which this procedure was used, Walster (1963) found some discrepancy between choices and verbal reports of the attractiveness of occupations. She asked men who had recently been drafted into the army to rate each of ten job descriptions on a 31-point scale, ranging from "would like extremely much" to "would dislike extremely much." Each subject was then given his choice between two jobs rated near the middle of the scale and separated by 3 to 7 scale points in ratings. He was then led to believe that the job that he chose would be his job assignment during his two years in the army. Fifty-one of the 244 subjects (21 percent) chose the job that they had earlier rated lower in attractiveness.

In the laboratory, it is possible to let subjects choose among different tasks or to let them structure a single task so that their preferences will be revealed. Such a procedure has been used (McClelland, 1958b; Atkinson and Litwin, 1960; Atkinson, Bastian, Earl, and Litwin, 1960), but the tasks have been simple in nature and do not approach the complexity of occupations.

Occupational Choices. Individuals not only have preferences concerning occupations but also make choices among them. Before entering the labor force each person must select from among the various forms of work that are available and then strive to implement his choice.

The term occupational choice is used here to refer to the process of selection among occupations. The chosen occupation is the result of this process and is the occupation that the person is attempting to enter. Our conceptual model would lead us to explain occupational choice (as distinct from preferences) in terms of the relative strength of forces acting on the person. The chosen occupation is assumed to be that occupation toward which there is the strongest positive force.

A frequent indicator of choice of occupation is enrollment in a training program for that occupation. Thus, enrollment in a medical school would indicate that the person had chosen to become a physician, whereas enrollment in a law school would signify that he had chosen to become a lawyer.

Occupational Attainments. Conceptually, the attainment of an occupation is very different from either a preference for it or a choice of it. Some individuals are unsuccessful in gaining entrance to occupations that they have chosen and for which they have devoted substantial proportions of their lives in preparation. Operationally, the assessment of occupational attainment is relatively simple. The occupation in which the person is presently working can usually be accurately determined from records or verbal reports.

Differences Among Preference, Choice, and Attainment. The significance of the distinction that has been made between the phenomena that we have labeled occupational preference, occupational choice, and occupational attainment depends on the existence of differences among them. If all people choose the occupations they most prefer and attain the occupation they choose, the conceptual and operational distinctions that we have made become unimportant. In that case investigators who are studying preferences will in fact be studying the same things as those who are studying choices or attainments.

On theoretical grounds, it can be argued that preferences among occupations should be related to, but not identical with, choices among them and that choice of an occupation by a person should be a necessary but not sufficient condition for its attainment. In the model presented in Chapter Two, we defined a preference between outcomes in terms of their relative valence. We also asserted (Proposition 1) that the valence of an outcome was at least partly explicable in terms of its expected relation to other outcomes and their valence. Preferences among occupations are also defined in terms of their relative valence and are predicted to be systematically related to the estimated consequences of entry into these occupations and the valence of these consequences for the person.

We have assumed choices among acts to reflect the relative strength of forces acting on the person. We have asserted (Proposition 2) that each of these forces is determined by the valence of outcomes and by the expectancy or subjective probability that the act will result in the outcome. Accordingly, we would view choices among occupations as the result not only of preferences among them but also of the subjective probability and expected costs of their attainment. Persons may not choose the most positively valent occupation if the subjective probability of attaining it is low or if the expected costs of attaining it are very high.

It is also clear that a decision to try for one outcome rather than another is no guarantee that a person will attain the outcome that he has chosen. A person's success in implementing his decisions is also affected by his abilities and, in many cases, by events that are beyond his control. Thus, a person's choice of an occupation will not lead to successful attainment of that occupation if, for example, he lacks the ability to complete the necessary training, or if he cannot find employment after completing the training.

Apart from these theoretical considerations, there is empirical evidence that preferences among occupations do not always coincide with choices. On the basis of data collected during the Great Depression, Williamson (1939) reported that 37 percent of college men and 46 percent of college women did not give the same occupation as both their chosen and preferred occupations. Rosenberg's data (1957), collected in 1952, show a comparable figure of 22 percent for a sample including both college men and women. The latter study also yields information concerning the occupations that are most frequently entered reluctantly, that is, in which the proportion of those choosing the field but not preferring it was relatively high. Business occupations head this list. Fifty-three percent of students choosing real estate or finance, 48 percent of those choosing business (unspecified), and 40 percent of those choosing sales-promotion occupations stated that they would have preferred some other field. At the other end of the list are medicine and art, with 7 percent and 14 percent, respectively.

What factors might be responsible for a difference between

choice and preference? Rosenberg's data indicate that the student reluctantly choosing a business career is relatively uncertain about his school work and is uninterested in it. He cuts classes more often and receives lower grades. It seems possible that these students may not feel that they have the ability needed for the occupations they would like to enter and, therefore, feel forced to compromise. Strong (1943) listed eight factors that might cause choices to deviate from preferences, including lack of necessary ability, personality, and health.

It is also clear that a disproportionately large number of persons state a preference for higher-status occupations than actually attain them (Kroger and Louttit, 1935; Sisson, 1938; Livesay, 1941). These studies do not indicate how much of this discrepancy comes about because individuals do not choose their preferred occupation or choose it but fail to attain it.

A discrepancy between occupational choice and occupational attainment occurs whenever a person fails to cross one of the necessary hurdles for entry into that occupation. Successful attainment of an occupation is a result of two sets of choices—one by an individual, the other by social institutions. People not only *select* occupations, they *are selected for* occupations. This latter process serves to maintain standards of performance in occupations through admitting only those who are expected to prove effective. It also helps to maintain the level of rewards received by members of occupations by keeping supply lower than demand.

The specific social institutions that execute the selective function vary greatly from one occupation to another. For the professions, the job of recruiting and selecting members rests largely with members of the occupation. The medical profession, for example, determines which persons shall call themselves, and practice as, physicians. Their judgment is enforced by the power of the state, which prevents an unqualified person from performing as a member of that occupation. For the semiskilled and unskilled trades, selection is largely carried out by the employer, whereas the principal control over entry into the skilled trades rests with labor unions. The only occupations for which there is no formal institutional selection are those involving self-employment, such as farming or ownership of a retail business. However, as Caplow (1954) points out, the necessary requirement of large capital investment and the dependence of persons seeking to enter these occupations on bank loans accords these institutions some selective function.

It seems safe to conclude, therefore, that the phenomena of occupational preference, choice, and attainment are sufficiently distinct to warrant their separate treatment. Preferences among occupations are important but by no means the only determinants of occupational choices. Similarly, choices of occupations are necessary but not sufficient conditions for the successful attainment of occupations.

Motives and the Occupational Choice Process

It is usually assumed that people's occupational choices are determined by their motives. To the extent to which this is true, we should be able to predict and explain differences in the occupational preferences, choices, and attainments of people through assessment of individual differences in motives. In the following section we will review the research evidence bearing on this hypothetical relationship. We will examine the relationship of motivational variables to occupational preferences, to occupational choices, and to occupational attainments.

Motives and Occupational Preferences. Most investigations of the role of motivational variables in occupational preference have utilized pencil and paper inventories of the motivational variables. The subject is asked to indicate the extent to which he likes or derives satisfaction from various objects or activities. These responses are scored according to some logically or empirically derived system, and the resultant scores are related to stated preferences among occupations.

The three tests most frequently related to occupational preferences are the Strong Vocational Interest Blank, the Kuder Preference Record, and the Allport-Vernon Study of Values.[1] The Strong test has an empirically derived scoring key. A respondent's answers

[1]This test appeared in revised form in 1951 as the Allport-Vernon-Lindzey Study of Values. For a more complete description of these three tests consult Cronbach, L., *Essentials of Psychological Testing.* New York: HarperCollins, 1960.

are scored for different occupations, each score indicating the similarity between his answers and those of members of that occupation. The Kuder and the Allport-Vernon tests, in contrast, have scoring keys that are logically or theoretically based. The Kuder provides scores on nine dimensions of interests: outdoor, mechanical, computational, scientific, persuasive, artistic, literary, musical, social service, and clerical.[2] The Allport-Vernon, which is based on Spranger's classification of values, provides data on six value dimensions: theoretical, economic, social, religious, aesthetic, and political.

There is considerable evidence that the Strong Vocational Interest Blank scores are related to people's reports of their occupational preferences. Strong (1943) computed the occupational scores on twenty-three scales for a group of college seniors and rank-ordered them for each person. The median ranking of the occupation that the student wanted to enter was 2.6. In another study similar in design but of college freshmen, Strong found that the score on the scale corresponding to the preferred occupation had a median rank of 3.5 when compared with all other scales. Similar results from a study of high school boys and girls were reported by Carter, Taylor, and Canning (1941).

The nature of the construction and scoring of the Strong test does not lend itself to a determination of the specific pattern of motives that are characteristic of individuals with different occupational preferences. The scores obtained from the test indicate not what activities and events are liked and disliked but the degree of similarity of the likes and dislikes of that person to members of various occupations. Consequently, these findings can be taken to mean that the interests of persons preferring a given occupation are more likely to be similar to the interests of persons actually in that occupation than to those in other occupations. Since preference is undoubtedly one of the determinants of occupational attainment, these findings should not be surprising. Their significance lies primarily in their implications for the validity of the test rather than

[2]Kuder has recently published a new interest inventory, the Kuder Preference Record—Occupational, which, like the Strong, yields scores on empirically derived occupational scales.

in any illumination concerning the motivational bases of occupational preferences.

Stone (1933) determined the preferred occupations of a group of college students and related them to their scores on the Allport-Vernon Study of Values. The various occupational preferences and associated values are expressed in Table 4.1.

Astin (1958) constructed his own interest test on the basis of a cluster analysis of scores on twenty-one items answered by two-hundred college freshmen. The test was scored to yield measures of the strength of three needs: (1) managerial-aggressive need, defined as a need to dominate and control others; (2) status need, defined as a concern for monetary and social prestige outcomes of work; and (3) organization need, defined as a desire to structure and organize both the work and the job environment. Students stating a preference for careers in sales, managerial, and persuasive occupations obtained the highest scores on the managerial-aggressive need, whereas those who were vocationally undecided, as well as those who preferred the occupations of farmer and engineer, had the lowest scores on this need. The status need measure did not discriminate among those preferring different occupations, whereas those with the highest scores on the organization need preferred scientific occupations.

McClelland (1955) reported a study of the relationship between the strength of achievement motive, measured by the thematic apperception method, and occupational preferences. College freshmen with various achievement motive scores were asked to state whether they liked, disliked, or were indifferent to one-hundred dif-

Table 4.1. Characteristic Allport-Vernon Values for
College Students Indicating Preferences for
Different Classes of Occupations.

Business:	High economic, low theoretical and aesthetic
Banking:	High economic, low religious
Medicine:	High theoretical, low economic and political
Education:	High aesthetic, low economic
Law:	High political, low theoretical
Literature:	High aesthetic and religious, low economic

Source: After Stone, 1933, p. 275.

ferent occupations. The top 20 percent on need for achievement were found to express significantly greater liking than the bottom 20 percent for the following six occupations: stockbroker, office manager, sales manager, buyer of merchandise, real estate salesman, factory manager. Apparently, a high level of achievement motivation tends to be associated with a preference for business occupations.

Other studies have indicated a tendency for persons with high need for achievement to prefer activities involving intermediate degrees of risk. McClelland (1958b), studying groups of kindergarten and third-grade children in a ring-tossing task, found that those with high need achievement tended to stand at a distance from the ring so that their probability of success was moderate (p = .11 to .30), whereas those with lower scores on need achievement stood either much closer or much further away. Similar preferences for activities involving intermediate probabilities of success on the part of high need achievers have been reported by Atkinson and Litwin (1960), Atkinson, Bastian, Earl, and Litwin (1960), and Scodel, Ratoosh, and Minas (1959). A theoretical model to account for these data has been proposed by Atkinson (1957). McClelland, in contrast, has focused on their societal implications. These findings constitute a link in his argument that the economic growth of a society is dependent on the existence in that society of a high level of need for achievement among people playing a key role in the economy. The reader who is interested in this broader question should consult his book, *The Achieving Society* (McClelland, 1961), for a comprehensive analysis of evidence regarding the relationship of achievement motivation to economic growth.

If the relationship between need achievement and preference for intermediate risks is corroborated in further research, it could have important implications for the problem of occupational choice. Risk is involved not only in the content of certain occupations but also in the content of many vocational decisions. Some persons take calculated risks in their choice of an occupation, selecting one in which the probability of attainment is considerably less than certainty. Persons with high need achievement may prefer occupations that permit the making of decisions which involve moderate degrees of risk and they may also tend to choose occupations that they have a moderate probability of attaining. Both of these possibilities represent interesting problems for further research. The latter possibility has been studied by Burnstein (1963). He found a tendency for persons with high need for achievement and low fear of failure to aspire to more prestigeful occupations, where the probability of attainment is less than certainty, than persons with low need for achievement and high fear of failure. However, individuals with high need for achievement and low fear of failure were *less* likely to aspire to occupations like United States Supreme Court justice and state governor where the risk was very great. An analysis of variance indicated that fear of failure, measured by the Mandler-Sarason Test Anxiety Scale, contributed more to these results than need for achievement.

Taken as a group, the studies that we have described in this section indicate considerable correspondence between the motives of individuals, as measured by both verbal reports and fantasy, and their preferences among occupations. People tend to express a preference for occupations providing outcomes that independent observations indicate to be positively valent. In none of these studies is the relationship between motives and occupational preferences a perfect one or even a very strong one. However, the absence of perfect correspondence is easily attributable to unreliability of measures and to the fact that the analyses dealt with the relationship between single motives and occupational preferences.

Motives and Occupational Choices. Many studies have been made of differences in the motivations of persons in training for different occupations. In one of the more comprehensive of these, Traxler and McCall (1941) report mean profiles on the Kuder Preference Record for freshmen enrolled in different fields of study at the University of South Carolina. The data show a marked consistency between measured interests and the content of the program of study. For example, engineering students were found to have relatively high scientific and computational interests; journalism students, high literary interests; and art students high artistic interests. Comparable findings concerning the relationship between Kuder scores and major field of study have been reported by Yum (1942), Marzolf (1946), and Kuder (1946).

Vernon and Allport (1931) compared the scores on the Allport-Vernon Study of Values of persons majoring in or working in a number of different specialties.[3] In general, the distinctive values of each of these groups were congruent with the nature of their chosen professions. Those in economics, business, and engineering had strong economic values; those in law and politics had strong political values; those in literature and languages had strong aesthetic values; and those in science, medicine, and psychology had strong theoretical values. Seashore (1947) compared the scores on the same test of 452 college men who were majors in health and physical education with 252 men majoring in the applied social sciences. The majors in health and physical education had high scores on the scales of social, religious, and political values and low scores on economic and aesthetic values while the applied social science majors had high social and religious values and low political, economic, and aesthetic values. Cantril and Allport (1933) found male commercial students to be high in economic and low in aesthetic values, whereas male salesmanship students were high in economic and political and low in aesthetic and religious values. Female students of literature were high in aesthetic and low in theoretical values, and female students of science were high in theoretical and low in economic values. Comparable evidence regarding differences in Allport-Vernon values for students in different fields of study has been reported by Pintner (1933); Duffy and Crissey (1940); Kelly and Fiske (1950); Allport, Vernon, and Lindzey (1951); and Conrad and Jaffe (1960).

Rosenberg (1957) has conducted a large-scale study of the relationship between the values of college students and the occupations they choose. Data were available from 3,905 college students selected on a representative basis from eleven universities throughout the country. In the course of an interview, each student was presented with a list of requirements (for example, permit me to be creative and original, provide me with adventure, and so on) and was asked to judge the extent to which a job or career would have to satisfy each of these requirements before he or she could consider it ideal. Using these judgments, three indices were constructed: (1) a

---

[3]Separate breakdowns were not given for persons majoring in a field and those actually working in the field.

Self-Expression-Oriented Index, based on rankings of importance of "permit me to be creative and original" and "opportunity to use my special abilities and aptitudes"; (2) a People-Oriented Index, based on rankings of importance of "opportunity to work with people rather than things" and "opportunity to be helpful to others"; and (3) an Extrinsic-Reward-Oriented Index, based on rankings of importance of "chance to earn a good deal of money" and "give me social status and prestige." Marked differences in scores on these three indices were found among students choosing different occupations. Highest scores on the Self-Expression-Oriented Index were observed for students choosing the fields of architecture, journalism, drama, and art, while lowest scores were obtained by students choosing business occupations such as sales, hotel management, real estate, or finance. These same business occupations stood highest on the Extrinsic-Reward-Oriented Index, while social work and teaching stood lowest. On the People-Oriented Index the highest scores were received by students choosing social work, medicine, teaching, and social science, and the lowest scores were received by those choosing natural science, engineering, and farming.

Rosenberg has also established that the degree of association between values and choices increases during the period of college training. In 1952, 712 students who had been interviewed concerning their values and occupational choices in 1950 were reinterviewed. Because the questions on values and choices were phrased identically both times, it was possible to observe that the degree of association between these two variables increased during the two-year span. To a large extent, this increase in consistency between values and choices came about because people changed their choices to agree with their reported values. For example, students with relatively low scores on the People-Oriented Index who, in 1950, had chosen teaching as a profession, usually had changed their choices to some other field by 1952. Similarly, those with low scores on the Extrinsic-Reward Index who had chosen business in 1950 usually had changed their choices to some other occupation by 1952.

Because preferences among occupations undoubtedly constitute one of the factors affecting choices among them, it is not surprising to find that motives are associated with occupational choices in a manner similar to that previously reported for occupational preferences. However, occupational choices are also influenced by what Ginzberg, Ginsburg, Axelrod, and Herma (1951) have called "reality" factors. According to our model the probability that a person will choose an occupation is a function not only of its valence but also of his expectancy that it can be attained and of the amount of "cost" that he expects to be associated with its attainment. Consequently we can argue that it should be more difficult to predict a person's occupational choice from his motives than to predict his preferred occupation. Unfortunately, the existing evidence does not permit the testing of this possibility. There are no studies of preference and choice using the same measure on the same population. Furthermore, investigators have typically emphasized the statistical significance of relationships and have failed to report their data in such a way as to permit determination of the strength of association between motives and either choices or preferences.

We would also predict that the degree of relationship between motives and occupational choices should vary with the degree to which the choice has been "constrained" by "reality" factors. People who expect that they can attain all occupations, and for whom considerations of time and cost are relatively unimportant, should choose the occupation they most prefer and their choices should be quite highly predictable from their motives. In contrast, those who are less confident of their abilities, and for whom cost differences are highly important, would be more likely to compromise. Their choices should reflect the influence of many factors other than their motives and should be less predictable from measures of motivational variables. There has been no really direct test of this proposition, but the findings of a study by McArthur and Stevens (1955) bear on it. They found that the expressed vocational interests of graduates of private schools correspond more closely with their ultimate occupations than do the expressed vocational interests of graduates of public schools.

Motives and Occupational Attainments. An extensive amount of research has been conducted in an attempt to determine motivational differences among people working in different occupations. In an early study, Cowdery (1926) was successful in differentiating among the interests of lawyers, physicians, and engineers. Subsequently Strong (1943) carried out a very broad study of the interests of persons in different occupations. No other empirical work on this problem approaches that of Strong, either in number of occupations studied or in number of variables employed. However, Strong was less concerned with the nature of the differences in interests among members of various occupations than he was with constructing an interest test to reflect the degree of similarity between the interests of a given person and the characteristic pattern of interests of people in different occupations. It is clear from his work that successful members of different occupations do report that they are interested in different activities, but the nature of these differences can only be revealed through content analysis of the large number of scoring keys for the test.

Kuder (1946) has reported the mean scores and standard deviations on each of the nine scales of the Kuder Preference Record for men and women working in a large number of different occupations. The results are generally consistent with the view that people tend to attain occupations that are consistent with their interests. Chemists are found to be particularly high on the scientific scale, writers on the literary scale, musicians on the musical scale, and accountants on the computational scale. A new edition of the Kuder test, the Kuder Preference Record—Occupational (Kuder, 1959) resembles the Strong Vocational Interest Blank in that it yields scores indicating the extent to which the preferences reported by the person taking the test are similar to those of members of different occupational groups.

Psychoanalytic theorists have emphasized the role of unconscious impulses and defense mechanisms in choice of occupation. Persons prefer, choose, and enter vocations that have some symbolic relationship to their inner conflicts and unconscious impulses. Brill (1949), for example, writes, "Because work or profession is nothing but a sublimating process in the service of hunger and love we may assume that it also must be guided by the individual's unconscious motives. Investigation has convinced me of the truth of this assumption" (p. 266). In a similar vein, Forer (1953) writes, "Choice of a vocation is not primarily rational or logical but is a somewhat blind, impulsive, emotional, and automatic process and is not always subject to practical and reasonable considerations" (p. 361).

Evidence in support of this position has typically been obtained by a study of members of various occupational groups, hence the inclusion of our discussion of this position here. The existing evidence is largely clinical in nature with no attempt to measure objectively the specific motivational variables that are assumed to affect occupational choice.

Brill (1949) presents a very extensive discussion of the psychodynamics of persons in different occupations. He describes the sadomasochistic impulses that he feels have been sublimated in the vocational choices of physicians, the unconscious guilt feelings that characterize lawyers and ministers, the sublimation of infantile exhibitionism of actors, soldiers, and lifeguards, and the voyeuristic tendencies of photographers. Even the choice of lower-level occupations is suggested to be a result of unconscious impulses. Brill reports that some "rubbers" in Turkish baths are sublimating their infantile desire for touching and that street cleaners are giving expression either to their infantile desires to "wallow in dirt" or to "clean up the rottenness of society."

Verifying these claims regarding the role of unconscious motives in occupational choice is hindered by the difficulty in measuring these motives. Unfortunately, the psychoanalysts have not provided us with any methods of measuring sadomasochistic impulses, unconscious guilt feelings, or desires to "wallow in dirt." Until reliable, valid, and objective methods have been developed for assessing such variables, it will be impossible to affirm or deny these clinical impressions.

Veroff, Atkinson, Feld, and Gurin (1960) used the thematic apperception method to obtain scores on needs for achievement, affiliation, and power from a national sample of men employed in different occupations. They found that strength of need for achievement was positively related to the status of the occupation. Sixty percent of the men working in the professions and 59 percent of the managers and proprietors obtained scores that were above the median on this variable, compared with only 45 percent of the unskilled workers and 44 percent of the farmers. Needs for affiliation and power were not systematically related to occupational status although there were differences in scores received by those in different occupations. The managers and proprietors and the semiskilled workers obtained relatively high scores on the need for power, whereas the professionals and clerical workers had relatively low scores. A strong need for affiliation was also characteristic of the managers and proprietors, but it was uncharacteristic of the farmers and unskilled workers.

Meyer, Walker, and Litwin (1961) obtained scores on the same motivational variables of a group of managers and of a group of specialists employed by the same organization. These two groups were matched in age, education, and level in the organization. The managers were found to have a higher level of need for achievement than the specialists. No significant differences were obtained on needs for affiliation and power.

Roe has carried out studies of the Rorschach profiles of scientists in various specialties including physicists (1950, 1951a), biologists (1949, 1951b,c), paleontologists (1946), psychologists (1953b), and anthropologists (1953b). She has found marked differences in their responses and has drawn inferences from these differences concerning the personalities of those in each field. For example, she reports

> The anatomists are generally the least intellectually controlled; the physiologists seem to show more free anxiety and more concern with immediate personal problems than do the others. The botanists appear to be a generally rather well-adjusted group, and rather placid, with no particular deviant tendencies. The geneticists are a more colorful group than the others, with somewhat more emotional dominance, but this is of a sort different from that shown by the anatomists (1956, p. 218).

The confidence to be placed in such interpretations must be tempered somewhat by the lack of empirical evidence for the "traditional" interpretations of Rorschach profiles. The Rorschach test may offer promise for the measurement of personality, but its usefulness in research requires greater attention to construct validation of the sort that has characterized the work on the measurement of the achievement, affiliation, and power motives with the thematic apperception test (TAT).

McClelland (1962) has summarized the results of investigations into the distinguishing characteristics of physical scientists. He proposes the following generalizations concerning the attributes of members of this occupational group:

1. Men are more likely to be creative scientists than women.
2. Experimental physical scientists come from a background of radical Protestantism more often than would be expected by chance, but they are not themselves religious.
3. Scientists avoid interpersonal contact.
4. Creative scientists are unusually hardworking to the extent of appearing almost obsessed with their work.
5. Scientists avoid and are disturbed by complex human emotions, perhaps particularly interpersonal aggression.
6. Physical scientists like music and dislike art and poetry.
7. Physical scientists are intensely masculine.
8. Physical scientists develop a strong interest in analysis, in the structure of things, early in life.

These generalizations are supported by a considerable body of evidence, including Terman's follow-up (1954) of the intellectually gifted children he had studied thirty years earlier (generalizations 2, 3, 4, 6, 7, 8), McClelland's content analysis (1956) of the answer key to the Strong Vocational Interest Test (generalizations 3, 6), Roe's studies of eminent scientists (1951a, 1953a, 1956) (generalizations 1, 2, 4), and Knapp and Goodrich's work (1952) on the collegiate origins of American scientists (generalization 2).

In an attempt to find a motivational explanation for these data, McClelland offers two possibilities. The first is based on Freudian conceptions of the Oedipus situation and of psychosexual stages.

> That is, in psychoanalytic terms, one can assume that for the first three or four years of his life the future scientist, like most boys, develops an intense love re-

lationship with his mother which produces acute anxiety arising simultaneously from the fear of the
strength of his own impulses, from guilt over hatred
of the loved father, and from fear of retaliation by the
father. Normally a boy is supposed to defend himself
against his anxiety by repression and identification
with the father. Perhaps the future scientist differs in
that he adopts the defense slightly earlier—in the
phallic rather than the genital period—so that all his
"symptoms" are more extreme than those of a normal
boy. He is particularly marked by a tendency to avoid
any cue associated with interpersonal relationships
which may rearouse the original anxiety. So the scientist dislikes interpersonal contacts, human emotion,
and even art and poetry, which frequently deal with
human emotions. Finally he is analytic and hardworking because his sexual drive has been repressed
earlier than usual and finds its substitute outlets in
intellectual curiosity—or more specifically in "looking" and seeking to "penetrate the secrets of nature,"
which in classical psychoanalytic terms are pregenital,
especially phallic, sexual activities (pp. 153–154).

The second explanation proposed by McClelland is based on
aggressive rather than sexual motivation. He suggests that future
scientists are characterized by a conflict between strong aggressive
impulses and an equally strong fear of expressing them. They deal
with this conflict by avoiding contacts with other persons. The
aggressive impulses are then sublimated in an attempt to conquer
and control nature through the methods of science. The tendency
for men rather than women to pursue careers in the physical sciences is attributed to the fact that controlling aggression is more of
a problem for boys because of their greater strength. The observation that scientists more frequently come from radical Protestant
households is explained by assuming more severe control of sexual
and aggressive impulses in such families.

These two explanations—one based on sexual and the other
on aggressive motivations—are offered by McClelland as highly ten-

tative and speculative first attempts to account for existing data and to suggest new lines of research. They represent important empirically based advances over the traditional treatments of the problem by psychoanalytic theorists, although, to this writer, the attempt to identify a single motivational basis for the choice of any occupation is likely to suffer the fate of all "simple and sovereign" theories.

Investigations of the psychological differences among persons in different occupations present major methodological difficulties for those interested in the occupational choice process. As we noted earlier in this chapter, occupational attainment may be regarded as the result of two sets of choices—a choice of an occupation by a person and a choice of a person for an occupation. It is impossible to determine from the observation that people in one occupation (for example, psychologist) have more of some psychological characteristic than people in a second occupation (for example, physicist) whether this association has resulted from the operation of an individual or an institutional selection process. It may mean that those with a large amount of this characteristic are more likely *to select* psychology than physics or that they are more likely *to be selected* for psychology than physics.

Another problem in inferring something about the occupational choice process from observations of differences among members of different occupations stems from the possibility that these differences may have resulted from (as well as preceded) occupational attainment. The fact that membership in occupations may produce psychological changes in individuals has long been recognized. As early as 1776 Adam Smith wrote, "the very different genius which appears to distinguish men of different professions, when grown up to maturity, is not upon many occasions so much the cause, as the effect of the division of labor" (p. 19).

In practice, it has been extremely difficult to separate the effects of occupational and institutional choices from the psychological changes that occur as a result of occupational membership. Distinguishing between these two types of processes requires a longitudinal study of persons before and after they have selected and have been selected for various occupations. Lieberman's investigation (1956) of factory workers who were later made foremen or shop stewards is one of the few that permit the separation of these effects.

He measured the attitudes toward management and the union of 2,354 rank and file factory workers. Subsequent to the measurement, 23 of these workers were promoted to foremen and 35 were elected to the position of union steward. After these personnel changes were made, the attitudes of these two groups were remeasured along with two matched control groups of workers who had not changed their work roles. A comparison of the attitudes toward union and management of the persons who were subsequently to be made either foremen or stewards showed no differences between the two groups. However, the data indicated differential changes in the attitudes of these two groups after they were placed in their new roles. Those who were made foremen developed more positive attitudes toward management and more negative attitudes toward the union, while those who were made stewards became more positive toward the union but did not change their attitudes toward management.

These findings demonstrate the changes in psychological variables that may occur as a consequence of entry into an occupational role. Although it would be incorrect to infer from these data that all psychological differences between persons in different occupations represent results rather than causes of occupational attainment, it is clear that at least some of the variance in psychological characteristics associated with occupational membership may have been created by conditions surrounding the entry or subsequent occupancy of a work role.

Abilities and the Occupational Choice Process

Individual differences in aptitudes and abilities have been the subject of study by industrial and educational psychologists for over a half century. Although the primary purpose of this activity has been the development and application of measures of these variables to increase the rationality of programs of selection, placement, and guidance of workers and students, there is some evidence concerning the role of these variables in the occupational choice process. In the following section we will briefly consider the data concerning the relationship between tests of mental ability or intelligence and occupational preferences, choices, and attainments.

Abilities and Occupational Preferences. Byrns (1939) analyzed the scores on a test of mental ability of 42,479 girls and 34,472 boys expressing various vocational preferences. There were marked relationships for both sexes. Boys indicating a preference for being a writer had the highest median percentile score (87.9) and those expressing a preference for being a chemical engineer were next (82.2). The lowest median percentile scores were obtained by boys indicating a preference for being a barber (31.0) and dairying or cheesemaking (30.0). Similarly, the girls preferring the occupations of writing and journalism had the highest median percentile scores (84.4 and 84.3), while those preferring to be a retail clerk or to work in beauty culture obtained the lowest scores (34.0 and 33.5).

Livesay (1941) obtained similar results in a study of the American Council on Education (ACE) scores of high school seniors indicating an interest in various occupations. Those preferring the professions had the highest scores while those preferring the skilled trades had the lowest. Teaching, business, semiprofessional occupations, and agriculture, in that order, were intermediate between the two extremes. Additional evidence for the relationship of intelligence to occupational preference was obtained in an early study by Fryer (1924) and by Terman in his classic study of gifted children (Terman, 1925).

These findings suggest a rough correspondence between the intelligence of persons and the intellectual requirements of the occupations they prefer. Individuals with a high level of mental ability tend to prefer occupations that seem to require a higher level of this ability, while those with less mental ability tend to prefer simpler, less demanding occupations. From a societal standpoint this correspondence is indeed fortunate, and, one hopes, would be represented in other dimensions of aptitude and ability. The process whereby the relationship between capacities and vocational preferences occurs is, however, far from evident.

There has been considerable exploration in vocational psychology of the possibility of a general relationship between interests and capacities. Empirical studies of this relationship (Hartman and Dashiell, 1919; Bridges and Dollinger, 1920; Uhrbrock, 1926; Adkins and Kuder, 1940; Darley, 1941; Gustad, 1951) have obtained mixed results. To some extent this may reflect the difficulties in obtaining measures of both variables for parallel activities. A study by Tyler (1951) suggests that the degree of relationship between interests and abilities may differ for the two sexes. She found significant correlations between interests and primary mental abilities for first-grade boys but not for girls.

Although the relationship between interest and *actual* ability has not been empirically demonstrated, there is a great deal of evidence for a relationship between interest and *perceived* ability. A number of investigators (Thorndike, 1917; King and Adelstein, 1917; Fryer, 1927) have found extremely high relationships between individuals' reports of their preferences among activities and their estimates of their ability to perform these activities. The activities that are most highly preferred tend to be those in which the person believes himself to possess the greatest ability.

Abilities and Occupational Choices. Wolfle and Oxtoby (1952) analyzed the scores on the Army General Classification Test of about 10,000 undergraduate students and 4,500 graduate students with various major fields in forty different colleges. As would be expected, graduate students in each field have higher mean scores than undergraduate students in the same field. The highest scores were obtained by students specializing in the physical sciences, psychology, and engineering, and the lowest scores were obtained by those in physical education and home economics.

Schultz and Angoff (1956) have reported the scores on the Graduate Record Examination for college seniors in various major fields. The findings roughly parallel those obtained by Wolfle and Oxtoby. A breakdown of the data into verbal and quantitative scores reveals some additional differences between fields. Students majoring in the physical sciences have higher quantitative than verbal scores, while those majoring in the social sciences and humanities have higher verbal than quantitative scores.

As with studies of occupational preference previously described, these findings indicate a tendency for persons with abilities corresponding to an occupation to choose that occupation. The basis for the relationship, however, may be more complex than that involved in the ability-preference relationship. The Wolfle and Oxtoby and Schultz and Angoff findings probably reflect, in part, different selective processes at work within educational institutions. Some college departments are more highly selective or select on the basis of different kinds of criteria than others. Thus, associations between aptitudes or abilities and field of study are not exclusively the reflections of individual choice processes but may be caused by institutional choice mechanisms.

Abilities and Occupational Attainments. Considerable evidence is available concerning the differences in abilities among people working in various occupations. Some of the data are based on relations between test scores of military personnel during World Wars I and II and their civilian occupation. Data from World War I showing the Army Alpha scores for persons in various occupations were reported in Yerkes (1921). This study was replicated by Stewart (1947) on a much larger sample during World War II using the Army General Classification Test. She obtained the scores of 83,618 white enlisted men classified according to their civilian occupation. The nature of the sample ensured a broad coverage of the lower-level occupations. The median AGCT scores ranged from 129 for accountants to 85 for lumberjacks. The variability in scores within an occupation was found to be greater for the lower-level occupations. Similar findings for army personnel using the AGCT, but embracing a somewhat smaller sample both of persons and of occupations, have been reported by Harrell and Harrell (1945).

Further evidence for occupational ability patterns was obtained in research carried out by the Minnesota Employment Stabilization Institute (Paterson and Darley, 1936) and by the United States Employment Service (Dvorak, 1947). In addition, some longitudinal studies have been carried out in which a person's abilities are measured at one point in time, typically before he has made his occupational choice, and a follow-up is made some years later to determine what occupation he subsequently attained. Bennett, Seashore, and Wesman (1952) followed up 2,900 high school students who had taken the Differential Aptitude Tests in 1947. They reported the mean test scores for various occupations. Individuals who at the time of the follow-up were continuing their education were classified according to their field of study. In general, people were working in or studying for occupations for which they possessed relevant abilities. For example, those who entered the mechanical, electric, and building trades had their highest scores on mechanical reasoning, while clerks had superior knowledge of grammar and spelling.

By far the largest study using this method was conducted by Thorndike and Hagen (1959). In 1955 and 1956 they obtained information concerning the educational and vocational histories of over 10,000 men who had received an extensive battery of aptitude tests as part of the Army Air Force program of air crew testing during World War II. The authors report aptitude profiles for 124 different occupations. The general intellectual tests showed the greatest discrimination among these occupations, followed by mechanical tests, tests of numerical fluency, visual perception, and psychomotor ability, in that order. There was a tendency for occupational groups that were superior in their performance on tests of one type also to perform well on tests of another type, but there were some marked exceptions to this. For example, college professors were well above the mean of all occupations on the general intellectual, numerical fluency, and visual perception tests but were well below average on the mechanical tests. In contrast, carpenters were well above the mean on mechanical tests but well below the mean on the general intellectual measures.

The use of the follow-up method minimizes the risk that obtained associations between abilities and occupations could result from formal or informal training received while in the occupation. There remains, however, the question of the relative role of self-selection and institutional selection mechanisms.

The Self-Concept and the Occupational Choice Process

Super (1951, 1953) has outlined a theory of vocational development in which the self-concept plays a primary role. He writes

> The process of vocational development is essentially
> that of developing and implementing a self-concept:
> it is a compromise process in which the self-concept
> is a product of the interaction of inherited aptitudes,
> neural and endocrine make-up, opportunity to play

various roles, and evaluations of the extent to which the results of role playing meet with the approval of superiors and fellows (1953, p. 190).

Since publication of Super's views, a number of investigators have carried out empirical studies of the relationship between self-conceptions and occupational preferences or choices. Blocher and Schutz (1961) asked 135 twelfth-grade boys to describe themselves and their ideal selves on a 180-item check list. Each boy also chose from a list of 45 occupations the one that interested him most and the one that interested him least. One week later he was given the same checklist and asked to describe the typical member of each of these two occupations. The authors computed the degree of similarity between self-descriptions (both actual and ideal) and descriptions of members of the most and least interesting occupation. As predicted, the boys' descriptions of members of the most interesting occupation were significantly more similar to their descriptions of themselves and their ideal selves than their descriptions of members of the least interesting occupation.

Englander (1960) compared the self-descriptions of a group of college students with their descriptions of elementary teachers. He found greater similarity between these two sets of descriptions for majors in elementary education than for noneducation majors. The degree of similarity for students majoring in fields of education other than elementary teaching was intermediate to the other two groups.

Morrison (1962) obtained similar results with nursing trainees and education majors. Both groups described themselves, nurses, and teachers using the Q-sort method (Stephenson, 1953). The self-descriptions of nursing students were found to be significantly more similar to their descriptions of nurses than to their descriptions of teachers. Furthermore, the self-descriptions of education majors were significantly more similar to their descriptions of teachers than to their descriptions of nurses. The greater the degree of commitment reported by the person to her chosen occupation, the greater the degree of correspondence between her self-description and her description of members of that occupation.

These studies imply a relationship between the valence of an occupation to a person and the extent to which he perceives similarity between his own attributes and those of members of the occupation. Such findings are quite common in social psychology. A large number of investigators have reported positive correlations between the extent to which a person is attracted to another person or group and the extent to which he describes that person or group as similar to himself (Fiedler, Warrington, and Blaisdell, 1952; Preston, Peltz, Mudd, and Froscher, 1952; Fiedler, 1954; Davitz, 1955; Farber, 1957; Wallin and Clark, 1958; Vroom, 1959b; Vroom, 1960b; Newcomb, 1961). The results of Blocher and Shutz, Morrison, and Englander can be interpreted as indicating either that an individual tends to choose an occupation on the basis of his estimate of his similarity to its members, or that he tends to project his own characteristics on members of the occupation that he has chosen. Because the findings are correlational they do not permit a determination of whether the perception of similarity precedes or follows the development of preferences and the making of choices.

Self-conceptions may affect occupational choices in another way. People may prefer and choose occupations that they expect will permit them to use their talents and skills. An individual who views himself as artistic and creative might be expected to prefer being an architect to being a physician, whereas someone who believes himself to be accurate at figures might be expected to prefer being a bookkeeper to being a policeman. In effect, believed possession of a skill could be tantamount to a desire to use that skill. If this assumption is correct, we would expect to find individuals preferring and choosing occupations that they believe will give them an opportunity to use whatever skills they believe they possess.

Vroom conducted an unpublished study on this problem. Undergraduate college students were asked to rank five occupations (lawyer, artist, personnel manager, physicist, accountant) in order of preference. In addition, they were asked which occupation they planned to enter on completing their education. Each student's self-concept was measured by means of the Q-sort technique. He sorted a set of fifteen attributes (for example, creativity, leadership, intelligence) into piles according to the extent to which he possessed and would like to possess each attribute. He then sorted the same attributes into piles according to the extent to which they were important for success in each of the five occupations, as well as for success in his chosen occupation. Using a method developed by Cohen (1957), Pearson product-moment correlation coefficients were computed between (1) each subject's actual self-concept and his concept of the requirements for success in each of the occupations, and (2) his actual self-concept and his ideal self-concept.

Table 4.2 shows the mean correlation coefficients between actual self-concepts and occupational requirements for subjects' occupational choices and for occupations that they ranked first through fifth in preference. The results are in agreement with the hypothesis. Considering the total sample, the amount of correspondence between conceptions of self and conceptions of the requirements of occupations is greatest for the chosen occupation and diminishes progressively for occupations ranked first through fifth.

It is possible that a person's desire to use a skill that he thinks he possesses may be greater when he values the skill than when he is relatively indifferent to it. The same data permit an indirect test of this hypothesis. The total sample was broken down into three approximately equal groups according to the degree of correspon-

Table 4.2. Mean Correlation Coefficients Between Subjects' Actual Self-Concepts and Their Concepts of Requirements of Occupations.

| | | Chosen | Occupation Ranked | | | | |
		Occupation[c]	1st	2nd	3rd	4th	5th
Total sample	N = 82[b]	.535	.412	.359	.199	.172	.094
High self-esteem[a]	N = 27[b]	.679	.541	.398	.257	.176	.152
Moderate self-esteem[a]	N = 26[b]	.535	.428	.410	.166	.134	.059
Low self-esteem[a]	N = 29[b]	.401	.282	.272	.175	.201	.093

[a]Self-esteem was measured by computing the correlation between actual and ideal self-concept. For the high self-esteem group the correlations ranged from 1.00 to .682; for the moderate self-esteem group, the correlations ranged from .636 to .455; and for the low self-esteem group, the correlations ranged from .386 to .087.

[b]The number of subjects for particular cells varied slightly from these values because incomplete or inconsistent data were discarded.

[c]Scores for those subjects whose chosen occupation was one of the five standard occupations are included in the means for both the chosen occupation and for the rank to which the chosen occupation was assigned.

dence between subjects' self- and ideal self-concepts. Table 4.2 shows separate analyses for these three groups, which we have termed high, moderate, and low self-esteem. It can be seen that the relationship between the valence of occupation and the amount of congruence between subjects' actual self-concepts and their concepts of occupational requirements is greatest for the high self-esteem group and lowest for the low self-esteem group. The differences among self-esteem groups are greatest for the chosen occupation and for the occupation ranked first in order of preference. For these relatively attractive occupations, the amount of correspondence between subjects' self-concepts and their concepts of occupational requirements diminishes when going from high to moderate, and from moderate to low self-esteem. There is no such tendency for occupations ranked third, fourth, and fifth in preference.

Although causality cannot be conclusively inferred from such a correlational study, these findings suggest a relatively strong tendency for the valence of an occupation to be directly related to the extent to which a person believes himself to have the attributes necessary for success in it. There is also some indication that this relationship is strongest when the person also values those attributes which he believes himself to possess.

Rosen (1961) obtained some experimental evidence regarding the effects on the valence of an occupation of subjects' conceptions of their ability to perform it successfully. Subjects rated the valence of an occupation before and after they were given information regarding the extent to which they had the aptitudes that it required. This information, although supposedly based on an aptitude test that the subjects had taken, was falsified. One-third of the subjects, chosen at random, were told they had very little chance of getting into the occupation; another third were told that they had a moderate chance; and the remaining third were told that they had an excellent chance of getting into the occupation.

The information about the extent to which subjects possessed the aptitudes required by the occupation produced systematic changes in their ratings of its valence. When the occupation about which they received information was initially highly valent, 50 percent of the subjects who were told that their lack of aptitude gave them little chance of entering it lowered their ratings, as compared with 17 percent of those who were told they had a moderate chance, and 9 percent of those who were told they had an excellent chance. In contrast, when the occupation was initially low in valence, the greatest change in valence occurred among persons who were told that their aptitudes gave them an excellent chance of entry. Ninety-one percent of this group rated the occupation as more attractive as compared with 48 percent of the moderate and 22 percent of the low probability groups.

Conceptions of Occupations and
the Occupational Choice Process

Clearly a person's choice among occupations is limited to those about which he knows something. If a person has no concept of what an ichthyologist or an epidemiologist is or does, it can have no effect on his vocational decisions. For most people the range of possible alternatives from which to choose is greatly limited by the restricted range of information that they have concerning the world of work. Furthermore, the conceptions that people have of the activities performed by and rewards accruing to members of occupations are seldom based on actual experience and may be greatly at variance with reality. Rosenberg (1957) has compared the person making an occupational choice to a hungry child with a coin looking at a long counter of sweets he has never tasted, who must decide on one purchase.

Vocational counselors are generally sensitive to the need for occupational information on the part of their clients, but empirical data on the role that conceptions of occupations play in the occupational choice process are limited. There are some studies (Recktenwald, 1946; Speer and Jasker, 1949) that purport to show that changes in people's reports of their preferences or choices can be brought about by providing them with information about themselves and about occupations. However, the absence of control groups makes the results inconclusive.

Walker (1958) has reported that people have stereotypes of occupations that are comparable in magnitude to the ethnic stereotypes reported by Katz and Braly (1933). He found considerable consistency in the adjectives attributed by college students to members of different occupational groups. For example, lawyers tended to be described as alert, calculating, well educated, shrewd, and clever, while politicians were usually described as ambitious, argumentative, power-seeking, talkative, and evasive. Some occupational groups were more stereotyped than others. There was least variability in the characteristics ascribed to doctors and factory owners, and greatest variability in those ascribed to trade union leaders and factory workers.

In contrast, Kuhlen (1963) found a great deal of variability in teachers' descriptions of the potential of their occupation for satisfying different needs. This variability was greatest in their ratings of the potential of teaching for satisfying needs for achievement, exhibition, and change. On each of these dimensions, there is evidence of bimodality in the ratings. For example, a large number reported that teaching would be highly satisfying to a person with high need for achievement and a large number reported that it would be highly frustrating to such a person. Relatively few viewed it as in between these extremes.

There are undoubtedly a large number of factors affecting the amount of similarity in individuals' descriptions of occupations and their members. These factors probably include the specificity of the dimension being rated, as well as the amount of exposure of the individuals to the occupation or to information concerning it. Further research on the nature, extent, and influence of occupational stereotypes may be expected to contribute to our understanding of the occupational choice process.

In Chapter Two, we stated a proposition that is relevant to the effects of a person's beliefs concerning occupations on his preferences among these occupations. We asserted that the valence of any outcome to a person was a function of the product of the valence of other outcomes to him and his beliefs concerning the instrumentality of the first outcome to the others (Proposition 1). Applied to occupational choice, the valence of an occupation to an individual should be predictable from (1) measures of goals, that is, the valence of other outcomes, and (2) measures of his conception of the relative probabilities of attaining these goals in the occupation and outside the occupation, that is, the instrumentality of the occupation for the attainment of these outcomes. The best predictor of the valence of the occupation should be an index obtained by multiplying the valence of each other outcome by the perceived instrumentality of the occupation for its attainment and summing over outcomes.

Two studies support this prediction. Englander (1960) used the Q-sort procedure to secure ratings from students concerning the relative desirability of various features of occupations. The students then rated these features (also by means of Q sorts) according to their availability in the occupation of elementary teaching. An index of the degree of congruency[4] between ratings of desirability and availability was obtained for each subject. Mean scores on this index were found to be significantly higher for majors in elementary education than for noneducation majors. The mean score for other education majors was in between the other two groups and was also significantly different from the mean for noneducation majors.

In an unpublished study, Vroom had college students state their occupational choice and rank order five occupations in order of preference. Each student then rated fifteen outcomes, for example, having authority over others, high social status, and so on, in terms of their desirability. Subsequently, the student rated the same outcomes in terms of the degree to which they were likely to be attained in the five occupations and in his chosen occupation. The ratings of all outcomes were made relative to one another and according to an assigned normal distribution. This procedure permitted the calculation of coefficients of correlation between ratings of desirability and ratings of instrumentality for each subject-occupation combination. Table 4.3 shows the mean correlation coefficients between the two sets of ratings for the chosen occupation and for occupations ranked first through fifth in preference. An inspection of these data shows that the mean correlation between ratings of

---

[4]The particular measure of congruency used by Englander is not specified. However, the reader should note that there is a perfect positive relationship between the product-moment correlation coefficient between a set of pairs of scores and the sum of the products of these same pairs of scores. This relationship also holds for the rank-difference correlation and for many other measures of association. Thus it appears justifiable to treat Englander's index of congruence as if it were equivalent to the sum of the products of the paired scores, and thereby use it to test our prediction.

**Table 4.3. Mean Correlation Coefficients Between
Ratings of Desirability of Outcomes and Ratings
of the Instrumentality of Occupations for the
Attainment of Outcomes.**

	Mean Correlation	N[a]
Chosen occupation[b]	.445	77
Occupation ranked first	.335	84
Occupation ranked second	.183	86
Occupation ranked third	.113	84
Occupation ranked fourth	.071	87
Occupation ranked fifth	−.035	83

[a] The number of subjects varies slightly because some subjects did not state a chosen occupation or gave incomplete ratings of desirability and instrumentality.

[b] Scores for those subjects whose chosen occupation was one of the five standard occupations are included in the means for both the chosen occupation and for the rank to which the chosen occupation was assigned.

desirability and ratings of instrumentality is greatest for the chosen occupation and declines progressively from occupations ranked first through fifth in preference. A further analysis, not shown in the table, indicates a relationship between correlations for the chosen occupation and subjects' ratings on a 7-point scale of the certainty of their occupational choice. For those who indicated that they were very certain of their occupational choice (a rating of 7 on a 7-point scale) the mean correlation between desirability and instrumentality ratings was .50 (N = 26); for those who were less certain (a rating of 6), the mean correlation was .47 (N = 26); and for those who were relatively uncertain (ratings of 3 to 5), the mean correlation was .42 (N = 33).

These results lend some degree of support to the hypothesis about the role of motivational and cognitive variables in determining the valence of occupations. The best test of the hypothesis is, however, an experimental one. If the hypothesis is correct, it should be possible to produce predictable changes in people's occupational preferences through experimental manipulation of their beliefs concerning the consequences of being in the occupation and the strength of their desire or aversion for these consequences. To date there have been no experimental attacks on this problem. It constitutes a very promising avenue for future work.

Occupational choices should be affected not only by conceptions of the benefits provided by membership in them but also by conceptions of the likelihood that they can be attained. In Chapter Two, we proposed that the force on a person to perform an act was equal to the sum of the products of the valence of outcomes and the strength of expectancies that the act would be followed by these outcomes (Proposition 2). A laboratory experiment by Rosen (1961), part of which was described earlier in this chapter, also tested the applicability of this proposition to occupational choice. The valence of the occupation and the subject's expectancy of attaining it were varied independently in a group of boys enrolled in two high schools. Each subject rated five occupations at approximately equal intervals along a linear rating scale. Some subjects were subsequently given information about an occupation that they had rated high on the scale, while others received information about an occupation that they had placed at the midpoint or neutral position on the scale. All subjects were then given the Differential Aptitude Test and were asked to return in a week to receive preliminary results and complete the testing. On returning, subjects were given falsified test profiles and estimates of the probability with which they would be able to attain the occupation about which they had received information. Some were told that they had .91 chance of entering that occupation, others that they had .51 chance, and a third group that they had .11 chance.

Thus, there were six conditions corresponding to the two values of the valence of the occupations and three values of the probability of entering the occupation. The force on the subject to enter the occupation was measured by the subject's willingness to return for further testing concerning his qualifications for the occupation and by his performance on a digit symbol test that was depicted as a device for the selection of candidates for the occupation.

The percentage of subjects in the six conditions who volunteered to return for further testing is shown in Table 4.4.

The results indicate that the percentage of subjects who agreed to return for further testing is a positive function of both the

**Table 4.4. Effects of the Valence of the Occupation and the
Expectancy of Attaining It on the Percentage of Subjects
Who Agreed to Return for Further Testing.**

	High Expectancy (.91)	Moderate Expectancy (.51)	Low Expectancy (.11)	Total
High valence	86% (N = 22)	83% (N = 23)	70% (N = 23)	79% (N = 68)
Low valence	68% (N = 22)	52% (N = 25)	35% (N = 23)	51% (N = 70)
Total	77% (N = 44)	67% (N = 48)	52% (N = 46)	

Source: Adapted from Rosen, 1961.

valence of the occupation and of the expectancy of attaining it. The higher the valence, the greater the percentage of persons who agreed to return. Similarly, the greater the expectancy of attaining the occupation, the greater the percentage of people who agreed to return. There is, however, no evidence of an interaction between these variables such as would be predicted by the multiplicative formulation. Possibly such an interaction would have appeared had a greater range of values of valence been used.

The analysis using the digit symbol test yielded no significant differences between groups. This finding may have come about because the level of motivation of all groups to do well on such a test was high and because differences that may have existed between the various experimental groups were not sufficient to yield differences in performance.

The Actual Properties of Occupations. The relative neglect of cognitive variables in the occupational choice process may be due, in part, to an implicit assumption that people's cognitions of occupations mirror the actual properties of these occupations. If, indeed, beliefs about occupations are highly realistic, then the problem becomes one of describing the real properties of occupations and of determining the part they play in the choice process. We can circumvent the methodological difficulties involved in the assessment of cognitions by measuring the properties of the objects of those cognitions, that is, the occupations themselves.

In order to accomplish this task, some taxonomic system is required for describing and classifying occupations. The most widely known system for this purpose is that of the *Dictionary of Occupational Titles,* developed by the U.S. Employment Service. In this system, occupations are broadly classified into seven types: (1) professional and managerial; (2) clerical and sales; (3) service; (4) agricultural, fishery, and forestry; (5) skilled; (6) semiskilled; and (7) unskilled. Within these broad classifications, progressively finer breakdowns are made, culminating in the differentiation of over 22,000 occupations. It is generally recognized that the DOT system has limited psychological usefulness. Super (1957) has pointed out that three different bases are used for classification. Professional-managerial, clerical-sales, and service are types of *activity;* agriculture, fishery, and forestry are types of *enterprise,* and skilled, semi-skilled, and unskilled are *skill levels.*

There have been many attempts by psychologists to develop a more useful system for describing occupations. Roe (1956) proposes a two-dimensional system, with a quantitative dimension referring to the level of the occupation and a qualitative one distinguishing eight fields of activity. Super (1957), on the other hand, suggests a three-dimensional descriptive system adding, to the level and field dimensions of Roe, nine types of enterprises.

Methods of classifying occupations are likely to be specific in their applicability. It is unlikely that a relatively simple, all-purpose system can be developed. The method that is useful to the labor economist to describe changes in the labor force may not suit the purposes of the personnel psychologist interested in the selection, placement, and transfer of workers or the occupational psychologist interested in the role of motivational variables in occupational choice. Each system must be set up to serve its particular purpose and must be capable of integration within a different conceptual scheme.

For the psychologist interested in the occupational choice process, occupations are most appropriately described in terms that bear some logical relation to the psychological variables assumed to influence this process. Because our model holds that the valence of an occupation to a person is a function of the algebraic sum of the products of the valence of outcomes and the instrumentality of the occupation for the attainment of these outcomes (Proposition 1), we would seek to describe occupations in terms of the outcomes that they provide their members. Conceivably, a person's preferences among a set of occupations could be predicted quite accurately from measures of the amounts of money, autonomy, status, and so on that these occupations provide, and from measures of the valence of these outcomes to that person.

The accuracy of predictions of preferences based on these data would, of course, be dependent on the veridicality or realism of people's conceptions of occupations. If each person had perfect knowledge about the consequences of being in each occupation, such predictions should be quite accurate. In contrast, if people's conceptions of the occupations were highly unrealistic, the predictions could be very inaccurate.

Even if people's conceptions of occupations are often unrealistic, measures of the actual properties of occupations may be useful in the construction of higher-order measures of the degree of realism. In the type of model that we have been considering, realism can be inferred, not from a cognition of an object alone or from a measurement of the actual properties of the object, but from the relationship between the two. The amount of realism of any cognition refers to the degree of correspondence between it and the actual properties of the object. If they agree perfectly, the cognition is realistic. If they are highly disparate, the cognition is unrealistic.

Because a number of beliefs are hypothesized to be involved in occupation choice, there are many different aspects of realism that can be considered. These include the following:

1. The correspondence between the perceived and actual instrumentality of the chosen occupation for the attainment of various outcomes. The criterion of this aspect of realism might be a test of the correctness and completeness of the person's information about the duties, income, working hours, and so on, of persons in his chosen occupation.

2. The correspondence between the valence of outcomes believed to be attained as a result of entry into the chosen occupation

and the actual value or satisfaction derived from the attainment of these outcomes. The old maxim, "all that glitters is not gold," points up the distinction between the attractiveness or valence of an outcome and its actual reward value. A person may, for example, choose the occupation of traveling salesman on the basis of the highly attractive freedom that it provides only to discover that the freedom affords him little satisfaction.

3. The correspondence between actual and perceived probabilities of entering the chosen occupation. The most appropriate criterion would be a comparison of the attributes of the person and the attributes necessary for entry into the chosen occupation.

4. The correspondence between actual and perceived methods and costs of entering the chosen occupation. The criterion could be a test of the correctness and completeness of a person's information concerning the training requirements for the chosen occupation.

We would expect that the amount of each of these four aspects of realism of occupational choices would be related to later occupational adjustment. If measures of them could be developed, they might prove to be useful criteria in evaluating the effects of vocational guidance.

Some research has been conducted on the determinants of realism of occupational choices. Small (1953) found that the first occupational choices of a group of normal teenage boys were more realistic than those of a matched group of emotionally disturbed boys. In his study, realism was inferred from the degree of correspondence between the requirements of the occupation and the personal characteristics of the boy. Tageson (1960) found significant correlations between the similarity of the self-descriptions of seminarians to their descriptions of the ideal and average seminarian and faculty and peer ratings of the realism of their vocational choices.

Mahone (1960) studied the relationship between the realism of occupational choices of male college students and their scores on a projective measure of achievement motivation and on Alpert's Debilitating Anxiety scale (Alpert, 1957). Four different criteria of realism were used: (1) judgments by clinical psychologists based on the discrepancy between the person's own measured ability and the ability judged to be required by his occupational choice; (2) the discrepancy between the person's estimate of his own ability and his estimate of the ability required to attain his chosen occupation; (3) the discrepancy between the person's estimate of his ability and his measured ability; and (4) the discrepancy between the person's vocational interests, as measured by the Strong Vocational Interest Test, and his occupational choice. On each of these criteria, the occupational choices of subjects who were low in achievement motivation and high in anxiety were found to be less realistic than the choices of those who were high in achievement motivation and low in anxiety. The anxiety measure was a better predictor of criteria (1) and (2), although the measure of achievement motivation was a better predictor of criterion (4).

The Stability of Occupational Choices

Ginzberg, Ginsburg, Axelrod, and Herma (1951) have emphasized the developmental nature of the occupational choice process. The decision concerning one's future vocation is not an *event* occurring at a single point in time but a *process* extending over a period of time. For most people it is appropriate to speak not of a single occupational *choice* but occupational *choices,* taking cognizance of the fact that vocational plans may be altered, both before and after they enter the labor market. Super and his associates (Super and others, 1957; Super, 1961) have extended this line of thinking by focusing on the prediction of career development, that is, the sequence of occupations, jobs, and positions in the life of the individual, rather than on occupational choice.

In this section we will consider one major problem raised by the conception of occupational choice as a sequence of decisions. To what degree and under what conditions are occupational choices stable and persistent or unstable and revoked?

Ginzberg, Ginsburg, Axelrod, and Herma have stressed the fact that occupational choices are irreversible. Decisions made at one stage of development seriously affect the limits within which subsequent decisions can be made. For example, a person deciding to major in sociology in college would, according to Ginzberg, have his ultimate choice constrained to occupations that require sociology or, more particularly, would have to eliminate from consideration occupations that require some other major.

Roe (1956) has disagreed with the emphasis placed on irreversibility in Ginzberg's position.

> It is true, as Ginzberg and his associates have emphasized, that there are irreversible elements: one type of education cannot be exchanged for another in retrospect: time spent on one job means that there is that much less time to spend on another, and so on. Nevertheless both individuals and society are much more flexible than Ginzberg seems to consider them. Individual occupational histories show shifts. Some of these may seem minor at the time, but they may mean personally significant changes, even within the framework of a superficially similar job, that lead to more congenial activities (p. 253).

According to the conceptual framework that we have proposed, occupational choices should be stable to the extent to which they result in marked and permanent changes in the force field on the person. If a person selects an occupation or class of occupations, and if, as a consequence of that selection, the strength of force acting on him in the direction of that occupation is permanently increased relative to that directed toward other occupations, the choice will not be reversed.

In order to understand the conditions under which occupational choices are revoked, it is necessary to examine the relationship between the decision-making process and changes in the force field. There are three conceptually distinguishable bases for predicting changes in the forces resulting from the act of making a decision. Changes in forces may occur as a consequence of (1) the decision itself; (2) actions taken to implement the decision; and (3) the receipt of further information about the alternatives.

Lewin (1951) has discussed the tendency for changes in force fields to occur as a result of the decision itself. If a person were in a situation deciding between two or more alternatives, the forces corresponding to these different alternatives might be approximately equal until the decision was made. The moment the person chose one of the alternatives, the forces corresponding to the others would seem to diminish in strength.

Festinger (1957) has attempted to account for this phenomenon in terms of his theory of cognitive dissonance. If a person is forced to choose between two attractive alternatives, the choice of one will result in dissonance between knowledge of his choice and both the attractive properties of the unchosen alternative and the unattractive properties of the chosen alternative. This cognitive dissonance is assumed to be unpleasant and is predicted to result in changes in cognitions, which have the effect of reducing the amount of dissonance.

Let us apply this model to the occupational choice situation. Consider a person who is in the process of choosing between being a physician and an engineer. The forces corresponding to each occupation are positive and approximately equal. If he decides in favor of becoming a physician, his choice is dissonant with any unfavorable aspects of being a physician as well as with any attractive aspects of being an engineer. The cognitive dissonance resulting from this choice would be predicted to decrease the extent to which unfavorable properties were ascribed to the occupation of physician and to decrease the extent to which favorable properties were ascribed to the occupation of engineer. In other words, as a result of choosing physician instead of engineer, the valence of physician is increased and that of engineer is decreased. Since valence is one of the components of force, the consequence of choosing one occupation over another is to increase further the disparity between the two forces, thereby stabilizing the decision.

Walster (1963) conducted an experiment that tests this theory. The subjects were men who had just been drafted into the army. Each was told that he had been randomly selected for a special job placement program that the army was conducting. He was given ten job descriptions and was asked to rate each on a 31-point scale of desirability. While he was taking a battery of tests, two jobs, which he had rated near the middle of the desirability scale, were selected. The subject was told that assignments to occupational specialties were being made on the basis of both interest and ability and that he could choose between two job assignments. After making his choice, he was asked to rerate the ten original jobs (including both the jobs he had chosen and the one he had rejected) on the original 31-point scale. If the prediction from dissonance theory is correct, the difference between the ratings of the chosen and the rejected alternative should increase. The chosen alternative should become more attractive and the rejected alternative less attractive.

While the procedure described above was followed for all subjects, there were differences in the amount of time that was permitted to elapse between the decision and the remeasurement of the attractiveness of the jobs. Subjects were randomly assigned to one of four experimental conditions with one-fourth rerating the jobs immediately after the decision, and the others rerating the jobs after intervals of 4 minutes, 15 minutes, and 90 minutes.

This time interval exerted a major influence on the results. The prediction from dissonance theory was substantiated for subjects in the 15-minute condition. The chosen job was rated as more attractive than it had been before the decision, and the rejected job was rated as less attractive. Similar results were obtained for the immediate and the 90-minute conditions, although they did not reach customary levels of statistical significance. The exception to this pattern occurred for subjects who waited 4 minutes between the decision and the rerating of the jobs. The data from these subjects show a decrease in the attractiveness of the chosen alternative and an increase in the attractiveness of the rejected alternative. Walster suggests that this is evidence for a short period of "regret" following the decision. She predicts that this phenomenon is most likely to occur when the alternatives are close in attractiveness and when they have nonoverlapping positive and negative qualities.

Choice of an occupation might be expected to result not only in an increase in the valence of that occupation relative to others but also in an increase in the valence of distinctive outcomes that the chosen occupation provides. For example, if a person chooses an occupation noted for its high level of pay but low job security, the choice might result in an increase in the importance he places on money and a decrease in the importance he places on job security.

Rosenberg's study (1957) of the occupational choices of college students supports this prediction. Students whose reported values did not coincide with their occupational choices tended to change their values to agree more closely with the occupations they selected. For example, 166 of the students who had scores above the median on Rosenberg's People-Oriented Value Index[5] had chosen occupations like natural science, engineering, and farming, typically selected by individuals with low scores on this index. When these same people were reinterviewed two years later, 49 of them, or about 30 percent, had changed their scores so that they were now below the median. A similar change was observed on the part of only 7 percent of the 226 students who were above the median and had chosen a "people-oriented" occupation. It should be noted that these students had not yet entered their chosen occupation. The changes in values are, therefore, to be interpreted as a consequence of having made a choice among occupations or of exposure to situations that are a natural outgrowth of this choice.

The fact that occupational choices are not only influenced *by* motives and values but also exert an influence *on* them indicates that a great deal of caution should be exercised in inferring direction of causality from associations between motivational variables and occupational choices. Although Rosenberg's results would suggest that the effects of values on occupational choices are greater than the effects of these choices on values, they clearly underscore the fact that both types of effects can and do occur.

Changes in the relative strength of forces toward the chosen and unchosen occupations might also be expected to result from action taken to implement the choice. Consider once again the individual choosing between being a physician or an engineer. The forces corresponding to each of the two occupations have been hypothesized to be a function not only of the valence of the two occupations but also of such factors as the expectancy that they can be reached, and the costs and deprivations expected to be involved in attaining them. If the person decides to become a physician and successfully completes one year of medical school, the subsequent costs of attaining the occupation of physician have been reduced,

[5]See the discussion of Rosenberg's study in Chapter Four for information on the composition of this index.

while the costs of becoming an engineer have not. Consequently, the force corresponding to the occupation of physician has increased in strength relative to that of engineer. The greater the extent to which the occupational choice has resulted in actions that have had the consequence of either decreasing the costs or increasing the expectancy of attaining the chosen occupation, the greater the increase in force corresponding to that occupation, and the less likely the choice will be reversed.

The probability of the occupational choice being reversed should also be an increasing function of the transferability of the person's investment in his chosen occupation. If the actions taken to implement the occupational choice are equally applicable to a number of occupations, the force corresponding to each should be increased, and the choice may be altered with little or no additional costs. In contrast, if the actions taken to attain the chosen occupation are believed to lead only to that occupation, the forces corresponding to it should have increased relative to all other occupations and the choice may not be reversed without additional costs. Thus persons who have undergone highly specialized training in order to implement their occupational choice would be predicted to be less likely to reverse their choice than those who have undergone more general training.

Rosenberg's study (1957) also supports this prediction. He observed that the number of college students changing their plans during a two-year period varied considerably from one occupation to another. In order to develop an adequate picture of this turnover, he determined the number of students adopting or revoking each occupation during the two-year period and divided it by the number who originally chose that occupation. Scores on this "index of changeability" varied from 3.48 for housewife to .51 for engineering. With the exception of social work, none of the seven most "changeable" occupations involved specialized or long-term training. In contrast, all of the seven least changeable occupations required specialized long-term training. Furthermore, the frequency of change varied with the stage at which students were in their occupational preparation. The lowest amounts of change occurred in engineering, home economics, hotel administration, and architecture, fields in which the students had already begun their specialized training as undergraduates. Slightly higher rates of change were observed for medicine, law, and teaching, fields in which students had completed some initial preparatory work but which required further postgraduate study. It appears to be safe to conclude that the more specialized training undergone by a student to implement his occupational choice, the less likely he is to revoke that choice later.

Finally, changes in force fields may be expected to occur as a result of learning. The person's conception of occupations or of himself may change as a result of experiences prior to or following entry into the labor market. These changes may serve to strengthen or weaken the original occupational choice. It seems likely that the amount of change will be inversely related to the degree of realism in the original beliefs. People who had accurately appraised such things as the outcomes provided by occupations and the amount of satisfaction they would derive from these outcomes would be less likely to revoke their occupational choice than those whose appraisals had been less accurate.

Social Influences on the Occupational Choice Process

Biographical studies of individuals have often pointed to the social nature of the occupational choice process. Such data clearly indicate the important influences that can be exerted by key persons—parents, teachers, or peers—on the individual's vocational decisions. However, reliable quantitative evidence on the effects of specific social relationships at different stages of development on subsequent occupational preferences, choices, and attainments is limited.

The Family. Since the family typically plays a principal role in socialization, it is not surprising to find considerable attention directed to the influence of family characteristics on the occupational choice process. One of the problems receiving the greatest amount of attention, perhaps because it is easy to study, is the relationship between fathers' occupations and the occupational choices of their sons. In a large-scale study of over three thousand college students in eighteen colleges and universities, Nelson (1939) found that students' stated choices tended to coincide with the occupations of their fathers more often than would be expected on a chance basis. Similar results have been obtained by other investigators (Dvorak, 1930; Berdie, 1942).

Rosenberg's study of college students (1957) demonstrated a marked relationship between the economic position of his family and the student's occupational choice. The greater the income received by the father, the more likely the student was to choose law, medicine, or some branch of business and the less likely he was to select one of the salaried professions. Seventy-one percent of the students whose fathers' annual income was in excess of $30,000 planned to enter law, medicine, or business compared with only 38 percent of the students whose fathers' annual income was less than $7,500. On the other hand, 16 percent of those whose fathers were in the over $30,000 bracket planned to enter engineering, teaching, social work, or science compared with 45 percent of those whose fathers earned less than $7,500. Rosenberg also found a relationship between father's income and the economic level of aspiration of the student. The more money currently earned by the father, the greater the amount the student expected to be earning in the future. The fact that these expectations rest on some foundation of realism is indicated by Havemann and West's finding (1952) that college graduates from wealthier families tend to earn more than those from poorer families.

There is also considerable evidence that sons tend to enter and remain in occupations that are similar to their fathers' (Davidson and Anderson, 1937; Centers, 1948a; Reynolds, 1951; Bendix, Lipset, and Malm, 1954; and Jenson and Kirchner, 1955). When the occupations of fathers and sons are categorized according to level, we can observe in the results of these studies evidence for a "regression toward the mean." Sons whose fathers were at very high levels tend to enter lower occupations than their fathers, and those whose fathers were at lower levels tend to enter higher occupations.

Other investigators have tried to determine whether there is any greater than chance similarity between the interest patterns of fathers and their sons. In an early study of this kind, Forster (1931) correlated the scores obtained by fathers and sons on the Strong Vocational Interest Blank. Correlations ranged from .49 for the scale of farmer to .00 for the scale of personnel manager. The median correlation for the twenty-five scales was .35. Further evidence that these correlations tend to exceed expectations based on chance has been obtained by Strong (1943) and by Gjerde (reported by Roff, 1950).

A few investigators have studied the relationship between the degree of similarity between fathers and their sons, either in interests or in occupations, and some third variable. Henderson (1958) sought to determine whether sons who strongly identified with their fathers would have interests that were more similar to those of their fathers than those who identified less strongly. He developed a comprehensive measure of identification including such variables as the extent to which father and son shared activities, the son's perception of his father's importance, and the son's affection for his father. For ninth-grade boys, he found a relationship between sons' scores on this measure and the extent of similarity between their scores and their fathers' scores on the Strong Vocational Interest Blank. However, there was no relationship between these same variables for boys who were in the twelfth grade.

Crockett (1961) studied the relationship between the strength of achievement motivation of the son and the similarity between the occupational levels of father and son. He observed the same tendencies noted above for downward mobility among those whose fathers were at high levels, and upward mobility for those whose fathers were at low levels. However, the magnitude of these tendencies varied with the sons' achievement motivation. Need for achievement was positively associated with upward mobility among the sons with fathers at lower occupational levels and negatively associated with downward mobility among sons with fathers at higher levels.

Galinsky (1962) attempted to test some predictions from psychoanalytic theory about the effects of parent-child relationships on occupational choice. He compared the life histories of twenty male graduate students in physics with those of twenty male graduate students in clinical psychology. These two occupations were selected because of the different objects of curiosity offered by each—curiosity about the physical world for the physicist and curiosity about interpersonal relations for the clinical psychologist. The subjects in each group were equated for religion and social class. Life histories were investigated by means of structured tape-recorded interviews, which were subsequently coded on variables that had been predicted to differentiate individuals who would choose these two occupations. The predictions were largely supported by the data. During childhood, the clinical psychology students were found to have had closer and warmer relationships with their mothers than did the physics students. The discipline of the psychologist was also more flexible, stressed appeal to feelings, and was more often meted out by their mothers, while the discipline of the physicists was more rigid, stressed obedience, and was more often meted out by their fathers. In general, the clinical psychologists had more opportunity to be curious about interpersonal matters while the physicists received more intellectual stimulation from their families. Additional support for psychoanalytically based predictions concerning the relationship between childhood experiences, as revealed in biographical interviews, and occupational choice may be found in a study of graduate students in law, dentistry, and social work by Nachmann (1960).

Religion. Religion has also been suggested to play an important part in the occupational choice process. Max Weber (1930) observed that "business leaders and owners of capital, as well as the higher grades of skilled labour, and even more the highly technically and commercially trained personnel of modern enterprises, are overwhelmingly Protestant" (p. 35). McClelland (1955) has elaborated on the Weber hypothesis and has suggested the nature of the process by which religious affiliation affects occupational choice. Protestant and Jewish parents have been found (McClelland, Rindlisbacher, and deCharms, 1955) to favor earlier independence training for their children than Catholic parents. Age of independence training has been demonstrated to be negatively related to the strength of the need for achievement of sons (Winterbottom, 1958). Finally, as indicated earlier in this chapter, persons with high need achievement scores have been found to prefer occupations involving business activity.

Havemann and West (1952) found a slightly greater tendency for college graduates who were Protestant to become proprietors, managers, and executives than for those who were Catholic. However, Faw (reported in Roe, 1956) found that Protestant high school boys exhibited a stronger preference for the professions and the trades, and Catholics expressed greater interest in managerial, clerical, and sales occupations. The argument that Catholics have lower achievement motivation is also weakened by data collected from a national sample of employed men (Veroff, Atkinson, Feld, and Gurin, 1960). Of the Catholics, 58.6 percent obtained scores on need achievement that were above the median compared with 49.3 percent of the Protestants (reported in McClelland, 1961).

Differences in the occupational level of members of various religious, social, and ethnic groups have been reliably demonstrated. Protestants are more likely to attain positions of eminence than Roman Catholics (Davis, 1953); Jews are more likely to attain high-status occupations than Italians (Strodtbeck, 1958); and whites are more likely to attain high-status occupations than African Americans (Anderson and Davidson, 1945).

Sex. There are obvious sex differences in occupational choices. In his study of college students, Rosenberg (1957) noted that one-half of the men planned to enter law, engineering, farming, or business, whereas only one-twentieth of the women chose one of these occupations. In contrast, half of the women selected teaching, social work, secretarial work, art, journalism, and drama, compared with one-seventh of the men. With the exception of farming, the occupations chosen more frequently by men provide relatively high status and economic rewards, values that Rosenberg found to be rated as more important by men than women. The occupations chosen more frequently by women than men tend to require creativity, for example, art, journalism, and drama, or to be humanitarian in nature, for example, teaching and social work. Consistent with this observation is Rosenberg's finding that women rate working with people, being helpful to others, and being creative and original more highly than do men.

The different values and occupational choices of men and women undoubtedly stem, at least in part, from different patterns of socialization. Conceivably, boys, through identification with their fathers, are more likely to learn the desirability of being "a good provider" for one's family, while girls may be more likely to acquire the "socioemotional" concerns of their mothers. Lehman

and Witty (1936) observed that these different vocational orientations are apparent to very young boys and girls. They asked children
of 8½ to 10½ years of age to choose from a list of two hundred
occupations the three in which they would be most willing to work.
Girls more frequently selected occupations involving teaching and
personal service, whereas boys more frequently chose those involving travel, physical danger, and giving orders.

Discussion and Summary

In this chapter we examined research bearing on the determinants
of occupational choice. We began by distinguishing the phenomena
of occupational preference, occupational choice, and occupational
attainment. Conceptual and operation definitions were proposed
for each, and hypotheses derived from the model were advanced
concerning their determinants.

Although very few of the studies were designed to test them,
our hypotheses are reasonably consistent with existing evidence.
Providing some support for our hypothesis about the psychological
determinants of the valence of occupations are a large number of
studies showing a correspondence between the motives of individuals, as measured both by verbal reports and analysis of fantasy, and
the nature of the occupations that they state that they prefer and that
they actually chose and attain. The degree of association between
any single motive measure and the strength of disposition to choose
an occupation is slight, but all associations seem consistent with a
subjectively rational model of the occupational choice process. Of
greater relevance to this proposition are the results of two studies
showing substantial relationship between people's stated preferences among occupations and index scores obtained by combining
data on the relative valence of a number of outcomes and the relative
instrumentality of occupations for their attainment.

The significance that can be attached to these data is restricted by their correlational nature. It is impossible to prove conclusively from a demonstration of an association between motives
and occupational choices that the motives caused the choices. The
fact that choices can also result in changes in motives is illustrated
by Rosenberg's finding (1957) that choice of an occupation reduces

the valence of outcomes not provided by the occupation and Walster's finding (1963) that choice of an occupation tends to change
ratings of its valence. In the light of these findings, we concluded
that experimentation, involving the manipulation of motives and/
or conceptions or occupations constituted the best approach to testing the hypothesis.

Our model led us to view occupational choices as determined
not only by preferences among them but also by the subjective probability and expected costs of their attainment. There are no direct tests
of this proposition, but a number of findings bear on it. There is
evidence that people do not always choose the occupation which they
state they prefer and that "reluctant entry" into occupations is typical
of persons who are lacking in ability. Of most direct relevance is
Rosen's finding (1961) that the probability that a subject would return
for further testing of his qualifications for an occupation was positively related to the valence of the occupation but negatively related
to the indicated probability that he could attain it.

No predictions were made about the relationship between
occupational choice and performance on tests of ability. Nonetheless, marked differences in ability were observed on the part of the
people (1) in different occupations, (2) preparing for different occupations, and (3) stating a preference for different occupations.
Differences in abilities among people who are members of or who
are in training for different occupations are attributable, at least in
part, to different criteria of selection used by social institutions
charged with selecting occupational members. However, relationships between measured ability and stated preferences among occupations cannot be so easily accounted for. Why is it that children
who have a high level of mental ability tend to state a preference
for occupations in which the duties are very difficult and complex
while those with lower mental ability tend to state a preference for
occupations that are simple and less demanding?

Conceivably, possession of an ability by a person, or to be
more exact, believed possession of an ability, is tantamount to a
motive to use that ability. If a person believes that he has a great
deal of a particular ability the strength of his desire to enter occupations may be directly related to the extent to which he believes

that they will permit him to use it. We have seen, in the studies reported in this chapter, considerable support for this view. Investigators have found marked correlations between reports of preferences among activities and estimates of ability to perform these activities, as well as relationships between occupational preference or choice and the amount of congruence between people's ratings of their abilities and of occupational requirements. To be sure, these studies are correlational and subject to the traditional limitations of such results. However, there is at least one experimental finding supporting the same interpretation. Rosen (1961) has shown that an occupation is rated as less attractive by a person after he has been told that he doesn't have the abilities that it requires and that it is rated as more attractive after he is told that he does have the necessary abilities.

We also found evidence that occupational preferences, choices, and attainments are related to demographic variables, like sex and the father's occupation, and to social variables, such as family relationships and child-rearing practices. These relationships must be regarded as largely irrelevant to the model. None of these variables was included in our list of empirical coordinates of valence and expectancy (see Figure 2.1) and we can only speculate concerning their possible basis.

Part Three

Satisfaction with Work Roles

5

The Determinants of
Job Satisfaction

Since Hoppock's monograph *Job Satisfaction* (1935), a substantial amount of research has been conducted on this topic. Variables like job satisfaction, employee attitudes, and morale have acquired an important place in the literature of industrial, vocational, and social psychology. In the next two chapters we will examine existing theory and research on job satisfaction and related concepts. Our focus in this chapter will be on the determinants or causes of job satisfaction. In Chapter Six we will examine the relationship of job satisfaction to behavior on the job.

The Concept of Job Satisfaction

The terms *job satisfaction* and *job attitudes* are usually used interchangeably. Both refer to affective orientations on the part of individuals toward work roles that they are presently occupying. Positive attitudes toward the job are conceptually equivalent to job satisfaction and negative attitudes toward the job are equivalent to job dissatisfaction.

The term *morale* has been given a variety of meanings, some of which correspond quite closely to the concepts of attitude and satisfaction. For example, Likert and Willits (1940) defined job morale as an individual's "mental attitude toward all features of his work and toward all of the people with whom he works" (p. 27). Similarly, Guion has defined morale as "the extent to which the individual's needs are satisfied and the extent to which the individual perceives that satisfaction as stemming from his total job situation" (1958, p. 62).

Job satisfaction, job attitudes, and morale are typically measured by means of interviews or questionnaires in which workers are asked to state the degree to which they like or dislike various aspects of their work roles. The degree to which a person is satisfied with his job is inferred from his verbal responses to one or more questions about how he feels about his job. Other more indirect methods have been developed (Weschler and Bernberg, 1950; Weitz and Nuckols, 1953) but they have not had very wide use.

Unfortunately, there has been little standardization of job satisfaction measures. Most investigators "tailor-make" an instrument for the particular population they are studying. There are exceptions to this, such as the Brayfield-Rothe job satisfaction scale (Brayfield and Rothe, 1951) and the Kerr Tear Ballot (Kerr, 1948), both of which have had repeated use. However, investigators more commonly "adapt" old instruments or devise new ones to meet their requirements at a given time. This practice greatly restricts the comparability of different studies and results in relatively little attention to problems of scaling and of reliability or validity.

Smith and her associates (Smith, Kendall, and Hulin, 1969) have recently completed an impressive program of research on the measurement of job satisfaction. The product of this research, an instrument called the Job Description Index, is without doubt the most carefully constructed measure of job satisfaction in existence today. The developers of the JDI have already obtained data from some 2,500 workers and 1,000 retirees in twenty-one different plants. The extensive methodological work underlying this measure as well as the available norms should ensure its widespread use in both research and practice.

Having discussed the conceptual and operational definitions of job satisfaction, let us now consider where it fits in the conceptual model presented in Chapter Two. Intuitively one would assume that the meaning usually accorded the term satisfaction comes very close to what we mean by valence. If we describe a person as satisfied with an object, we mean that the object has positive valence for him. However, satisfaction has much more restricted usage. In common parlance, we refer to a person's satisfaction only with reference to objects that he possesses. Thus we might speak of a person's satisfaction with his present job but not with jobs that he has never performed. No such restriction has been placed on the concept of valence.

The use of verbal reports to measure job satisfaction further supports the assumption that it can be equated conceptually with the valence of the job. Although verbal reports are not the only behavioral indicators of valence, we have regarded them as acceptable indicators, particularly when other measures are impractical. On these grounds, we maintain that the term job satisfaction, as used in the literature of industrial psychology, is the conceptual equivalent of the valence of the job or work role to the person performing it. While we will adhere to convention and use job satisfaction in describing the findings of other investigators, the reader should keep in mind, particularly in theoretical discussions, the assumed correspondence between satisfaction and valence.

Job Satisfaction—General or Specific?

Although we have been referring to job satisfaction as if it were a single variable, most investigators have treated it as a rather complex set of variables. The reasons for doing so are quite compelling. For example, workers can be found who report that they are very satisfied with their supervisor, indifferent toward company policies, and very dissatisfied with their wages. Which one, or combination of these, represents their level of job satisfaction? Is it not both theoretically and practically useful to consider specific referents for satisfaction within the work role?

If we consider job satisfaction as the valence of a work role to its occupant, it becomes clear that there can be different valences associated with different properties of work roles. The general valence of the work role might be of most value in predicting behavior in relation to the work role as a whole (that is, actions that lead a person toward or away from it). In contrast, the valence of particular sets of properties of the work role (that is, task content, promotional possibilities, and so on) might be of value in predicting how individuals would respond to changes in work roles as well as the degree to which they might seek to initiate changes on their own.

If we decide that, for our purposes, job satisfaction is best treated as a set of dimensions rather than a single dimension, we are immediately faced with the problem of specifying these dimensions. How can the characteristics of work roles be divided in order to arrive at useful dimensions of job satisfaction?

In our discussion of choice of work role we distinguished between choices among occupations and choices among organizations. This distinction is necessitated by the fact that, for most persons, occupational and organizational choices are temporally separated. A parallel distinction can be made for job satisfaction. We can determine the extent to which a worker is attracted to his occupation and its associated activities, as well as the extent to which he is attracted to his employing organization. Such a distinction is found frequently in the writings of those interested in scientific and professional personnel. Thus, Pelz (1956) refers to the degree to which scientists are scientifically as well as institutionally oriented. Marvick (1954) distinguishes specialists from institutionalists in a federal agency. And Gouldner (1957) distinguishes between cosmopolitans who are "high on commitment to specialized role skills" and locals who are "high on loyalty to the employing organization."

The early Survey Research Center studies (Katz, Maccoby, and Morse, 1950; Katz, Maccoby, Gurin, and Floor, 1951; Morse, 1953) used four dimensions of morale: intrinsic job satisfaction, company involvement, financial and job status satisfaction, and pride in group performance. Morse obtained measures of each of these four dimensions in a study of white collar workers. Each of the measures was significantly correlated with the others (Pearson r's from .35 to .43), with the exception of pride in group performance, which was not significantly related to any of the other three dimensions.

One basis for making conceptual distinctions among various dimensions of attitudes toward or satisfaction with the work situation is to determine the amount of association between measures of these dimensions. Measures of persons' attitudes toward a large number of aspects of the work situation can be obtained and intercorrelated. A factor or cluster analysis can then be performed on either single items or scales in order to determine the number and nature of the dimensions needed to account for the results. This method has been used by a number of different investigators (Ash, 1954; Baehr, 1954; Wherry, 1954; Dabas, 1958; Roach, 1958; Twery, Schmid, and Wrigley, 1958; Kahn, 1960; Clarke and Grant, 1961; Harrison, 1961; Smith, Kendall, and Hulin, 1969). The results have invariably shown positive intercorrelations between measures of different aspects of satisfaction, a finding that has led some (Wherry, 1954, 1958; Dabas, 1958) to suggest a general factor of attitude toward the work situation analogous to Spearman's "general intelligence." Although the other results vary somewhat from study to study, more specific factors that have frequently emerged from such studies are attitudes toward the company and its management (Wherry, 1954; Ash, 1954; Dabas, 1958; Roach, 1958; Twery, Schmid, and Wrigley, 1958; Kahn, 1960; Harrison, 1961), promotional opportunities (Harrison, 1961; Smith, Kendall, and Hulin, 1969), the content of the job (Baehr, 1954; Ash, 1954; Roach, 1958; Smith, Kendall, and Hulin, 1969), supervision (Baehr, 1954; Ash, 1954; Dabas, 1958; Roach, 1958; Twery, Schmid, and Wrigley, 1958; Kahn, 1960; Harrison, 1961; Smith, Kendall, and Hulin, 1969), financial rewards (Wherry, 1954; Ash, 1954; Dabas, 1958; Roach, 1958; Kahn, 1960; Harrison, 1961; Smith, Kendall, and Hulin, 1969), working conditions (Wherry, 1954; Dabas, 1958; Harrison, 1961) and co-workers (Roach, 1958; Twery, Schmid, and Wrigley, 1958; Smith, Kendall, and Hulin, 1969).

There are at least four possible explanations of the fact that different measures of satisfaction are positively interrelated:

1. It is possible that there are characteristics of individuals which similarly condition their reactions to objectively different aspects of the work situation. One such possibility is that persons have developed different adaptation levels or standards of judgment as a result of differences in the amount or kind of experience in work situations. As a result of these differences some people might be "easily satisfied," reporting satisfaction if the work situation meets certain minimal requirements, whereas others have much higher thresholds.

2. It is also possible that the positive interrelationships among measures of satisfaction are the result of response sets. On

many satisfaction measures, a tendency to choose the first alternative, or to choose the "yes" or agree response, results in high scores indicating a high level of satisfaction. There is conclusive evidence that people vary in the extent to which they will agree with a statement regardless of its content (Jackson and Messick, 1958; McGee, 1962), which lends support to the idea that acquiescence, as it has been called, might be the basis for a generalized satisfaction with the job. The role of acquiescence can be eliminated by changing half of the items so that an "agree" response connotes dissatisfaction. However, another form of response set—social desirability—cannot be so easily handled. Because in many situations reporting a high level of job satisfaction may be construed as a socially desirable response, it is possible that individual differences in the tendency to give such responses may be the basis for associations between specific satisfaction measures. If, in fact, this is the case, we would expect to find a relationship between job satisfaction scores and measures of the strength of the tendency to give socially desirable responses such as those developed by Edwards (1957) and Crowne and Marlowe (1960).

3. A third possibility is that work situations providing one type of reward tend also to provide other types of rewards. For example, jobs that are highly paid also tend to offer greater variety of stimulation, high status, and many other frequently mentioned sources of rewards. The positive correlations between persons' satisfaction with these different aspects of the work role may be due to the fact that situational conditions, which determine these attitudes, are associated with one another.

4. Finally, it is possible that the measures of satisfaction with different aspects of work roles are associated because they are functionally interdependent. Changes in satisfaction with one aspect, for example, supervision, may result in changed satisfaction with another aspect, for example, the content of the work, and vice versa.

The research necessary to determine which of these explanations is correct has not yet been carried out. Since all are intuitively plausible, it is possible that each is contributing to some portion of the common variance among measures of satisfaction. We will have to await further research to evaluate their relative contribution.

At present there appear to be conditions under which both

general[1] and specific satisfaction measures are useful. In the review of the literature that follows later in this chapter, we will find that most studies dealing with the determinants of job satisfaction use specific measures, whereas those dealing with the relationship of job satisfaction to job behavior tend to use more general measures. The reasons for this are simple. If one is interested in the effects of a specific work role variable, such as amount of wages, on job satisfaction, it is likely that these effects will be more evident on workers' reports of their satisfaction with their wages than on their reports of their satisfaction with their job as a whole or with other aspects of their jobs. For example, Smith and Kendall (1963) reported that mean annual earnings are correlated more highly with satisfaction with wages than with either satisfaction with supervision or people. In contrast, there is as yet no convincing empirical evidence that the relationship between specific measures and behavioral indices such as absences, turnover, or performance will be any different from that obtained through the use of general measures of comparable reliability.[2]

Let us now turn to the principal subject of this chapter—the determinants of job satisfaction. One of the problems confronting the industrial psychologist is to account for the fact that people differ in the extent to which they report satisfaction with their jobs. It is generally assumed that the explanation of these differences lies in the nature of the jobs that these people perform. They express different amounts of job satisfaction because they have different supervisors or different co-workers, because they work for different companies or because they have different duties. While we will have reason, later on in the chapter, to question this assumption, it has had such a pervasive influence on the research conducted that we can conveniently organize this research according to the various

---

[1]It should be noted that general measures of job satisfaction fall into two distinct types. They may be obtained by combining workers' responses to a large number of questions, each of which deals with a specific aspect of their jobs, or by asking the workers one or more questions concerning how much they are satisfied with their jobs as a whole.
[2]Katzell, Barrett, and Parker (1961) have found no consistent trend for specific satisfaction measures to differ from one another in their relationship to performance criteria.

kinds of job or work role variables that have been thought to affect job satisfaction. We will consider, in turn, the effects on job satisfaction of (1) supervision, (2) the work group, (3) job content, (4) wages, (5) promotional opportunities, and (6) hours of work.

Supervision

There is some disagreement concerning the importance of immediate supervision in worker satisfaction. Putnam (1930), in discussing the results of the program of interviewing in the Hawthorne works of the Western Electric Company, takes the position that supervision is the most important determinant of worker attitudes.

> Finally, the comments from employees have convinced us that the relationship between first line supervisors and the individual workman is of more importance in determining the attitude, morale, general happiness, and efficiency of that employee than any other single factor (p. 325).

On the basis of their study of accountants and engineers, however, Herzberg, Mausner, and Snyderman (1959) suggest that the importance of supervision has been overrated.

> The negligible role which interpersonal relationships play in our data tallies poorly with the assumption basic to most human-relations training programs that the way in which a supervisor gets along with his people is the single most important determinant of morale (p. 115).

Quantitative evidence concerning the importance of supervision is inconclusive. Herzberg, Mausner, Peterson, and Capwell (1957) have compiled data from fifteen studies in which workers were asked what made them satisfied or dissatisfied with their jobs. Supervision was mentioned as a source of satisfaction more frequently than security, job content, company and management, working conditions, and opportunity for advancement and wages.

The only aspect of the job mentioned more frequently was relationships with co-workers. However, supervision appears fourth in the same list of job factors when they are ordered in terms of the frequency with which they are mentioned as sources of dissatisfaction.

When workers are asked to rank order job factors in terms of their importance, following a procedure used by Jurgenson (1949), supervision is accorded an even lower position on this list. Herzberg, Mausner, Peterson, and Capwell have compiled the results of sixteen studies using this method. The highest rank is accorded the factor of security, followed by opportunity for advancement, company and management, wages, intrinsic aspects of jobs, supervision, social aspects of jobs, communications, working conditions, and benefits, in that order.

There is some experimental evidence that extensive changes in satisfaction follow changes in supervision. Using an attitude questionnaire patterned after one developed by Mahoney (1949), Jackson (1953) measured the attitudes of members of nine work groups, each concerned with the installation or repair of telephone equipment. Subsequent to this measurement, three foremen whose men had relatively positive attitudes toward the leadership they were receiving from them, were exchanged with three foremen whose men had relatively negative attitudes toward their leadership. The remaining three foremen remained with their original sections and served as controls. Approximately four months after the original attitude measurement the same questionnaire was readministered. The three work groups who initially had positive attitudes toward their foreman changed in a negative direction. In two of these groups the differences were statistically significant. Similarly, the three work groups who initially had more negative attitudes toward their foreman changed in a positive direction. In two of these groups the differences were significant, while the significance of the third was not tested because the newly acquired foreman had become ill and had to be replaced. The attitudes of the three work groups who had served as controls remained unchanged.

In a laboratory experiment of somewhat similar design, Bell and French (1950) have shown that it is possible to predict with considerable accuracy the attitudes of members of a group toward the quality of leadership exercised by a given person through judgments of his leadership ability by members of a different group. In their experiment each subject participated in six discussion groups. In each group his fellow participants were four different students with whom he was unacquainted. At the end of the discussion session, the five group members were asked individually to rank other group members on their ability to lead the discussion for an expected next meeting. The rankings for a given person by the other four members were averaged and correlated with the leadership rankings that the same person received in the other five groups. The correlation coefficients between leadership rankings in different groups ranged from -.03 to .96, with a mean of .75.

Both of these experiments demonstrate that the satisfaction of group members with the leadership they receive are affected to a large extent by attributes of the person providing the leadership. They do not indicate, however, what characteristics of supervision produce positive and negative attitudes. Other methods must be used in order to determine the traits of supervisors or methods of supervision that are most likely to result in a high level of job satisfaction on the part of subordinates.

In explaining the effects of supervision on job satisfaction, it is necessary to find some basis for describing and measuring differences in supervision. An examination of the literature reveals two somewhat different approaches to this problem—one directed toward the "personality" of the supervisor and the other directed toward his behavior in the work situation. The "personality" of the supervisor is usually assumed to be reflected in his behavior in standardized tests constructed to yield information concerning his intelligence, dominance, extraversion, and so on. In contrast, his behavior in the work situation is determined through descriptions of this behavior by the supervisor himself, by his subordinates, peers, superior, or by outside observers.

Reviews of the empirical evidence of the role of personality variables in leadership have been prepared by Jenkins (1947), Stogdill (1948), and Mann (1959). The criteria of leadership used in such studies are extremely varied, as are the situations in which the research was conducted. In general, the correlations between personality variables and leadership criteria are low, with considerable variation in the size and direction of the relationship from study to study. Few of these studies were carried out in work situations or used measures of worker satisfaction or attitudes as criteria of leadership, so a detailed examination of them will not be undertaken here.

In one of the few investigations relating personality characteristics of supervisors in an industrial organization to the attitudes of their subordinates, Vroom and Mann (1960) found substantially different relationships between the authoritarianism of the supervisor, as measured by the F scale (Adorno, Frenkel-Brunswik, Levinson, and Sanford, 1950) and the attitudes of subordinates in two situations within the same organization. Employees in small, highly interdependent work groups, which were characterized by a great deal of interaction among workers and between workers and their supervisor, had more positive attitudes toward equalitarian leaders. The correlation between the supervisors' F-scale scores and the mean attitude toward the supervisor of their subordinates was -.41 for twenty-four groups. In contrast, employees in large work groups, in which opportunities for interaction among workers and between workers and their supervisor were greatly restricted and in which individual employees were highly independent, were found to have more positive attitudes toward authoritarian leaders. The correlation between the F-scale scores of these supervisors and the mean attitude toward the supervisor of their subordinates was +.41 for twenty-eight groups.

There are good reasons for thinking that measures of supervisory behavior should constitute better predictors of job satisfaction of subordinates than measures of the "personality characteristics" of supervisors. We can assume that the only aspects of the behavior of the supervisor that can affect the job satisfaction of his subordinates are those that are perceived by the subordinates. Usually this behavior would occur in the work situation as part of the normal interaction between these persons in performing their work roles. However, the personality variables are generally inferred from the behavior of the supervisor in situations that are very different from the work situation. This dissimilarity in the situations should greatly reduce the predictability of behaviors in one from another and restrict the usefulness of personality variables in explaining differences in job satisfaction.

Operationally, however, there are some advantages in favor of personality variables. The behavior from which "personality" is inferred is exhibited in situations created by the researcher and the problems of objective observation are minimized. It is relatively easy to determine how the person has responded to the test situation and to develop and apply standard procedures for "scoring" these responses. In contrast, obtaining a systematic picture of a supervisor's behavior in situations involving his subordinates can be an extremely difficult task. Relying on descriptions by participants in this interaction produces inevitable bias and distortion, whereas the use of specially trained nonparticipant observers is very costly and their presence may affect the behavior being observed.

The problems of measurement of the behavior of supervisors is bypassed if this behavior is subject to experimental manipulation. It is possible to create different kinds of leadership styles or supervisory methods in the laboratory or under certain field conditions. Their effects on satisfaction and performance can then be observed. Examples of this approach can be found in the classic experiments by Lewin, Lippitt, and White (1939) on the effects of autocratic, democratic, and laissez-faire leadership, and in more recent experiments on group decision by Maier (1963). These investigations combine a focus on the effects of leader behavior with the greater rigor of controlled experimentation. Furthermore, they permit the possibility of determining the effects of leadership methods that are not used in existing organizations with sufficient frequency to permit their study by correlational methods.

We turn now to consider the evidence concerning the effects of supervisory behavior on the job satisfaction of their subordinates.

Consideration. Much of the research on supervision has been based on the assumption that supervisors can be characterized in terms of the degree to which they are considerate of the desires of their subordinates. Various terms have been used to describe this aspect of supervisory behavior including employee orientation (Kahn and Katz, 1960), consideration (Halpin and Winer, 1957; Fleishman, 1957a,b), and attitude toward the men (Likert, 1958b). None of these terms has been very precisely defined, but each refers to the extent to which an individual supervisor's acts facilitate the attainment of rewards or the avoidance of punishments by his subordinates. The early studies of the Survey Research Center (Katz, Maccoby, and Morse, 1950; Katz, Maccoby, Gurin, and Floor, 1951) contrasted employee-oriented and production-oriented supervision. An employee-oriented supervisor established a supportive personal relationship with his subordinates, took a personal interest in them, and was understanding when mistakes were made. In contrast, a production-oriented supervisor viewed his subordinates as "people to get the work done" and was concerned primarily with achieving a high level of production.

It was initially assumed that employee orientation and a production orientation were at opposite ends of a single continuum. As a supervisor became more employee oriented he was assumed to become less production oriented and vice versa. This assumption was inconsistent with the empirical findings of the Ohio State Leadership Studies. Using factor analysis, Halpin and Winer identified two major independent dimensions of leader behavior that are very similar to employee and production orientation. These two dimensions have been called Consideration and Initiating Structure. Consideration includes supervisory behavior "indicative of friendship, mutual trust, respect, and warmth" (p. 42), while Initiating Structure includes behavior in which the supervisor organizes and defines group activities and his relation to the group (Halpin and Winer, 1957).

Methods for the measurement of these two variables have been developed by researchers associated with the Ohio State Leadership Studies. The primary instrument is called the Leader Behavior Description Questionnaire originally developed by Hemphill and Coons (1957), and subsequently modified for use in military and educational situations by Halpin (1957) and Halpin and Winer (1957), and in industrial situations by Fleishman (1957a). It is typically given to subordinates who are asked to describe the behavior of their supervisor. A related instrument called the Leadership Opinion Questionnaire has also been developed by Fleishman (1957b). It also provides scores on Consideration and Initiating Structure but is completed by supervisors who are asked to describe how they think they should behave.

The relationship between scores on Consideration and In-

itiating Structure seems to depend greatly on the particular version
of the measuring instrument used. Although their factor analysis of
the Leader Behavior Description Questionnaire showed consideration and initiating structure to be orthogonal factors, Halpin and
Winer found positive correlations between measures of them, because few items were factorially pure. In his revision of the instrument for use in industry, Fleishman set out to minimize the
association between these measures by selecting items for one factor
with zero or negative loadings on the other factor. As a result he
reports essential independence of the two scales in both industrial
and military settings (1957a).

Scores on Consideration and Initiating Structure, obtained
from giving the Leadership Opinion Questionnaire to supervisors
and asking them how they should behave, also appear to be un-
correlated. Fleishman (1957b) found a correlation of -.01 based on
a sample of 122 foremen in an industrial plant and reports correlations ranging from -.23 to .08 for nine other military and industrial populations.

There is considerable evidence that the satisfaction of subordinates is related to the consideration or employee orientation of
their supervisors. In a study of twenty-nine aircraft commanders,
Halpin and Winer (1957) found a correlation of .64 between consideration as measured by the Leader Behavior Description Questionnaire and an index of crew satisfaction. A later investigation of
eighty-nine aircraft commanders by Halpin (1957) indicated a correlation of .75 between consideration and crew satisfaction with their
commander. In other investigations Seeman (1957) reports a positive relationship between the consideration of school superintend-
ents and the job satisfaction of elementary school teachers; Fleishman, Harris, and Burtt (1955) have found a positive relationship
between the consideration of foremen and the morale of their
subordinates.

Likert (1961) described findings from a study of a public
utility, which bear on the effects of consideration. The data in Table
5.1 show the percentage of employees in work groups with favorable
and unfavorable attitudes on job-related matters who state that their
supervisor engages in various behaviors. It shows quite striking
differences in the frequency with which employee-oriented behav-

Table 5.1. Relationship Between Supervisor's Behavior
and Attitudes of Subordinates.

Supervisory Behavior	Percentage of Employees in Work Groups with Favorable Attitudes Who Report That Their Supervisors Engage in the Stated Activity	Percentage of Employees in Work Groups with Unfavorable Attitudes Who Report That Their Supervisors Engage in the Stated Activity
Recommends promotions, transfers, pay increases	61	22
Informs men on what is happening in the company	47	11
Keeps men posted on how well they are doing	47	12
Hears complaints and grievances	65	32
Thinks of employees as human beings rather than as persons to get the work done	97	33
Will go to bat or stand up for me	87	30
Usually pulls for the men or for both the men and the company, rather than for himself or for the company only	86	29
Takes an interest in me and understands my problems	81	29
Is really part of the group; interests are the same as those of the people in the group	66	16
Likes to get our ideas and tries to do something about them	62	17

Source: Adapted from Likert, 1961, pp. 16–17.

iors are attributed to supervisors by employees in satisfied and dissatisfied work groups.

There is other evidence that the amount of consideration displayed by a supervisor is negatively related to such behavioral measures as absences, turnover, and grievances. Fleishman, Harris, and Burtt (1955) report correlations of -.49 and -.38 between the consideration of supervisors as measured by the Leader Behavior Description and subordinates' absenteeism in studies of seventy-two production and twenty-three nonproduction foremen. No significant relationship was found between Consideration and either grievances or turnover, although Initiating Structure was found to correlate .45 with grievances among production foremen and .51 with turnover among the nonproduction foremen.

In a more recent investigation in a motor truck manufacturing plant, Fleishman and Harris (1962) found relationships between Consideration and Structure measured by subordinates' descriptions of their supervisor, and grievances and turnover rates. In general, low consideration and high structure were found to go with high grievances and turnover. However, these relationships were not linear. There appeared to be critical levels beyond which increased consideration and decreased structure had no relationship to grievances or turnover rates. Furthermore, there was evidence of an interaction between consideration and structure. Amount of structure was more positively related to turnover among foremen who had low consideration than among those with high consideration.

We are tempted to conclude from these findings that consideration of subordinates on the part of a supervisor results in a high level of satisfaction, which in turn is reflected in relatively low turnover rates, grievances, and absences. Although this is probably the most likely explanation of these data, it is by no means the only one. Their use of correlational rather than experimental methods and of subordinates' reports to measure supervisory behavior makes a number of additional interpretations possible.

One such possibility is that the direction of causality is opposite to that previously discussed. Conceivably, supervisors display a greater degree of consideration for subordinates, both individually and collectively, whom they perceive to be satisfied and accepting of them. In contrast, subordinates who are critical and dissatisfied may be more likely to elicit controlling and structuring behavior from their supervisors and less likely to be the recipients of warmth and personal support. Such an explanation has some degree of plausibility and cannot be ruled out completely on the basis of existing data. It could be seriously weakened by correlational evidence (not yet obtained) that the relationship between the amount of consideration shown by a supervisor and the satisfaction of subordinates varied with such personal characteristics of subordinates as the strength of their need for affiliation. However, the experimental manipulation of consideration and observation of the effects on satisfaction would provide a more conclusive test of the direction of causality.

Another possible interpretation of these data stems from their use of subordinates' reports to determine supervisory behavior. There is considerable evidence in the literature of social psychology that descriptions of the behavior of one person by another tend to be subject to biases, including a tendency to attribute favorable behaviors or motives to liked persons and unfavorable behaviors or motives to disliked persons. Possibly the observed association between supervisory consideration and subordinate attitudes reflects the fact that subordinates who, for one reason or another, like their supervisors describe them in a systematically different way than do subordinates who dislike their supervisors. This possibility could be rejected if one could demonstrate that (1) subordinates' descriptions of supervisory behavior agreed with those obtained from other sources, or (2) similar relationships between consideration and satisfaction are obtained when other types of measures of supervisory behavior are used. At present the data concerning both (1) and (2) do not permit us to reject this explanation. There is a growing body of evidence that subordinates' descriptions of the behavior of their supervisors are not highly related to such descriptions by the supervisor himself (Gross, 1956; Vroom, 1960a), by the supervisor's superior (Besco and Lawshe, 1959; Vroom, 1960a), by the supervisor's peers (Vroom, 1960a), or to observations based on the use of time sampling methods (Gross, 1956). Similarly, there is a paucity of evidence that consideration of the supervisor, as measured by data from other sources, is related to subordinate satisfaction. Morse (1953) found that members of high morale groups were significantly more likely to describe their supervisor as taking a personal interest in them and as more satisfied with the way he handles complaints. However, interviews with supervisors about handling complaints and amount of personal interest did not reveal differences between high and low morale groups.

The use of nonparticipant observation and interaction recording techniques to measure supervisory consideration might enable us to determine whether the frequency of considerate acts on the part of a supervisor is related to the measured satisfaction of their subordinates. However, such techniques would probably require a more precise definition of the concept of consideration. It is not clear that considerate and inconsiderate acts could be distinguished without knowing something about the motives of the subordinates. To choose an extreme example, let us consider a subordinate who is a masochist. Let us further assume that his supervisor is aware of this masochistic tendency. Acts on the part of the supervisor that have the consequence of inflicting pain and punishment on this subordinate could be termed considerate, although identical acts performed in relation to other subordinates would be classified as inconsiderate. Certainly, this example is extreme but the point is general. People vary in their desires and aversions and a classification of the acts of another on a dimension of consideration cannot be undertaken simply on the basis of the nature of these acts. Such a classification must also be based on a knowledge of the nature of these desires and aversions or, at the very least, on the supervisor's conception of them.

Kay, French, and Meyer (1962) have used nonparticipant observation methods to assess supervisory behaviors that are relevant to consideration. They coded the number of times during a performance appraisal interview that the supervisor praised or criticized the subordinate and related this to measures of the satisfaction of the subordinate. Number of criticisms or threats by the supervisor was found to be negatively related to subordinates' reports of the amount of understanding that existed between themselves and their supervisor, as well as to their satisfaction with the appraisal system. There was also a marked relationship between the number of times a subordinate was criticized and the number of times he defended his performance in the appraisal interview. The relationship between number of praises and both attitude measures and measures of number of defenses was less marked, approaching significance only for subordinates' reports of the amount of trust they had in their manager and the amount of his supportiveness.

Pelz (1951) reports findings that suggest that the effects of consideration on satisfaction depend upon the amount of influence exercised by the supervisor on his own superior. Forty work groups in a public utility in which employees were high in satisfaction and thirty work groups in which employees were low in satisfaction were selected on the basis of employees' responses to questionnaires. The practices of the supervisors in charge of each of these seventy work groups were determined by means of personal interviews with the supervisors. Two scales of supervisory behavior were developed, one dealing with the degree to which the supervisor sided with employees in cases of employee-management conflict and the second dealing with the "social closeness" of the supervisor to his employees. Separate correlations were computed between these two aspects of supervisory behavior and several measures of employee attitudes toward supervisors for those groups in which the supervisor had considerable influence with his own superior and for those in which he had little such influence. Significant differences emerged between the two influence conditions. The relationships between the two indices of supervisory behavior and employee attitudes were more positive where supervisors had a high level of influence with their own supervisors. Pelz concludes that attempts by influential supervisors to help their subordinates achieve their goals will usually succeed and will result in higher employee satisfaction, whereas similar attempts by noninfluential supervisors are less likely to succeed and to affect satisfaction. In a hierarchical organization the degree to which a supervisor satisfies the needs of his subordinates may be dependent not only on the supervisory methods and practices that he uses but also on the amount of his power in the larger organization.

Influence in Decision Making. One of the basic assumptions of those associated with the human relations movement is that persons obtain satisfaction from influencing decisions and controlling their work environment. Terms such as group decision, democratic leadership, and participative supervision, all of which have an important place in the literature on human relations, refer to supervisory styles that permit subordinates a substantial degree of influence on decisions that affect them.

There is considerable evidence that the satisfaction of subordinates is positively associated with the degree to which they are permitted an opportunity to participate in making decisions. Baumgartel (1956) studied the effects of patterns of leadership on the attitudes of scientists in eighteen research laboratories. On the basis of questionnaire responses by subordinates, six of the laboratory directors were characterized as providing laissez-faire leadership, seven as providing participative leadership, and five as providing directive leadership. This threefold typology of leadership patterns is similar to the conception used in the classic field experiment on mask-making in children by Lewin, Lippitt, and White (1939). The scientists working under participative leadership were found to have significantly more positive attitudes toward their director than those under directive leadership. Those who were working under laissez-faire directors were generally intermediate in attitudes compared with those exposed to the other two leadership styles, although there were attitude items in which they demonstrated more positive responses than either of the other two groups.

In an investigation in an automobile manufacturing plant, Jacobson (1951) related the attitudes of workers toward their foremen and toward their shop stewards to their reports of the extent to which they were involved in decision making by occupants of each of these roles. As predicted, there was a positive relationship between the amount of participation in decision making and attitudes toward both foremen and shop stewards. In another study Wickert (1951) compared the questionnaire responses of telephone operators and service representatives who were still in the employ of the company with those who had left. The major differences were in responses to questions about the degree to which they could influence conditions on their jobs. Persons remaining on the job more frequently reported that they had a chance to make decisions on the job and that they were making an important contribution to the success of the company.

The Wickert study is weakened by the fact that the completion of the questionnaire by those who left the company followed their resignation. Perhaps the act of resigning results in changes in the way in which persons describe their work roles. This weakness was overcome in an investigation by Ross and Zander (1957). Questionnaire results were obtained on 2,680 female workers in a large company, 169 of whom resigned during the four-month period following the administration of the questionnaire. Each resigned employee was matched with 2 employees still with the company on the basis of a number of demographic variables. The largest differences between the resigned workers and the matched continuing workers occurred in their responses to questions about the amount of autonomy and the amount of recognition they received. The resigned workers reported less frequently that they were on their own when they worked and that they were fully informed about the quality of their work.

All of the above studies suffer from the limitations imposed by the use of subordinates' reports to measure the amount of their influence. Consequently, it is possible that the findings reflect a tendency for subordinates to ascribe what they conceive to be favorable practices to supervisors toward whom they have positive attitudes and unfavorable practices to those toward whom they have negative attitudes. This "halo effect" constitutes an alternative interpretation of any correlational study in which reports of the supervisors' behavior are obtained from the subordinates.

This difficulty is overcome in a study of white collar workers by Morse (1953). She used supervisors' reports of their behavior as the basis for distinguishing between those giving close and those giving general supervision. A comparison of the attitudes of the workers under these two types of supervisors showed few clear-cut differences. Employees receiving general supervision described their supervisors as more effective in handling people and more frequently showed a strong degree of identification with their division, but they manifested less positive attitudes toward overall company policies than did employees receiving close supervision.

In addition to these correlational studies, there are three field experiments that deal with the effects of participation on job satisfaction. The first of these was carried out by Morse and Reimer (1956) in four parallel divisions of the clerical positions of a large insurance company. Two programs of change were employed. One of these, the autonomy program, was introduced into two of the divisions and was designed to increase the role of rank and file employees in decision making. The second, the hierarchically controlled program, was introduced into the other two divisions and was designed to increase the role of upper management in decision making. The introduction of the changes required approximately six months, and the entire experiment was carried on for about a year. Job satisfaction was measured just before and just after the experimental year. As predicted, there was an increase in satisfaction under the autonomy program and a decrease in the hierarchically controlled program. Both programs, however, significantly increased productivity, with the hierarchically controlled program resulting in the greater increase.

The second field experiment was carried out by French, Israel, and Ås (1960) in a Norwegian factory. Nine four-man groups were given new products to produce. In the four control groups the change was introduced in the usual manner. The other five experimental groups were allowed to participate more in the decisions involved in the change. They met with their foremen and representatives of the planning department to decide which of the five new products would be assigned to each group. Also, two of the experimental groups held additional meetings in which they helped to decide about the division of labor into four jobs, the assignment of these jobs to group members, and the training for these new jobs. The experimental groups were found to display a higher level of satisfaction than the control groups on ten out of fourteen satisfaction items but only three of these differences were significant.

The third experiment was carried out by Kay, French, and Meyer (1962) in a plant manufacturing aircraft engines. Amount of participation on the part of individual salaried employees was varied within goal-planning sessions with their supervisors, which followed performance appraisal interviews. Half of the subjects in the study were given an opportunity to participate to a major degree in the setting of their goals for the future. At the end of the performance appraisal interview, they were instructed by their superior to prepare a set of goals for review at the goal-planning session. During the session, the high participation subjects presented their list of goals to the manager, who was instructed to be sure that his subordinates had more influence than he did on their final formulation. The other half of the subjects were given much less opportunity to participate in the goal-setting process. The list of goals for each was written by their supervisor who presented them during the planning session, and allowed them to react and make suggestions. Interviews conducted with both high and low participation subjects after the goal-planning sessions revealed few differences in attitudes. The only significant difference was in the subordinates' reported acceptance of the job goals, which was higher under the high than under the low participation condition.

To sum up the findings described so far, there is fairly clear-cut evidence that people who are satisfied with their jobs tend to report that they have greater opportunity to influence decisions that have effects on them. For the reasons we have indicated, this evidence cannot be regarded as proof that greater influence increases job satisfaction and that less influence decreases job satisfaction. Field experiments in which changes were made in amount of influence and its effects on satisfaction were measured have produced mixed results. Morse and Reimer's experiment (1956) provides rather strong evidence that amount of influence does affect job satisfaction, while experiments by French, Israel, and Ås (1960) and Kay, French, and Meyer (1962) have obtained results that are in the same direction but are less conclusive.

Intuitively, one would assume that the amount of satisfaction obtained from a given amount of influence might vary considerably with the nature of the decision, the desires of the person, and the nature of the social situation in which the influence is exercised. Taking such variables into account may help explain discrepancies in findings. The importance of individual differences has been documented in a number of recent studies. In the Morse and Reimer experiment previously described, Tannenbaum and Allport (1956) investigated the role of personality variables in determining adjustment to the two experimental programs—one permitting workers greater opportunity for decision making and the other restricting existing activities. Using pencil and paper tests, they obtained scores that they assumed to represent the strength of various personality trends. They then classified individuals on the basis of the estimated suitability of their personalities to each of the experimental programs. It was found that persons "suited" to the program in which they were placed wanted their respective programs to last longer and were more satisfied than persons who were less suited to the program in which they were placed.

Vroom (1959a, 1960a) also obtained evidence suggesting that the effects of participation in decision making on satisfaction depend on the personality of the participant. In a field study in a package delivery organization, he found that the relationship between an employee's psychological participation and both job satisfaction and job performance varied with the strength of his need for independence and the degree of his authoritarianism (Adorno Frenkel-Brusnwik, Levinson, and Sanford, 1950). Amount of participation was most positively related to the satisfaction and performance of those low in need for independence and high in authoritarianism. There was no evidence of any unfavorable effects of participation either on satisfaction or performance.

Vroom's finding that the relationship between participation and job satisfaction depended on the extent to which the employee was authoritarian and on the strength of his need for independence is consistent with the results of two other investigators. Sanford (1950) found that authoritarian personalities are more likely to state a preference for high status, strongly directive leadership, and Trow (1957) found that subjects with a strong need for autonomy (as measured by a questionnaire) expressed significantly lower satisfaction with roles in which they were made highly dependent on others than did subjects with a weaker need for autonomy.

The Work Group

Elton Mayo vigorously opposed principles of management based on the assumption that workers were strictly "economic men." To Mayo, "man's desire to be continuously associated in work with his fellows is a strong, if not the strongest, human characteristic" (1945, p. 111). This point of view has been reflected in a consistent focus by Mayo and his followers at the Harvard Business School on the influence of the face-to-face work group on worker satisfaction and productivity.

It is difficult to take issue with the view that social interaction can be highly rewarding to most persons or that experiences with one's co-workers may be a major satisfaction in work. These statements are, however, neither more nor less true than are their opposites. They are useful only as points of departure. We must develop an understanding of the attributes of social interaction that are satisfying and dissatisfying to individuals. The problem that besets the industrial psychologist is to identify the affective consequences of particular forms of social interaction within the work situation.

Relatively little work has been carried out by industrial psychologists that is relevant to this problem. There has been, however, some research by social psychologists on the determinants of group cohesiveness and attraction to the group. Using the methods of laboratory experimentation, this research is highly relevant to a determination of the conditions under which membership in a face-to-face work group is a source of satisfaction.

Explanations of the determinants of attraction to the group usually stress the valence of group-mediated outcomes. Thus, Bass hypothesizes, "A group is more *attractive,* the greater the rewards which may be earned by membership in the group and the greater the anticipation or expectancy of earning them" (1960, p. 60). Similarly, Cartwright and Zander suggest that the valence of the group for a given person "depends upon the nature and strength of his needs and upon the perceived suitability of the group for satisfying these needs" (1960, p. 72). It can be seen that these are restatements of our more general proposition (Proposition 1) about the determinants of valence. If the work group is believed by an individual to be instrumental to the attainment of positively valent outcomes, it will acquire positive valence for him; if, in contrast, it is perceived to be instrumental to negatively valent outcomes, it will acquire negative valence for him. We will now consider some of the specific group characteristics or outcomes that have been related, both theoretically and empirically, to member satisfaction and attraction.

Interaction. One of the necessary conditions for exchange of rewards to occur between persons is some degree of interaction between them. The role of interaction in the development of attitudes between persons has been emphasized most strongly by Homans. He hypothesized, "If the frequency of interaction between two or more persons increases, the degree of their liking for one another will increase, and vice versa" (1950, p. 112). Strict application of this hypothesis to the work situation would suggest that work groups would be attractive to their members to the extent to which the nature of the situation permits or requires interaction. Furthermore, the degree of attraction between any two members should be directly related to the extent to which they interact with one another while performing their work.

Business organizations provide ample opportunity for studying the effects of interaction between workers. There is a great deal of variation in the extent to which interaction is required by interdependent role relationships among workers, sanctioned by management of the organization or facilitated by the physical structure of the work situation. If Homans' hypothesis is correct, measures of these conditions over work groups should be related to measures of group cohesiveness. Within work groups, sociometric preference should be predictable from measures of the frequency of interaction among group members.

There is some evidence supporting Homans' hypothesis from research carried out in both work and nonwork settings. In a field study of a housing development, Festinger, Schachter, and Back (1950) found that the frequency of social choices between families was an inverse function of the physical distance between the houses that they occupied. Similarly, Newcomb (1956, 1961) found propinquity to be a major determinant of interpersonal attraction between college students living in the same house; and Strodtbeck and Hook (1961) found that sociometric preferences among jury members were positively related to their physical nearness and visual accessibility around the table. In a sociometric study of air force bomber crews, Kipnis (1957) found a relationship between interaction and attraction. The amount of attraction between two crew members was positively related to their physical proximity in the plane, as well as to the extent to which they were required to work together by the nature of their job responsibilities.

There are also some data suggesting that workers' satisfaction with their jobs is related to their opportunities for interaction with others on the job. On the basis of interviews with workers in an automobile plant, Walker and Guest (1952) state, "Isolated workers disliked their jobs and gave social isolation as the principle reason" (p. 76). Kerr, Koppelmeir, and Sullivan (1951) found a significant tendency for departments providing the least opportunity for conversations among workers to have the highest turnover rates; and Sawatsky (1951) found that machine operators, who have restricted opportunity for communication because they work under conditions of intense noise and are confined to the area of their machine, have much higher turnover than nonmachine operators. These findings are consistent with Richards and Dobryns' (1957) observations that the morale of a group of workers in an insurance company was greatly lowered by an environmental change that restricted their opportunity for social interaction.

In addition, there is evidence concerning the correlates of size of work groups. Larger work groups have been shown to have lower cohesiveness or morale (Worthy, 1950; Seashore, 1954; Hemphill, 1956) and more frequent unexcused absences per person than smaller groups (Hewitt and Parfit, 1953). Merrihue and Katzell (1955) also report a tendency for smaller work groups to have more favorable scores on an employee relations index, obtained by combining objective data on such variables as absences, turnover, and grievances. The implications of these results for Homans' interaction hypothesis are not completely clear. While it seems reasonable to expect that the amount of interaction between any two group members would be inversely related to group size, it is not obvious that the total amount of interaction by any group member with all other group members would bear any necessary relation to size. Persons in large work groups presumably interact to the same degree with others even though their interaction may be distributed over a larger number of persons.

When we attempt to reconcile Homans' position that interaction causes liking with our proposition about the determinants of valence (Proposition 1) we are forced to assume that all interaction involves the exchange of rewards. Intuitively, one would find this highly unlikely. There are many circumstances in which interaction with other persons is unpleasant and does not result in greater liking for them but in an increase in disliking. A more conservative statement of the role of interaction in the formation of attitudes toward persons and groups is that interaction may lead to the emergence of both positive and negative attitudes. Although there may be a general tendency for interaction to be pleasant and satisfying, and hence one may find some support for Homans' hypothesis, a more complete explanation of the effects of interaction on attraction would require a specification not only of the amount of interaction but also of its content. This position is suggested by Seashore who states, "Even though heightened interaction thus in some instances may accompany high cohesiveness, there is no basis for assuming that it is a necessary relationship" (1954, p. 26). Similarly, Cartwright and Zander maintain, "There is no convincing evidence, however, that interaction which is unpleasant will make persons better like one another" (1960, p. 80).

In understanding the effect of interaction on the attractiveness of work groups and roles, it appears to be necessary to specify the conditions under which interaction will be rewarding and the conditions under which it will be frustrating. This is by no means a simple problem, but we will consider what appear to be some of the more promising attempts to solve it.

Similarity of Attitudes. Newcomb has hypothesized that interaction is rewarding when it results in the cognition of similar attitudes. "Insofar as communication results in the perception of increased similarity of attitude toward important and relevant objects, it will also be followed by an increase in positive attraction" (1956, p. 579). Perceiving another person as having similar attitudes toward some object X is assumed to be rewarding because it permits the "ready calculability of the other's behavior" as well as "the validation of one's own orientation toward X" (1953, p. 149).

It follows from this hypothesis that the interaction between members of work groups will be satisfying and will result in increased attractiveness of the work group to the extent to which the members of the groups have similar attitudes. Evidence concerning the effects of similarity on attraction is mixed. In a study of industrial work groups, Seashore (1954) found no consistent relationship between the similarity of group members in age and in education and their cohesiveness. Hoffman (1958) constructed groups in the laboratory in which members were homogeneous and heterogeneous in personality. After both types of groups had interacted during a series of problem-solving sessions, measures of the degree to which members were attracted to their group were obtained. No differences were found between the homogeneous and heterogeneous groups. However, Newcomb (1956, 1961), in a study of college students living in a cooperative house, found significant correlations between a number of different measures of the amount of similarity in attitudes of pairs of students and measures of their attraction to one another. The measures of similarity that were most significantly related to attraction were agreement in values as measured by the Allport-Vernon Scale of values and agreement in their liking for other persons in the house.

These discrepant findings may be caused by the different aspects of interpersonal similarity studied. Newcomb's theory deals only with similarity in attitudes. Furthermore, he suggests that the effects of similarity on attitudes and attraction is a function of the importance of the attitudes to the individuals and their relevance to interaction between them.

Acceptance. Another variable that has been hypothesized to affect the attractiveness of groups for their members is the degree to which the members are accepted or valued by other group members. The notion that a person derives satisfaction from interacting with others who like or value him has an appealing simplicity and appears in many different forms in the writings of both industrial and social psychologists.

Bellows, for example, expressed his view of the importance of this variable as follows:

> The manner in which a new employee is accepted by and adjusts to his fellow workers may determine to a large extent his satisfaction with his job, his attitude toward his job, employer, boss and the firm, his amount of production and quality of work, . . . and even the length of time he remains with the company (1949, p. 288).

Jackson (1959) takes a similar position in his hypothesis that a person's attraction to membership in any group or organization will be directly related to the magnitude of his social worth.[3] He further suggests that the magnitude of this relationship will vary directly with the volume of interaction the person has with other members of the group or organization under consideration.

There is considerable evidence concerning the affective consequences of the degree to which a person is liked or positively valued by other members of his own work group. Some of this evidence is correlational in nature. In a field study among construction workers, Van Zelst (1951) found a correlation of .82 between the interpersonal desirability of rank and file workers, as measured by ratings of their co-workers, and their job satisfaction as measured by the Kerr Tear Ballot. Similarly, Zaleznik, Christensen, and Roethlisberger (1958) found that only 43 percent of "isolates" in work groups in a manufacturing plant were highly satisfied with their jobs, whereas 75 percent of regular group members fell in this category; and Jackson (1959) in a study of a child welfare agency, found a significant positive correlation between measures of a person's attraction to the group and measures of the degree to which he was valued by other group members. Experimental evidence for the effects of acceptance by others on attraction to the group may be found in laboratory investigations by Dittes and Kelley (1956), Dittes (1959), Kelley and Shapiro (1954), and Zander and Cohen (1955).

If a person's acceptance by other group members affects the valence of the group for him, it should also affect the probability that he will withdraw from the group. Sagi, Olmsted, and Atelsek (1955) were able to predict voluntary withdrawal from campus groups by previously obtained measures of their social status. Two hundred and ninety-three college students, who were members of twenty-three different student groups, were asked to name their closest friends in their group. A measure of the social status of each person was obtained by dividing the number of choices he received by the number received by the most popular group member. A follow-up, six months later, indicated a highly significant differ-

[3]Jackson uses the term social worth to refer to the degree to which the person is objectively valued by other members of the group or organization.

ence (p < .001) between the social status of those remaining in the group and those voluntarily dropping out.

Goal Interdependence. It is reasonable to assume that interactions between two persons would be satisfying to both if this interaction has the consequence of facilitating the progress of each of the persons toward the attainment of his goals. In contrast, interaction would be frustrating if it had the consequence of impeding progress toward goal attainment. One of the conditions that should greatly affect this aspect of social interaction is the relationship between the goals of the interacting persons. Deutsch (1949) has used the terms promotive and contrient to contrast two extreme types of relations among goals that are predicted to affect the cooperative or competitive nature of the ensuing interaction. The goals of two persons are *promotively interdependent* if entry into the goal region by one person results in entry into the goal region by the other person. In contrast, the goals of two or more persons are *contriently interdependent* if entry into the goal region by each person precludes entry into the goal region by other persons.

There are many conditions in organizations that may affect the nature of the goal interdependence among members of the same work group. Group incentive or profit sharing plans result in promotive interdependence since attainment of financial rewards by one group member is accompanied by the attainment of similar rewards by other group members. However, the opportunity for a highly attractive promotion to a higher level position would create contrient interdependence among group members since the attainment of the promotion by one person precludes its attainment by others.

There are two experimental studies of the consequences of promotive interdependence among goals on the affective qualities of the interaction among group members. Using five-person discussion groups made up of students enrolled in an introductory psychology course, Deutsch (1949) created promotive and contrient interdependence by instructions to students about how grades would be assigned. Persons in the promotively interdependent situation were told that each person in the group would receive the same grade and that this grade would be determined by comparing the group with other groups. Those in the contriently interdependent condition were told that grades would be assigned by evaluating group members in relation to others in the same group. Both sets of groups met for about three hours a week for five weeks during which time they worked on puzzles and human relations problems. Observer ratings and questionnaires filled out by the participants showed many significant differences between the two conditions. The promotively interdependent groups were more productive and their members exhibited a more favorable evaluation of the group and its products than did the contriently interdependent groups.

Jones and Vroom (1964) obtained similar results with two-person groups working on jigsaw puzzles. All subjects worked for financial incentives. Those in the promotively interdependent condition were told that they would receive the incentive if their combined performance exceeded the average for all groups. Those in the contriently interdependent condition were told that they would receive the incentive if their individual performance exceeded that of their partner. Measures of the attitudes of subjects taken after the task performance indicated that subjects in the promotively interdependent condition had a higher degree of liking for their partner and were more satisfied with their own performance than those in the contriently interdependent condition.

Individual Differences. The investigations considered in this section have been relevant to a determination of the effect of social relationships between members of the same work group on their attitudes or satisfaction. There has been virtually no consideration given to the role of individual differences in this relationship. The probability that individual personality and work group characteristics may interact in the determination of affective orientations toward the group or the group setting has not been explored in existing research on this topic.

There are important theoretical reasons for expecting that individual differences, particularly differences in motives, would be extremely important. Cartwright and Zander, for example, propose that, ". . . attraction to the group will depend upon two sets of conditions: (a) such properties of the group as its goals, programs, size, type of organization, and position in the community; and (b) the needs of the person for affiliation, recognition, security, and other things which can be mediated by groups. Both the nature of the group and the motivational state of the persons involved must be treated in any adequate formulation of group cohesiveness" (1960, p. 72).

It would seem to be crucial to go beyond the implicit assumption that all persons equally value interaction with their co-workers or acceptance by their co-workers, and to attempt to establish the nature of the interactions between these environmental states and individual motives.

Job Content

The assumption made by Mayo and others associated with the "human relations movement"—that the social relationships which the worker establishes are the crucial determinants of his satisfaction and productivity—has contributed to the wealth of research on such problems as the effects of supervision and the effects of the informal organization. However, this point of view has been accompanied by a comparative neglect of the effects of job content. Relatively little research has been carried out on the motivational consequences of job or task variables.

The number and nature of the functions that individual workers are called upon to perform vary tremendously from one work role to another. The duties of the doctor, the assembly line worker, the policeman, and the corporation president differ so extensively from one another that it is difficult to see how the psychological consequences of these differences could have received so little attention.

Interestingly enough, we find that psychologists who are concerned with occupational choice assume that individuals select occupations at least partly on the basis of content of the work. Whether little John prefers to become an engineer or a doctor depends on what engineers do and on what doctors do and on the implications of this difference for John's motives or values. However, psychologists interested in the determinants of job satisfaction are prone to overlook the content of the work in favor of the effects of social relationships. Whether John likes or dislikes his job is assumed to be dependent on his relationships with his supervisor and co-workers.

Interest on the part of industrial psychologists in the motivational consequences of job content has recently been generated by a book by Herzberg, Mausner, and Snyderman (1959), *The Motivation to Work*. The book describes an investigation into the sources of job satisfaction and dissatisfaction of accountants and engineers. The methods used were neither correlational nor experimental. The authors assumed that people have the ability and the motivation to report accurately the conditions that made them satisfied and dissatisfied with their jobs. Accordingly, they asked their subjects in interviews to tell them about times during which they felt exceptionally good and exceptionally bad about their jobs. They found that the stories told about "good" periods most frequently concerned the content of the job. Achievement, recognition, advancement, responsibility, and the work itself were the most frequently coded themes in such stories. In contrast, stories concerned with "bad" periods most frequently concerned the context of the job. Company policy and administration, supervision, salary, and working conditions more frequently appeared in these stories than in those told about "good" periods.

These findings have recently been replicated in a study of male supervisors employed by public utility companies (Schwartz, Jenusaitis, and Stark, 1963). Job-related factors were more frequently mentioned in connection with positive experiences and job-context factors were more frequently mentioned in connection with negative experiences. These investigators also found no significant relationships between story content and their demographic variables, such as age and education, or personality characteristics as measured by the Edwards Personal Preference Test.

Herzberg and his associates attribute these findings to the fact that the favorable job-content factors, such as achievement and the work itself, tend to produce satisfaction, but their absence does not tend to produce dissatisfaction. In contrast, the unfavorable job-context factors like poor supervision or working conditions tend to produce dissatisfaction, but their absence does not produce satisfaction. In effect, this explanation asserts a nonlinearity in the effects of job-content and job-context variables on job satisfaction. Increases in some desirable job-context variable will result in an increase in job satisfaction to the point where the worker is indifferent or neutral concerning the job. Increases in some desirable job-content variable are required to increase further the worker's job satisfaction to a positive level.

This interpretation of the fact that different factors are mentioned as sources of satisfaction and dissatisfaction may be correct, but it is not the only possible interpretation. One could also argue that the relative frequency with which job-content or job-context features will be mentioned as sources of satisfaction and dissatisfaction is dependent on the nature of the content and context of the work roles of the respondents. This interpretation is consistent with the results of Walker and Guest's study (1952) of assembly line workers in an automobile plant. The findings in this investigation are diametrically opposed to those obtained by Herzberg and his associates in their interviews with accountants and engineers. They found job content, particularly the paced repetitive nature of the work, to be the chief factor reported as disliked about jobs. In contrast, the economic factors of pay and security (both job-context characteristics) were the principal liked features. Furthermore, Herzberg's own review (Herzberg, Mausner, Peterson, and Capwell, 1957) of the results of fifteen studies involving over 28,000 employees in which workers were asked to indicate what made them satisfied or dissatisfied with their jobs is not consistent with his subsequent conclusion that job content can produce satisfaction but not dissatisfaction, while job context can produce dissatisfaction but not satisfaction. The relative frequency with which eight different factors are reported by workers as contributing to their satisfaction and dissatisfaction are reported. The results for six of the eight factors are in a direction opposite to what would be predicted from Herzberg's theory. Five job-content factors (security, wages, supervision, social aspects of jobs, and working conditions) are more frequently mentioned as contributing to satisfaction rather than dissatisfaction, and one factor that pertains at least in part to the job content (opportunity for advancement) is more frequently mentioned as contributing to dissatisfaction. It is true that the specific method used by Herzberg, Mausner, and Snyderman (having workers tell stories about "good" and "bad" periods) was not used in these studies or by Walker and Guest. Nonetheless, the marked difference in findings suggests the desirability of further research using the same methods on a large number of different populations.

Even if such research were to replicate perfectly the Herzberg, Mausner, and Snyderman findings on widely different populations, their inference concerning a qualitative difference between satisfiers and dissatisfiers could not be unequivocally accepted. It is still possible that obtained differences between stated sources of satisfaction and dissatisfaction stem from defensive processes within the individual respondent. Persons may be more likely to attribute the causes of satisfaction to their own achievements and accomplishments on the job. In contrast, they may be more likely to attribute their dissatisfaction not to personal inadequacies or deficiencies but to factors in the work environment, that is, obstacles presented by company policies or supervision. This type of explanation is invoked by Gurin, Veroff, and Feld (1960), who explain similar findings to those of Herzberg, Mausner, and Snyderman as follows:

> . . . this finding suggests that there is relatively little
> introspection in analysing the sources of distress on
> the job—that complaints tend to be externalized rather
> than cast in personality terms (p. 153).

Herzberg's conclusion that the variance in job satisfaction below some hypothetical level can be explained in terms of one set of variables, whereas the variance above that level requires another set of variables, can neither be accepted nor rejected on the basis of evidence available at this time. Corroboration of his position will require correlational or experimental evidence of nonlinearity in relationships, a problem that is worthy of much more attention than it has received. Regardless of the outcome, Herzberg and his associates deserve credit for directing attention toward the psychological effects of job content, a problem of great importance in a world of rapidly changing technology.

Job Level. One of the most frequently studied correlates of job satisfaction is job level. A positive relationship between the level or status of the worker's job and his job satisfaction has been reported by a large number of investigators (Uhrbrock, 1934; Hoppock, 1935; Thorndike, 1935; Super, 1939; Miller, 1941; Paterson and Stone, 1942; Heron, 1948; Centers, 1948b; Katz, 1949; Mann, 1953; Morse, 1953; Gurin, Veroff, and Feld, 1960; Kornhauser, 1965). Gurin, Veroff, and Feld's findings on this point are of most interest because they are recent and are based on a national sample. The results shown in Table 5.2 indicate substantial differences between the level of satisfaction reported by persons in different occupational categories. Forty-two percent of persons employed in professional-technical occupations report that they are very satisfied with their jobs compared with only 13 percent of workers in the unskilled category. In general, reported job satisfaction declines with occupational level. However, the relatively low level of satisfaction reported by clerical and sales workers should be noted. Only 61 percent of clerical workers and 68 percent of salespeople state that they are very satisfied or satisfied with their jobs compared with 80 percent, 76 percent, and 75 percent for farmers, skilled, and semiskilled workers, respectively.

Baldamus (1951) found a negative relationship between the level of jobs within a single factory and the rate of turnover within these jobs. He reports the length of training period required by twenty-three different jobs and the rate of turnover for each of these jobs. The rank-difference correlation between these variables was computed by Vroom and found to be -.82.[1] These data are in agreement with Reynold's finding (1951) that unskilled workers change jobs more frequently than semiskilled workers, who in turn change jobs more frequently than skilled workers.

Most investigators have suggested that the positive relationship between level and satisfaction is due to the fact that positions at high levels provide more rewards to their occupants than those at lower levels. However, the nature of these rewards is not clear. Job level is a highly gross variable and includes a number of empirically related but conceptually separable properties. Jobs that are high in level, either in a single organization or in society as a whole,

---

[1]For those jobs in which a range was given for the training period (for example, three to six months) the midpoint was used.

Table 5.2. Relationship Between Occupational Status and Job Satisfaction Among Employed Men.

Job Satisfaction	Occupational Status							
	Professionals, Technicians	Managers, Proprietors	Clerical Workers	Sales Workers	Skilled Workers	Semiskilled Workers	Unskilled Workers	Farmers
Very satisfied	42%	38%	22%	24%	22%	27%	13%	22%
Satisfied	41	42	39	44	54	48	52	58
Neutral	1	6	9	5	6	9	6	4
Ambivalent	10	6	13	9	10	9	13	9
Dissatisfied	3	6	17	16	7	6	16	7
Not ascertained	3	2	–	2	1	1	–	–
Total	100%	100%	100%	100%	100%	100%	100%	100%
Number of cases	119	127	46	55	202	152	84	77

Source: After Gurin, Veroff, and Feld, 1960, p. 163.

are generally more highly paid, less repetitive, provide more freedom, and require less physical effort than jobs low in level. If we are to gain any understanding of the psychological basis of the correlation between level and job satisfaction, we must deal with these different variables separately.

A recent study by Porter (1962) sheds some light on the basis for the relationship between level within the managerial hierarchy and job satisfaction. He obtained ratings from nearly 2,000 managers concerning the amount of different outcomes, for example, security, autonomy, esteem, and so on, which were now connected with their positions and the amount that they thought should be connected with their positions. The degree of perceived deficiency in fulfillment of a manager's need for a particular type of outcome was measured by subtracting his rating of the amount of the outcome now connected with his position from his rating of the amount that should be connected with his position. Respondents were classified into five managerial levels: presidents, vice presidents, upper-middle managers (for example, division managers and plant managers), lower-middle managers (for example, department managers), and lower managers (first- and second-level supervisors). Holding age constant, Porter observed a tendency for the amount of difference between ratings, that is, perceived deficiencies in need fulfillment, to increase at each successive lower level of the management hierarchy. However, the strength of this relationship varied markedly from one need category to another, being highly significant for esteem, autonomy, and self-actualization but not significant for social and security need categories. These findings imply that the greater satisfaction of higher level managers is the result, at least in part, of greater opportunities to satisfy esteem, autonomy, and self-actualization needs.

Specialization. Virtually all occupations have undergone increased specialization during this century. This change has probably been most marked for rank and file factory workers. The development of the techniques of mass production has resulted in a substantial increase in the repetitiveness of the jobs of most factory workers. Although most social scientists acknowledge the increases in efficiency that have stemmed from greater specialization, many of them feel that specialization has led to a decrease in job satisfaction. Such writers as Merton (1947), Krech and Crutchfield (1948), and Katz (1954) have commented on the deprivations associated with greater repetitiveness of tasks.

The terms repetitiveness and specialization have often been used without adequate definition. Although any precise definition would, at this point, have to be an arbitrary one, it seems important to distinguish between the number of different responses made, or operations performed by the worker, and the frequency with which he can alternate from one response or operation to another. Thus, a job may be made less repetitive by increasing the number of operations that the worker performs or by increasing the frequency with which he can change from one operation to another. Herein lies the distinction between industrial programs of job enlargement and job rotation, both designed to decrease the repetitiveness of work. Job enlargement refers to increases in the number of operations making up a single work role. It provides workers with a larger number of operations to perform and usually increases the frequency with which they can change from one operation to another. In contrast, in job rotation, the content of single work roles remains the same, although workers are enabled to move periodically from one work role to another. The effect, as far as repetitiveness is concerned, is to increase the total number of operations that the worker performs over some long time period but not to increase the frequency with which he can alternate from one operation to another.

The effects of repetitive work received considerable attention during the 1920s in the work of the Industrial Fatigue Research Board in Great Britain. A large number of studies were carried out in both laboratory and industrial settings on the determinants and consequences of monotony and boredom in tasks. The major conclusions of these studies were summarized by Wyatt, Fraser, and Stock as follows:

> The amount of boredom experienced bears some relation to the conditions of work. It is less liable to arise

(a)   when the form of activity is changed at suitable
       times within the spell of work,
(b)   when the operatives are paid according to output
       instead of time worked,
(c)   when the work is conceived as a series of self-
       contained tasks rather than as an indefinite and
       apparently interminable activity,
(d)   when the operatives are allowed to work in com-
       pact social groups rather than as isolated units,
(e)   when suitable rest pauses are introduced within
       the spell of work (1929, pp. 42-43).

In a more recent investigation Walker and Guest (1952) found that the degree to which employees in an automobile assembly plant expressed interest in their jobs was related to the number of operations that they carried out. Only 33 percent of workers performing a single operation reported their jobs as very or fairly interesting. But, 44 percent of those performing two to five operations and 69 percent of those performing more than five operations reported their work as very or fairly interesting. In addition, many workers, particularly those on jobs involving few operations, expressed dissatisfaction in interviews with the repetitive nature of their work.

In another study, Walker (1950, 1954) described the results of the introduction of job enlargement into a factory making calculating machines. Before the introduction of the change, the tasks of setting up the work on the machines, operating the machines, and inspecting the product were performed by three different groups of workers. As a result of management decision, the three tasks were combined into one. The machine operator was given the added duties of making his own set-ups and doing his own inspection. After a year of experience with the enlarged job content, according to Walker, the workers declared their preference for the new arrangement. "Feelings of frustration and boredom, which had formerly existed in the shop, diminished or disappeared. At the same time, management was pleased because the rate of production was maintained and an improvement in quality was recorded" (1954,

p. 349). Similar results have been described by Guest (1957), based on work in an insurance company and in a manufacturing organization, and by Elliott (1953), based on work in a public utility.

An intensive case study of the consequences of a decrease in the number of operations performed by workers can be found in Trist and Bamforth's account (1951) of the conversion to the long-wall method of coal mining in Britain. Coal had traditionally been mined by two-person groups who performed all the mining operations (that is, loosening the coal, collecting it, and loading it). Subsequently, greater specialization was introduced, with large groups assigned to perform a single operation. Although greater productivity was expected to result from this change, the expectation was not realized. Furthermore, Trist and Bamforth report, on the basis of observations and interviews, a marked drop in job satisfaction occurred and both absenteeism and psychosomatic illnesses increased. The complex nature of this particular change makes it impossible to attribute these effects solely to the change in the number of operations performed. The authors mention a number of possible contributing factors, including the increased group size and the new functional basis of group organization.

Baldamus (1951) showed that repetitiveness is also reflected in turnover. He compared the labor turnover rates of workers in a number of different jobs in a single company with the length of the work cycle for each of these jobs. For those jobs ($N = 11$) in which the work cycle was less than thirty minutes, the median turnover rate was 25 percent, compared with a median of only 11 percent for those in which the work cycle ranged from thirty minutes to twelve weeks ($N = 11$).

Mann and Hoffman (1960) studied workers in an automated power plant who had recently been transferred from an older plant. Because of technological changes and management decisions the jobs in the new plant had been enlarged by increasing the number of duties of workers. In addition, workers in the new plant were rotated among different types of jobs. Questionnaires filled out by operators in the new plant indicated that they felt more interested in and more satisfied with their new jobs. One hundred percent of the workers studied in the new plant stated that their new job was much more interesting, and 94 percent stated that they were either a little more or much more satisfied with their new job than with their old. Further evidence concerning the effects of the programs of job enlargement and job rotation in the new plant was obtained by comparing the level of job satisfaction of workers in the new plant with that of workers in another plant that had not adopted these changes. Eighty percent of workers in the new plant stated that they liked their jobs very much or fairly well compared with only 40 percent in the old plant.

Kennedy and O'Neil (1958) carried out one of the few studies whose results do not support the effects of repetitiveness on worker satisfaction. They compared the attitudes of assembly operators with those of utility men in an automobile plant. Each of the assembly operators performed a single task or set of tasks as the line passed his work station. Utility men, in contrast, had more varied duties, including relieving assembly operators for scheduled or emergency breaks, helping operators who were unable to keep up with the line, and demonstrating jobs for new operators. No differences were observed between the attitudes of these two groups. Vroom and Maier (1961) have suggested that these negative results may reflect the fact that the size of increments in satisfaction following increases in the number of duties is dependent on the relatedness of the added duties.

> Greater variety of tasks may not increase satisfaction unless the tasks form a unified, integrated, and meaningful whole. Enlarging the job by adding diverse unrelated activities or rotating the worker from one job to another unrelated job may not have the intended positive consequences on either satisfaction or motivation (p. 434).

Some attention has been given to individual differences in negative affective reactions to repetitive work. In his textbook on industrial psychology, Viteles observed that individuals vary in their susceptibility to monotony.

> Monotony must then be conceived not solely as a function of the task, but to a large extent as a function of the individual to whom the task is assigned. It is more

apt to occur in uniform than in varied tasks, in simple
than in complex tasks, in the operation of a machine
than in hand work, but, in the final analysis, it is to
the susceptibility of the individual, and not to the
task, that the responsibility for the feeling of boredom
must in large part be ascribed (1932, p. 547).

It has often been suggested that intelligence accentuates negative reactions to repetitive work. On highly repetitive tasks, highly
intelligent persons have been predicted to experience greater monotony and boredom than those of lesser intelligence. Some support for
this view may be found in investigations showing greater turnover
on highly repetitive jobs among the most intelligent workers (Kornhauser, 1922; Viteles, 1924; Kriedt and Gadel, 1953). A more appropriate test of the idea that the person's aversion to repetitive work
is directly related to his intelligence would be to determine the
relationship between intelligence and job satisfaction, or some related variable, for workers on jobs of different degrees of repetitiveness. If a negative correlation is found on repetitive jobs but
diminishes as the job becomes less repetitive, we are in a better
position to conclude that it is repetitiveness which is the basis for
the dissatisfaction of the more intelligent worker.

Bills (1923) found that this was indeed the case. One hundred
and thirty-three clerical workers in five jobs representing different
degrees of difficulty were given a test of mental alertness. Two and
a half years later, a follow-up was made to determine if they still
remained on the job. The results are shown in Table 5.3. They
indicate a marked tendency for the intelligent workers to leave the
less difficult jobs and to remain on the more difficult ones. In contrast, those with a relatively low degree of intelligence tended to
leave the more difficult jobs and to remain on jobs that were less
difficult.

Other investigators have related verbal reports of monotony
and dissatisfaction to measured intelligence. Wyatt, Fraser, and
Stock (1929) found that workers of low intelligence liked repetitive
work more than those of high intelligence, and Reynolds (1951)
found a positive relationship between education and expressed dissatisfaction among manual workers. However, Smith (1955), in a

Table 5.3. Percentage of Turnover of Workers in the Upper and
Lower Thirds of the Distribution of Scores on a Test of Mental
Alertness on Five Different Jobs.

Job	Number of Persons Originally on Job	Number Remaining after 30 Months	Percentage of Turnover for Workers in Upper Third on Mental Alertness	Percentage of Turnover for Workers in Lower Third on Mental Alertness
A (least difficult)	16	7	100	37
B	15	6	100	62
C	24	11	72	50
D	56	26	53	58
E (most difficult)	22	13	41	66

Source: Adapted from Bills, 1923.

study of women workers in a knitwear mill, found no significant
relationship between educational level, which she assumed to reflect
intelligence, and reported monotony. In the same study, Smith
found a relationship between other individual characteristics and
reports of monotony. Workers reporting a high level of monotony
were more likely to be young, to report a preference for variety in
their daily habits and leisure time activities, and to report less satisfaction with personal, home, and plant situations in aspects not
directly concerned with uniformity or repetitiveness.

We have not yet considered the nature of the process by
which repetitiveness affects satisfaction. Why should a job that permits the performance of a large number of operations be more rewarding than one calling for a single operation to be performed
over and over? There are a number of possible answers to this question, each of which may have some degree of validity.

One of these answers involves the physiological process of
fatigue. Physiologists have long recognized that the continuous ac-
tivation of a muscle results in a decrease in the probability and
amplitude of its response. This decreased responsiveness is called
fatigue and is associated with an accumulation of lactic acid in the
muscle. It seems reasonable to assume that performing the same
operation over and over again would be more fatiguing than per-

different operations involved the use of different muscles. If one makes the further common assumption that fatigue is an aversive state, it follows that persons would prefer varied to repetitive work.

This is a rather neat, simple explanation that may have some applicability, but it is doubtful if it is any more than partially correct. Many of the repetitive jobs that are disliked are not fatiguing in the usual sense of the term. The muscular activity involved in the performance of a single operation is not so great nor is the pace of the work so fast that the activity cannot be continued without fatigue. Furthermore, these jobs are described not as fatiguing by workers but as boring. It is not the amount of physical effort that they require but their "sameness" that workers point to in describing the source of their displeasure.

An alternative explanation of the aversive consequences of repetitive jobs takes as its point of departure the lack of variety in stimulation that they provide the worker. Hebb (1949) and McClelland, Atkinson, Clark, and Lowell (1953) have proposed similar conceptions of the source of pleasure, which are consistent with such a view. According to these theories, the affective consequences of a stimulus pattern are dependent on the amount of disparity between the stimulus and some structure or adaptation level established in the person as a result of past experience. Mild disparities are pleasant; large disparities are disruptive and unpleasant; and the absence of disparity (that is, the identity of the stimulus and the adaptation level) is boring and unpleasant. If a worker is performing a highly repetitive operation, the sources of stimulation, from kinesthetic as well as other sense modalities, are highly constant and predictable. Virtually no disparity between the stimulation received by the worker and previous cognitive or neural organizations could be assumed. The result would be a high degree of displeasure that is not due to fatigue in the physiological sense but to the absence of novelty or change.

A classic experiment by one of Lewin's students at the University of Berlin, Anitra Karsten (1928), demonstrated the aversive qualities of a highly repetitive task. The subjects, college students, were asked to perform simple tasks like drawing lines in a particular rhythm. As soon as the subject filled a sheet of paper, he was given another, followed by another, and so on. Gradually the subjects introduced variations in their work. The lines were made heavier or lighter, tilted or curved, larger or smaller. Eventually, the subject reached a point where he was unable to continue.

Lewin (1935) attributes this result not to fatigue but to psychological satiation. After the repeated performance of an activity, the subject becomes satiated for the activity. Even though it might have been initially pleasurable, the repetition of an activity results in deterioration characterized by efforts to vary the activity, followed by a complete intolerance for the activity. Hebb (1949) assumes that a similar process occurs when a person rereads a novel that he read the previous week or hears the same piece of music over and over. On the basis of existing evidence, it seems likely that the unattractiveness of repetitive tasks is based more on the constant stimulus pattern with which they provide the worker than on their greater demands on his musculature. Further work needs to be done, however, in establishing the relative effects of varied stimulation in different sense modalities. Ultimately, it will be necessary to refine the concept of repetitiveness to express the extent to which the content of the work provides variety in a number of different stimulus dimensions.

Control Over Work Methods. The increased *specialization* that has accompanied technological innovations has been paralleled by greater *standardization* of work methods. The methods of science have been used not only to create machines and equipment but also to determine the optimal means of using them. The result has been a marked decrease in the amount of control exercised by industrial workers over the methods that they use in carrying out their jobs. Among the pioneers in this development were F. W. Taylor (1911) and Frank and Lillian Gilbreth (1919). Taylor believed that a great deal of inefficiency in industry stemmed from the fact that workers who were given a job to do were also permitted to decide how that job should be done. He felt that the *planning* of a job should be separated from the *doing* of it. The doing of the work could be entrusted to the workers themselves, but the planning was a highly complex activity that required the application of special techniques.

Taylor's methods are illustrated in the often-told story of his work with a Pennsylvania Dutchman by the name of Schmidt.

Schmidt was one of seventy-five laborers whose job it was to load pig iron onto railway cars. Production averaged 12½ tons a day, a figure that Taylor felt could be markedly increased by the use of more efficient working methods. Taylor told Schmidt that he could earn substantially more money if he were to do exactly as he was told. When Schmidt expressed interest, Taylor accompanied him on his job and gave him precise directions—to walk, to lift, to put the iron down, to rest, and so on. At the end of the day, Schmidt had loaded 47½ tons of pig iron and continued to load this amount for the three years he was under observation.

The basic assumption of Taylor and the Gilbreths—that there is one best way of doing the work—has been criticized by industrial psychologists. Viteles, for example, argued for some attention to individual differences:

> According to this viewpoint personal differences in physical and mental make-up must be recognized, and the possibility allowed that the worker may discover a method of work better suited to his requirements than a prescribed one. Moreover, the criticism of the one-best-way denies that speed of work is the best criterion for judging the effectiveness of a movement. The logical development of this viewpoint is the contention that increased output cannot serve as the only gauge of the value of a method of work. There must be combined with speed of work and output a yardstick showing the ease with which the worker can perform the series of movements—i.e., the cost in fatigue and malaise of a prescribed method of work (1932, p. 435).

The Taylor-Gilbreth philosophy, which led to development of time and motion study, has had its principal application in work roles in which the number of operations performed by the worker is small. There has been little attempt to apply these principles to higher level positions, including those in management. The reasons for this are simple. The number of situations with which the worker in a managerial position is confronted is exceedingly large. In most cases the consequences of alternative responses to a given situation are uncertain and the criteria in terms of which they can be evaluated are many and complexly interrelated. Under such circumstances the codification of work methods is an extremely difficult, if not impossible, task.

Viteles' observations cited above suggest that depriving the worker of control over his own methods of work has negative affective consequences. Prescribing a single method for all workers to follow may increase productivity but will lead to a reduction in worker satisfaction. There is considerable evidence from naturalistic observation to support such an observation but surprisingly little systematic empirical evidence.

Control over Work Pace. Work roles vary not only in the extent to which the worker is free to choose the methods he will use in doing the work but also in the extent to which he can choose his own pace of work. There is no necessary relationship between these two different aspects of control. A worker may be able to decide how he will do his job but not how fast he will work, or he may be able to set his own pace of work but have to follow a prescribed method.

The pace at which a worker performs his job may be regulated either socially or mechanically. The term close supervision is typically used to refer to a relationship between supervisor and worker in which the worker's choice of work pace is constrained by the presence of his supervisor. Presumably workers subject to close supervision have less freedom to vary their pace of work without incurring penalties than those who are subject to more general supervision. Pace of work may also be controlled mechanically by conveyer systems, which regulate the speed with which the worker must carry out his job. The use of a conveyer demands that the worker's energy be expended at regular and unchangeable intervals and at a rate set by the machine. When the conveyer brings the work to the worker, he must perform his operation quickly before it "gets past" him. As Walker and Guest (1952) express it, "The worker cannot apply his own work rhythm but must adapt to the rhythm of the machine" (p. 11).

Walker and Guest found that automotive assemblers rated mechanical pacing as the most disliked feature of their work. While a small minority expressed some enjoyment at the excitement of a moving line, the majority regarded it as highly undesirable. Although not presenting quantitative data, the authors cite comments of a number of workers not working on the line indicating a decided preference for the greater freedom in their present positions.

In a study of automobile plants in the United Kingdom, Walker and Marriott (1951) found a similar difference between the job satisfaction of persons working on mechanized operations, "where the rate of working was controlled by a mechanically operated moving conveyer" (p. 183), and those on nonmechanized operations, where the pace of the work was physically under the worker's control. Of persons employed on nonmechanized operations, 72 percent in one plant and 77 percent in another stated that they were very or moderately satisfied with their jobs. The comparable percentage for workers on mechanized operations was 54 percent in both plants. Similar findings were reported by Marriott and Denerley (1955). Their findings suggest that the inability to control one's pace of work may be highly detrimental to worker satisfaction.

Use of Skills and Abilities. It is often asserted that an individual derives satisfaction from jobs that permit him to use his skills and abilities. For example, Maslow (1943) has stated

> A musician must make music, an artist must paint, a poet must write, if he is to be ultimately happy. What a man can be, he must be. This need we may call self-actualization (p. 382).

Such a proposition is basically testable. If we assume that the extent to which a person has a particular ability is reflected in his score on a test that purports to measure that ability and that the relevance of the ability for performance on a job is reflected in the validity coefficient of the test for that job, then we can make predictions about the relationship of abilities to job satisfaction. For example, we would predict that persons receiving high scores on a test would be more satisfied than those receiving low scores if the test is positively correlated with performance on the job.

Such predictions are so simple that it is surprising that there is so little evidence concerning them. Psychologists who have been interested in test validation have tended to look primarily at the relationship between test scores and criteria of performance and have neglected the affective consequences of a "mismatch" of abilities and job requirements. There are, however, a few studies on the relationship between abilities and turnover that have some relevance to this problem. We have previously noted that intelligence is negatively related to turnover on highly routine jobs (Kornhauser, 1922; Viteles, 1924; Kriedt and Gadel, 1953) and that this relationship becomes increasingly positive as the difficulty of the job increases (Bills, 1923). Brown and Ghiselli (1953) also found greater turnover among taxicab drivers with aptitude scores markedly above or below the average for their occupation; and Kephart (1948) found greater turnover in the job of lens inspector for persons with visual phorias.[5]

The relevance of these findings for the hypothesis that workers are more likely to be satisfied with jobs that permit them to use their skills is based on the assumption that turnover is a useful index of dissatisfaction. While these variables are undoubtedly related to one another, it is clear that turnover rates are affected by a number of other variables, such as level of unemployment and the availability of other jobs. As Viteles (1932) has pointed out, the higher turnover among highly intelligent workers on repetitive jobs may be due to the fact that they find it easier to obtain other employment. Furthermore, in most of the studies of ability and turnover, no distinction was made between dismissal and voluntary resignation as sources of turnover. It is consequently possible that some portion of the common variance between ability measures and turnover rates may be attributed to a greater probability of dismissal for workers with lower ability. The data reported above are consistent with the hypothesis that persons prefer jobs for which they have the necessary skills, but they cannot be regarded as a direct or unequivocal test of this hypothesis.

We can modify Maslow's hypothesis slightly by stating it in cognitive rather than objective terms. Thus, we would now predict

---

[5] A phoria is a tendency to deviation of the visual axis of one of the eyes from the normal.

greater job satisfaction on the part of people who believe their jobs require abilities that they believe they possess. If this modified hypothesis is correct, we should be able to find some lawful relationship between job satisfaction and measures or experimental manipulations of the extent to which people believe themselves to possess the abilities needed for their jobs.

Brophy's data (1959) provide a correlational test of this modified hypothesis. She obtained ratings from each of eighty-one female nurses concerning the extent to which they believed themselves to possess each of forty-nine different traits, for example, accurate, logical, efficient, and so on. Each nurse also rated the extent to which the job permitted her to be the kind of person represented by each of the forty-nine traits. The amount of discrepancy between these two sets of ratings was found to correlate -.41 with scores on a scale of vocational satisfaction. In other words, the less she saw her job as demanding the qualities she possessed, the lower her job satisfaction.

Kornhauser (1965) found a marked positive relationship between workers' reports of the extent to which their job enabled them to use their abilities and their mental health. This relationship appeared across occupational levels and within a given occupational level for both young and middle-aged workers. The index of mental health was obtained by combining scores for each worker on separate measures of anxiety, self-esteem, hostility, sociability and friendship, overall life satisfaction, and personal morale.

In another study, Vroom (1962) reported a correlation of .59 between opportunity for self-expression on the job and job satisfaction for 489 hourly blue collar workers in a Canadian oil refinery. A worker's opportunity for self-expression was determined by combining his responses to nine questions such as, "How much chance do you get to use the skills you have learned for this job?" and "How much chance do you get to do the kinds of things you are best at?" (p. 166). Similar evidence concerning a positive relationship between workers' reports of the extent to which their job permits them to use their abilities and their job satisfaction has been obtained in unpublished studies by the Survey Research Center in a public utility and in an equipment manufacturing organization.

The motivation of people to utilize their abilities is termed a self-actualization need by Maslow (1943, 1954). According to his hierarchical theory of motivation, there should be substantial individual differences in the strength of this need, and these differences should be positively related to the extent to which lower order needs like those for food and water, safety, and acceptance by others have been satisfied. When such lower order needs have been satisfied, higher order needs will emerge; when they have not been satisfied, higher order needs will remain inactive. If this hypothesis is correct, we should find that the effects on job satisfaction of the extent to which the job permitted the use of skills would vary inversely with the intensity of other deprivations experienced by the worker. If a worker was inadequately clothed or fed, in a dangerous or threatening situation, or rejected by others, the opportunity to utilize his skills or abilities would be predicted to be much less important to him than if these lower order needs were satisfied.

There have been some observations that are consistent with this hypothesis. Davis's interviews with underprivileged workers in Chicago (1946) strikingly demonstrated the lack of ambition or concern with the nature of the work that characterizes this worker population; Pellegrin and Coates (1957) reported that executives were more likely to define success as career accomplishment, whereas first level supervisors tended to view it in terms of security and being a good provider for one's family; Centers (1948b), Morse and Weiss (1955), and Lyman (1955) found that ratings of the importance of accomplishment and self-expression in work were directly related to job level, and Veroff, Atkinson, Feld, and Gurin (1960) have found that scores on need for achievement, as revealed in fantasy, are directly related to occupational level. However, it is not clear to what extent these differences in motives are a consequence of occupancy of different positions, as implied by the Maslow theory, or preceded occupancy of the different positions. Conceivably persons who attach great importance to achievement and accomplishment are more likely to choose and be chosen for higher level positions.

Although not bearing specifically on the Maslow hypothesis, the data reported by Vroom (1962) shed some light on individual differences in satisfaction derived from the use of abilities in work. Blue collar workers in an oil refinery were asked the question, "If a problem comes up in your work and it isn't all settled by the time you go home, how likely is it that you will find yourself thinking about it after work?" (p. 163). Responses to this question were assumed to provide some indication of the respondent's ego involvement in his job. Those stating that they were "almost sure to think about it" were termed highly ego involved; those stating that "there's a pretty good chance" that they would think about it were termed moderate in ego involvement; whereas those stating that they probably or surely "wouldn't think about it" were termed low in ego involvement (p. 163). Table 5.4 shows the correlations between the amount of opportunity for self-expression reported by individual workers and various measures of their satisfaction with or adjustment to their jobs.

It may be seen that, in general, opportunity for self-expression was most highly related to the satisfaction and adjustment of workers with the highest ego involvement in their jobs (a positive relationship in the case of the three satisfaction measures and a negative relationship for tension and absences) and least highly related for those with lowest ego involvement in their jobs. Two of the five differences between the correlations for the high and low groups (on job satisfaction and satisfaction with self) are significant at the .01 level, while one of the differences between moderate and low groups reaches that level. The only reversal to this general trend is the correlation between opportunity for self-expression and job satisfaction, which is higher (.65) for the moderate than for the high group (.62).

Table 5.4. Relationship Between Perceived Opportunity for Self-Expression and Measures of Satisfaction and Adjustment Among Persons with High, Moderate, and Low Ego Involvement.

Correlation Between Opportunity for Self-Expression in Job and	*Ego Involvement*			*Pt H-L*	*Pt H-M*	*Pt M-L*
	High (H) N = 121	*Moderate (M)* N = 270	*Low (L)* N = 98			
Job satisfaction	.62	.65	.36	.01	ns	.01
Satisfaction with self	.30	.15	−.05	.01	ns	ns
Satisfaction with health	.20	.16	.09	ns	ns	ns
Work-related tension	−.32	−.20	−.20	ns	ns	ns
Absences (from company records)	−.14	−.03	.04	ns	ns	ns

Source: After Vroom, 1962, p. 169.

Success and Failure in Work Performance. It seems circular to propose that success and failure might have affective consequences. Inherent in popular usage of the term success is the experience of attaining a positively valent outcome, whereas failure usually refers to the experience of attaining a negatively valent outcome. The circularity disappears, however, if we define success and failure in terms that are independent of the subject's reactions to them. In this case, we are using the terms success and failure to refer to effective and ineffective task performance, respectively. The question with which we are concerned is whether, and under what conditions, a person's liking for or satisfaction with a work role is influenced by the effectiveness of his performance in it. This question is at least theoretically separate from the question with which we dealt in the preceding section. Although the degree to which a job requires abilities or skills possessed by the worker should be related to his success or failure in that job, these two variables can be kept separate in the laboratory and are not perfectly related in "real life."

The effects of success and failure in task situations have most frequently been investigated in the laboratory. Researchers have experimentally manipulated success and failure on tasks and have studied its effects on such variables as (1) the subject's level of aspiration on the same or different tasks (Hoppe, 1930; Jucknat, 1937; Frank, 1935); (2) the subject's estimate of his likelihood of succeeding on subsequent trials (Diggory, Riley, and Blumenfeld, 1960; Diggory and Ostroff, 1962); (3) the subject's performance on the same or different tasks (Hurlock, 1924; Forlano and Axelrod, 1937; Sears, 1937; Lantz, 1945; Thompson and Hunnicutt, 1944); (4) the subject's liking for or preferences among tasks (Cartwright, 1942; Gebhard, 1948; Gewirtz, 1959; Bachman, 1962); and (5) the subject's self-esteem (Diggory and Magaziner, 1959; Stotland and others, 1957; Stotland and Zander, 1958). The results are generally consistent with the assumption that telling a subject that he has performed well on a task is rewarding, whereas telling him that he has done poorly is punishing.

To this writer's knowledge there have been no experimental investigations of success and failure in industrial situations. There are, however, a large number of correlational studies of the relationship of job performance to job satisfaction. These studies have been reviewed elsewhere (Brayfield and Crockett, 1955; Herzberg, Maus-ner, Peterson, and Capwell, 1957) and will be taken up in more detail in the next chapter. It will suffice at this point to quote the conclusion reached by Brayfield and Crockett:

> In summary, it appears that there is little evidence in the available literature that employee attitudes of the type usually measured in morale surveys bear any sim-ple—or, for that matter, appreciable—relationship to performance on the job (1955, p. 408).

If success and failure on tasks serve as rewards and punish-ments in highly artificial laboratory situations, why is there no substantial association between performance and satisfaction in in-dustrial situations? One kind of explanation of this discrepancy takes as its point of departure the difference between the operational definitions of performance in these two types of investigations. In the laboratory experiment performance is manipulated; individuals are told that they have performed effectively or ineffectively, regard-less of their actual performance. But field studies use measures of actual performance. It is possible that the performance as measured bears no relation to workers' conceptions of their performance. The latter is the variable that would be expected to affect satisfaction; a relationship between actual level of performance and satisfaction is predicated on the assumption that workers have accurate knowledge concerning their performance. If this explanation is correct, then we would expect to find a positive relationship between estimates by the worker of his level of performance and his job satisfaction, even though there was no association between the latter variable and actual performance. In support of this interpretation is Hoppock's finding (1935) that satisfied teachers more frequently said that they were making a success of their job than dissatisfied teachers. It is also consistent with Gurin, Veroff, and Feld's finding (1960) from a study of a national sample of employed men that job satisfaction was positively related to workers' reports of their adequacy on their jobs.

It is also possible that this discrepancy between the results of laboratory and field investigations may be caused by differences in the persons used as subjects and in the task situations. It might be argued that college students (used as subjects in most of the laboratory experiments) are very likely to be motivated to attain a favorable evaluation from a researcher concerning their performance on a task, particularly one that they are told is a measure of some aptitude or ability. In contrast, rank and file workers (studied in most industrial investigations) may be relatively indifferent to information from a supervisor or other source concerning their performance on their job. This line of argument would lead us to predict that, under conditions in which workers had some degree of involvement in their jobs, information concerning the effectiveness of their performance would have greater affective consequences. Likert (1961) has suggested that, as tasks become more varied and require greater use of skill, the relationship between job satisfaction and performance becomes increasingly positive. However, there is, as yet, no conclusive evidence in support of this suggestion.

Vroom (1962) hypothesizes that the effects of task performance on satisfaction varies with the extent to which the task is relevant to the worker's self-conception. If a person believes that a task requires abilities that he values and believes himself to possess, then success will be consonant with his self-concept and accompanied by satisfaction, whereas failure will be dissonant with his self-concept and accompanied by dissatisfaction. But, if he believes that the task does not require any abilities that he values and believes himself to possess, then his level of performance will be irrelevant to his self-concept.

Kaufmann (1962) carried out a laboratory experiment that was designed to test one aspect of this hypothesis. He was interested in determining whether the effects of failure in a task on satisfaction depended on the extent to which the subject conceived the task as a test of a possessed ability and on the value that he placed on the ability. Subjects who were tested individually were first given a short version of the Raven Progressive Matrices Test. Each was told that he had done extremely well and had scored at the 96th percentile for a college population. He was further told that his performance indicated that he possessed a high degree of "speed of closure." To half of the subjects speed of closure was represented as a highly valuable characteristic. They were shown evidence that it was an important determinant of success in almost every walk of life. The other half of the subjects were told that "speed of closure" was unimportant except for the occupation of textile spotter—a person whose job is to examine material for irregularities. It was assumed that these manipulations would result in all of the subjects regarding themselves as possessing "speed of closure" with one-half of them highly valuing this trait and the other being indifferent to it. Subsequently, all subjects were given a second task to perform (a modified version of the Digit Symbol subtest of the Wechsler Adult Intelligence Scale). One-half was told that this was an alternate test of their speed of closure while the other half was told that this test had nothing to do with this ability. Thus, there were four groups of subjects: (1) a group who were told that the second task measured an ability that they possessed and highly valued, (2) a group who were told that the second task measured an ability that they possessed but to which they were indifferent, (3) a group who were told that the second task did not measure an ability that they possessed and highly valued, and (4) a group who were told that the second task did not measure an ability that they possessed but to which they were indifferent. All four groups were made to fail on the second task and were given another attempt that also resulted in failure. Subsequent to these failures, they were given a questionnaire to complete that included questions dealing with their satisfaction with and liking for the task situation.

If failure has frustrating consequences because it provides information that is inconsistent with valued components of the self-concept, then the level of satisfaction of subjects with the task situation should be lower among subjects who believed that the second task measured an ability they possessed and highly valued than in the other three groups. The data support this prediction. Ratings by subjects of their level of satisfaction with their performance show that subjects who failed on a task that they had been led to believe measured a valued ability (group 1) expressed significantly greater dissatisfaction than those who believed that they had failed on a task measuring an ability to which they were indifferent (group 2). Subjects failing on a task that was irrelevant to their abilities (groups 3 and 4) were in between the first two groups in satisfaction and were not significantly different from one another. Although further research is needed in order to test this hypothesis more completely, these results suggest that the affective consequences of success and failure on tasks may depend on the nature of the task and its relationship to the self-concept of the task performer.

Interruption of Work on Tasks. A number of laboratory experiments by Lewin and his associates have been conducted on the motivational effects of interruption of work on tasks. Lewin (1951) has hypothesized that the intention to reach a certain goal, or carry out a certain action leading to the goal, corresponds to a tension system within the person that is released when the goal is reached. When a person intends to carry out a task, a tension system is created that is dissipated by completion of the task. If, however, the person is interrupted and prevented from completing the task, the tension persists and is reflected in a somewhat higher probability of recall of the incompleted task.

Ovsiankina (1928) has shown that there is a strong tendency for individuals to complete tasks on which they have once been interrupted. Zeigarnik (1927) and Marrow (1938) have further demonstrated that persons are more likely to recall tasks on which they have been interrupted than those that they have completed. While Zeigarnik's original findings have not always been replicated (Rosenzweig, 1943; Lewis and Franklin, 1944; Ericksen, 1952), the conditions in these investigations are such as to combine completion with success and interruption with failure. As Cartwright (1959) has pointed out, "When Zeigarnik's original conditions have been exactly reproduced the same findings have been obtained" (p. 33).

Maier (1955) has stressed the industrial implications of task interruption. He suggests that the amount of satisfaction that workers derive from their jobs may be increased by decreasing the frequency of interruptions that they experience and by creating opportunities for additional task completion experiences. The evidence from actual work situations concerning the satisfying effects of task completion and frustrating effects of task interruption is largely anecdotal. Maier describes an instance in which a worker struck and killed a foreman who tried to take him off a job he was doing and another instance in which a secretary's job satisfaction was increased when her supervisor gave her greater opportunity to finish her work when he called her for dictation. There is considerable need for more systematic investigation of the operation of this variable in actual work situations.

It is important to distinguish two different meanings that are sometimes associated with task completion. The first of these meanings pertains to the size or importance of the functions performed by the worker. A worker may be regarded as being prevented from completing a task whenever he shares with others the responsibility for creating some meaningful product or performing some service. In this sense, any assembly line worker who builds less than the entire airplane or any surgeon who performs less than the entire operation is unable to complete a task. The second meaning is independent of the first and derives directly from the laboratory experiments that we have described. It refers not to the nature of the task but to the frequency and length of interruptions that the worker incurs in executing it. An essential ingredient is the workers' intention to complete the task, which may be prevented from realization by a number of obstacles within the work situation. If these obstacles are experienced infrequently and their duration is brief, the work role may be described as providing considerable opportunity for task completion. But if there are frequent and lengthy interruptions, the work role may be characterized as providing very little opportunity for task completion.

Intuitively, one would assume that the force on a worker to complete a task is inversely related to the length of the task. If the task is a long one, interruptions may be less disturbing and even welcomed. This assumption is consistent with Smith and Lem's finding (1955) that the frequency of voluntary work stoppages among workers was directly related to the size of the lot on which they were working.

Wages

There has been a persistent controversy over the importance of wages to workers. Economists and many executives are prone to stress the importance of the size of the paycheck in determining a worker's job satisfaction and the probability that he will remain in his job. This assumption is decried by social scientists associated with the "human relations movement," who typically view economic factors as highly overemphasized and stress the importance of the satisfaction of social and ego needs.

Both sides can find some support for their position. When workers are asked to rank different aspects of the work role in terms of their importance, wages tend to be rated as less important than security, opportunity for advancement, and company and management, but as more important than job content, supervision, the social aspects of the job, communication, working conditions, and benefits (Herzberg, Mausner, Peterson, and Capwell, 1957). However, when they are asked to describe what makes them satisfied or dissatisfied with their jobs, wages are found to be the most frequent source of dissatisfaction but the least frequent source of satisfaction. Clearly, neither side to the controversy may be said to have scored a complete victory when the criteria are workers' descriptions of their motivations!

When one considers correlational evidence, some data show that income level is positively associated with job satisfaction. Several follow-up studies of college graduates (Thompson, 1939; Miller, 1941; Barnett, Handelsman, Stewart, and Super, 1952) provide support for such a relationship, as do investigations in British factories (Marriott and Denerley, 1955) and on a national sample in the United States (Centers and Cantril, 1946). Terman and Oden's follow-up (1959) of the gifted children whom they had studied thirty-five years earlier also support this relationship. And Lawler and Porter (1963) determined the level of wages received by almost 2,000 managers and found that this variable was positively related to satisfaction with wages with managerial level held constant.

In a recent paper, Smith, Kendall, and Hulin (1969) reported a correlation of .78 between the mean annual earnings of men in twenty-one plants and their mean job satisfaction as measured by the Job Description Index. Within plants, the correlations varied from .46 to -.16 with a mean correlation of .25. In contrast, Hoppock (1935) reported no significant difference in average earnings between one hundred well-satisfied and one hundred poorly satisfied teachers matched for age and sex. The latter's results probably reflect the relatively restricted range of wages received by respondents in his study.

It has been suggested that satisfaction stemming from the receipt of wages is dependent not on the absolute amount of these wages, but on the relationship between that amount and some standard of comparison used by the individual. The standard may be an adaptation level (Helson, 1947) derived from wages received at previous times or a conception of the amount of wages received by other people.

The latter of these two possibilities has been most thoroughly explored. Patchen (1961) formulated the problem of satisfaction with wages in terms of social comparison theory. He assumed that individuals compare their own earnings with those of others and evaluate differences or similarities in terms of their relative standing on dimensions believed to be the basis of pay (for example, skill, seniority, and education). Satisfaction with a specific wage comparison was hypothesized to be a function of the objective dissonance of the comparison. A comparison is termed objectively dissonant by Patchen when the ratio of the comparer's position on dimensions relevant to pay to another's position on these dimensions is culturally considered congruent with, or appropriate to, the ratio of their earnings. For example, if one person compared himself with another person who was earning more but who was similar in his standing on dimensions related to pay, the comparison would be dissonant and would be expected to lead to dissatisfaction on the part of the comparer. Similarly, if he compared himself with someone who was earning the same but who was inferior in standing on dimensions related to pay, the comparison would also be objectively dissonant and accompanied by dissatisfaction. In contrast, if a person compared himself with someone who was earning more and who was superior on dimensions related to pay, or with someone who was earning the same and was similar on dimensions related to pay, it would be objectively consonant and would be expected to result in satisfaction.

Evidence in support of the predicted relationship between the dissonance of wage comparisons and satisfaction has been obtained by Patchen in a study of workers in an oil refinery. Each person was asked to (1) name two other persons whose wages were different from his own, (2) state whether each person named was earning more or less than he, (3) state the occupation of the comparison person, (4) state his satisfaction with the way the earnings compared, and (5) state his reasons for his satisfaction or dissatisfaction with the comparison. The results are generally consistent with the predictions. He found that individuals who choose comparison persons who earn more but who are on a higher occupational level are more satisfied with the comparison than are men who choose comparison persons who earn more but are on the same occupational level. The greater the similarity between the occupational level of the person earning more, the less the reported satisfaction with the comparison. Furthermore, most men who were satisfied with comparisons with men earning more explained their satisfaction in terms of some other differences (for example, skill or seniority), which made the wage difference appropriate. Those who were dissatisfied about earning less than comparison persons gave as their reasons their own equality or superiority on pay-related dimensions.

These findings support the long-held contention of many personnel managers that satisfaction is dependent on relative rather than absolute wage levels. However, complete acceptance of the specific formulation proposed by Patchen must await the existence of experimental evidence. The existence of an association between choice of comparison person and satisfaction cannot be taken as evidence of a causal relation between these variables. It is as reasonable to expect that a person's satisfaction with his wages may affect the kind of comparisons he makes as it is to propose that the causal relationship is reversed. Ultimately, the fruitfulness of invoking an intervening process of choice of comparison person in explanations of job satisfaction depends on the degree to which it aids in identifying objectively definable conditions that can be demonstrated to affect measured satisfaction.

Promotional Opportunities

Economic organizations can be described as a hierarchy of roles with the chairman of the board of directors at the top and rank and file workers at the bottom. Role occupants may remain in the same role throughout their organizational membership or they may be "promoted" to a role involving greater wages, power, and status.

The opportunities for promotion afforded organization members are highly variable and are often assumed to have a marked effect on job satisfaction.

Promotional opportunities are difficult to describe in any systematic fashion. A position at a higher level in the same organization usually involves changes in supervision, co-workers, job content, and pay. Consequently it cuts across each of the topics that we have discussed. Furthermore, the specific outcomes that constitute a particular promotion differ greatly from one situation to another. Two persons in the same organization may expect a promotion within a six-month period, but for one person the expected promotion is to the presidency of the company with a $40,000 a year increase in salary, whereas for the other it is to the job of group leader with 25 cents an hour additional pay.

If we are willing to overlook the differences in the outcomes represented by promotions, we can describe promotions in terms of their probability of occurrence. The likelihood that an individual will be promoted to a given position within a specified time period may be assumed to vary from 0 (representing no possibility) to +1 (representing certainty) and may be defined in both objective and psychological terms. Such variations in *amount* of promotional opportunity have most frequently been studied as possible determinants of job satisfaction or morale.

Using data from a study in an electric utility company, Morse (1953) found a positive relationship between persons' statements of their promotional opportunities and their satisfaction with these promotional opportunities. She also found a negative relationship between workers' ratings of importance of promotion to them and their satisfaction with their promotional opportunities. Scores on the satisfaction measure could be predicted better by subtracting the ratings of importance from the ratings of promotional opportunities than from either index alone. Similarly, in an investigation in an electronic manufacturing organization, Sirota (1959) found a negative relationship between measures of promotional frustration (obtained by subtracting persons' estimates of how soon they would like a promotion from their estimates of when they expected to receive it) and measures of attitudes toward the company.

Patchen's study (1960) in a Canadian oil refinery demonstrated a higher frequency of absences among persons who felt that they deserved to have been promoted compared with those who stated that they did not feel that way at all. He also found significantly greater absences among persons who stated that their present promotional chances should be better than among those who stated they were as good as they should be. There was no significant relation between absences and persons' reports of their present promotion chances.

Spector (1956) conducted a laboratory experiment on the effects of amount of promotional opportunity on job satisfaction. His subjects were assigned to four-person groups to work on a simulated military intelligence problem. They were to operate as a team in which each man was to decode a different part of the group's message. Subjects were seated in such a manner as to prevent them from observing other group members. Some groups were told that three of the four men would be promoted after completion of the first message, while others were told that only one out of every four men would be promoted. Subsequent to completion of the first message, all of the members of half of the groups were informed that they were promoted, whereas none of the members of the other half of the groups were promoted. Thus, there were equal numbers of subjects under the following conditions: (1) subjects who believed they had a high probability of being promoted and were in fact promoted; (2) subjects who believed they had a high probability of being promoted but were not promoted; (3) subjects who believed that they had a low probability of being promoted and were in fact promoted; (4) subjects who believed that they had a low probability of being promoted and were not promoted.

Following completion of the second message, each person completed a six-item morale scale. Morale was found to be higher among subjects who were induced to believe they had a low probability of promotion than among those who believed they had a high probability. Furthermore, those receiving a promotion had higher morale than those who did not, regardless of their expectations. There was no interaction between expectations and attainment of promotion. Spector concluded that "personnel managers might be wise to underplay, rather than overplay, the opportunities for advancement in their organizations" (1956, p. 55).

There is a discrepancy between the Spector finding of higher
morale among those with low promotional expectations and those
of Morse (1953) and Sirota (1959) of a positive correlation between
promotional expectations and satisfaction. A reconciliation of these
discrepant findings might take the following form. Insofar as the
outcomes associated with a promotion (for example, more wages)
are positively valent to the person, the valence of his work role (that
is, his job satisfaction) will be positively related to the likelihood
that his occupancy of it will result in his promotion. Thus, we
might expect to find, as did Morse and Sirota, that a person's evaluation of his present position is directly related to his expectations
regarding promotion. However, we might also reason that receiving
a promotion will be more rewarding to persons who do not expect
it than to those who do. Similarly, failure to receive a promotion
might be less frustrating to those who do not expect it than to those
who do. Consequently, we would predict that receiving a desired
promotion would result in a greater increment in job satisfaction
on the part of workers who do not expect it than on the part of those
who do expect it; and failure to receive a desired promotion would
result in a greater decrement in the job satisfaction of those expecting it than those not expecting it.

Given these assumptions, it follows that the effects of promotional expectations on job satisfaction would vary from positive,
before information about success and failure in attaining the promotion was received, to negative after it was received. In the Morse
and Sirota studies, measures of promotional expectations and job
satisfaction were taken concurrently. Therefore, workers might be
assumed to be reporting what they believed to be their chances for
a promotion *before they received information concerning the final
awarding of these promotions.* Consequently, a positive association
between expectation and satisfaction would be predicted. However,
Spector induced promotional expectations and then let subjects
know about the ultimate realization of these expectations *before*
measuring satisfaction. Since subjects possessed final and irreversible information concerning their attainment (or lack of attainment) of a promotion, a negative relationship between their earlier
expectations and satisfaction would be predicted. According to this
interpretation, we would predict that, if Spector had taken his sat-

isfaction measures before telling persons whether they had been promoted, the reverse relationship between expectations and satisfaction would have been obtained.

Hours of Work

The work role occupied by a person affects not only how he will use his working hours but also how he can spend his leisure time. A person's job usually influences the community in which he lives, the way in which other members of the community respond to him, and the amount of time he can spend with his children. The implications of work roles for use of leisure time have generally been overlooked in studies of job satisfaction. With the exception of wages, which certainly affect how a person can use his leisure hours, little is known about the nonwork environments associated with various kinds of work roles and the effects of these nonwork environments on satisfaction and adjustment.

One of the properties of the work role that has obvious implications for the nonwork environment is the work schedule of patterns of normal working hours during which the person is expected to be performing his regular duties at his place of work. Although the majority of workers in our society work from early morning to late afternoon, Monday through Friday, and have weekends and major holidays "off," this is by no means the only pattern. There are many different kinds of work schedules, some requiring evening work (approximately 4:00 P.M. to 12:00 P.M.), others requiring night work (12:00 P M to 8:00 A.M.), and still others requiring the worker to rotate from one set of working hours to another.

The increased capital investment associated with automation and consequent pressures to make greater use of equipment is resulting in the employment of greater numbers of persons on what is called "shift work." Evidence concerning the effects of shift work on worker satisfaction is incomplete, but there are indications that these effects depend on the nature of the work schedule as well as on the personality of the individual worker. Mann and Hoffman (1960) studied the attitudes of rotating shift workers in two power plants and found a general dislike for shift work. There were, however, important differences in the extent of this dislike between the two plants. Thirty-five percent of the workers in one of the plants and 73 percent of the workers in the other plant reported disliking shift work very much or somewhat. The differences in results between the two plants might be attributable to differences in work schedules. Even though both work schedules were rotating (that is, workers changed periodically from the day to the night to the evening shift), there were many differences. At the plant in which workers manifested the greatest dissatisfaction with shift work, the rotation was monthly, whereas at the other plant it was weekly; in the former plant, the men and supervisors rotated together, whereas at the latter, they rotated individually; at the former, shift workers had weekends off once every fourth week, whereas at the latter, workers had them off only every twenty-five weeks; and the shifts at the former plant started at 12 P M , 8:00 A.M., and 4:00 P M , whereas at the latter, the starting times were 11:00 P.M., 7:00 A.M., and 3:00 P.M

The generally negative picture of attitudes toward shift work shown by Mann and Hoffman is in striking contrast to the findings reported by Blakelock (1959) from a study in a Canadian oil refinery. In this study, only 13 percent of the shift workers expressed dissatisfaction with shift work. Furthermore, shift workers reported significantly greater satisfaction with their jobs than nonshift workers.

In an unpublished theoretical paper, Vroom provides a model for predicting the affective consequences of work schedules. The basic assumption is that the valence of a given work schedule for a person will be an inverse function of the extent to which that work schedule restricts his ability to perform satisfying leisure activities. One of the central concepts in the model is the *time pattern for an activity*. It is obtained by plotting the probability that an activity can be performed at various times of day. Some activities are highly flexible,[6] that is, they can be carried out at any time of day or night. Many individual hobbies are essentially of this order. Other activities are inflexible and may be performed only at highly specific times. Watching a particular TV program or attending meetings of a particular organization are examples. Figure 5.1

---

[6]The concept of flexibility of activities originated with Blakelock (1960).

Figure 5.1. Time Patterns for Three Hypothetical Activities.

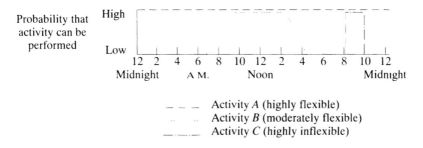

shows the time pattern for three hypothetical activities during a single 24-hour span.

A second major concept—the *discordance of a work schedule for a given activity*—is defined as the amount of overlap between the work schedule and the time pattern for that activity. It can be represented schematically by superimposing the work schedule on the time pattern. Figure 5.2 shows the discordance of three typical work schedules for each of the activities shown in Figure 5.1.

It can be seen that the three work schedules are equally discordant with respect to activity *A*. There is no difference in the likelihood that workers on each of the three work schedules would be able to perform that activity. However, activity *B* presents a different picture. The times that it is most easily performed fall almost completely during the time at which workers on the second work

Figure 5.2. Discordance of Three Work Schedules for Three Hypothetical Activities.

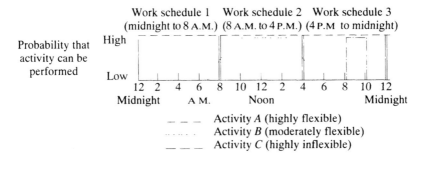

schedule are at work. Consequently, work schedule 2 is most discordant with respect to that activity, followed by work schedule 3 and work schedule 1, in that order. Activity C, the least flexible activity, can be performed only during the working hours of those on the third work schedule. Thus, this schedule is most discordant with respect to activity C, with schedules 1 and 2 both having least (in this case zero) discordance.

Vroom's major hypothesis may be stated as follows: the greater the positive valence of an activity for a person, the greater the negative effects of discordance of his work schedule with respect to that activity on his satisfaction with the work schedule. If an activity has strong positive valence for a person, decreases in the discordance of his work schedule with respect to that activity should result in increases in the valence of his work role and increases in discordance should result in decreases in valence. In contrast, if a person is indifferent to an activity, changes in the discordance of his work schedule with respect to that activity should have no effect on the valence of his work role. It can be seen that this hypothesis is a specific case of our first proposition in Chapter Two. The term discordance is merely another name for the fact that a work schedule restricts, that is, is negatively instrumental to, performance of an activity.

It should be noted that this hypothesis provides for extensive individual differences in reactions to the same work schedule. Two persons with markedly different interests in inflexible activities might have opposite preferences among work schedules. For example, a man who enjoyed participation in community organizations or playing with his school-age children would be expected to dislike working on the evening shift, whereas another person who was exclusively interested in outdoor sports such as fishing or golf might prefer working evenings to all other schedules.

Differences in the valence of activities or in the time patterns for activities on the part of workers in different plants or communities could lead to substantial differences in reactions to the same work schedule. The dissatisfaction with rotating shift patterns reported by Mann and Hoffman and the relative satisfaction reported by Blakelock may be the result of differences between the communities in which the research was conducted. The power plants studied by Mann and Hoffman were located in or adjacent to one of the largest American cities, whereas the oil refinery studied by Blakelock was located in a small Canadian town. The latter community was distinguished by the ample opportunities for swimming, sailing, and fishing. In addition, it is a community in which a relatively large proportion of the community works shifts and where shift work is accepted as a part of the way of life in the community.

A large multiplant, multi-industry study of the effects of shift work has recently been conducted by staff members of The Institute for Social Research of the University of Michigan. One of the purposes of this investigation was to test hypotheses about the effects of discordance. Unfortunately, at the time of this writing, the results are still being analyzed and no information concerning them has been released.

Some Theoretical Issues

Throughout this chapter we have presented many findings from specific research investigations concerning the conditions affecting job satisfaction. Although most of the investigations have been designed to shed light on important practical problems rather than to test any general theoretical models, they do have some theoretical implications. The choice of variables to be studied and the choice of the methods for measuring these variables are based on some kind of model of behavior, however vague or unformulated. We will now consider some of the theoretical issues involved in an understanding of the determinants of job satisfaction.

The Effects of the Work Role. An extremely large proportion of the studies cited in this chapter has been directed toward the establishment of a causal relation between some characteristic of work roles and job satisfaction. The underlying assumption is that there is a difference between the properties of a satisfying and a dissatisfying work role. Consequently, most of the studies have dealt with only two sets of variables, one a measure of a characteristic of a work role and the other a measure of job satisfaction.

The tendency to view job satisfaction as environmentally

caused rather than a reflection of personality mechanisms within the individual has been discussed by Gurin, Veroff, and Feld (1960). They point out that negative attitudes toward the job are thought to reflect an "unhealthy situation" rather than a lack of personal resources in the person. Therefore, attempts to solve job frustrations usually involve changing the work situation rather than attempting to effect personality changes in the dissatisfied individual.

> In these respects, attitudes toward the job differ from those on marriage or parenthood, roles that are assumed to have broad possibilities that any "healthy" individual should be able to maximize. This difference is implicitly recognized in the fact that personal therapy is more often recommended as a solution to problems and dissatisfactions in marital and parent-child relationships than it is with respect to problems and dissatisfactions in the job (1960, pp. 148–149).

Furthermore, the effects of work role characteristics on job satisfaction have usually been assumed to be linear. Those work role variables that are most frequently studied are expressed in terms of amounts or probabilities of certain kinds of outcomes (for example, pay, promotional opportunities, consideration from supervisor, interaction with co-workers, and so on) and the hypotheses, where stated, deal with simple linear relations between these amounts and job satisfaction.

There is no well-developed basis in these investigations for determining what kinds of outcomes should raise or lower job satisfaction and to what degree. Most investigators make very simplified gross assumptions about human motivation (for example, people have a need to be accepted by others or people have a need for self-actualization), and this leads them to predict that certain classes of events will act as rewards and other classes as punishments.

The assumption that job satisfaction is environmentally determined has been rather useful. Despite the frequent use of rather imprecise research methods, investigators have tended to find the correlations and differences between groups that they have predicted. These findings, although usually statistically significant, are seldom very impressive. In correlational studies, the amount of the variance in job satisfaction attributable to any single work role variable is quite small, and in experiments the variance among subjects exposed to the same condition is usually quite large. We might argue that these negative cases are due to errors of measurement or to other methodological weaknesses, but it is more likely that they are due to an oversimplified theory that does not do justice to the complexity of the phenomena with which it purports to deal.

Personality Variables. Although environmental factors have received the greatest amount of attention as determinants of job satisfaction, some investigators have focused their explanations on the personalities of workers. Persons who are satisfied with their jobs are assumed to differ systematically in their personalities from those who are dissatisfied.

The approach that attempts to link attitudes and personality variables has its roots in the early development of social psychology. The first studies were directed toward the relationship between personality traits (for example, intraversion-extraversion) or abilities (for example, intelligence) and attitudes. Later investigations attempted to explain attitudes and opinions in terms of unconscious needs and conflicts. Freud (1930) set the pattern for this line of research in his explanation of religious sentiments in terms of unresolved dependency needs and a resulting need for a strong protective parent to guard against lingering feelings of infantile helplessness. Subsequent research in this tradition was carried out by Lasswell (1948) on political attitudes and by Adorno, Frenkel-Brunswik, Levinson, and Sanford (1950) on racial prejudice.

There has been little attempt to deal with the relationship between personality variables and job satisfaction in theoretical terms and most of the empirical work represents an effort to establish a relationship between measures of adjustment or neuroticism and job satisfaction. A large number of methods of measuring adjustment have been used, including personality inventories (Heron, 1952, 1955), interviews (Kornhauser and Sharp, 1932; Hoppock, 1935; Smith, 1936), situational tests (Heron, 1955), and projective tests (Kates, 1950). Herzberg, Mausner, Peterson, and Capwell (1957) summarize the results with the following descriptions of satisfied and dissatisfied workers:

> The satisfied worker is, in general, a more flexible, better adjusted person who has come from a superior family environment, or who has the *capacity to overcome the effects of an inferior environment.*[7] He is realistic about his own situation and about his goals. The worker dissatisfied with his job, in contrast, is often rigid, inflexible, unrealistic in his choice of goals, unable to overcome environmental obstacles, generally unhappy and dissatisfied (1957, p. 20).

The assumption that dissatisfaction with one's job reflects a more basic maladjustment forms the basis for the field of employee counseling, which had its origins in the program developed at the Hawthorne plant of the Western Electric Company (Roethlisberger and Dickson, 1939). By creating a warm and permissive atmosphere, the counselor encourages the person to express his anxieties and feelings. This expression is assumed to permit the worker to gain greater insight into the inner problems and conflicts that form the basis of his dissatisfaction with his work.

The Joint Effects of Work Role and Personality Variables. The two approaches to the analysis of conditions affecting job satisfaction that we have described are based on the assumption that it is possible to explain data on satisfaction *either* by looking at the nature of his work role *or* by looking at the nature of his personality. Although we can muster evidence for each of these approaches, there is an alternative approach to the determination of job satisfaction that is growing in favor. This approach assumes that explanations of satisfaction require the use of both work role and personality variables. It further asserts that there are important interactions between these two types of variables, which can be revealed only if they receive simultaneous study. Evidence concerning the effects of job content, supervisory behavior, or any other characteristic of a work role on

[7]Italics are those of the original authors.

job satisfaction, represents only average effects for the population studied and obscures the fact that, within that population, different people react in markedly different ways to the same environmental conditions. Similarly, relationships between personality variables and job satisfaction may be expected to vary markedly depending on the nature of the job and work environment.

The last ten years have witnessed the proposal, by a number of different researchers, of theories regarding the causes of job satisfaction that encompass both work role and personality variables. In these theories, the satisfaction that an individual derives from a work role, or more precisely the valence of a work role to its occupant, is assumed to be a function not only of the objective properties of that work role but also of the motives of the individual. Insofar as people differ in their motives, the "optimal" or most satisfying work role will differ for each person.

Morse stated this point of view as follows:

> At first we thought that satisfaction would simply be a function of how much a person received from the situation or what we have called the amount of environmental return. It made sense to feel that those who were in more need-fulfilling environments would be more satisfied. But the amount of environmental return did not seem to be the *only* factor involved. Another factor obviously had to be included in order to predict satisfaction accurately. This variable was the strength of an individual's desires, or his level of aspiration in a particular area. If the environment provided little possibility for need-satisfaction, those with the strongest desires, or highest aspirations, were the least happy (1953, pp. 27–28).

Schaffer presented a similar point of view in the following hypothesis:

> Overall job satisfaction will vary directly with the extent to which those needs of an individual which can be satisfied are actually satisfied; the stronger the need,

the more closely will job satisfaction depend on its fulfillment (1953, p. 3).

Similar emphases on the importance of differences in both individual motivational variables and work roles in determining job satisfaction may be found in the work of Tannenbaum and Allport (1956), Ross and Zander (1957), Vroom (1960a), and Kuhlen (1963).

Some investigators have gone further by attempting to state mathematically the manner in which work role variables and individual motivational variables combine in determining job satisfaction. Obviously, the status of the methodology does not warrant highly complex mathematical models of the sort found in psychophysics and the study of learning. Nonetheless, it is possible to distinguish between (1) models that assert that job satisfaction or some conceptually similar variable is a function of the *difference* between the amount of some outcome provided by a work role and the strength of a related desire or motive on the part of the person and (2) those that assume that job satisfaction is a function of the *product* of a work role variable and a related motivational variable. The first of these types we may call subtractive models and the second multiplicative models.

Ross and Zander (1957) and Morse (1953) have proposed subtractive models. The Ross and Zander model, which is the simpler of the two, assumes that need satisfaction is a function of the difference between the extent to which a need is met in a work situation and the strength of the need. Accordingly, in determining amount of need dissatisfaction, they subtract an individual's report concerning conditions in his work role (for example, How much do you feel you are on your own on your job?) from his report concerning the strength of a parallel motivation (for example, How much do you want to be on your own when you work?).

In Chapter Two we outlined a multiplicative model. From Proposition 1, it follows that the valence of a job is a monotonically increasing function of the algebraic sum of the *products* of the valence of other outcomes and the cognized instrumentality of the job for the attainment of these outcomes. A similar formulation specifically dealing with job satisfaction may be found in Vroom (1960a).

In spite of the primitive state of the methods of measuring the variables contained in the models, the differences between subtractive and multiplicative models are considerable and potentially testable. The subtractive model is not an interactive one. In this model the effects of an increase in the frequency or probability of attainment of a particular kind of reward on job satisfaction is always positive and does not depend on the strength of a person's desire for that reward. Similarly, the relationship between strength of desires or motives and job satisfaction is always negative and does not depend on the extent to which these desires or motives are satisfied on the job. In contrast, the multiplicative model implies an interaction between motivational and work role variables. The effect of changes in frequency or probability of attainment of an outcome in a work role on the valence of that work role is predicted to depend on the valence of the outcome. If the person desires the outcome, an increase in the extent to which it is provided by the work role should result in an increase in the valence of the work role. If he is indifferent toward the outcome, this increase should have no effects on the valence of the work role, while if he has an aversion for the outcome, this increase should decrease the valence of the work role. Similarly the relationship between differences in strength of desires and aversions and the valence of the work role is predicted to depend on the extent to which the desired or aversive outcomes are provided by the work role. If a work role facilitates the attainment of an outcome there should be a positive relationship between strength of desire for it and the valence of the work role. But if the work role impedes the attainment of the outcome, the relationship between desire for it and the valence of the work role should be negative.

At present there is considerable evidence that the prediction of job satisfaction can be improved by considering individual differences in motivational variables as well as differences in the nature of the work role (Morse, 1953; Schaffer, 1953; Tannenbaum and Allport, 1956; Vroom, 1960a). However, the optimal method of combining data on these two types of variables is less clear. Supporting the subtractive model, Morse (1953) found a positive association between individuals' reports of their chances of being promoted and their satisfaction with their promotional opportunities. In addition, there was a negative association between individuals' reports of the importance of promotion to them and their satisfaction with their promotional opportunities. There was no evidence of an interaction between promotional opportunities and desires. In other words, the relationship between promotional opportunities and satisfaction did not vary with the strength of the worker's desire for promotion.

Kuhlen (1963) also tested a subtractive model. Using the Edwards Personal Preference Schedule, he measured the strength of needs of 203 teachers. Each teacher also rated the potential of the teaching profession for satisfying each need. Scores on need strength and potential of the occupation for satisfying the need were converted to comparable 5-point scales, and the former subtracted from the latter. Kuhlen predicted that negative discrepancies (that is, need score is higher than occupational potential score) would be associated with low satisfaction, whereas no discrepancies (that is, need score equals potential score) and positive discrepancies (that is, the need score is lower than potential score) would be associated with higher satisfaction. The total discrepancy score, obtained by summing discrepancies for fourteen needs, was found to correlate .25 with ratings of satisfaction with occupation for 108 men and .02 for 95 women. These low correlations do not indicate strong support for the subtractive model. No attempt was made to test for interactions between need strength and potential such as would be predicted by the multiplicative model.

Vroom (1960a) reports results favorable to the multiplicative model. He found that the relationship between the extent to which a person reported participating in making decisions in his job and his satisfaction with that job depended on the strength of his need for independence. The correlation between psychological participation and job satisfaction was .55 for persons high in need for independence; .31 for those moderate in need for independence; and .13 for those low in need for independence. Similarly, the relationship between need for independence and job satisfaction varied from negative under conditions of low psychological participation to positive under conditions of high psychological participation.

These findings clearly support the existence of an interaction between a work role variable (psychological participation) and a personality variable (need for independence), and this interaction takes the form predicted by the multiplicative theory.

Schaffer (1953) also obtained results that support a multiplicative model. Using a questionnaire, he measured the strength of twelve needs of each of seventy-two employed persons. In the same questionnaire he measured the extent to which each need was being satisfied in the work situation and the individual's overall job satisfaction. In general, the greater the relative strength of the need, the greater the positive correlation between the measure of the degree to which the need was described as being satisfied and overall job satisfaction. For the highest ranking need this correlation was .54; for the lowest ranking need it was .13.

On balance, it would appear that the multiplicative model is more consistent with existing data than is the subtractive one. However, the evidence is by no means conclusive. Experimental methods should provide more insight into the nature of the interaction between work role and motivational variables.

Changes in Level of Reward. We have been reviewing methods for predicting job satisfaction from measures of the amount or probability of attainment of outcomes in the job and the valence of these outcomes for the worker. It is possible that there is another variable which must be considered in these predictions—the expected level of reward. Starting with William James, psychologists have speculated that man's affective response to the level of reward that he receives is dependent on the level that he expects. If a person expected to earn $20,000 and earns $18,000, he will be much less satisfied than a person who earns the same amount but expected to earn only $10,000.

There is considerable support in the literature of both experimental and social psychology for this supposition. In a typical experiment, subjects are led to expect a particular level of reward through training or communication from the experimenter, and the attained level of reward is set experimentally at a level greater or lower than the expected level. Crespi (1942) found that upward shifts in the amounts of reward given animals trained to run in a runway resulted in "elation effects." These animals increased their running speed to a level significantly greater than that of animals who had been receiving the larger amount throughout their training. In contrast, downward shifts in level of reward resulted in "depression effects." The animals decreased their speed to a level that was lower than that of animals who had been receiving the smaller amount throughout their training. Similar effects on response time were observed by Zeaman (1949).

In other experiments it has been shown that the effects of amount of food and strength of shock on response probability depend on the previous amounts of food and shock received by the subjects. A given amount of food was more effective in reinforcing a response when animals had been accustomed to receiving lower amounts than when they had been accustomed to receiving the same amount, and more effective when they had been accustomed to receiving the same amount than when they had previously received a greater amount (Collier and Marx, 1959). Similarly, a given strength of shock was less effective in decreasing the probability of a response when the subject had previously been receiving a shock with greater intensity than when he had been receiving a shock of the same strength or one of less intensity (Bevan and Adamson, 1960; Black, Adamson, and Bevan, 1961). In terms of our model, the valence of a particular amount of reward or punishment seems to be affected by the previous amounts received by the subject.

Spector's experiment (1956), described earlier in this chapter, illustrates the relevance of expected level of reward for predicting job satisfaction. By means of instruction, he induced some subjects to believe that they had a high probability of receiving a promotion and others to believe that the probability was low. The morale of persons receiving an unexpected promotion was higher than the morale of those who received an expected promotion. Similarly, for subjects who did not receive a promotion, the morale of those expecting it was found to be lower than the morale of those who did not expect it.

A similar process is apparent in research on level of aspiration. The results of this research have been summarized by Lewin, Dembo, Festinger, and Sears (1944). They conclude:

The experiments show that the feeling of success and failure does not depend on the absolute level of achievement. What for one person means success means failure for another person, and even for the same person the same achievement will lead sometimes to the feeling of failure and sometimes to the feeling of success.

What counts is the level of achievement relative to certain standards, in particular to the level of aspiration . . . (pp. 374-375).

The significance of these findings for industrial psychology depends on the stability of expectations. If the expected level of reward quickly adjusts to the new level, then the effects discussed above will be transitory and have little applied significance. But if adaptation takes place more slowly, this process could be exceedingly important. Consider the example of a worker who has been making under $5,000 a year all his life and is suddenly given a raise to $15,000 a year. We assume that the valence of his job increases markedly and would be greater than that of some person who has been making $15,000 for an extended period. But how long does it remain this way? A week? A month? A year? If the adaptation to changed levels of reward is rapid, we can, for all practical purposes, disregard them in our predictions. But if this adaptation takes a long period of time, we cannot ignore them for in so doing we would fail to account for a major source of variance.

The question of speed of adaptation to changed levels of reward is one on which there has been little work in industrial psychology. We have no firm empirical basis in the applied literature on which to judge whether increases in reward are adapted to more quickly than decreases, whether speed of adaptation is inversely related to the amount of change, or whether the whole process is a slow or a lengthy one.

The Concept of Equity. It follows from our model that the attractiveness of a work role for a person is directly related to the extent to which it provides him with rewarding outcomes and inversely

related to the extent to which it provides him with aversive outcomes. Thus, if money constitutes a reward for a person then the
more money he makes from his work the more attracted he will be
to his work role. If rejection by other people constitutes an aversive
outcome, then the more he is rejected by his co-workers the less
attracted he will be to his work role.

A somewhat different starting point is represented in the assumption that persons do not strive to maximize the attainment of
desired outcomes like money but rather strive to obtain an equitable
or fair amount. Basic to this position is the belief that individuals
are guided by a moral system that has as a basic tenet the fair
distribution of rewards. If a person receives less than a fair amount
he feels that an injustice has been done him; if he receives more than
the fair amount he feels guilty.

In effect, this point of view would lead us to regard job satisfaction as a function of the amount of difference between the
amount of reward that the person believes he should receive and the
amount of reward that in fact he does receive. The greater the difference between these two amounts, the greater the tension or disequilibrium experienced by the person.

Although such a model may be applicable to any dimension
of reward, it is most frequently regarded as applicable to wages. All
systems of wage and salary administration contain the implicit assumption that there is a fair and equitable level of compensation
for each worker on each job. Jaques (1961) has provided a psychological basis for this assumption with his hypothesis that a state of
disequilibrium is created within a person whenever his actual level
of payment deviates from the equitable level, regardless of the direction of the disparity. According to this hypothesis, if a person
believes that he should receive a salary of $100 a week but in fact
receives $75 per week, he will experience feelings of tension and
inequity and strive to reduce the discrepancy. If the same person
receives a salary of $125 a week he will also experience tension and
inequity and seek to reduce the discrepancy.

Jaques (1956, 1961) has tried to determine, through interviews, the level of payment that supervisors and manual workers in
six different British firms consider proper or equitable for their jobs.
He has related these equitable levels of payment to a measure of the

time span of discretion of their jobs. This measure indicates the "period of time during which marginally sub-standard discretion could be exercised in a role before information about the accumulating sub-standard work would become available to the manager in charge of the role" (1961, p. 99). Jaques states that "with only slight variations" persons having the same time span report the same pay as proper for their job. Furthermore, he reports that the level of equitable payment is a constantly increasing function of the time span of discretion. A graph relating these two variables (Jaques, 1961) shows a gradual rate of increase in equitable level from time spans of one-half day to six months with a much sharper rate of increase from six months to ten years. Jaques professes to have uncovered "the existence of an unrecognized system of norms of fair payment for any given level of work, unconscious knowledge of these norms being shared among the population engaged in employment work" (p. 124). We find it difficult to share his enthusiasm without having information on the degree of dispersion around the curve, data that Jaques fails to report.

Jaques also finds evidence for the state of disequilibrium that he assumes to be created by disparities between equitable and actual levels of payment. He summarizes his findings as follows:

> If the actual salary bracket for a person's role coincides with equity, he expresses himself as being in a reasonably paid role. If his actual payment bracket has fallen below the equitable bracket, he expresses himself as dissatisfied with the financial recognition for his role. If, on the other hand, his actual payment bracket has risen above the equitable bracket, then he reacts with a sense of being paid within a rather higher range than he can ever hope to maintain. The intensity of his reaction varies with the size of the discrepancy between the actual and equitable brackets (1961, p. 132).

Once again it should be noted that Jaques does not point out, in any systematic way, the basis for these conclusions. He does not specify in his report what methods were used in measuring dissatisfaction, the number of persons on whom observations were made, or even the means and variances in scores on the dependent variables. The scientifically oriented reader cannot help but be cautious in his evaluation of such conclusions.

Zaleznik, Christensen, and Roethlisberger (1958) also studied the effects of wage inequity on worker satisfaction. They tried to infer what workers would regard as equitable pay from their age, seniority, education, ethnicity, and sex, all of which are assumed to indicate the extent of their "investment" in their jobs. They predicted that workers whose degree of reward was favorable in comparison with their investments would express a greater degree of satisfaction than workers whose degree of reward was unfavorable in relation to their investments. To test this prediction, they constructed a reward-investment index[8] and obtained a score for each of forty-seven workers. The index was intended to express the difference between what the workers received from their jobs and what they invested in it. Contrary to prediction, satisfaction scores were not associated with scores on this reward-investment index. However, the authors acknowledge the weaknesses in this crude test and tend to regard this finding as a result of methodological inadequacies rather than of defects in their theory.

A more elaborate and detailed conception of equity has appeared in recent writings. Equity and its opposite, inequity, are defined in relative rather than absolute terms. Inequity is assumed to result, not from a discrepancy between rewards received from and investments made in one's job, but from discrepancies in the relative magnitudes of rewards and investments of a person and those of other persons with whom he compares himself. An individual's perception of the rewards and investments of others is thought to provide him with a standard against which he judges the fairness and equity of rewards that he himself receives.

There are many examples in social psychology of persons and groups who have reported being much more or much less satisfied than one would have expected from a knowledge of their

[8]Values were assigned to different levels or types of age, seniority, education, ethnicity, and sex. Each was subtracted from the worker's pay multiplied by 5. The differences were summed and added to 100 to yield his score on the reward-investment index.

actual situation. Such findings have typically been interpreted, in an ad hoc fashion, in terms of reference groups, that is, groups that serve as comparison or reference points when individuals make judgments of an evaluative nature. For example, the authors of *The American Soldier* (Stouffer and others, 1949) noted that the job satisfaction of noncombat soldiers overseas was much higher than expected. They suggest that this finding reflects the tendency of these soldiers to compare their situation with that of the combat troops.

> In general, it is of course true that the overseas soldier, relative to soldiers still at home, suffered a greater break with home ties and with many of the amenities of life in the United States to which he was accustomed. But it was also true that, relative to the combat soldier, the overseas soldier not in combat and not likely to get into combat suffered far less deprivation than the actual fighting man. If he was in war areas of an active theater he could be, and was, thankful that he was escaping the risks of death and the grueling life of the front lines (pp. 172–173).

Formal conceptions of equity based on relative rewards and deprivations have been developed independently by Patchen (1961), Homans (1961), and Adams (1963). While these applications use different language, they are, in fact, very similar and there do not appear to be testable differences among them. Consequently, it will suffice to illustrate the general nature of these theories by treating one in some detail. The specific formulation that we will consider is that of Adams (1963). Adams treats the employment relationship as a case of an exchange between an employer and an employee. The employee exchanges his services for pay from the employer. On the employee's side of the ledger are his *inputs*, which include his education, intelligence, experience, training, skill, seniority, age, sex, ethnic backgrounds, social status, and the effort he expends on the job. On the employer's side of the exchange are the *outcomes* or rewards provided the employee for his services. These include pay, rewards intrinsic to the job, seniority benefits, fringe benefits, and status symbols.

Inequity is said to exist for an employee *"whenever his perceived job inputs and/or outcomes stand psychologically in an obverse relation to what he perceives are the inputs and/or outcomes of others"* (Adams, 1963, p. 424). (Italics are his.) If a person's inputs exceed those of another, but his outcomes are the same or less, then inequity exists. Similarly, if the person's inputs are less than those of another, but his outcomes are greater or the same, inequity also exists. In computing the amount of inequity existing in a given person-other relationship, Adams employs the following mathematical formula. Inequity = |(person's inputs-person's outcomes) – (other's inputs-other's outcomes)|.

In addition to specifying the determinants of inequity, Adams discusses its behavioral and cognitive effects. Since inequity is regarded as involving tension, persons are assumed to be motivated to reduce it. They may do this through actual or psychological changes in the inputs or outcomes of either "person" or "other."

There are two somewhat different kinds of hypotheses that we can derive from this line of theorizing: (1) hypotheses about the determinants of inequity and associated dissatisfaction or tension; and (2) hypotheses about the behavioral or cognitive consequences of inequity. Our interest in this chapter is primarily in evidence relating to hypotheses of the first kind. In the section of the book dealing with performance, we will consider some data bearing on the implications of equity theory for worker performance.

If we assume that equity is reflected in satisfaction with a work role and inequity is reflected in dissatisfaction, we can use the kind of model described above as the basis for predictions about the determinants of job satisfaction. The conditions that affect the employee's assessment of the equity of the exchange between himself and his employer would also be expected to affect the employee's job satisfaction. However, attempts to use equity theory as a basis for explaining differences in job satisfaction are hindered by the large number of variables that it encompasses, the complexity of the interactions among these variables, and the relative inadequacy of our operational definitions. Following the statement of equity theory set forth by Adams (and substituting job satisfaction for equity) would lead one to predict that the job satisfaction of a worker would be a function of: (1) his beliefs concerning the degree to which he possesses various characteristics; (2) his convictions concerning the degree to which these characteristics should result in the attainment of rewarding outcomes from his job, that is, their value as inputs; (3) his beliefs concerning the degree to which he receives these rewarding outcomes from his job; (4) his beliefs concerning the degree to which others possess these characteristics; (5) his beliefs concerning the degree to which others receive rewarding outcomes from their jobs; and (6) the extent to which he compares himself with these others. None of the functional relations between these six types of variables and job satisfaction is simple; the effect of each variable depends on a number of the others.

Our emphasis on the complexity of equity theory should, by no means, be construed as relevant to its validity. There is no reason to assume, on the basis of existing evidence, that simpler models are more appropriate. However, the complexity of equity theory makes conclusive tests very difficult. A great deal of theoretical and methodological refinement remains to be carried out before this approach can be properly evaluated. The study carried out by Patchen (1961) described earlier in this chapter provides a start in this direction. Further investigation is certainly warranted.

One problem, which deserves more attention than it has received, is whether the nature and manner of resolution of the hypothetical states of tension produced by over-reward and under-reward are identical. Intuitively, one would find possible that feelings of inequity produced by over-reward may be less frustrating and less stable, because they may be resolved by an increase in the value that the person attaches to his own inputs to the job.

Discussion and Summary

In this chapter we have focused on the determinants of job satisfaction. For more than twenty-five years social scientists have been using quantitative methods in an attempt to ascertain the events and conditions that result in different levels of job satisfaction. The prevailing assumption guiding investigations of this problem is that differences in job satisfaction reflect differences in the nature of the jobs or work situations of individuals. Using a variety of methods, researchers have attempted to establish the nature of the effects on job satisfaction of such aspects of work roles as the nature of supervision the worker receives, the kind of work group of which he is a member, the content of his job, the amount of his wages, his chances for promotion, and his hours of work. Research of this type has certainly been useful. A large number of work role variables have been isolated and the general nature of their effects on job satisfaction determined. The outcome of this research has been a general picture of a "satisfying work role." A work role most conducive to job satisfaction appears to be one that provides high pay, substantial promotional opportunities, considerate and participative supervision, an opportunity to interact with one's peers, varied duties, and a high degree of control over work methods and work pace.

There is no way of assessing the amount of variance in job satisfaction that can be accounted for by means of such work role variables. It is safe to say, however, that there is a great deal of variance in job satisfaction that remains to be explained. Some further progress can undoubtedly be made by refining our conceptual and operational definitions of previously identified work role variables and by the discovery of new ones. However, in this writer's view, a substantial advancement in our knowledge of the causes of job satisfaction requires that we discard the assumption, on which so much existing work is based, that differences in job satisfaction are the exclusive results of differences in work roles.

Individuals differ greatly in their motives, values and abilities, and these differences probably have an important bearing on the "optimal" characteristics of their work role. Such personality differences have traditionally played little part in research on job satisfaction, although, as we saw in the previous chapter, they have been the major focus of those interested in the occupational choice process. If differences in the attractiveness of a work role to persons about to enter the labor market can be accounted for in terms of personality differences, is it not reasonable to assume that such personality differences might have similar effects on the attractiveness of the work role to those occupying it?

A somewhat different assumption from the environmental one that we have been discussing is represented in the idea that differences in job satisfaction are the direct result of individual differences in personality. Some persons are satisfied and others are dissatisfied *regardless of the nature of their work roles.* Research based on this assumption usually seeks to determine the relationship between measures of such personality variables as neuroticism or adjustment and job satisfaction.

In the view of this writer, neither of these assumptions—one based on situational and the other on personality variables—is likely to enable us to proceed very far in our understanding of the causes of job satisfaction. Job satisfaction must be assumed to be the result of the operation of both situational and personality variables. It is only through simultaneous study of these two sets of factors that the complex nature of their interactions can be revealed. Very few investigators have attempted to deal with differences among work roles and among individuals in the same study. However, the results of those studies in which this has been done are promising and indicate the fruitfulness of this approach. It seems likely that greater exchange between psychologists interested in occupational choice and job satisfaction would expedite the discovery of interactions between personality and work role variables. Conceivably, the psychological conditions that make a work role attractive to a person just about to enter the labor market are analogous or identical to those that make it attractive to its occupant.

Much of the evidence reported in this chapter on the determinants of job satisfaction is consistent with our proposition about the determinants of valence (Proposition 1). People's reports of their satisfaction with their jobs are, in fact, directly related to the extent to which their jobs provide them with such rewarding outcomes as pay, variety in stimulation, consideration from their supervisor, a high probability of promotion, close interaction with co-workers, an opportunity to influence decisions that have future effects on them, and control over their pace of work. Furthermore, individual differences in motives seem to have the effects predicted in the proposition. The more a person reports valuing these outcomes, the greater the positive effect on his job satisfaction of an increase in the extent to which it is provided by his job.

Not all of the evidence reported in this chapter is directly interpretable in terms of the model. Exceptions include those studies showing that the affective consequences of a given level of reward depend on the level that was expected and studies dealing with the concept of equity. Interpreting these findings in terms of the model is not impossible but would require adding to our list of assumptions about motivation presented in Chapter Two.

6

Job Satisfaction and
Job Behavior

In the previous chapter, we examined conditions affecting the satisfaction of workers. We turn now to the implications of this satisfaction for their behavior on their jobs. In what ways do persons who report being satisfied with their jobs behave that distinguishes them from those who are dissatisfied? In an effort to find an answer to this question we shall examine evidence concerning the relationship of job satisfaction to turnover, absences, accidents, and job performance.

Job Satisfaction and Turnover

If we assume that measures of job satisfaction reflect the valence of the job to its occupant, then it follows from our model that job satisfaction should be related to the strength of the force on the person to remain in his job. The more satisfied a worker, the stronger the force on him to remain in his job and the less the probability of his leaving it voluntarily.

This hypothesis can be tested in two ways: (1) by determining if the same conditions are associated with measures of turnover as are associated with measures of satisfaction or, (2) by determining if measures of satisfaction are related to measures of turnover. In our review of the evidence concerning the determinants of job satisfaction we found many instances in which parallel relationships were obtained between work role variables and both job satisfaction and turnover. Evidence of this kind is, however, indirect and does not provide as good a test of the hypothesis as evidence that job satisfaction and turnover are negatively related to one another. If individuals who report a high level of job satisfaction are less likely to leave their jobs than individuals who report a low level of satisfaction, or if organizational units with a high mean level of satisfaction have a lower rate of turnover than organizational units with a lower mean level of satisfaction, the hypothesis can be regarded as supported.

There are seven studies dealing with the satisfaction-turnover relationship, four of them using individuals as the unit of analysis and three using groups. All studies indicate the expected negative relationship between these variables although the magnitude and significance of this relationship varies considerably from study to study.

Weitz and Nuckols (1953) assumed that job satisfaction would be negatively related to turnover and consequently sought to determine the relative validity of indirect and direct job satisfaction measures by seeing which one best predicted future turnover. They mailed questionnaires containing both direct and indirect measures of job satisfaction to 1,200 insurance agents representing a single company in the southern states. Forty-seven percent of these replied. The authors related the satisfaction data obtained in this manner to subsequent information they received about terminations. The satisfaction scores obtained by the direct method correlated .20 with survival (significant at the 1 percent level). The scores obtained through the indirect method (in which agents were asked to estimate the attitudes of other agents toward their jobs) correlated only .05 with survival. The latter correlation was not significant.

Webb and Hollander (1956) obtained three different measures of morale from each of 210 cadets enrolled in a preflight curriculum in a naval air training situation. The three measures were the following: (1) a questionnaire pertaining to "interest in and enthusiasm for the naval air program" (p. 17); (2) peer nominations of interest and enthusiasm for naval aviation; (3) self-rankings on interest and enthusiasm for naval aviation. Subsequent to the morale measurement, 16 of the 210 cadets voluntarily withdrew from the program. All three of the measures had some relationship to withdrawal, with peer nominations and self-evaluations being the better predictors. Of the 16 persons who withdrew, 14 were below the median on these two measures, whereas 10 were below the median on the questionnaire.

Sagi, Olmstead, and Atelsek (1955) obtained questionnaire measures of personal involvement from each of 293 college students who were members of groups concerned with "the creation of products or services for the student body" (p. 308). A follow-up six months later revealed that 60 persons had voluntarily dropped out of their group. Scores on the personal involvement measure discriminated significantly between those maintaining their group membership and those voluntarily withdrawing.

Libo (1953) carried out a laboratory experiment to test the effects of attraction to the group on the decision to stay in or leave the group. Subjects, recruited from undergraduate courses, were asked to participate in newly formed discussion groups. Each group was made up of four to eight students of the same sex who did not know one another. Half of the groups were exposed to conditions designed to generate a high level of attraction to the group. They were given an interesting topic to discuss (a case in human relations), were told that their answers to previously administered questionnaires indicated that their congeniality potential was high, and that various professional groups were interested in their opinions. The other half of the groups were exposed to conditions designed to create low attraction to the group. They were given a relatively uninteresting problem to discuss (a problem in accident prevention), were told that their cogeniality potential was low, and were told nothing about the interest of professional groups.

At the conclusion of the discussion, each person completed a questionnaire measure of his attraction to the group and a projective measure designed to assess the same variable. He was then given a choice between staying in the group for future meetings and permanently leaving the group. The results show that a much larger proportion of subjects in the high attraction groups chose to remain in the group than in the low attraction groups. Scores on both the questionnaire and projective measures of attraction to the group were affected by experimental conditions and were found to be significantly related to the outcome of the decision to leave or to remain.

In group analyses, Giese and Ruter (1949) found a correlation of -.42 between the morale and turnover rates of twenty-five departments in a small mail-order company; Fleishman, Harris, and Burtt (1955) found a correlation of -.21 between the turnover rates and morale of production and nonproduction departments at International Harvester; and Kerr, Koppelmeir, and Sullivan (1951) found a correlation of -.13 between the average job satisfaction scores and turnover rates of twenty departments in a metal fabrication factory.

Some insight into the small magnitude of these correlations, as well as the differences among them, might be obtained by a consideration of the kinds of variables that our model would suggest to be involved in the decision to resign from one's job. The probability of resignation would be expected to be a function of the difference in the strength of two sets of forces—those acting on the person in the direction of remaining in his present job and those acting on him in the direction of leaving. Only the former set of forces are assumed to be reflected in job satisfaction scores. Forces on a person to leave his present position are assumed to be a function of the valence of outcomes that cannot be attained without leaving his position (most notably the valence of other positions) and of the expectancy with which these other outcomes can be attained. It seems reasonable to assume that simultaneous measurements of the valence of one's present position (that is, job satisfaction), the valence of other positions, and the expectancy that these other positions can be attained would yield a better prediction of the outcome of an individual's decision to stay or resign from his job than would measurements of job satisfaction alone.

If the probability of resignation is affected not only by job satisfaction but also by the availability of other positions, one should find higher turnover in times of full employment than in times of considerable unemployment. Behrend (1953) found evidence of this. Studying fifty-five factories in five large engineering and metal working companies in England, he found a marked reduction in rate of voluntary turnover from a period of full employment to a period of less than full employment. Similar results have been reported by Brissenden and Frankel (1922) and Woytinsky (1942).

Job Satisfaction and Absences

In a sense, workers make daily decisions concerning whether they will appear for work. We would assume these decisions to be predictable from information about the anticipated consequences of the alternatives. If, on a given day, the consequences expected from not working are more attractive than those expected from working, the worker would be predicted to be absent. In contrast, if the reverse is true, the worker would be predicted to report for work.

The large number and the variable nature of the consequences of being present and being absent from work on a given day make any precise determination of who will be absent, and when, unfeasible if not impossible. However, there may be some measurable outcomes of this decision that are sufficiently important to bear a relationship to absences. One such factor is the extent to which working is satisfying or rewarding to the person. To the extent to which the worker derives satisfaction from participating in his work role, we would assume that there would be a force acting on him to be present at work. It would seem to make little difference what characteristics of the work role are the source of these rewards. The only requirement is that the attainment of the rewards is dependent on being present at work.

The preceding analysis constitutes a rationale for the hypothesis that job satisfaction would be negatively related to absences. It does not assert that workers who are highly satisfied with their jobs would never be absent. On some occasions, the advantages of doing so would far outweigh the loss of one or two days' work. However, these occasions should be less frequent for those who are satisfied than for those who are dissatisfied with their jobs.

Let us turn to the evidence concerning the relationship between job satisfaction and absences. We were able to find ten studies bearing on this problem. The earliest investigation was carried out by Kornhauser and Sharp (1932), who studied the absences of women factory workers. While no data on the magnitude of the relationship are given, they report that "unfavorableness of job attitudes is slightly correlated with lost time because of sickness and with ratings of health by the foreladies" (p. 402). In more recent studies, Fleishman, Harris, and Burtt (1955) have found a correlation of -.25 between the morale and absence rates of departments in International Harvester; Van Zelst and Kerr (1953) found that the job satisfaction of 340 employees in fourteen firms correlated .31 with the favorableness of their reported absence record; and Harding and Bottenberg (1961) found a multiple correlation of -.38 between eight measures of satisfaction and absences in a group of 376 airmen.

In contrast, Vroom (1962) found a correlation of only -.07 between job satisfaction and absences for 489 employees in an oil refinery; Bernberg (1952) found correlations ranging from .00 to .06 between four dimensions of morale and absences for 890 workers in an aircraft plant; and Mann, Indik, and Vroom (1963) reported correlations of .14 and -.32 between the mean overall work satisfaction and the absence rates of twenty-eight groups of drivers and twenty-four groups of positioners in a large package delivering company.

The findings of Kerr, Koppelmeir, and Sullivan (1951) indicate that the kind of absence measure used greatly affects the size and direction of the relationships obtained with job satisfaction. Studying twenty-nine departments in a metal fabrication factory, they correlated the mean job satisfaction for each department with six different types of absence measures. While job satisfaction correlated .51 with total absenteeism, it correlated -.44 with unexcused absenteeism. If one assumes that total absence figures are heavily influenced by long illnesses, these findings appear consistent with those of Metzner and Mann (1953). The latter found the negative relationship between employee attitudes and absences more marked when frequency of absence was used rather than a count of actual days lost. They suggest that this relationship is most likely to appear when absence figures are used that minimize the weight of absences caused by illness and maximize the weight of absences of persons whose attendance pattern is irregular.

Metzner and Mann also found the relationship between attitudes and absences to depend on the sex of the worker and, for male workers, on the nature of the job. There was no relationship between attitudes and absences for white collar women but a fairly consistent negative relationship for both blue and white collar men. When the data for the white collar men were broken down by skill level, there was practically no relationship between these variables for those at a high skill level and a consistent negative relationship at low skill levels.

Job Satisfaction and Accidents

Hill and Trist (1953) have suggested that accidents, like turnover and absences, reflect the strength of motivation on the part of the individual to withdraw from a work situation. In support of this view they found that accident rates are positively associated with other forms of absences and most strongly associated with the least sanctioned forms of absence. If this interpretation is correct, we should also expect to find a negative relationship between satisfaction and accidents. Dissatisfied workers should be more likely to have accidents in order to remove themselves from their unpleasant work situation. There is relatively little data on this relationship. Stagner, Flebbe, and Wood (1952) found a correlation of -.42 between the mean job satisfaction scores and accident rates of ten divisions and -.23 between these two variables for twelve shops in a railroad. However, Fleishman, Harris, and Burtt (1955) found a correlation of only -.03 between morale and accident rates of departments in International Harvester. Certainly more data are required, preferably using individuals as the unit of analysis, before we can conclude that dissatisfaction is associated with a predisposition toward accidents.

Even if this association should be conclusively demonstrated, the Hill and Trist interpretation that accidents are a means of withdrawal from the work situation cannot be completely accepted. This interpretation implies that dissatisfaction motivates persons to have accidents and is contrary to the more traditional view, implied in the term, that accidents are unintended consequences of acts. Since accidents are often highly painful and otherwise costly to those who have them, it is not easy to see why they should be adopted as a solution to an unpleasant work situation. Dissatisfied employees may be more likely to make trips to the dispensary for minor reasons but this does not mean that they are more motivated, either consciously or unconsciously, to have accidents.

The more conventional view leads us to a different interpretation of a negative relationship between satisfaction and accidents. This interpretation assumes that accidents cause dissatisfaction. Having an accident in the work situation, or working in an environment in which accidents are likely, creates anxiety and reduces the attractiveness of the job. This, in fact, is the explanation offered by Stagner, Flebbe, and Wood for the negative correlation between satisfaction and accidents that they obtained in their study.

Job Satisfaction and Job Performance

It was typically assumed by most people connected with the human relations movement that job satisfaction was positively associated with job performance. In fact human relations might be described as an attempt to increase productivity by satisfying the needs of employees.

The results of the widely publicized early studies of the Survey Research Center in an insurance company (Katz, Maccoby, and Morse, 1950) and in a railroad (Katz, Maccoby, Gurin, and Floor, 1951) cast some doubt on this assumption. No differences were found in either study between the satisfaction with wages, satisfaction with job status, or satisfaction with the company of workers in high and low productivity sections. In the insurance study, those in highly productive groups tended to be more critical of certain aspects of company policy; and in the railroad study, those in highly productive groups reported less intrinsic job satisfaction than those in less productive groups. More devastating, however, was the review of the extensive literature on this question by Brayfield and Crockett (1955), who concluded that there was little evidence of any simple or appreciable relationship between employees' attitudes and the effectiveness of their performance.

Before attempting our own evaluation of the empirical evidence, let us analyze the relationship between satisfaction and productivity in terms of our model. If we assume that job satisfaction reflects the valence of the job for its occupant, what consequences would job satisfaction be expected to have on job behavior? It follows from our proposition about the relationship between valence and force (Proposition 2) that the strength of the force on a worker to remain in his job is a monotonically increasing function of the valence of his job. Supporting this proposition is the evidence, just reviewed, that satisfaction is negatively related to turnover and absences. However, it is much less clear why job satisfaction should result in greater productivity. The valence of the job might be related to the probability that workers will perform at a sufficient level to avoid being fired but, in most situations, retaining one's position requires a level of performance far short of the potential of the worker. Furthermore, it is likely that most of the workers studied in investigations of the relationship between satisfaction and performance have reached or exceeded the minimal level of performance necessary to avoid being fired.

We could argue that satisfaction would result in higher performance above this minimum level if we were willing to assume that the valence of the job generalizes to other objects and events the attainment of which is contingent on performance. Thus, it has been suggested that workers will demonstrate their gratitude for rewards received from management by increasing their output or that a satisfied worker is more likely to accept managerial goals of higher production. However, these proposals seem tenuous in the absence of direct evidence.

So far we have been considering ways in which increases in satisfaction might result in higher performance. The correlation between these two variables is also dependent on any effects that performance had on satisfaction. We would expect to find these two variables correlated if satisfaction caused performance or if performance caused satisfaction. A more plausible case can be made for the latter alternative. It is frequently the case that workers are rewarded for effective performance or punished for ineffective performance. Under such conditions they would be expected to be highly motivated to perform effectively. The more successful they are in achieving effective performance, the more rewards (or fewer punishments) they receive. In contrast, those conditions associated with relatively low motivation, that is, no association between the attainment of rewards and performance, should produce little or no effect of performance on satisfaction.

The association between job satisfaction and job performance in a given situation is also affected by any variables that are uncontrolled. If members of the population studied differ in the degree to which they possess some third variable, and if that variable is similarly related (either positively or negatively) to both job satisfaction and job performance, then a positive association would be observed between the latter two variables. But if the third variable has opposite relationships with job satisfaction and job performance, then a negative association would be observed.

The preceding discussion suggests that predicting the relationship between job satisfaction and performance is no simple problem. There are probably many factors affecting the magnitude and direction of the relationship in any given situation. Correlations between these two variables are affected by any effects of satisfaction on performance, any effects of performance on satisfaction, and by uncontrolled variables.

Let us turn now to an examination of the empirical evidence. Because there exist other reviews of this literature (Brayfield and Crockett, 1955; Herzberg, Mausner, Peterson, and Capwell, 1957) and because there are an unusually large number of investigations bearing on this topic, we will not describe each study in detail. Instead, we will restrict ourselves to the studies that shed some light on the strength of association between job satisfaction and job performance. In so doing we will examine some of the variables that might affect the magnitude and size of the association.

Table 6.1 shows data from twenty studies. In each of these, one or more measures of job satisfaction or employee attitudes was correlated with one or more criteria of performance.[1] Some of the studies used individuals as the unit of analysis; others used groups

---

[1]Where more than one measure of satisfaction was used, the table shows the correlation obtained with the most comprehensive measure. For example, if the investigator computed correlations between performance, and both single satisfaction items and a global index of satisfaction, the latter is reported. Similarly, if a number of satisfaction indices are used, the one with the broadest referent, for example, satisfaction with the overall work situation rather than satisfaction with pay, is shown. If both objective and subjective (ratings) criteria of performance were used, both are shown; if more than one of each type of criterion was used, the median correlation is shown in the table.

Table 6.1. Correlational Studies—Job Satisfaction and Job Performance.

Author	Type of Analysis	Population	Correlation	Type of Criterion of Productivity	N
Baxter cited in Brayfield & Crockett (1955)	Ind.	Insurance agents	.23 .26	Ratings Objective	233
Bellows cited in Brayfield & Crockett (1955)	Ind.	Air force control tower operators	.005	Ratings	109
Bernberg (1952)	Ind.	Hourly paid workers	.05	Ratings	890
Brayfield cited in Brayfield & Crockett (1955)	Ind.	Female office employees	.14	Ratings	231
Brayfield & Mangelsdorf cited in Brayfield & Crockett (1955)	Ind.	Plumber's apprentices	.203	Ratings	55
Brayfield & Marsh cited in Brayfield & Crockett (1955)	Ind.	Farmers	.115	Ratings	50
Brody (1945)	Ind.	Production employees on piece work	.68	Objective	40
Fleishman, Harris & Burtt (1955)	Gr.	Work groups in an equipment mfg. plant	-.31	Ratings[a]	58
Gadel & Kriedt (1952)	Ind.	IBM operators	.08	Ratings	193
Giese & Ruter (1949)	Gr.	Departments in mail-order company	.19	Objective	25
Hamid (1953)	Ind.	Insurance agents	.22	Objective	552
Heron (1954)	Ind.	Bus drivers	.308	Objective[b]	144
Lawshe & Nagle (1953)	Gr.	Departments in an office	.86[c]	Ratings	14
Lopez (1962)	Ind.	Administrative-technical personnel	.12	Ratings	124
Mann, Indik & Vroom (1963)	Gr.	Truck drivers—large work groups	.14 -.21	Ratings Objective	28

Table 6.1. Correlational Studies—Job Satisfaction and Job Performance, Cont'd.

Author	Type of Analysis	Population	Correlation	Type of Criterion of Productivity	N
Mann, Indik & Vroom (1963)	Gr.	Positioners—small work groups	.18 .02	Ratings Objective	24
Mossin (1949)	Ind.	Female sales clerks	−.03	Ratings	94
Sirota (1958)	Ind.	Employees in an electronics firm	.11	Ratings	377
Sirota (1958)	Ind.	Supervisors in an electronics firm	.13	Ratings	145
Vroom (1960a)[d]	Ind.	Supervisors in a package delivery co.	.21	Ratings	96

[a] Ratings of foremen's proficiency.

[b] A composite criterion based on five objective measures and one supervisory rating. Correlation reported is between job satisfaction and value to the employer with age partialled out.

[c] Correlation reported is between attitude toward the supervisor and productivity.

[d] These data were not reported in the original publication.

or organizational units. For all studies, the median correlation between satisfaction and performance is .14[2] with a range of .86 to −.31. The median correlation is virtually identical for studies using individuals and for studies using groups as units of analysis. For individuals it is .135 (N = 16); for groups it is .14 (N = 7).

Katzell (1957) has suggested that the lack of satisfactory production data in many of the investigations may have affected the size of the relationships between performance and satisfaction. In order to test this possibility the median correlation for studies using objective criteria and for those using ratings was computed. For objective measures of performance, the median correlation with satisfac-

[2] For three studies, correlations were computed using both objective criteria and ratings. Both were included in calculating the median. Hence, the number of cases is twenty-three rather than twenty.

tion was .22 (N = 7), for ratings it was .12 (N = 16). The results are in the expected direction but the difference is not significant.

Katzell, Barrett, and Parker (1961) have recently shown that some kinds of objective criteria of performance are more highly related to satisfaction measures than others. They obtained measures of the quantity of work, quality of work, and profitability of each of seventy-two wholesale warehousing divisions concerned with the storage and distribution of drug and pharmaceutical products. Aggregate scores on forty-seven different job satisfaction items were correlated with these three performance criteria. The mean correlation between the forty-seven items and each criterion was computed and found to be .28 for profitability, .21 for quantity, and –.02 for quality. The basis for these different relationships is not clear.

Likert (1961) has suggested that the relationship between satisfaction and performance becomes more positive as the level of skill required by the job increases. Although some of the populations on which the results in Table 6.1 are based are too heterogeneous to make a meaningful determination of level, a small number of the investigations have been based on relatively homogeneous samples of workers in administrative, professional, or technical positions. Those analyses based on insurance agents, supervisors, IBM operators, and air force control tower operators seem to have these characteristics. The median correlation obtained in these studies is .17 (N = 8), whereas in the remainder of the studies it is .14 (N = 15). Once again, the difference is in the proposed direction but is not statistically significant.

The number of studies in which data are presently available and the lack of detail with which some are reported make further analyses of this type unfeasible. It is impossible to determine from existing data whether the size and direction of the relationship depends on whether the worker is paid by the piece or by the time he works, on the nature of the supervision he receives, or on a wide range of other potentially relevant variables. Recently, Smith, Kendall, and Hulin (1969) reported different relationships between job satisfaction and job performance for men and women. They found a positive relationship between the total satisfaction of men as measured by the Job Description Index and performance ratings in eighteen of twenty companies. A similar relationship was found for women in only eight of thirteen companies. Because no data on the strength of association is reported for either sex, these results cannot be compared with those presented here.

Summary

On the basis of the evidence that we have reviewed in this section, it is possible to draw the following conclusions:

1. There is a consistent negative relationship between job satisfaction and the probability of resignation. This relationship appears when scores on job satisfaction are obtained from individuals and used to predict subsequent voluntary dropouts and when mean scores on job satisfaction for organizational units are correlated with turnover rates for these units.

2. There is a less consistent negative relationship between job satisfaction and absences. This relationship appears to emerge most consistently with measures of unexcused absences, and when frequency of absence rather than actual days lost are used.

3. There is some indication of a negative relationship between job satisfaction and accidents. However, the number of existing studies of this relationship is too small to permit any firm conclusions.

4. There is no simple relationship between job satisfaction and job performance. Correlations between these variables vary within an extremely large range and the median correlation of .14 has little theoretical or practical importance. We do not yet know the conditions that affect the magnitude and direction of relationships between satisfaction and performance. Obtained correlations are similar for analyses based on individuals and groups and do not seem to depend, to any appreciable extent, on the occupational level of the subjects or on the nature of the criterion (objective or ratings) employed.

An attempt was made to interpret these findings within the framework of our model. The negative relationship between job satisfaction and both turnover and absences was derived from the proposition that the valence of the work role to its occupant is directly related to the strength of the force acting on him to remain within that work role. In other words, workers who are highly attracted to their jobs should be subject to stronger forces to remain in them than those who are less attracted to their jobs. These stronger forces to remain should be reflected in a lower probability of behaviors that take the person out of his job, both permanently and temporarily.

The bases for the relationship between satisfaction and performance are more complex. It has been argued by some writers that greater satisfaction should result in higher performance and by others that higher performance should result in greater satisfaction. With respect to the former, there is no obvious theoretical basis for assuming that an increase in the valence of the work role should result in greater performance. In order for this to occur, one must assume that the increased valence of the work role generalizes to other objects and events, for example, recognition from management, the attainment of which is contingent on performance. However, effects of performance on satisfaction are somewhat more plausible and would be expected to occur when effective performance brings with it greater rewards, at not appreciably greater cost, than ineffective performance. When workers are highly motivated to perform effectively, their success in attaining effective performance might be expected to affect the attractiveness of their job.

The absence of a marked or consistent correlation between job satisfaction and performance casts some doubt on the generality or intensity of either effects of satisfaction on performance or performance on satisfaction. It also suggests that the conditions that determine a person's level of job satisfaction and his level of job performance are not identical. Some conditions may produce high satisfaction and low performance, others low satisfaction and high performance, and still others high satisfaction and high performance or low satisfaction and low performance. We will have more to say about possible differences between the determinants of job satisfaction and job performance after we have considered the motivational determinants of performance in Chapter Eight. At this point it is sufficient to note that the lack of any marked association between two variables suggests the desirability of regarding them as both conceptually and empirically separable outcomes of the person-work role relationship.

Part Four

Performance in
Work Roles

7

The Role of Motivation
in Work Performance

Industrial psychologists have long been interested in the conditions that make a worker effective in his job. A substantial proportion of the research in this field has been concerned with explaining individual differences in performance, and many of the methods used by the professional industrial psychologist are directed toward increasing the level of performance of workers.

It is only within the last three decades that there has been much attention to the role of motivation in performance. Earlier technologies for increasing performance, such as the simplification and standardization of work methods and the development of tests of aptitudes and abilities for use in personnel selection, made important contributions but were not successful in eliminating widespread restriction of output (Mathewson, 1931; Roy, 1952). The widely publicized studies in the Hawthorne plant of the Western Electric Company (Roethlisberger and Dickson, 1939) gave important impetus to the study of motivational influences in performance as did the experiments of Kurt Lewin and his associates in group decision making and democratic leadership (Lewin, Lippitt, and White, 1939; Coch and French, 1948).

The role of motivational processes in determining a worker's level of performance is now widely recognized by industrial psychologists. Viteles (1953) has identified the development of the "will to work" as industry's core problem in the utilization of its manpower; Maier (1955) indicates the need for greater attention to problems of motivation and frustration by industrial firms; and McGregor (1960) and Likert (1961) have outlined theories of management based largely on assumptions about human motivation.

The Meaning of Motivation for Effective Performance

Let us consider what is meant by the term motivation when applied to performance. Terms like *motivation to produce* or *motivation for effective performance* are frequently used without adequate conceptual definition. It will be helpful to consider this concept in terms of the model outlined in Chapter Two. When a worker attempts to perform a job, a number of different outcomes are possible. In most work situations, there exist standards in terms of which these performance outcomes can be evaluated. If a worker turns out 300 units per hour, this is regarded as representing a higher level of performance than 200 units, which in turn can be regarded as representing a higher level of performance than 100 units.

In addition to placing each performance outcome on a dimension of level of performance it is also meaningful to refer to its valence or attractiveness for a particular person. For example, performing at a level of 300 units per hour may be preferred to producing at 200 units, which in turn may be preferred to producing at 100 units. It should be noted that there is no necessary relationship between the relative position of performance outcomes on a dimension of level of performance and on a dimension of valence. The highest levels of performance may be the most positively valent performance outcomes, but they may also be the least positively valent outcomes.

Consider a simple task permitting only two performance outcomes, *x* and *y*, which represent effective and ineffective performance, respectively. Table 7.1 depicts the hypothetical valence of each of these two outcomes for four persons.

For Persons 1 and 2, the demands of the task are highly consistent with their own desires. They prefer performing at a high rather than at a low level. In the case of Person 1 this preference is based on a desire for the high level outcome whereas for Person 2

**Table 7.1. The Relationship Between the Valence and Level of
Performance Outcomes for Four Hypothetical Persons.**

	Level of Performance	Valence for Person 1	Valence for Person 2	Valence for Person 3	Valence for Person 4
Performance Outcome x	High	+1	0	0	0
y	Low	0	-1	0	+1

it is based on an aversion for the low level outcome.[1] For Person 3
there is no relationship between the demands of the task and his
own desires. He is indifferent to whether he performs at a high or
a low level. For Person 4 the demands of the task are diametrically
opposed to his desires. He prefers performing at a low level to
performing at a high level.

The term *motivation for effective performance* could be
meaningfully used to refer to the degree of correspondence between
the results of these two methods of classifying performance outcomes—level and valence. If the two are in high agreement (as in
the case of Persons 1 and 2) the individual is motivated to perform
effectively; if the two are unrelated (as in the case of Person 3) he
is unmotivated; if the two are negatively related (as in the case of
Person 4) he is motivated to perform ineffectively.

If we wish the concept of motivation for effective performance to refer to the amount of task-related effort exerted by a
person, a more complex formulation is required. The reader will
recall that in Chapter Two we proposed that the force on a person
to perform an act is equal to the product of the valence of outcomes
and the strength of expectancies that these outcomes will follow
that act. If this proposition is correct, it follows that attempts to
predict or explain the amount of task-related effort must consider
both the valence of possible outcomes to that person and his expectancies regarding the consequences of different levels of effort for
attaining them.

Let us consider how the model introduced in Chapter Two

[1]This difference between individuals who are motivated by desire for success and those who are motivated by fear of failure has been noted by Lewin,
Dembo, Festinger, and Sears (1944) and amplified by Atkinson (1957).

might deal with the problem of explaining choices among different levels of task-related effort.[2] In the interest of simplicity, we will assume that there are only two different levels of effort, *a* and *b*, from which workers have to choose. Level *a* involves more effort than level *b*. According to our model, a worker's choice between level *a* and *b* should be dependent not only on the valence of performance outcomes but also on the expected relationship of *a* and *b* to these outcomes.

In Table 7.2 we have taken one of the individuals shown in the previous table (Person 1) and have attempted to show how his choice between these two levels of effort would vary with his expectancies. Three separate cases are illustrated. In each case, the worker is assumed to have the same strength of preference for performing at a high level. However, all three have different conceptions of their chances of doing so.

Case 1 is confident of his success regardless of how hard he tries. The hypothetical forces corresponding to levels of effort *a* and *b* are equal, signifying that they would be predicted to be equally probable. Despite the fact that Case 1 prefers success to failure, it would be misleading to describe him as highly motivated to perform effectively.

Case 2 is also depicted as preferring success to failure. However, he believes that the greater level of effort is certain to result in success whereas the lesser level of effort is certain to result in failure. Consequently, he is predicted by the model to choose to exert the greater amount of effort. Case 2 *is* appropriately regarded as highly motivated to perform effectively.

Case 3 is shown as expecting failure regardless of whether he chooses *a* or *b*. Although he prefers success to failure neither set of choices available to him is believed to lead to success. The situation is "hopeless" and his choice of level of effort is predicted to be similar to that of Case 1.

---

[2]The term *level of task-related effort* is used throughout this part of the book to refer to the degree to which energy is expended in responses that lead to the performance of task functions. Relevant behavioral measures would include amount of time worked, frequency of task-related responses per unit time, and amplitude of task-related responses.

Table 7.2. Hypothetical Effects of Valence and Expectancy
on Choice of Level of Effort.

	Outcome x (high performance) Valence = +1	Outcome y (low performance) Valence = 0	Force (valence × expectancy)
Case 1 Expectancy that effort level a will result in indicated outcome	1.00	.00	1.00
Expectancy that effort level b will result in indicated outcome	1.00	.00	1.00
Case 2 Expectancy that effort level a will result in indicated outcome	1.00	.00	1.00
Expectancy that effort level b will result in indicated outcome	.00	1.00	.00
Case 3 Expectancy that effort level a will result in indicated outcome	.00	1.00	.00
Expectancy that effort level b will result in indicated outcome	.00	1.00	.00

Clearly these cases do not exhaust the possibilities even for our simple and artificial situation involving only two levels of effort and two levels of performance. However, they do illustrate the kind of predictions that can be derived from the model. Workers' choices among different levels of effort expenditure on their jobs are predicted to be the result of *both* their preferences among performance outcomes and their expectancies concerning the consequences of each level of effort on the attainment of these outcomes. If we wish the concept of motivation for effective performance to include more of the variables that influence the amount of effort expended by the worker, it should be linked to the strength of force corresponding to different levels of effort rather than to differences in the valence of performance outcomes.

It should be noted that there are some motivational variables that undoubtedly influence level of effort expended but are not in-

cluded in the above formulation. One of these variables is the valence of level of effort itself. If, as is often assumed, people seek to
avoid the expenditure of effort,[3] then, other things being equal, the
force to exert higher levels of effort would be weaker than the force
to exert lower levels of effort. Cases 1 and 3 (in Table 7.2), who
believe the consequences of high and low effort to be identical,
would choose the lesser of the two amounts.

Task-related effort, as we are using the term, is not expended
in diffuse, undirected activity but in specific behaviors, the nature
of which varies from task to task. A person may prefer not only to
exert less effort than more effort but also to perform some behaviors
than others. For example, he may prefer being honest to being
dishonest or he may prefer helping others to hurting others. If the
attainment of a high level of performance is believed to require
dishonesty or hurting others, his desire to perform effectively and
his desire to avoid dishonesty or hurting others will be in conflict,
and the amount of effort that he is predicted to exert in his job is
correspondingly reduced. In contrast, if the attainment of a high
level of performance is believed to require honesty or helping others, the amount of task-related effort should be increased.

It can be argued that the valence of means will be reflected
in the ends that they serve. Thus, the valence of effective performance would be reduced if negatively valent methods were believed
to be required to attain it and increased if positively valent methods
were believed to be required to attain it. However, it is not at all
clear that this is the case. In fact, we saw in Chapter Three that the
valence of outcomes may be increased if their attainment is made
effortful or costly.

It follows that the valence of different levels of performance
and the expected consequences of different levels of effort are not the
only variables involved in determining a person's decision about the
amount of effort that he will exert in the performance of a task or job.
The definition of motivation for effective performance that we have

[3]See Chapter Three for a discussion of the evidence bearing on this
assumption.

proposed specifically excludes the valence of the particular responses believed to be necessary to achieve a high level of performance.

The Meaning of Level of Performance

In the preceding section we assumed that each of the possible performance outcomes can be ordered on a single scale of level of performance. We will now briefly consider some of the problems involved in making judgments of this kind.

The overall basis for the judgments is reasonably simple. We obtain information concerning the results or accomplishments of a worker during a given period of time and compare these results or accomplishments with certain evaluative standards. The nature of these evaluative standards is related to the worker's role or job definition. For example, if the worker's job calls for him to assemble widgets, then the number of widgets assembled during a given period of time would serve as a measure of his level of performance.

It should be noted that a determination of the standards to be used in evaluating performance is not a psychological problem. There is no psychological basis for specifying the performance outcomes that are "good" and "bad" in any given work role. Such judgments must be made in terms of a value system, and measures of level of performance based on them are always relative to these values.

If a work role is part of a formal organization, the objectives of the organization provide some guidelines in the development of standards for evaluating performance. For example, if the organization's principal objective is to "make a profit," the standards for evaluating member performance will be largely economic.[4] However, these guidelines are far from absolute and, particularly in more complex work roles, the standards are often subjective and matters of administrative judgment.

To the extent to which there exist clearly defined standards for evaluating performance in a given job, the concept of level of

[4]For a discussion of an approach to criterion development based exclusively on economic considerations see Brogden and Taylor (1950).

performance becomes meaningful.[5] In simple jobs and tasks these standards are usually clearly specified and objective criteria of level of performance can often be obtained. However, as the number of functions included in the work role increases, it becomes more difficult to find suitable performance criteria. The psychologist is usually forced to rely on judgments of other persons whose standards remain unspecified. The problem of obtaining adequate measures of level of performance—the criterion problem—has frequently been cited as the Achilles heel of the industrial psychologist. Although the importance of this problem has been most thoroughly recognized in work on personnel selection and placement, the difficulty of defining and measuring performance in a work role places no less important limitations on the study of motivational influences on performance.

Ability and Motivation as Joint Determinants of Performance. Attempts by industrial psychologists to predict or explain differences in level of performance among workers on the same task have been based on two somewhat different assumptions. The first of these assumptions is that the performance of a person is to be understood in terms of his abilities and their relevance to the task to be performed. More briefly, it can be represented by the proposition that the level of performance of a worker on a task is a direct function of his ability to perform that task. This assumption has led to efforts to measure abilities, usually by observation of performance in standardized tests, and to use these measurements in the selection and placement of workers. It has also led to efforts to increase performance by developing and increasing workers' abilities through training.

The second of these two assumptions is that the performance of a person is to be understood in terms of his motives (or needs or preferences) and the conditions for their satisfaction in the work

[5]If there are two or more standards for evaluating performance, for example, quantity and quality of output, they may be treated as separate performance dimensions or combined to yield a single dimension. For reasons of parsimony we will, in this section of the book, refer to level of performance as though it were a single dimension.

situation. It can be stated more succinctly in the proposition that the level of performance of a worker on a task or job is a direct function of his motivation to perform effectively. This assumption has led to an attempt to identify the conditions that generate a high level of motivation and to establish them in work situations.

How can these two assumptions be reconciled? The most obvious solution is to suggest that both are correct but only partially so. A worker's level of performance on his job is dependent *both* on his ability and on his motivation. This solution has, in fact, been most frequently adopted. Thus, Mace (1935) and Viteles (1953) distinguished between the "capacity to work" and "the will to work" and propose that both determine level of performance; Maier (1955) hypothesized that performance is a function of both ability and motivation; and Gagné and Fleishman (1959) propose that performance is dependent on skill level and on motivation.

Seldom have investigators attempted to specify precisely which determinants of performance are included under ability and which are included under motivation. The term *ability* usually denotes a potential for performing some task that may or may not be utilized. It refers to what a person "can do," not to what he "does do." The added requirement for effective performance is typically a motivational one. In order to achieve a high level of performance a person must have both the ability and the motivation to perform effectively (Baldwin, 1958).

This distinction between what a person can and does do is difficult to translate into operational terms. We can only observe directly what a person does do. There is no way of measuring his ability except insofar as it is reflected in actual performance in some situation. A person's score on any test designed to measure one of his abilities is consequently affected by a large number of factors, including the amount of his motivation in the test situation. In an attempt to circumvent this difficulty an effort is typically made to equate the motivation of all persons taking the ability test by standardizing instructions and other aspects of the conditions under which the test is given. Implicit in such operational definitions of ability is a conceptual definition that is more explicit about what ability is not than what it is. A person's ability to perform a task refers to the degree to which he possesses all of the psychological attributes necessary for a high level of performance excluding those of a motivational nature.

What are some of these nonmotivational determinants of performance? While an exhaustive examination of this problem exceeds the scope of this book, it is relatively easy to show that there are a number of such nonmotivational determinants and that they have diverse psychological bases. In discussing these determinants it will be helpful to keep in mind the types of psychological demands made by a work role. In the context of any work role, the role occupant is exposed to a variety of stimuli, some of which constitute signals for action on his part. The required behavior on the part of the worker depends on the nature of these stimuli, for example, he must respond differently if the light is on or off, if the thread is broken or unbroken, if the needle on the dial points to 150 or to 60, and so on. To each of these stimuli the worker must select among a number of possible responses such as pulling a lever, braking or accelerating, or turning a wheel to the right or left.

Consider a simple task in which a worker is presented with just two signals for action, S_1 and S_2. Let us further assume that there is only one appropriate response to each of these signals. We will designate the appropriate response to S_1 as R_1 and to S_2 as R_2. By definition, the more consistently the worker responds to S_1 with R_1 and to S_2 with R_2, the more effective is his performance. Even in this highly limited and programmed task one can identify a number of different determinants of level of performance that fit the conceptual definition of ability mentioned above. These include the following:

The probability that the worker will discriminate between stimuli requiring different responses (that is, S_1 and S_2). If the worker has poor vision and the stimuli are visual, his effectiveness will be lower than if he had normal vision. Similarly, if the cues are auditory, gustatory, olfactory, cutaneous, or kinesthetic and the worker has deficiencies in the corresponding sense modality, performance will be impaired. However, sensory deficiencies are not the only conditions affecting the probability that two stimuli will be discriminated. Hebb (1949) has shown that the discrimination of even elementary stimulus patterns like triangles and circles is not innate but requires a long period of learning with extensive exposure to the stimuli to be discriminated. It can also be demonstrated that the capacity of a person to discriminate reliably and quickly more complex patterns of stimulation (for example, a 1964 Ford and a 1964 Chevrolet) can be increased by appropriate training. It must be assumed, therefore, that those aspects of "ability" that reflect the probability of a worker making the relevant discriminations among task-related stimuli include both sensory and cognitive conditions, the latter modifiable by experience.

The worker's knowledge of the correct response to perform to each stimulus. In the simple task described, the worker may reliably discriminate between S_1 and S_2 but not "know" which response to make to each. Such knowledge of how to perform the task may be represented conceptually by the "correctness" of the worker's expectancies concerning the effects of task responses on level of performance.

The worker's capacity to execute the correct responses (that is, R_1 and R_2). A person may be able to make the necessary discriminations among task-related stimuli and may know which response may be made to each of the stimuli but may not be able to make the necessary responses. For example, two persons working on a task involving the repeated lifting of a very heavy weight may reliably discriminate between those situations in which they are to lift and those in which they are not to lift, and may be equally motivated to perform the task effectively, but may differ markedly in their level of performance. The differences could be attributable to the fact that they differ in the extent to which they have the muscular attributes needed to perform the necessary responses.

It can be seen that the concept of ability as typically used is a kind of "catch-all," including a number of highly different psychological characteristics relevant to task performance. The only conditions that are intentionally excluded are motivational, and there is some reason to think that they may account for some of the differences among scores on measures of ability. It is little wonder that the concept of ability has not proven very useful theoretically.

No attempt will be made here to refine this concept. Our primary interest is in the motivational determinants of performance and whenever we refer to a worker's ability to perform a task, we mean the degree to which he possesses the necessary nonmotivational attributes for attaining a high level of task performance.

If the possibility of some kind of conceptual and operational distinction between ability and motivation as determinants of level of performance is admitted, it becomes meaningful to ask whether their effects are independent of one another or whether they interact in some way in determining performance. There is surprisingly little data on this question. Traditionally, the assumption that performance is a function of ability has been made by personnel psychologists interested in personnel selection, placement, and training. In contrast, the assumption that performance is a function of motivation has been the basis for the work of social psychologists interested in social influences in job performance. As a result there has been little attempt to study directly the joint effects of these two types of variables on job performance.

The evidence that does exist suggests rather strongly that ability and motivation, as typically measured or manipulated, do not have independent effects on performance but rather interact with one another. Elizabeth French (1957) studied the joint effects of intelligence and achievement motivation on the problem-solving success of airmen and found a significant interaction between these two variables. Among those subjects high in achievement motivation, problem-solving success was positively related to their intelligence. However, among those who were low in achievement motivation, there was no relationship between intelligence and problem-solving success.

Similar results were obtained by Fleishman (1958). He manipulated degree of motivation experimentally by telling one group of two hundred air force trainees that their performance on a complex coordination task would be important in determining their future assignments (high motivation condition), while a second group of two hundred was given no such instruction (low motivation condition). The results show that performance was significantly higher under the high motivation condition than under the low motivation condition. However, the difference in performance between the two motivation conditions was significantly greater for subjects high in ability (as measured by previous performance on the task) than for those low in ability. Similarly, as with the findings of French, the difference in performance of high and low ability subjects was greater under the high motivation condition than under the low.

In a study of the effects of participation in decision making on supervisors' satisfaction and performance, Vroom (1960a) examined the correlations between scores on four tests of ability and scores on four measures of job performance for supervisors who were classified as high, moderate, and low in motivation for effective performance.[6] He found fairly high positive correlations between the ability and performance of supervisors high in motivation, generally lower positive correlations for those moderate in motivation, and zero or slightly negative correlations for those low in motivation. These results are essentially in accord with those of French and Fleishman.

Further corroborating evidence for the fact that a given increment in motivation has greater positive effect on the performance of those high in ability than of those low in ability may be found in the results of an early experiment on the effects of economic incentives carried out by Wyatt (1934). This experiment, to be described in more detail in the next chapter, compared the level of performance achieved by the same group of ten female workers in a candy factory under hourly, bonus, and piece-rate methods of pay. When the girls were changed from the hourly system of payment to a competitive bonus method, production increased markedly. A further increase occurred later when the girls were placed on a piece-rate system. Apparently these increases were the result of changes in the degree of motivation of the girls.

The evidence for an interaction between motivation and ability in determining performance comes from Wyatt's analysis of individual differences under the three payment conditions. Throughout the experiment the ten girls worked on five different jobs. There

[6]Two different measures of amount of motivation were used. The results described here are based on a measure obtained by combining data on the degree to which workers participated in decision making with data on the strength of their need for independence. The results obtained from use of the other measure of motivation showed little difference in correlations between ability and performance. For a more complete account of the rationale and procedure for these measures, see Vroom (1960a).

were always two girls performing the same job and these girls rotated from job to job together as well as simultaneously experiencing the change in methods of payment. Table 7.3 shows that the percentage difference in output between the members of the five pairs of workers increased as the method of payment was changed from the time rate to the bonus rate and from the bonus rate to the piece rate.

If we assume that the differences in performance between two girls working on the same tasks under the same conditions are largely a function of differences in their skill or ability, then these findings are consistent with those previously cited. As level of motivation was increased by changes in method of payment, these differences in ability became more significant in affecting performance. The increased motivation resulting from the use of economic incentives had greater effect on the level of performance of those who were initially performing at a relatively high level than on those who were initially performing at a relatively low level.

Insofar as the ability of workers is increased by experience on a task, we should find that motivational effects on performance become more pronounced as workers acquire greater experience in carrying out the task. Such a result is indicated in two other experiments described by Wyatt (1934). In the first experiment, the relative effectiveness of time and bonus methods of payment was ascertained for female workers who had just been assigned the job of filling small cartons with tablets. During the initial weeks on this

Table 7.3. Percentage Difference in Output Between the
Two Members of Each Pair Under Each System of Payment.

Workers	Time Rate	Bonus Rate	Piece Rate
A and B	3.6	8.7	9.7
C and D	6.4	9.7	9.8
E and F	5.6	7.5	9.6
G and H	13.0	25.6	29.4
I and J	6.3	10.1	7.7
Average	7.0	12.3	13.2

Source: From Wyatt, 1934, p. 11.

new operation, payment by the bonus rate resulted in only moderately greater output than payment by the time rate, but this difference increased as the workers acquired more skill. At the end of the ninth week the output of those paid by the bonus method was almost 35 percent greater than that of those paid by the time method. The comparable difference at the end of the second week was only 8 percent.

The second experiment dealt with the performance of nineteen operatives who were also filling cartons. Ten of these workers were paid by time throughout the entire learning period while the remaining nine were put on a piece rate after five days of time payment. During the first five days, the output of the two groups increased moderately at the same rate. After the introduction of the piece rate for the second group, its output began to increase at a faster rate than that of the group remaining on time payment. The difference between the output of those on piece and time rates increased progressively from the fifth day to the thirty-fifth day, at which time it was approximately 25 percent.

The general picture emerging from these studies is that the effects of motivation on performance are dependent on the level of ability of the worker, and the relationship of ability to performance is dependent on the motivation of the worker. The effects of ability and motivation on performance are not additive but interactive. The data presently available on this question suggest something more closely resembling the multiplicative relationship depicted in the following formula:

$$\text{Performance} = f(\text{Ability} \times \text{Motivation}).$$

It follows from such a formula that, when ability has a low value, increments in motivation will result in smaller increases in performance than when ability has a high value. Furthermore, when motivation has a low value, increments in ability will result in smaller increases in performance than when motivation has a high value. It makes little sense to ask which is the more important determinant of performance—a person's level of ability or his level of motivation. Such a question would be analogous to asking whether the length or height of a rectangle is more important in determining its area. The consequences of a given increment in each depends on the preexisting value of the other. More is to be gained from increasing the motivation of those who are high in ability than from increasing the motivation of those who are low in ability. Similarly, more is to be gained from increasing the ability of those who are highly motivated than from increasing the ability of those who are relatively unmotivated.

If such an interaction between ability and motivation were to be corroborated in further research, it would have considerable implications for managerial practice. It would suggest that managerial efforts to obtain and develop persons with skill and ability and to motivate these persons must proceed concurrently. The value of programs of selection and training depends on the organization's previous success in creating conditions conducive to a high level of individual motivation. Similarly, the value of programs designed to motivate employees depends on the skill level of these employees.

The Nature of the Relationship
Between Motivation and Performance

Up to now we have been assuming that, given some value of ability greater than zero, level of performance is a constantly increasing function of amount of motivation. In other words, the more motivated the worker to perform effectively, the more effective his performance. This kind of relationship is shown by the straight line in Figure 7.1.

There are at least two other plausible alternatives to this type of relationship. The first of these is a negatively accelerated curve approaching an upper limit. This possibility is shown in Figure 7.1 by a dotted line. It implies a law of diminishing returns—successive increments in motivation of identical amounts result in smaller and smaller increments in performance until a point is reached at which there is no further increase in performance. The second of these two alternative possibilities, an inverted U function, is shown by a broken line. It is similar to the first except for a reduction in performance under high levels of motivation. Performance is low at low levels of motivation, reaches its maximum point under mod-

**Figure 7.1. Hypothetical Relationships Between Amount of Motivation
and Level of Performance.**

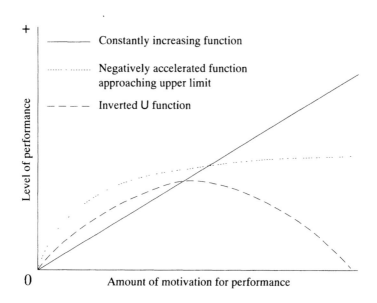

erate levels of motivation and then drops off again under high levels
of motivation.

Difficulties in measuring amount of motivation with any
degree of precision make any very accurate determination of the
value of the functional relationship between amount of motivation
and level of performance impossible. At best we can measure or
manipulate motivation on an ordinal scale, that is, we can specify
that one level is higher than another but not how much higher it
is. The admittedly imprecise nature of this measurement rules out
the determination of the slope of the relationship between these two
variables (for example, positively accelerated, linear, or negatively
accelerated). It should still be possible, however, to determine
changes in direction of the relationship (for example, from positive
to zero to negative). Thus, we can determine whether increases in
motivation, when level of motivation is already at a high level, have
positive effects on performance (as shown in the straight line), have
no effect on performance (as shown in the dotted line), or have
negative effects on performance (as shown in the broken line).

There is considerable evidence that performance increases with an increase in the magnitude of the reward offered for successful performance. However, a few investigators have shown decrements in performance under very high levels of motivation. In a very early study, Yerkes and Dodson (1908) showed that maximum motivation did not lead to the most rapid learning, particularly if the task was difficult. They attempted to train mice to choose a white box over a black one by shocking them for entering the black box. Amount of motivation was varied by using different intensities of shock, and the difficulty of the task was varied by changing the difference in brightness between the white and black boxes. When the boxes differed only slightly in brightness, and consequently the task of discriminating among them was difficult, the relationship between amount of motivation and performance approximated the inverted U function. The optimal level of motivation was neither the highest nor the lowest. When the task was made somewhat easier (by increasing the brightness difference between the boxes), the optimal level of motivation increased but there was still a decrement in performance under the highest motivation levels. Only when the brightness difference between the boxes was made very great was there a continuous increase in performance with increases in level of motivation.

Patrick (1934) obtained further evidence for the inverted U function. In his experiment, he placed human subjects in a compartment that contained exit doors. Their problem was to escape from the compartment by discovering which one of the doors was unlocked. Inasmuch as the unlocked door was varied in random fashion from one trial to another and was never the same on two adjacent trials, there was no possibility for the subjects to learn a permanent solution to the problem. Under normal motivation, subjects went about trying to solve the problem in a highly rational fashion, avoiding repeated attempts to open the same door or avoiding the door that was unlocked on the previous trial. However, when the experimenter increased their motivation to escape by spraying them with a cold shower, shocking them through their bare feet, or sounding a loud Klaxon horn, the subjects demonstrated more stereotyped and less efficient performance on the task.

Additional data suggesting the disruptive effects of high levels of motivation are found in an experiment carried out by Birch (1945). Six young chimpanzees were given a series of problems to solve under various lengths of food deprivation. The solution of each of the problems required the animals to use the materials provided (for example, string, rope, or sticks) to obtain food. Birch found the intermediate lengths of food deprivation, which we can assume to represent the intermediate levels of motivation to get food, to be most conducive to problem-solving efficiency. Relatively short and relatively long periods of food deprivation resulted in less efficient behavior. Birch's description of the behavior of the animals illuminates the different bases for the ineffective performance of animals under conditions of very low and very high motivation.

> When motivation is very low the animals are easily diverted from the problem by extraneous factors and behavior tends to deteriorate into a series of non-goal-directed acts. Under conditions of very intense motivation, the animals concentrated upon the goal to the relative exclusion of other features of the situation which were essential to the solution of the problem. Also, the frequent occurrence of frustration responses, such as tantrums and screaming, when a given stereotyped pattern of response proved to be inadequate, hindered the animals in their problem-solving efforts (1945, p. 316).

Although the form of the relationship between amount of motivation and level of performance may vary somewhat with the nature of the task confronting the subject, most investigators have suggested that the inverted U function most closely approximates the actual state of affairs. McClelland (1951) concludes that

> . . . *as a motive increases in intensity it first leads to an increase in the efficiency of instrumental activity and then to a decrease.* Thus it would appear that as far as adjustment is concerned there is a certain optimum level of motive intensity, a level of "creative anxiety," which leads to maximum problem-solving

efficiency. Too little motivation leads to sluggishness
and inertia, too much to disruption and defense
against anxiety. The theoretical problems still unsolved are the discovery of what this area of optimum
intensity is and why higher intensities lead to inefficiency (1951, p. 485).

How can the decrement in performance under very high levels of motivation be accounted for? There are at least two possible
explanations. One explanation is based on the assumption, made
by Tolman (1948), that a high level of motivation is accompanied
by a "narrowing of the cognitive field." A highly motivated person
may attend only to those cues which he expects to be useful in the
attainment of his goals. If the task or problem is a novel or difficult
one, his intense motivation may lead to his ignoring relevant information. Supporting Tolman's assumption are at least two experiments (Johnson, 1952; Bruner, Matter, and Papanek, 1955) showing
substantially less incidental learning among animals trained under
high levels of motivation. The possibility that a narrowing of the
cognitive field represents the basis for the decrement in performance
under very high motivation is further suggested by Birch's observation that the chimpanzees who had been deprived of food for forty-
eight hours concentrated so intensely on the food that they ignored
other objects in the cage that could be used to solve the problem.

The second explanation involves the supposition that a high
level of motivation to attain a goal tends to be associated with
anxiety or some other strong emotional state, which in turn impairs
performance. The idea that high levels of motivation tend to be
accompanied by anxiety is not intuitively unreasonable. Anxiety
has been defined by Mowrer (1939) as a learned anticipatory response to cues that have in the past been followed by injury or pain.
It might be argued that the anticipation of failure in a situation in
which failure has high negative valence could be the source of considerable anxiety. Because such a situation would also tend to be
one in which the subject strongly prefers success to failure, anxiety
and intense motivation may frequently accompany one another.

What about the assertion that anxiety impairs performance?
There is considerable anecdotal and experimental evidence that sug-

gests that this is in fact the case. On the anecdotal side are the frequently heard stories about the student who was so frightened by the prospects of failing an examination that his mind went "blank" or the actor who forgot on opening night the lines that he knew so well during rehearsal. In experiments, it has been shown that when individuals are placed in a stressful situation designed to create anxiety, their performance tends to be lower than when the situation is nonstressful (McKinney, 1933; Sears, 1937; Lantz, 1945; Alper, 1946a; Williams, 1947; McClelland and Apicella, 1947). It has also been found that persons obtaining high scores on the Taylor Manifest Anxiety Scale (Taylor, 1953) perform less effectively on relatively complex verbal and nonverbal training tasks than those obtaining low scores (Taylor and Spence, 1952; Raymond, 1953; Montague, 1953; Farber and Spence, 1953).

Why should anxiety impair performance? For one thing, there are involuntary autonomic responses associated with anxiety that could interfere with execution of a task. The pianist may find it difficult to play when his hands are perspiring and his heart pounding and the actor may find his mouth so dry that he is incapable of delivering his lines. It is also possible that the highly anxious person's actions will become directed toward reducing his anxiety rather than performing the task. The anxious soldier may flee from the battlefield and the anxious executive may lapse into fantasy or turn to alcohol for the solution of his problems.

The disruption in performance resulting from anxiety seems to be greatest for relatively difficult tasks. Studies by Montague (1953), Farber and Spence (1953), and Raymond (1953) show that the superiority in rate of learning of nonanxious subjects (as measured by the Taylor Manifest Anxiety Scale) increases with the difficulty of the material to be learned. It has even been shown that, in the very simple eye-blink conditioning situation, anxious persons learn more quickly than nonanxious persons (Taylor, 1951; Spence and Taylor, 1951; Spence and Farber, 1953, 1954).

A recent series of field experiments by Schachter, Willerman, Festinger, and Hyman (1961) demonstrates that situationally produced emotional disturbances result in a greater impairment in workers' performance of novel nonstereotyped tasks. These experiments were conducted on groups of assembly workers in General

Electric factories. The experiments were similar in design, although details varied from factory to factory. In each experiment, matched groups performing identical operations were selected. Half of the groups, called disfavored, were subjected to a series of annoyances with the intent of making them "disturbed and upset." The other half of the groups, called favored, were confronted with situations designed to produce "contentment and satisfaction." Production data was gathered before these manipulations and during the manipulation period which lasted from two to four weeks. At the end of this time, the manipulations were halted and identical changes in work procedure were introduced into the favored and disfavored groups. The results indicate little difference in productivity between the favored and disfavored groups before the changeover. However, after the changeover, when the task required relearning on the part of the workers, the disfavored groups displayed lower productivity than the favored groups. The authors conclude, "Emotional disturbance has little effect on stereotyped activity, but does have a disrupting effect on nonstereotyped activity" (p. 211).

Both explanations of the decrement in performance under intense motivation are logically plausible and consistent with some empirical observations. Further research on the relationship between strength of motivation and performance for a wide range of different tasks and subjects should shed further light on the underlying processes.

Summary

In this chapter, the role of motivation in work performance has been examined. Two related definitions of motivation for effective performance were discussed—one in terms of the relative valence of different performance levels and the other in terms of the relative strength of the force on the person to exert different levels of effort in performance of the task. The latter, while somewhat more complex, appears to describe more accurately the motivational conditions that would be expected to affect level of performance in a task or job.

Industrial psychologists have proposed that the performance of a worker on a task or job is not to be understood solely in terms of motivational factors but is also dependent on his ability to do the task. An examination of the concept of ability reveals that it is typically defined in such a manner as to exclude motivational influences but to include all other conditions affecting performance. A logical analysis of a simple task led to an identification of at least three types of nonmotivational determinants of performance that must be considered in such a definition of ability.

An examination of the results of studies that attempted to measure or manipulate both the ability of the person to do a task and the amount of his motivation to perform it effectively revealed that there is an interaction between these variables. The effects on performance of a given increment in motivation are negligible for those low in ability and positive for those high in ability. Similarly, the relationship between ability and performance varies with the amount of motivation, being negligible for those low in motivation and positive for those high in motivation.

The form of the functional relationship between amount of motivation for effective performance and level of performance was examined. There are some indications in existing data that the relationship is not a constantly increasing one but is approximated by an inverted U function. On tasks in which effective performance requires insight or higher level mental processes, extremely high levels of motivation appear to result in a lower level of performance than more moderate levels. Two interpretations of this performance decrement were discussed. One interpretation is based on the assumption that high motivation involves a narrowing of the cognitive field, while the second assumes that highly motivated persons tend to be anxious over failure. Both interpretations are consistent with some empirical data. Further research is needed on the conditions affecting the amount of performance impairment under intense motivation.

8

Some Motivational Determinants
of Effective Job Performance

In the previous chapter we discussed the role of motivation in determining the effectiveness with which a person performs a task or job. We also noted that there were many psychological variables other than those of a motivational nature that influence a person's level of performance and we briefly discussed their nature as well as the way in which they might interact with motivational variables. In this chapter we will consider the influence of some specific motivational variables on level of performance.

As in our discussion of the determinants of job satisfaction, we will proceed from the specific to the general. First, we will consider evidence pertaining to the consequences on workers' performance of their (1) supervision, (2) work group, (3) job content, (4) wages, and (5) promotional opportunities. In each case we will be concerned with only those aspects of these conditions that are typically assumed to affect or have some logical relationship with the motivation of workers to perform effectively on their jobs. Second, we will look at the problem of worker motivation from a broader perspective, attempting to integrate what we now know about the conditions affecting it and to identify some fruitful areas for further inquiry.

Supervision

The influence of supervision on productivity of work groups was dramatically illustrated in a field experiment reported by Feldman

(1937). This experiment was carried out in twenty-two work sections in the home office of an insurance company. Each section was composed of forty to fifty clerks doing roughly the same kind of work. During the year preceding the experiment, a group bonus plan was introduced in an attempt to reduce costs. There were marked differences in the amount of cost reduction achieved in each of the sections subsequent to the introduction of the plan, and these data provided the basis for a large-scale transfer of supervisors. Each of the twenty-two supervisors was transferred from his old section to a different one, with the aim of putting those who were above average in achieved amount of cost reduction in charge of below-average groups and vice versa.

One year after the transfer took place, the cost savings effected in the twenty-two sections were examined once again. There were still large differences among the sections, but the order of supervisors in terms of amount of cost reduction remained practically the same. Those supervisors who had succeeded in reducing costs to a major degree in their previous work section had similar results in their new sections. In contrast, those supervisors who had been relatively unsuccessful in reducing costs were also relatively unsuccessful in their new sections. Changes in rank order among the twenty-two supervisors were limited to three supervisors and these changed only slightly. If the amount of cost reduction achieved is treated as a measure of productivity, it seems clear from these results that the supervisor plays a very important role in determining the productivity of his work group.

The methods used by different supervisors in attempts to reduce costs are not revealed in this experiment, nor is it clear to what extent their different results reflect their ability to motivate subordinates to perform effectively. The motivational effects of supervision have been studied most frequently, but they are but one of a number of bases for supervisory control over productivity. Supervisors affect the productivity of their units in ways that have nothing to do with the motivation of their subordinates. They may differ in their skill in training subordinates, coordinating activities, or developing new and better work methods. Although these different bases for the influence of supervision on productivity make it difficult to isolate the effects that are due to motivation, we will restrict our attention to those aspects of supervisory behavior that seem most likely to have motivational consequences.

Consideration. It is frequently suggested that consideration by a supervisor for the needs or feelings of his subordinates has positive effects on their motivation to perform their jobs effectively. The more "considerate," "supportive," or "employee-oriented" the supervisor, the greater the extent to which his subordinates will strive to do their jobs well. Thus, Davis (1962) concludes that "employee-oriented supervisors tend to get better productivity, motivation, and worker satisfaction" (p. 130), and Likert (1959b) asserts that the supervisor who obtains the highest productivity is "supportive, friendly, and helpful rather than hostile" and "endeavors to treat people in a sensitive, considerate way" (p. 190).

Evidence for a positive relationship between amount of consideration shown by supervisors for their subordinates and productivity was obtained in a field study carried out by Katz, Maccoby, and Morse (1950) in a life insurance company. Twelve work sections with high productivity and twelve with low productivity were selected for study. The behavior of supervisors in these two sets of work sections was assessed by means of interviews with both supervisors and their subordinates. The results indicate substantial difference in the amount of consideration that low and high productivity supervisors showed their subordinates. The highly productive supervisors were typically characterized as "employee-centered," for they tended to describe as most important the "human relations" aspects of their jobs. In contrast, those in charge of low productivity work groups were typically characterized as "production-centered" for they tended to consider their subordinates primarily as "people to get the work done."

In an attempt to determine the generality of this finding, Katz, Maccoby, Gurin, and Floor (1951) carried out a second investigation among railroad maintenance-of-way workers. The research design was similar, but the setting was different in a number of respects. The workers studied were manual laborers instead of clerical employees; they were primarily middle-aged instead of young people just out of high school; and they were men instead of girls. Despite the differences, there was a marked similarity in the results.

The men in high productivity groups more frequently described their supervisors as taking a personal interest in them, being helpful in training them for better jobs, and being less punitive than did the men in low productivity sections.

Similar results have been obtained in more recent studies. Likert (1958a) reports a correlation of .64 between supervisors' "attitude toward the men" and the productivity of thirty-two geographically separated work units in a large package delivery organization. Argyle, Gardner, and Cioffi (1958) found a significant positive relationship between the degree to which foremen were nonpunitive in their dealings with subordinates and the productivity of their work groups in a study of ninety work groups in seven British factories, and Besco and Lawshe (1959) found correlations with departmental effectiveness of .46 and .59 for foreman consideration as judged by their subordinates and superiors, respectively.

Not all of the results fit this same pattern. Halpin and Winer (1957) report correlations of -.23 between the consideration of 29 air crew commanders, as measured by the Ohio State Leader Behavior Description Questionnaire, and ratings of their overall effectiveness. In contrast, scores on initiating structure, which are assumed to reflect the extent to which the commander organized and defined the relationship between himself and members of his crew, correlated .28 with overall effectiveness ratings. A subsequent study of 89 air crew commanders revealed correlations with overall effectiveness ratings of .17 for consideration and .25 for initiating structure (Halpin, 1957). Using a modified version of the Leader Behavior Description Questionnaire adapted for use in industry, Fleishman, Harris, and Burtt (1955) obtained scores on consideration and initiating structure for 112 foremen in production and nonproduction divisions of International Harvester. For production foremen, the correlations between proficiency ratings and consideration and initiating structure were -.31 and .47, respectively. For nonproduction foremen, the correlations were .28 for consideration and -.19 for initiating structure. In another industrial study, Rambo (1958) found no relationship between scores of supervisors on consideration or on initiating structure and rankings of overall supervisory effectiveness.

Fleishman (1957a, 1960) has developed a different type of

questionnaire, the Leadership Opinion Questionnaire, which yields scores for supervisors on the same two dimensions of leader behavior. Unlike the Leader Behavior Description Questionnaire, which is generally completed by subordinates who describe the supervisor, the Leadership Opinion Questionnaire is intended to be completed by supervisors and consists of forty questions dealing with how they think they should behave in supervisory situations. Using this measure in a study of fifty-three first-line supervisors in a petrochemical plant, Bass (1956) found a correlation of .29 between consideration and forced choice performance ratings obtained two years later. In a replication of this study on forty-two sales supervisors he found a correlation of .32 between consideration and rank order performance ratings (Bass, 1958). The correlations between performance and initiating structure in these two studies were -.09 and -.01, respectively.

In summary, it appears that measures of the amount of consideration shown by a supervisor for his subordinates are frequently positively related to the effectiveness of his work unit. However, there are some inconsistencies in findings from study to study, which may reflect the fact that different situations require different supervisory methods. Recent discussions of leadership (Stogdill, 1948; Gibb, 1954; Likert, 1961) have emphasized its situational nature. The leader traits and methods that result in effective group performance are assumed to depend on such situational variables as the objectives of the group, its structure, and the personalities of its members. Conceivably, consideration was more of a liability than an asset in the combat situations studied by Halpin and Winer (1957) and in the production divisions studied by Fleishman, Harris, and Burtt (1955).

Before situational differences are concluded to be the basis for different relationships between consideration and group effectiveness, one note of caution should be sounded. Each of the studies that we have described is correlational in nature and subject to the traditional difficulties associated with this method. Even if supervisory consideration and work group effectiveness were always perfectly and positively associated with one another, we could not unequivocally conclude that differences in consideration are the source of differences in group effectiveness. It is possible that the direction of causality is reversed. Supervisors may display more consideration when their subordinates perform effectively than when they perform ineffectively. Indeed, productivity on the part of subordinates may be the cause of consideration on the part of their supervisor rather than the other way around. There is also the possibility that the association between consideration and effectiveness is the result of the lack of control of one or more additional variables that are associated with both.

Experimental methods are necessary to decide among these alternative interpretations. If we could increase or decrease the amount of consideration of supervisors at will, it could then be ascertained if any changes in group effectiveness occurred. This kind of experimentation is exceedingly difficult. There is, as yet, no reliable procedure for creating the amount of change in supervisory behavior required by such an experiment. Human relations training methods, which are widely used for changing the behavior of supervisors, have not proved very effective when evaluated against a criterion of behavior change (Hariton, 1951; Fleishman, Harris, and Burtt, 1955). Until more effective methods are developed, the possibility of verifying the hypothesized "effects" of consideration on group performance in actual field situations must be discounted.

It is conceivable that laboratory experimentation might present a "way out" of this dilemma. In the laboratory it is relatively easy to subject groups of persons working on tasks to different forms of supervision. One might, therefore, expose matched groups of workers to "considerate" and "inconsiderate" supervision, or alternatively expose each group to both forms of supervision in counterbalanced order. The relative productivity achieved under these two different forms of supervision could then be assessed, and the hypothesis that consideration "causes" productivity could be adequately tested. This kind of research is made difficult by the fact that researchers using the concept of consideration have not provided very objective guidelines concerning the acts that define this variable. It is not possible to designate, in any objective manner, supervisory acts as "considerate" or "inconsiderate" without knowing something about the motives of subordinates. The same act may be "inconsiderate" from the point of view of one subordinate but be highly "considerate" from the point of view of another.

This situation is recognized by Likert (1958a), who points out that it is the subordinate's view of the supportiveness of the supervisor that is important and that the character of interactions which are viewed as supportive depend on the experience and expectations of the particular subordinate. Likert does not point out, however, the difficulty that a subjective definition of supportiveness or consideration presents for carrying out the experiments that are necessary to test his theory conclusively.

One of the behaviors that is likely to be part of an objectively defined concept of consideration is the frequency with which the supervisor praises or criticizes his subordinates. Supervisors high in consideration or some conceptually similar dimension are assumed to praise their subordinates more frequently and to be less punitive than those supervisors who are low in consideration. Consequently one might be able to acquire some experimental evidence concerning the effects of consideration by inquiring into the consequences of praise or criticism on performance.

A large number of experiments on this problem have been carried out, primarily by educational psychologists. Hurlock's experiment (1925) will serve to illustrate the kind of procedure employed. She gave a group of 106 children a series of addition problems to perform each day for five days. At the end of the first day, and on each succeeding day, one preselected group was publicly praised for its performance. A second group matched in initial performance, age, and sex were publicly reproved for their performance, and a third matched group heard the praises and criticisms given to others but were themselves ignored. Changes in performance on the addition problems of these three groups were observed during the five days and were compared with one another and with the changes in performance of a control group who were tested in a different room and received no feedback. The data indicate that the praised group showed the most marked improvement in performance, followed by the reproved group, the ignored group, and finally the control group.

Similar results have been obtained by other investigators (Gilchrist, 1916). However, some experimenters have found no difference between the effects of praise and criticism (Hurlock, 1924;

Thompson and Hunnicutt, 1944) and others have found superior results under criticism (Brenner, 1934; Forlano and Axelrod, 1937).

These discrepant findings may reflect, in part, substantial individual differences in responses to praise and criticism. Forlano and Axelrod (1937) and Thompson and Hunnicutt (1944) found that intraverts increased their performance more readily following criticism than did extraverts; and Bernadin and Jessor (1957) found that criticism lowered the performance of subjects who were dependent as measured by the Edwards Personal Preference Scale more than that of subjects who were independent.

In each of these experiments a subject's receipt of praise or criticism was independent of his actual level of performance. It is questionable whether continued application of either unconditional praise or criticism would result in high levels of performance. Our model would lead us to predict that a person who expects to be praised for ineffective as well as effective performance will be no more motivated to perform effectively than one who expects to be criticized regardless of his level of performance. Both praise and criticism would be expected to be effective sources of task motivation only if their attainment is believed by workers to be contingent on their level of performance of the task.

By the same token, unconditional consideration on the part of the supervisor may be less effective in motivating subordinates than consideration, which is dependent on the effectiveness of the subordinate. To be of maximal value in motivating subordinates to perform effectively, consideration or supportiveness must be a response to effort and accomplishment rather than an indiscriminate supervisory style. If we are seeking to understand the effects of the supervisor's behavior on the motivation of subordinates to carry out their jobs effectively, it would seem to be important to conceptualize it in terms of his responses to effective and ineffective performance on the part of his subordinates rather than in more general or "average" terms. It is necessary to "capture" the differences between supervisors who reward effective performance and do not reward ineffective performance, those who punish ineffective performance but do not punish effective performance, those who reward or punish both effective and ineffective performance, and those who are inconsistent in their application of both rewards and punishments.

Although existing research on supervision and productivity has primarily been concerned with effects of the frequency with which supervisors reward or punish subordinates rather than the conditions under which they do so, it has sometimes been proposed that rewarding subordinates for effective performance and withholding rewards—and even punishing subordinates—for ineffective performance is a necessary component of effective leadership. For example, McGregor (1944) states

> Given a clear knowledge of what is expected of him, the subordinate requires in addition the definite assurance that he will have the unqualified support of his superiors so long as his actions are consistent with those policies and are taken within the limits of his responsibility. Only then can he have the security and confidence that will enable him to do his job well. At the same time the subordinate must know that failure to live up to his responsibilities, or to observe the rules which are established, will result in punishment (p. 151).

In support of this view, Kahn (1958) reported that differences in productivity among work groups in a tractor factory were related to the extent to which their supervisors developed the belief in subordinates that productivity would lead to supervisory approval.

> . . . there are a few findings which suggest that supervisors who have actually achieved high levels of productivity have done so in part by making such behavior on the part of the employee a path to supervisory approval and a condition for the exertion of supervisory influence. For example, among employees in a tractor factory, those in the high producing groups were more likely to say that their foreman considered high productivity one of the most important things on the job. Employees in low producing groups more often said that other things were equally or more important to their foreman. The implication of such a

finding is that the high-producing supervisor not only
wants to attain high productivity but has successfully
communicated to his employees that at least one of the
paths to supervisory approval is to produce at a high
rate (p. 69).

There is some evidence (Fleishman, 1953; Mann and Hoffman, 1960) that supervisory styles tend to be similar between adjacent hierarchical levels within an organization. Although there are
a number of plausible explanations for this state of affairs, Bowers
has suggested that it is brought about by a tendency of supervisors
to pattern their behavior after that of their superior in order to
attain his recognition and approval. A recent study in a manufacturing organization (Bowers, 1963) lends some support to this
explanation.

Fiedler's research (1958) on leadership and group performance suggests that group performance is dependent on the kinds
of behaviors that are rewarded and punished by the leader rather
than on the frequency of his rewards and punishments. He measured a leader variable that he calls Assumed Similarity Between
Opposites (ASO). A person obtained a high ASO score if his descriptions of the personalities of his most and least preferred co-
workers were highly similar. Fiedler assumes that such a person
"feels the need for the approval and support of his associates"
(p. 22). A person obtained a low ASO score if his descriptions of his
most and least preferred co-workers were very different. He is assumed by Fiedler to be "relatively independent of others, less concerned with their feelings and willing to reject a person when he
cannot accomplish an assigned task" (p. 22).

Fiedler correlated the ASO scores of leaders with measures of
the effectiveness of their groups in a wide range of situations, including high school basketball teams, surveying parties, B-29 crews,
tank crews, open-hearth steel shops, and farm cooperatives. Generally, he found a negative correlation between ASO scores and group
effectiveness. In other words, leaders whose descriptions of most and
least preferred co-workers were similar usually had less effective
groups than those whose descriptions were different. However,
Fiedler did not find this negative correlation among groups that did

not accept their leader. He explained this by suggesting that acceptance of the leader by his men is a necessary condition for the
leader's characteristics to affect their behavior. If the subordinates
do not accept their leader, then they are relatively indifferent to his
acceptance or rejection of them.

Fiedler's interpretation of his results seems at variance with
the conclusions of Likert and others associated with the human relations movement. The real significance of this difference is difficult
to determine without knowing more about the behavioral correlates
of ASO scores in actual leadership situations. How do leaders with
high and low ASO scores differ in their treatment of subordinates?
Fiedler's inference that the latter are more likely to base rewards and
punishments on the subordinate's level of performance is consistent
with evidence concerning the usefulness of rewards and punishments
in controlling behavior, but such an inference cannot be completely
accepted without empirical verification.

Let us now attempt to sum up the evidence regarding the
effects of supervisory consideration on performance. We noted eight
situations in which there was a positive relationship between measures of consideration and performance, two in which there was a
negative relationship, and one in which there was essentially no
relationship. Although these findings may be construed as support
by the advocates of better human relations in industry, the two negative correlations and typically small positive correlations hardly
represent a solid foundation for a general approach to management.

We are inclined to regard the negative correlations, in the
production division studied by Fleishman and the combat bomber
crews studied by Halpin and Winer, as evidence that the effects of
consideration on performance depend on situational requirements.
However, it is inappropriate to conclude that consideration has *any*
effect on performance without experimental evidence. Correlations
between supervisory consideration and performance may result
from the fact that consideration results in effective performance,
that effective performance results in consideration, or that both are
affected by some third variable. Attempts to determine the effects of
consideration on performance by the use of experimental methods
are hampered by the difficulty of changing supervisory behavior
and by the lack of specificity in the concept of consideration itself.

There is nothing in the conceptual model outlined in Chapter Two that would lead us to predict any necessary effect of consideration on performance. We would expect the effects of any reward on behavior to be dependent on the conditions under which the reward is given. Rewards given unconditionally, that is, rewards that are not contingent or are not expected to be contingent on the choices made by individuals, should have no effect on the choices they make. In contrast, either rewards or punishments that are contingent on behavior should have a very marked effect, decreasing the probability of those choices that lead to punishment and increasing the probability of those that lead to reward. On the assumption that considerate behavior on the part of a supervisor is rewarding behavior, we would predict that it would be effective in motivating subordinates to the extent to which it is a response by the supervisor to effective performance on the part of his subordinates and not an invariant supervisory style. The effects of this "conditional consideration" have not been adequately investigated. There are isolated findings that are consistent with this position, but they cannot be taken as conclusive evidence.

Influence in Decision Making. Contemporary writers on human relations in industry have often asserted that supervisory methods that permit subordinates to influence decisions that have effects on them result in more effective performance than methods that deny them this influence. Participation in decision making by subordinates is assumed to result not only in greater job satisfaction but also in higher productivity (Scott, 1962; Davis, 1962). Let us consider the evidence bearing on this belief in the efficacy of participation and discuss some of the mechanisms by which it may affect individual and group performance.

There are a large number of concepts that have been used to refer to the amount of influence exerted by subordinates upon the decision-making process of a work group or organization. Some of these concepts are defined in terms of specific methods of supervision or leadership, for example, democratic, autocratic, and laissez-faire (Lewin, Lippitt, and White, 1939), group decision (Maier, 1952), and consultative supervision (Carey, 1942). Other concepts are descriptive properties of entire organizations, for example, locus of organizational control (Morse and Reimer, 1956) and degree of centralization (Marschak, 1959; McNulty, 1962). Still other concepts are defined in terms of the amount of influence that a particular person has had in a single joint decision, for example, participation in decision making (French, Israel, and Ås, 1960; Vroom, 1959a, 1960a).

One of the earliest investigations into the effects of participation in decision making was an experiment on the behavior of eleven-year-old boys under democratic, autocratic, and laissez-faire leadership (Lewin, Lippitt, and White, 1939; White and Lippitt, 1960). Twenty boys were organized into four clubs that met after school. Each club received at least six weeks of autocratic and six weeks of democratic leadership, and two of the clubs also received a six-week period of laissez-faire leadership. The results show that the laissez-faire leaders had the poorest productivity record. The highest level of productivity occurred under autocratic leadership, although the boys tended to stop working when the autocratic leader left the room. Under democratic leadership, productivity was also high and was maintained at a similar level regardless of the presence of the leader in the room.

An experiment by Coch and French (1948) in the Harwood manufacturing plant suggests the value of democratic methods in the introduction of change. The nature of the product in this plant required continual changes in work methods and they were generally resisted by workers, many of whom preferred to quit rather than make the changes. Four groups of workers about to undergo a change in work methods were used in the experiment. These groups were roughly equivalent with respect to their efficiency before the change, the amount of change required, and their amount of "we-feeling." In one of the four groups, the control group, the change was introduced in the usual manner. The jobs were modified by the production department, new rates were set, and a meeting was held with workers in which they were told of the change. The other three groups, designated as experimental groups, were given an opportunity to participate in making decisions concerning some aspects of the change. In one of these experimental groups, workers were given a chance to influence the change only through their elected representatives. They were told of the plan to introduce the change and selected two of their members to assist in working out the details. The elected representatives contributed many useful suggestions and shared in establishing the new methods and rates. In the other two experimental groups, each operator had a chance to participate directly in making decisions regarding the change.

An analysis of the productivity of the four groups on the new job revealed marked differences. The productivity of the control group dropped substantially following introduction of the change and did not improve appreciably with time. Resistance developed and there were numerous instances of aggression toward management. Seventeen percent of this group quit during the first thirty-two days following the change, at which time the group was broken up. The productivity of the first experimental group, who participated through their representatives, also dropped when they were placed on the new job but rapidly increased as the workers acquired experience. None of its members resigned during the first forty days following the change, and after fourteen days they regained their previous mean production level. The most favorable results were achieved in the two experimental groups whose members each had the opportunity to participate in making decisions regarding the change. These groups recovered their prechange level of production after four days and continued to improve until they reached a level of performance that was 14 percent above that which they had attained before the change.

In another experiment in the Harwood plant, Bavelas (reported in French, 1950) showed that productivity could be increased by worker participation in the setting of production goals. Groups of women sewing machine operators, ranging in size from four to twelve workers, met with the experimenter in the management conference room. In these meetings the experimenter asked the group if they would like to set a group goal for higher production. In most cases the group agreed and then proceeded to make group decisions concerning the level of production that they hoped to reach and the length of time in which they would try to reach it. The experimenter then arranged for further meetings with the group in which he provided them with graphs showing changes in group productivity. Each experimental group was matched with a control group for type of job, social setting, and supervision. An analysis of the changes in productivity for experimental and control groups showed striking differences. In the control groups the level of production remained relatively constant over the four-month period of observation. In contrast, in the experimental groups, there was an average increase in production of 18 percent following the goal setting that was maintained for over two months.

Lawrence and Smith (1955) carried out an experiment to determine whether work groups making a decision concerning production goals attained higher productivity than those that just took part in group discussions. Two groups participated in weekly meetings for the purpose of setting production goals and, in addition, discussed a wide range of employee and company matters. Two other groups participated in group discussions without making decisions concerning production. The groups setting production goals showed a significantly greater increase in production than those not setting goals.

Strauss (in Whyte, 1955) described an experiment dealing with the effects of increasing workers' influence over their work pace. The experiment was carried out in the paint room of a toy factory. The painting operation had recently been reengineered so that the girls' pace of work was controlled by a moving belt. This change had resulted in a marked increase in absenteeism and turnover. Even though the girls were being paid on a bonus plan, production was low and they made frequent complaints concerning the speed of the belt. In an attempt to deal with these problems, the foreman, on the advice of a consultant, decided to give the girls an opportunity to decide how fast the belt should operate. The group leader was provided with a control by which she could set the belt speed. The girls usually spent their lunch hours deciding how the speed should be varied from hour to hour. Production increased markedly following the introduction of this system, but the increase was so great that it created serious difficulties in relations with other parts of the plant. The girls' earnings on the bonus were so high that serious inequities were created with those received elsewhere in the plant. Furthermore, the extra production on the operation performed by the girls resulted in a pile-up of work on subsequent operations and a "vacuum" behind. As a result of these difficulties, control over the belt speed was taken away from the girls. Production dropped again and within a month all but two of the eight girls had quit.

Each of the investigations described has dealt with the effects of involving a group of subordinates in making decisions that are not part of their defined responsibilities. There is further evidence concerning the consequences of the amount of autonomy or freedom provided individual subordinates during the execution of their regular duties. In a field study in an insurance company, Katz, Maccoby, and Morse (1950) found that supervisors in charge of low productivity sections were more likely to supervise closely than were those in charge of high productivity sections. The low productivity supervisors more frequently "checked up" on their subordinates, gave them detailed and frequent instructions, and generally limited their freedom to do the work in their own way.

A subsequent study of maintenance-of-way workers in a railroad failed to replicate this finding (Katz, Maccoby, Gurin, and Floor, 1951). There was little difference between high and low productivity supervisors in the extent to which they attempted to exercise close control over their subordinates. The authors suggest that the difference in results in the railroad and insurance company may be the result of a difference in the nature of the two situations.

> In the insurance company, work methods are sufficiently standardized so that employees get little help of a technical nature out of close, detailed supervision. Such supervision may, instead, be a threat and an annoyance to them. Among the railroad section gangs, on the other hand, there is less routinization of working procedure and more opportunity for individual attention from the foreman. Sections are small enough to permit the foreman to give each man the benefit of his superior technical knowledge and to contribute to the effective performance of his men in this way. However, there is no positive relationship between productivity and close supervision in the railroad study and it is likely that the foreman's technical contribution is not sufficient to outweigh possible detrimental effects of close supervision on worker motivation (pp. 33-34).

A large-scale field experiment was carried out by Morse and Reimer (1956) in an attempt to determine whether changes in the amount of influence of rank and file employees in a wide range of decisions would result in changes in productivity. The experimental design is summarized by the authors as follows:

> Using four parallel divisions of the clerical operations of an organization, two programs of changes were introduced. One program, the Autonomy program involving two of the divisions, was designed to increase the role of rank-and-file employees in the decision-making process of the organization. The other two divisions received a program designed to increase the role of upper management in the decision-making processes (the Hierarchically controlled program) (p. 129).

While the satisfaction of employees increased in the autonomy program and decreased in the hierarchical program, productivity was significantly increased under both programs, with the hierarchically controlled program resulting in the greater increase. In accounting for the superior productivity achieved under the hierarchically controlled program, Likert (1961) emphasized that the experiment was terminated at the end of one year, at which time this program was "in a state of unstable equilibrium." He stated

> The results . . . give every reason to believe that had the clerical experiment been continued for another year or two, productivity and quality of work would have continued to increase in the participative program, while in the hierarchically controlled program productivity and quality of work would have declined as a result of the hostility, resentment, and turnover evoked by the program (p. 69).

Vroom (1959a, 1960a) carried out a study that suggests that there are important individual differences in the effects of participation in decision making on performance. He studied 108 supervisors in a parcel delivery company. Responses to a series of questions were obtained from each supervisor concerning the amount of his influence in decision making. These responses were combined to yield a measure that was called "amount of psychological participation." Supervisors' scores on this measure were found to correlate significantly with a number of different measures of their job performance. However, the size of these correlations varied systematically with the supervisors' needs for independence and authoritarianism. Amount of psychological participation was most highly related to the level of performance of those supervisors who were high in need for independence and low in authoritarianism. It was unrelated to the level of performance of those who were low in need for independence and high in authoritarianism.

It has often been suggested that the effects of participation in decision making are highly variable from culture to culture. Thus Young (1944) commented on the experiment by Lewin, Lippitt, and White, described above, as follows:

> The same results might not follow from similar experimental work among children with a rigid class system and a different cultural setting of dominance. Children in Nazi Germany or in Japan, for instance, might do very well under a dictatorial regime and rather poorly under a democratic one (pp. 245–246).

In the same vein, Krech and Crutchfield (1948) state

> All the experimental evidence to be reported has been obtained by the study of so-called "authoritarian" and "democratic" leadership situations *in our democratic culture.* It is entirely possible that similar studies in other cultures might yield different results (p. 423).

Since these observations were made, a number of investigations of the effects of democratic leadership methods in other countries have been carried out. French, Israel, and Ås (1960) have studied participation in decision making in Norway; Maier and Hoffman (1962) have attempted to replicate some of their findings concerning the effects of group decision in England; and Misumi (1959) has conducted a series of experiments on the effects of democratic leadership and group decision on group productivity in Japan. While "identical" experiments are not always possible in different cultures, none of these investigators found much evidence for cultural differences. Misumi's findings—that democratic leadership resulted in superior productivity than either autocratic or laissez-faire leadership and that group decision was a more effective method for achieving behavioral change than the lecture—are probably of most interest because, even today, the Japanese culture is less similar to that of the United States than is either England's or Norway's.

When the entire pattern of results is considered, we find substantial basis for the belief that participation in decision making increases productivity. There is experimental and correlational evidence indicating that higher levels of influence by workers in making decisions that they are to carry out result in higher productivity than lower levels of influence. It should be noted, however, that not all the findings are consistent with this generalization. The results of both Lewin, Lippitt, and White (1939) and Morse and Reimer (1956) suggest that, under some conditions, higher productivity may be achieved with the use of more autocratic methods.

Perhaps our understanding of the reasons for these differences may be increased by examining the possible ways in which the amount of influence of subordinates in decision making may affect their subsequent performance. There appear to be at least two major ways. The degree of influence of subordinates in decision making may affect the "quality" of the decision reached and it may affect the speed and efficiency with which the decision is carried out. Let us consider each of these in more detail.

Subordinate Influence and Decision Quality. The nature of the decisions reached in a work group may have considerable effect on the subsequent productivity of the group. This is particularly true where the decision concerns such "key" matters as equipment, staffing, and work methods. Some decisions may be found later to be of high quality, because their implementation increases productivity, while others may be found to be of low quality, because their implementation decreases productivity.

It is clear that the amount of influence afforded subordinates in the decision-making process can have important effects on the nature of the decisions reached. A supervisor who attempts to solve a problem without consulting his subordinates may adopt a very different course of action than his subordinates would if they were permitted to make the decision. This raises the possibility that the relative effectiveness of democratic and autocratic methods of supervision may be due to a tendency for these methods to generate decisions that differ in their quality.

The most intensive exploration of the effects of supervisory methods on decision quality has been carried out by Maier and his associates (Maier, 1952, 1955; Maier and Hayes, 1962; Maier, 1963). Their results cast some doubt on the belief of many managers that releasing control of the decision-making function impairs decision quality. In a series of laboratory experiments they have found that leaders trained in the group decision method achieve higher quality decisions than those who are untrained or who have had less training (Maier, 1950, 1953; Maier and Hoffman, 1960).

It cannot be concluded that higher "decision quality" is a necessary consequence of the introduction of democratic methods. There may be situations in which organizational objectives and the desires of a particular group of its members are in conflict. The highest "quality" decision from an organizational standpoint might be to eliminate the jobs or reduce the pay of its members. It is difficult in such a situation to see how increasing the amount of influence that these individuals have on the decision would result in greater "decision quality."

Such a situation is represented in the field experiment by Morse and Reimer (1956) described earlier. These experimenters attributed the increased productivity in the hierarchically controlled divisions to an administrative decision to cut staff by 25 percent. Since there was, at any one time, a fixed volume of work to be done, a reduction in staff was the most effective method of increasing productivity and this decision was, from a productivity standpoint, of very high "quality." Understandably, there was greater reluctance to reduce staff in the divisions in which rank and file workers were given greater influence in decision making. To be sure, some reduction in staff was effected, but this resulted when the workers did not feel the need for replacing persons who left and/or were willing to try to find other jobs for some of their members whose jobs were redundant.

Differences in the quality of decisions reached democratically and autocratically are probably dependent on a large number of factors, including the extent to which supervisors and subordinates have information relevant to judging the organizational consequences of different courses of action and the extent to which the interests of each are in harmony with organizational objectives. It is extremely unlikely that democratic decisions are always higher in quality than autocratic ones or vice versa. We need further research on the conditions under which each of these effects occurs.

Subordinate Influence and the Execution of Decisions. The productivity of a work group is affected not only by the quality of the decisions reached but also by the speed and efficiency with which they are carried out. A high quality decision that is opposed by those expected to carry it out may result in lower productivity than a lower quality decision that is enthusiastically endorsed. Although the specific contribution of each of these variables is difficult to ascertain in most investigations, it is clear that the effects of participation in decision making are not confined to the nature of the decision but extend to the probability that the decision will be effectively implemented.

Why should persons be more likely to carry out decisions that they have helped to make than those over which they have had no influence? One possibility is that the use of democratic leadership methods results in the formation of group norms that are favorable to the successful execution of the decision. If a decision has been jointly made by members of a work group, they may exert pressure on one another to carry it out effectively. Successful execution of the group decision by any worker then becomes instrumental to his acceptance by other group members. Coch and French (1948) stressed the importance of changes in group norms in accounting for the superior productivity of groups who participated in making decisions concerning changes in work procedure; and Lewin (1947) attributed the superiority of group decision over lectures in changing behavior largely to the fact that the former changed group norms. This interpretation is consistent with Bennett's finding (1955) that the amount of consensus in the group affects the probability that group members will execute the decision.

It is also possible that people become "ego involved" in decisions in which they have had influence. If they have helped to make a decision it is "their decision," and the success or failure of the decision is their success or failure. Intuitively one would assume that the amount of personal involvement of people in decisions is dependent on the amount of influence they have had in the decision and on the extent to which they pride themselves on their ability to make that kind of decision. If, for example, a person who conceives himself to be a brilliant scientist shares in the making of a decision that he believes requires scientific judgment, the outcome of that decision is a test of the adequacy of his self-conception. A successful decision confirms his self-concept; an unsuccessful decision threatens it. In contrast, when he helps to make a decision on an administrative matter he has less "at stake." Neither a successful nor an unsuccessful decision would be greatly inconsistent with his self-concept.

Vroom's field study (1959a, 1960a) and a subsequent experiment by Bachman (1962) are among the few investigations of the motivational effects of individual influence in decision making. Both found a relationship between the performance of a single worker and the extent to which he perceives that he has influenced decisions which he is later expected to carry out. Vroom's finding that the relationship between amount of participation and level of performance is affected by the strength of the worker's need for independence and the degree of his authoritarianism is also consistent with an explanation emphasizing ego involvement rather than group norms.

In summary, it would appear that there are a number of different ways in which greater influence in decision making by subordinates can increase performance. It can increase the quality of decisions made, the strength of group norms regarding execution of the decisions, and the worker's "ego involvement" in the decisions. Each of these three effects seems to be a frequent—but probably not a necessary—consequence of increased influence in decision making by subordinates. It seems important for future research to proceed beyond the demonstration that "participation works" to determine the conditions under which it "works most" and "works least." The usefulness of participation both as a managerial method and as a social psychological concept can be greatly enhanced by further knowledge concerning the conditions under which the effects of participation on decision quality, group norms, and ego involvement are maximized and minimized.

The Work Group

Social psychologists have conducted a great deal of research on the determinants of group effectiveness. Experiments have been carried out in an attempt to ascertain the effects on group effectiveness of such variables as the homogeneity or compatibility of member personalities (Hoffman, 1959; Schutz, 1955, 1958; Cattell, Saunders, and Stice, 1953), the amount of cohesiveness or friendship existing among group members (Van Zelst, 1952; Schachter, Ellertson, McBride, and Gregory, 1951; Berkowitz, 1954), the size of the group (Marriott, 1949; Gibb, 1951), the degree of cooperation or competition among group members (Deutsch, 1949; Jones and Vroom, 1964), and the communication structure in the group (Bavelas, 1950; Leavitt, 1951; Shaw, 1954; Mulder, 1960).

The problem with which we are concerned is much more restricted. We are interested in the performance of individuals rather than of groups and are focusing primarily on those determinants of individual performance which are motivational in nature. Accordingly, we seek to determine the influence of the work group on the motivation of its members to perform their jobs effectively.

Social Facilitation. Allport (1920) carried out an early series of experiments illustrating the effects of co-workers on individual performance. His subjects were upper classmen and graduate students at Harvard and Radcliffe. They performed the same tasks under an "alone" condition, in which they worked in separate rooms, and under a "together" condition, in which they worked in a group seated about a common table. The results indicated that the presence of co-workers increased the speed of work, leading Allport to introduce the term "social facilitation." He found that the amount of social facilitation (that is, the degree of superiority of performance in the together condition to performance in the alone condition) was greater on more mechanical and motor tasks than it was on the more highly mental tasks. Further evidence for the facilitating effects of co-workers was obtained in an experiment in a factory carried out by Lorenz (described in Dashiell, 1935) and in laboratory experiments by Weston and English (1926), Anderson (1928), and by Abel (1938). The latter two investigations also demonstrate that the difference between performance in the "alone" and "together" conditions is a function of the intelligence of the subject.

The psychological basis for "social facilitation" is not completely clear. Possibly the presence of co-workers stimulated a competitive spirit among workers. Subjects in the "together" condition may have desired to work faster in order to outperform their co-workers. While Allport specifically told his subjects that their results would not be compared, he admits the possibility that his findings reflect the influence of competition. Subsequent research supporting this interpretation has demonstrated that experimental situations designed specifically to generate competition among co-workers performing independent tasks result in higher levels of performance than those designed to minimize competition (Hurlock, 1927; Maller, 1929; Moede, reported in Dashiell, 1935; and Wickens, 1942).[1]

Group Norms Regarding Performance. Interest in the role of the work group in performance was stimulated by the widely publicized investigations conducted in the Hawthorne plant of the Western Electric Company (Roethlisberger and Dickson, 1939). In the experiments conducted in the Relay Assembly Room, the investigators found that production continued to increase in a way that was independent of the experimental changes being made in physical conditions of work. In their search for an explanation for this finding, they turned to the informal relations among the workers. The high level of productivity was attributed to a unique kind of informal organization that developed in the group. In contrast, in the

[1]It should be noted that competitive relationships among those working on a *group task* result in less effective performance than cooperative relationships (Deutsch, 1949; Jones and Vroom, 1964).

Bank Wiring studies in the same company, the investigators found widespread reduction of output, a finding that was also attributed to the informal organization. Roethlisberger and Dickson commented on this difference as follows:

> In the case of the Relay Assembly Test Room there was a group, or informal organization, which could be characterized as a network of personal relations which had been developed in and through a particular way of working together; it was an organization which not only satisfied the wishes of its members but also worked in harmony with the aims of management. In the case of the Bank Wiring Observation Room there was an informal organization which could be characterized better as a set of practices and beliefs which its members had in common—practices and beliefs which at many points worked against the economic purposes of the company. In one case the relation between the formal and informal organization was one of compatibility; in the other case it was one of opposition (pp. 560–561).

Apparently the informal relations among members of the same work group are a kind of "two-edged" sword that can influence performance positively or negatively. But what is the nature of these two types of patterns and how are they produced? These are the questions raised, but not answered, by the Hawthorne findings.

It is sometimes suggested that the performance of a work group is directly related to its cohesiveness. If the group is highly cohesive, that is, co-workers are strongly attracted to one another, its members will be highly motivated to carry out their jobs effectively. In contrast, if the group is uncohesive, that is, co-workers are indifferent to or dislike one another, its members will not be highly motivated to carry out their jobs effectively. There is very little support for such a proposition. R. L. French (1949) found no relationship between a sociometric index of cohesiveness and a variety of measures of performance among naval recruits; Schachter, Ellertson, McBride, and Gregory (1951) and Berkowitz (1954) found no overall difference in productivity between experimentally created groups of high and low cohesiveness; and Seashore (1954) found only a slight tendency for groups with high measured cohesiveness to be higher in productivity than those with low measured cohesiveness in a plant manufacturing heavy machinery.

The only strong evidence for a positive effect of cohesiveness on productivity comes from a field experiment carried out by Van Zelst (1952) in the building trades industry. The subjects in the experiment were two groups of carpenters and bricklayers who had been working together on a large housing project for an average of five months. The experimental manipulation consisted of a re-grouping of workers into teams of two on the basis of their socio-metric choices. Each worker was requested to nominate, in order of preference, three of his co-workers as his choice of work partner. Twenty-two workers received their first choice, twenty-eight received their second choice, and eight were isolates. As a result of the regrouping, there was a marked reduction in turnover and a decrease in both labor and material costs.

The results of an experiment of Schachter, Ellertson, McBride, and Gregory (1951) indicated that cohesiveness affects the amount of influence that a group has on its members but does not necessarily determine the direction that the influence will take. Their subjects were female students recruited from undergraduate education and psychology classes. Prior to the experiment, potential subjects were told that the study was concerned with "people who really like one another." It was asserted that it was now possible to select people who would be genuinely fond of one another on the basis of their questionnaire responses. Volunteers were given such questionnaires to fill out. When they arrived for the experiment, they were given information by one of the experimenters designed to create groups of high or low cohesiveness. Subjects in the high cohesiveness condition were told that they were members of a highly cohesive group and that there was every reason to believe that "the other members of the group will like you and you will like them." In the low cohesiveness condition they were told that scheduling difficulties had made it impossible to bring together a congenial group and that "there is no particular reason to think that you will like them or that they will care for you" (p. 232).

Each experimental group consisted of three people. They were introduced to one another and told that their job was to produce cardboard checkerboards. It was made clear that there were three jobs to be done: cutting the cardboard, mounting and pasting it on heavier stock, and painting the boards through a stencil. Each subject was taken to a separate workroom where she was given the job of cutting cardboard. She was led to believe that the other members of her group were painting and pasting. Members of the same group were allowed to communicate with one another only by written notes, which were to be delivered by a messenger.

Actually all notes were intercepted by the messenger, who substituted a prewritten set of notes that were delivered at specified times. During the first twelve minutes of the work period, all subjects received notes, ostensibly from other group members, that were not designed to influence their behavior. Starting with the sixteenth minute, each subject received notes "from her co-workers" designed to influence her either to increase her level of performance (positive induction) or to decrease her level of performance (negative induction). Examples of the positive induction notes are "Can you hurry things up a bit?" signed PAINTER (delivered after sixteen minutes), and "Time's running out, let's really make a spurt," signed PASTER (delivered after twenty-eight minutes). Comparable negative induction notes are "Let's try to set a record—the slowest subjects they ever had," signed PAINTER (delivered after sixteen minutes) and "We've done a lot of these things. Let's take it easy now," signed PASTER (delivered after twenty-eight minutes) (p. 233).

The principal dependent variable in the experiment is the difference in the number of cardboards cut before and after the beginning of the delivery of the induction notes. Table 8.1 shows the mean change in production between the 8- to 16-minute period (before the induction) and the 24- to 32-minute period (after the induction). It can be seen that the largest increase in productivity occurred for subjects in highly cohesive groups who received the positive induction. In contrast, the largest decrease in productivity occurred for subjects who were also in the highly cohesive groups but who received the negative induction. The type of induction had greater effect on the highly cohesive groups than on those low in

Table 8.1. Mean Change in Production Level
Following Induction.

Experimental Conditions	
High cohesiveness, positive induction	+5.92
Low cohesiveness, positive induction	+5.09
High cohesiveness, negative induction	-2.16
Low cohesiveness, negative induction	- .42

Source: After Schachter, Ellertson, McBride, and Gregory, 1951, p. 234.

cohesiveness. The difference between the level of production of groups high and low in cohesiveness was statistically significant under the negative induction but was not significant under the positive induction.

Berkowitz (1954) carried out an experiment to determine whether the group influences on level of production obtained in the above experiment would persist after communications between group members had ceased. Using male students recruited from ROTC, government, and economics classes, he replicated the experiment by Schachter, Ellertson, McBride, and Gregory with a longer work period to explore the persistence of the group influences on performance. The task was to make ash trays on an assembly line basis. The first 12 minutes of the work period were used to determine the base level of production; the 12- to 24-minute period was used to communicate high and low production standards through passing of notes; and the 24- to 32 and 32- to 40-minute periods were used to determine performance after communication had ceased. Table 8.2 shows the mean changes from the baseline period to the standard-setting and poststandard-setting periods.

Again, the largest increase in productivity was obtained for subjects in highly cohesive work groups who received the positive induction, while the smallest increase was obtained for subjects in highly cohesive groups who received the negative induction. Attempts to influence subjects to increase and decrease their production were significantly more effective when they were believed to be coming from co-workers in highly cohesive groups than when they were believed to be coming from co-workers in groups that were low

Table 8.2. Mean Change in Production Level Following Induction.

Experimental Conditions	0'-12' to 12'-24'	0'-12' to 24'-32'	0'-12' to 32'-40'
High cohesiveness, positive induction	+2.21	+3.39	+4.67
Low cohesiveness, positive induction	+ .49	+1.62	+2.06
High cohesiveness, negative induction	−1.09	+ .55	+ .61
Low cohesiveness, negative induction	− .06	+2.12	+2.31

Source: After Berkowitz, 1954, p. 515.

in cohesiveness. These findings are essentially in agreement with those reported in Table 8.1 and demonstrate further that the social effects studied persist after communication among group members has ceased.

In a large-scale field study in a factory manufacturing heavy machinery, Seashore (1954) obtained results that are consistent with those obtained in these two laboratory experiments. He measured the cohesiveness of 228 work groups by averaging the responses of group members to a series of questions about the satisfactions that they obtained from being a part of their group. He also obtained, from company records, measures of individual productivity for a three-month period. Seashore found significantly less within-group variance in the productivity of members of groups high in cohesiveness than in those groups that were low in cohesiveness. In other words, workers in highly cohesive groups were more likely to produce at the same level as their co-workers than were workers in groups low in cohesiveness. He attributed this result to the greater power of highly cohesive groups to induce conformity to group standards regarding productivity.

Seashore also found significant differences in the amount of between-group variance in productivity for high and low cohesiveness work groups. Highly cohesive work groups differed from one another in their mean productivity level to a greater extent than those low in cohesiveness. They were more frequently at the extremes of productivity, either very high or very low. Although there was no measure of the extent to which group members attempted to influence one another either to produce at a high or a low level,

Seashore did have data on the extent to which group members felt supported by the organization of which the group was a part. On the assumption that this variable might reflect the nature of group norms regarding productivity, he correlated these measures of "support" with mean productivity for both high and low cohesiveness groups. He found that these measures were positively correlated with the productivity of highly cohesive groups but slightly negatively correlated with the productivity of groups low in cohesiveness. If we accept the assumption that the "support" measures reflect group norms with respect to productivity, these data appear highly consistent with the results of Schachter, Ellertson, McBride, and Gregory, (1951) and Berkowitz (1954). The results of all three investigations suggest that groups high in cohesiveness can exert greater influence over the behavior of their members than those that are low in cohesiveness. The direction that this influence will take cannot be inferred from the degree of cohesiveness of the group but requires a knowledge of the group norms or standards regarding productivity. Cohesiveness in the informal work group may have either positive or negative consequences on the level of performance of individual group members, depending on the nature of the norms or standards with respect to performance adopted in the group.

Let us relate these findings to our model. If it is assumed that the strength of a person's desire to be accepted by other group members is directly related to the extent of his attraction to the group, it follows that the strength of the force that the group can exert over its members would be greater in highly cohesive groups than in groups with low cohesiveness. If we wish to predict the direction of the force it is necessary to know the behaviors that will receive approval from other group members and the behaviors that will receive disapproval. The valence of effective performance should be positive where the worker strongly desires acceptance by his co-workers and anticipates that he will receive this acceptance only if he performs effectively, that is, effective performance is instrumental to acceptance. In contrast, the valence of effective performance should be negative where he strongly desires to be accepted by his co-workers and expects that he will be accepted only if he performs ineffectively, that is, effective performance is negatively instrumental to acceptance. Changes in an individual's conception of the level of performance acceptable to his co-workers should have little effect on the valence of effective performance where he is indifferent to his acceptance or rejection by them. Similarly, changes in attraction to the group should have little effect on the valence of effective performance where the person believes that his co-workers are indifferent to his level of performance.

Job Content

Although it has long been recognized that the content of the job or task to which a worker is assigned has considerable bearing on the strength of his motivation to perform it effectively, psychologists have given little attention to the motivational consequences of job or task variables. There seem to be at least two principal reasons for this neglect. The first of these is a characteristic assumption that such consequences have little administrative significance. Job content is assumed to be dictated by the requirements of the production process and cannot be altered without incurring substantial inefficiency. We can consider the motivational consequences of the design of wage and salary systems and the social and physical environment of the work situation, but the job content is fixed by technology.

The second reason for the neglect of the consequences of job content for the worker's motivation for effective performance is the difficulty in carrying out research on the problem. If we assume that the strength of a person's motivation to perform a task or job effectively can be observed only insofar as it is reflected in his actual level of performance in that task or job, then the motivational effects of task variables become very difficult to determine. There are no reliable or objective methods by which we can compare the level of performance of individuals doing different tasks. Objective criteria of performance are task specific, that is, they permit comparisons among people carrying out the same task but not among people carrying out different tasks. Thus, we can usually ascertain whether one typesetter is performing at a higher level than another, but we cannot say whether a typesetter is performing at a higher level than a musician.

To be sure, it is sometimes possible to determine whether a particular change in a job increases the efficiency with which an operation is performed. However, there is no way of isolating the role of motivation. There are many ways in which jobs can be changed that will greatly affect efficiency but have no necessary effect on the workers' preferences. For example, task stimuli that require different responses may be made more discriminable, controls may be made easier to operate, and the responses that workers must make to task stimuli may be made more compatible with their previous training.

There is no easy solution to this problem. Although it seems likely that the content of the task affects the strength of the worker's desire to perform it effectively, there is no way of inferring conclusively the nature of these effects from observations of performance on different tasks.

Specialization. Specialization has been a major guiding principle in the design of jobs for optimal productivity. In 1776, Adam Smith noted the causal relationship between specialization and productivity in his statement that "the division of labor, however, so far as it can be introduced, occasions, in every act, a proportionable increase of the productive powers of labor" (p. 7). Application of this principle has resulted in a substantial increase in the repetitiveness of jobs and a decrease in the number of different operations that a worker performs. There is little doubt that specialization has also resulted in an increase in industrial productivity and in the standard of living of countries in which it has been introduced.

The bases for the functional relationship between productivity and amount of specialization are fairly clear. Different operations require somewhat different abilities and skills for their successful performance. Specialization enables organizations to select and place workers in jobs that are most conducive to their particular skills and to train workers in just those skills required for the functions they are to perform. Furthermore, different operations frequently have to be performed in different locations. Specialization decreases the amount of time required for the worker to move from one location to another and consequently increases the amount of time that can be devoted to productive effort.

Some social scientists have argued that industry has gone too far in introducing specialization. They assert that the increased repetitiveness of jobs has not only resulted in greater dissatisfaction and turnover[2] but has also reduced the motivation of workers to perform their jobs effectively. Supporting this assertion is evidence that frequent rotation of workers from one job to another has resulted in greater productivity (Vernon and Wyatt, 1924; Wyatt and Fraser, 1928) and that increases in the number of operations performed by workers has resulted in greater productivity (Walker, 1950, 1954; Elliott, 1953; Guest, 1957; Marks, reported in Davis, 1957). Such findings are usually attributed to greater motivation on the part of workers to carry out their jobs effectively. Workers given highly simplified jobs to perform (consisting of a very small number of operations) are assumed to be less motivated to perform effectively than workers given jobs that require a larger number of operations.

There is little doubt that increased specialization may increase—as well as decrease—productivity. The pressing administrative problem is to achieve an understanding of the conditions under which each of these results will be obtained. To say that "too much specialization" will lower productivity really circumvents the major question. How much is too much? The complexity of the problem belies such a simple approach to its solution. Not one but many variables affect the productive consequences of a given increase in specialization. A workable administrative strategy requires that these variables be delimited and the nature of their effects be more clearly understood than they are at present.

Knowledge of Results. Tasks may be designed to provide the worker with different amounts of information concerning his performance. The terms "knowledge of results" and "feedback" have frequently been used to refer to this aspect of job content.

Knowledge of results may take many different forms. The worker may be told that he is "right" or "wrong" following the performance of correct or incorrect responses (Thorndike, 1927); he may observe the effectiveness of his performance through specially

[2]See Chapter Five for evidence bearing on this issue.

constructed dials or instruments (Bingham, 1932; Payne and Hauty, 1955); he may hear clicks through earphones when he is not performing effectively (Smode, 1958); or he may be provided with charts showing daily or weekly changes in his performance. The common element in all methods of providing knowledge of results is the presence of discriminable stimulus correlates of level of performance. It can easily be seen that all task situations provide some knowledge of results. At the very least there are discriminable proprioceptive cues associated with different motor responses, and in most tasks the worker's behavior produces changes in visual or auditory stimulus fields. Consequently, it is appropriate to speak of different amounts and kinds of knowledge of results rather than its presence or absence.

There is a wealth of evidence that the level of performance of workers can be increased by enhanced knowledge of results.[3] In the following discussion we will attempt to make a case for the idea that knowledge of the results of one's actions serves at least three different functions in a task situation. Increases in the amount of knowledge of results received by a person performing a task or job may (1) increase the probability of arousal of correct expectancies concerning the consequences of actions for successful task performance, (2) increase the strength of correct and decrease the strength of incorrect expectancies concerning the consequences of actions for successful performance, and (3) increase the valence of successful performance. We will refer to these as the cue function, the learning function, and the motivational function of knowledge of results and will discuss them separately.

The Cue Function. In performing many operations the worker can observe his relative success or failure before the operation is completed. He is, therefore, enabled to alter his responses, thus increasing his chances of being successful. For example, if we ask a person to draw a line three inches long, he normally receives visual cues concerning the length of line that he has drawn before his work is completed. These cues permit him to modify the length

---

[3]See Ammons (1956) and Bilodeau and Bilodeau (1961) for reviews of the literature on this question.

of his line to approximate more closely his judgment of the desired length. If we artificially prevent the person from observing the length of line that he has drawn, his performance on this task will be hindered (MacPherson, Dees, and Grindley, 1948).

The extent of workers' dependence on cues received during the performance of a task, even one that they have carried out many times, can be illustrated by the difficulty that a person would experience in driving an automobile home from work blindfolded, or in the difficulty that Beethoven experienced in attempting to conduct his compositions when partially deaf. The information that individuals receive during their performance of a task is often of critical importance in their decisions concerning the actions that they will perform. Increases in the extent to which they are provided with information of this type can usually be expected to increase their level of performance, while decreases can be expected to decrease their level of performance. Knowledge of results, which serves a cue function, has been called action feedback by Annett and Kay (1957) who predict sudden increases in performance with greater action feedback and sudden decreases in performance with reduced action feedback.

The Learning Function. Learning to perform any task involves a great deal of trial and error. A worker makes some responses that turn out to be successful and others that turn out to be unsuccessful. If success on the task is rewarding and failure punishing, a gradual increase in his level of performance throughout the learning period would be predicted. However, if the worker is prevented from observing the success or failure of his responses, learning is impaired and little or no improvement in performance will occur. Thus, the knowledge of results that the worker receives will greatly affect the rate at which he learns to perform the task.

The importance of knowledge of results or feedback in learning is widely recognized in training (McGehee and Thayer, 1961). Many training programs are set up in such a way that they maximize the amount and immediacy of the feedback the trainee receives. The training activities for which increased feedback has proven useful include such diverse tasks as management development (Mann, 1957; Argyris, 1962) and Morse code reception (Keller, 1943).

Much of the experimental literature on the effects of knowledge of results on performance can be interpreted in terms of its consequences for skill learning. In his classic experiment on line drawing, Thorndike (1927) found that subjects showed no improvement in drawing lines of specific lengths unless they were told whether they were "right" or "wrong." Elwell and Grindley (1938) found no improvement in subjects' performance in hitting a bull's eye on a target unless they could see the point reached, and Bilodeau, Bilodeau, and Schumsky (1959) found no improvement in performance on a lever-displacing task unless subjects were told the amount and direction of their errors.

To be optimally effective in facilitating learning, knowledge of results must be provided following the performance of specific task responses or operations and must immediately *follow* that response or operation. We would expect increases in the extent to which a worker receives such knowledge of results to be of maximal benefit before he has "mastered" the task and to be accompanied by a gradual improvement in performance. In comparison, knowledge of results is valuable as a *cue* only when it occurs *during* the performance of the response or operation.

The Motivational Function. It has frequently been suggested that knowledge of results motivates workers to perform tasks or jobs effectively (Viteles, 1953; Maier, 1955). Although there is no commonly accepted basis for separating the motivational consequences of knowledge of results from those previously described, there are some findings that are not easily explicable in terms of either its cue value or the information that it provides during the learning period. In an early experiment, Arps (1920) required subjects to continue lifting a weight by flexing a finger until the finger was completely exhausted. Eleven such tests were conducted at intervals of forty-eight hours. Subjects were tested under two different conditions: a *known* condition in which they were made aware of the number of lifts during the present work period and during each of the previous work periods, and an *unknown* condition in which they were not told their results. He found that both the absolute amounts of work and the rate of work done were greater under the known than under the unknown condition. These results cannot be attributed to the cue function since the results were not given during the course of making a response. Similarly, they cannot be easily attributed to the acquisition of skill since the task was a simple one that had been overlearned by the subject. It appears as though the subjects working under the known condition were motivated by a desire to better their previous performance.

Similar results were obtained by Manzer (1935). He had sixty-eight men and sixty women college students strive to achieve maximal contractions on a Smedley hand dynamometer. Half of the subjects were instructed to squeeze the dynamometer as hard as they could on each of fifty trials given at intervals of fifteen seconds with no knowledge of results. The other half made the first ten contractions without knowledge of results, the next twenty with knowledge of results, and the remaining twenty without knowledge of results. There were no significant differences in performance between the two groups of subjects on the first ten trials when they were working under identical conditions. However, on the middle twenty trials, the group receiving knowledge of results performed significantly better than those not receiving it. This difference persisted to some degree after removal of the knowledge of results on the last twenty trials. Further evidence indicating that knowledge of results increases the performance of subjects who have overlearned the task has been obtained in experiments by Johanson (1922) and Smode (1958).

It is seldom possible to attribute increments in performance following increases in knowledge of results to one and only one of the functions that we have described. The psychological basis for improvements in performance in most experiments, particularly those in which the knowledge of results takes more than one form, is difficult to determine. The field experiment in an electric generating plant reported by Bingham (1932) is a case in point. Instruments were installed on each of twelve boilers to let the firemen stoking it know how efficiently or inefficiently it was working. In addition, graphic daily and weekly records of the performance of each boiler were posted. According to Bingham, these changes enabled the men to know, for the first time, when they were being successful in their jobs. Their previous indifference was replaced by a new pride in their work. The efficiency of the twelve boilers increased so markedly that similar instruments were installed in other boilers and later in all of the power plants. Increased profit to the company in the form of savings in the cost of coal were estimated to be $330,000 in the main plant alone.

This experiment lacked the necessary controls to permit determination of what actually caused the increase in productivity. Let us assume, along with Bingham, that knowledge of results was a major factor. The question then becomes by what psychological process did these effects occur? Did the instruments and graphic records constitute cues that elicited previously learned responses? Did they provide information to the workers that enabled them to develop a higher level of skill on their jobs? Or did they, as Bingham suggests, replace a previous indifference on the part of workers to their level of performance with a new desire to perform effectively?

There is no way of definitely answering these questions from the data reported by Bingham. It is quite possible that these two different forms of knowledge of results performed all three functions, with the instruments serving as cues and as a source of information concerning successful and unsuccessful task responses and the graphic records serving to motivate workers by enabling them to determine whether they had bettered their previous performance.

Knowledge of Results and Group Performance. One can vary the amount of information given to groups about the effectiveness of their performance in ways that are similar to those used for single persons. There has been comparatively little experimentation about the effects on performance of increases or decreases in the amount of knowledge of results that groups receive. The data that are available indicate that increased knowledge of results increases group performance, although there is less evidence concerning when and why this occurs than was true for individual performance.

Pryer and Bass (1959) found that groups receiving feedback concerning their performance made significantly more accurate group decisions concerning the relative population of cities than those not receiving it. Because the nature of the task ruled out the learning of content, the authors inferred that feedback increased group effectiveness either by enabling group members to learn how to tackle problems effectively or by stimulating group motivation or interest in the task.

Lott, Schopler, and Gibb (1955) have distinguished between two types of group feedback: feeling-oriented feedback, dealing with the personal interaction of group members, and task-oriented feedback, dealing with degree of accomplishment of the group task. They found that feeling-oriented feedback produces higher task efficiency than task-oriented feedback.

In a follow-up study, French (1958) found that the effects on performance of these two types of feedback depend on the characteristic motivation of group members. Groups composed of members with high achievement motivation performed significantly better when they received task feedback than when they received feeling feedback. In contrast, groups composed of members with high affiliation motivation performed significantly better under feeling-oriented feedback than under task-oriented feedback. The interaction between type of motivation and type of feedback was significant well beyond the .001 level.

The use of increased feedback or knowledge of results to improve organizational performance has recently been suggested as the basis for implementing a new theory of management (Likert, 1959a, 1959b, 1961). Likert outlines an approach to management development in which each work unit evaluates its own performance on the basis of periodic measurements of such variables as production, costs, waste, and of such aspects of the "interaction-influence system" as the extent of group loyalty and the adequacy of communication. According to his program each manager works with his own subordinates in setting objectives for the forthcoming period. At the end of this period the success of the group in attaining these objectives is measured, and the results studied by the manager and his subordinates, who use them in setting new objectives and plans.

Psychological Versus Actual Job Content. Throughout this section we have been discussing evidence concerning the motivational consequences of task variables based on observations of what happens to level of performance when the actual properties of tasks are changed. We have examined changes in performance when the properties of tasks or jobs are altered and have tried to isolate the role of motivation in these changes. Although it is clear that task design is an important factor in productivity, we have found it difficult to extricate the motivational consequences of changes in tasks from other variables that also influence productivity. This problem can be largely overcome by varying the psychological properties (not the actual properties) of the task for the person performing it. The person's conception of the task can be systematically varied even though the actual task remains constant.

This approach is most suited to the laboratory, where subjects can be given a task or job with which they have had little or no experience. Their conceptions of the task can be varied by means of instructions given by the experimenter, and the effects of differences in instruction on their subsequent level of performance can be observed. Although task instruction can have a number of different psychological effects, our focus will be on those intended to influence the person's motivation to perform the task effectively.

The Extent to Which the Task Requires Valued Abilities. One frequently used method of increasing the task motivation of subjects in laboratory situations is to tell them that the task is a measure of some valued ability, usually their intelligence. The level of performance of these subjects can then be compared with that achieved by comparable groups who are told that it is the task rather than the subject that is being tested. Alper (1946b, 1948) has used the terms ego-orientation and task-orientation to refer to the psychological states induced by these types of instructions. If one assumes that these instructions are believed by the subjects, it follows that subjects receiving the ego-oriented instructions will expect that their level of intelligence will be reflected in their level of performance. If they do well on the task it means that they are intelligent; if they do poorly it means that they are not intelligent. In contrast, subjects receiving the task-oriented instructions will expect that their level of performance has no bearing on their intelligence.

Alper (1946b) gave two groups of subjects a list of nonsense syllables to memorize. One group was told that the task was a test of intellectual ability, and the second was merely told to memorize the list. There were no differences in the number of nonsense syllables recalled by these two groups immediately following learning. However, a second recall test, given twenty-four hours later, showed substantial differences in recall, with the subjects who were told that the task was a test of intellectual ability showing much greater retention. A subsequent experiment by Russell (1952) failed to replicate this finding. He did, however, observe significantly greater variability in rate of learning among subjects receiving the ego-oriented instructions. This finding is consistent with the observation made in the previous chapter that individual differences in performance increase with greater motivation.

Kaustler (1951) compared the rate of learning and level of performance of subjects who were told that the task was an intelligence test with that of subjects who were told that it was simply a classroom demonstration of a learning test. He found that the performance of the "ego-involved" subjects was significantly higher than that of the "task-involved" subjects. There was no difference in the amount of their "incidental learning" during performance of the task.

Elizabeth French (1955) compared the effects of "relaxed" instructions, "task-motivated" instructions, and "extrinsically motivated" instructions on the performance of students in Officer Candidate School on a digit-letter code test. The "relaxed" instructions closely resemble Alper's task-oriented instructions. Subjects receiving the "relaxed" instructions were told the experimenter was merely interested in determining what kinds of scores people make on the test; those receiving the "task-motivated" instructions were told that the task measured the ability to deal quickly and accurately with unfamiliar materials; and those receiving the "extrinsically motivated" instructions were told that the five persons making the best scores could leave, while the others would have to endure more practice periods and tests. Performance was highest under the "task-motivated" instructions and lowest under the "relaxed" instructions. Performance under the "task-motivated" instructions was also found to be a function of the subject's need for achievement (as measured by French's Test of Insight given five months earlier). Subjects with high need for achievement performed significantly better in this condition than those with low need for achievement. No significant differences were found between the performance of subjects with high and low need for achievement under the two other kinds of instructions. Further evidence that task performance is increased by instructions that lead the subject to believe that the task measures a valued ability was obtained in an experiment by Atkinson (reported in McClelland, Atkinson, Clark, and Lowell, 1953). Atkinson also found that subjects with high need for achievement performed at a higher level under these instructions than subjects with low need for achievement.

In the previous chapter it was argued that the effects of motivation on performance depend on the ability of the person to perform the task. Castaneda and Palermo (1955) found that the relative performance of subjects who were told that a task was a measure of their learning ability and those not receiving this instruction was dependent on the amount and appropriateness of past training that they had received. Telling subjects that the task was a measure of their learning ability resulted in greater performance only when subjects had received substantial training appropriate to the task. Subjects who had been trained in habits that were inappropriate to the task performed less effectively when they were given such instruction.

The findings that we have been considering indicate that the level of performance of subjects on a task tends to be increased by instructions designed to induce them to believe that the task measures a highly valued ability. Some of the results are inconsistent with this conclusion, but these exceptions appear attributable to conditions where increases in performance would not be expected to result from increases in motivation. We can tentatively conclude that credible instructions to subjects to the effect that a task which they are about to perform requires an ability that they highly value will increase the strength of their desire to perform the task effectively. This greater desire will tend to increase the level of their performance, although this increment will not occur when subjects are highly motivated without the instructions or lack abilities that are necessary for effective performance of the task.

We should exercise caution in drawing conclusions about the factors affecting the motivation of workers to perform their jobs effectively from the laboratory experiments that have been considered. Workers' conceptions concerning the ability requirements of their jobs are undoubtedly less easily manipulated by instructions. Nonetheless, researchers in industry have frequently been led, by very different evidence, to rather similar conclusions concerning the effects of job content on worker motivation. It is frequently asserted, for example, that jobs that require important and valued skills are more highly motivating than those with minimal skill requirements.

A study by Slater (1959) of blue collar workers in an oil refinery bears on this proposition. She studied the effects of job characteristics on the extent of a worker's "internalization of motivation toward occupational role performance." Motivation was defined as internalized to the extent to which it is independent of externally mediated sanctions. Amount of internalization was assumed to be reflected in the extent to which workers would report thinking about job problems after working hours. Consequently, workers were asked how likely it was that they would think about work-related problems after work. Their responses to this question were found to be related to management's ratings concerning the amount of aptitude required by the worker's job, as well as to the worker's report of the amount of his self-determination on his job. Workers on jobs for which the aptitude requirements were high and who reported considerable opportunity for self-determination were more likely to describe themselves as thinking about work-related problems after work than were those whose jobs had lower aptitude requirements and who reported less opportunity for self-determination.

If the extent to which workers strive to perform effectively on a task is positively related to the extent to which they believe that the task requires a valued ability, then we should be able to demonstrate the existence of an interaction between conceptions of the ability requirements of a task and individual differences in the value placed on abilities. Inasmuch as individuals differ in the value they place on different abilities, the psychological or actual properties of jobs that create the highest levels of task motivation should vary. Thus, the task motivation of a person who highly values intelligence, but is indifferent to artistic ability, would be expected to vary with the extent to which he believes the task to require intelligence but be unaffected by the extent to which he believes it to require artistic ability. The opposite would be expected for a person who is indifferent to intelligence but values artistic ability. Research aimed at uncovering possible interactions between the extent to which persons value different attributes and their conceptions of the psychological requirements of tasks would shed greater light on the validity of our explanation of the findings reviewed on the preceding pages.

The Extent to Which the Task Requires "Possessed" Abilities. In a book published after his death, Lecky (1945) outlined a theory of self-consistency. His central thesis was that people seek out events that confirm their conceptions of themselves and seek to avoid events that are inconsistent with their conceptions of themselves. He applied this principle in his efforts to understand the educational and adjustment problems of students. For example, he viewed inadequate spelling or reading performance as caused by the fact that the student defined himself as a poor speller or poor reader and was behaving in a way that was consistent with his self-definition.

Although he did not concern himself with the industrial applications of his ideas, Lecky's thesis, if true, does have considerable bearing on the problem of explaining workers' motivation to perform their jobs effectively. It suggests the relevance to work performance of the worker's conception of himself and his conception of the attributes required by the task or job.

Vroom (1961, 1962) has elaborated on these ideas. He hypothesized that if a person believes himself to possess an ability and believes that successful performance of his task requires that ability, he will prefer performing the task effectively to performing it ineffectively. If he believes that effective performance is irrelevant to the ability that he possesses, he will be indifferent to whether he performs the task effectively or ineffectively, and if he believes that effective performance is negatively relevant to the ability (that is, possession of the ability is a handicap to effective performance) he will prefer to perform the task ineffectively.

Predictions of this kind can be viewed as a special case of theories of cognitive balance (Heider, 1946, 1958) or cognitive dissonance (Festinger, 1957). They share with these more broadly stated positions the assumption that consistency among cognitions is pleasant and inconsistency among cognitions is unpleasant.

Lecky and Vroom deal explicitly with the motivation of persons to confirm their existing self-conceptions rather than with their motivation to achieve valued self-conceptions discussed in the previous section. If, as has sometimes been suggested, degree of possession of an attribute and valuation of it vary together, the effects of these two motivations may be difficult to separate empirically. Kaufmann (1962) carried out an experiment to test some derivations from Vroom's theory and at the same time to investigate the effects of degree of liking for the attribute. Subjects[4] who were told that a digit symbol task that they were about to perform was a test of speed of closure—an ability which they had previously been informed that they possessed to a large degree—performed at a much higher level than those who were told that the task was unaffected by "speed of closure." There was no effect on performance of the amount of value placed on speed of closure. The performance of subjects who had been told that speed of closure was a highly valuable ability did not differ from the performance of those who had been told that it was of little value, regardless of whether speed of closure was "being tested." Apparently subjects were motivated to perform effectively to the extent to which effective performance would be consistent, and ineffective performance inconsistent, with their conception of the amount of ability they possessed.

Further evidence that persons strive to perform at a level that is consistent with their conception of their abilities has been obtained by Aronson and Carlsmith (1962). They gave forty female subjects a test of "social sensitivity." The test consisted of one-hundred cards, each containing three photographs of young men, one of whom was purportedly a schizophrenic. The test was divided into five sections, with a three-minute rest between sections. After the subject had completed four of the five sections the experimenter reported a false prearranged score to her. Half of the subjects were given very high scores indicating that they had a great deal of "social sensitivity" while half were given very low scores indicating that they had little "social sensitivity." All subjects then completed the final section of the test and learned that they had either done very well or very poorly on it. The prearranged scores on the final

---

[4]For a more complete description of the procedure used in this experiment, and for other findings, see Chapter Five of this book.

section were independent of those on the first four sections, resulting in four experimental conditions: (1) a High-High Condition, in which the information given subjects concerning their performance on the final section was consistent with previously induced beliefs that they had a great deal of "social sensitivity;" (2) a High-Low Condition, in which the information given subjects concerning their performance on the final section was inconsistent with their previously induced belief that they had high "social sensitivity;" (3) a Low-Low Condition, in which the information provided subjects concerning their performance on the final section was consistent with their previously induced belief that they had low "social sensitivity;" and (4) a Low-High Condition, in which the information provided subjects concerning their performance was inconsistent with the previously induced belief that they had low "social sensitivity."

Conditions (1) and (3) were predicted to produce consistent cognitions while conditions (2) and (4) were predicted to produce inconsistent cognitions. Accordingly, Aronson and Carlsmith hypothesized that subjects under conditions (2) and (4) would be more likely to change their level of performance to make it more consistent with their previous conceptions of their ability. In order to test this hypothesis, they allowed all subjects to respond to the fifth section of the test again. This was done by having the experimenter confess his failure to time the subjects' responses to this part of the test. The subject was told to pretend that it was a completely new set of pictures so that the experimenter could get a fairly accurate estimate of time taken. The dependent variable was the number of responses that the subject changed on the repeat performance. The mean number of changed responses is shown in Table 8.3. It can

Table 8.3. Number of Responses Changed on Repeat Performance.

		Score Obtained on Fifth Section	
		Low	High
Score expected	High	11.1	3.9
on fifth test	Low	6.7	10.2

Source: From Aronson and Carlsmith, 1962, p. 181.

be seen that the largest number of changes occurred when the subject received inconsistent information (that is, the High-Low and Low-High Conditions), supporting the hypothesis that subjects strive to perform at a level that is consistent with their conceptions of their abilities. The interaction between the two experimental variables was significant at the .001 level.

Success and Failure in Work Performance. In performing a task or job a person typically receives information concerning the effectiveness of his performance. Earlier in this chapter, we considered the effects on performance of the amount of such feedback and of the process by which it was transmitted. Here our concern is with the consequences on the worker's performance of the content of this information. What happens to level of performance when a worker learns that he has performed very effectively or that he has performed very ineffectively?

A number of laboratory experiments have been carried out in an attempt to answer this question. Subjects have been given "false feedback" concerning their performance on a task, with one or more groups told that they have done very well and other matched groups told that they have done very poorly. The effects of this feedback are then determined by assessing changes in the level of performance of the two sets of groups, or by comparing the subsequent level of performance of the "successful" and "unsuccessful" subjects.

In one such experiment, Diggory and Loeb (1962) found that subjects who had been told that they succeeded estimated their probability of success on a second similar task to be greater, and actually performed at a higher level on a second similar task than those who had been told that they had failed. The authors concluded that failure had convinced the subjects that their abilities were inadequate and that, as a result, they did not try as hard on subsequent tasks.

There is additional evidence that failure results in a decrement in performance (McKinney, 1933; Sears, 1937) and that experimentally induced success results in more effective performance than experimentally induced failure (Gilchrist, 1916; Hurlock, 1925; Sears, 1937). However, some investigators have found no difference between the effects of success and failure (Hurlock, 1924;

Thompson and Hunnicutt, 1944; Lazarus and Ericksen, 1952) and others have found that experimentally induced failure results in a higher level of performance than experimentally induced success (Brenner, 1934; Forlano and Axelrod, 1937).

Diggory, Klein, and Cohen (1962) studied the effects of information about performance on the amount of effort exerted by subjects while they worked on a digit symbol task. All subjects were encouraged to attempt to achieve a fixed goal of performance on at least one of ten trials. Falsified information about performance was provided at the conclusion of each trial and was displayed in such a way that each person could observe changes in his performance over time. Effort was measured by recordings of muscle action potential. After each trial, subjects were told that their performance was below the fixed goal, but the amount of discrepancy and their rate of progress toward the fixed goal were varied experimentally. The results show an overall tendency for subjects who were informed that they were relatively close to the fixed goal to exert more effort during performance of the task than those who were informed that they were far from the goal. However, this difference was reversed for subjects told that their performance was increasing at a positively accelerated rate. Among subjects whose rate of improvement was slow during the first five trials but thereafter increased rapidly, those who were initially close to the goal exerted less effort than those who were initially distant from the goal.

Apparently, giving a person information to the effect that he has attained a low level of performance may either increase or decrease the amount of effort he exerts and the level of his subsequent performance. Similarly, giving him information to the effect that he has attained a high level of performance may either increase or decrease the amount of effort he exerts and his level of performance. How can one account for these findings? Let us begin by examining the possible meaning of success or failure to a person. A subject who is told that he has done poorly on a task may believe that he cannot succeed regardless of how hard he tries and therefore, he "gives up." In contrast, he may believe that he failed because of insufficient effort and that his future success will be assured if he works harder. Similarly, a subject who is told that he has done well on a task may be "spurred on" to greater effort, or may feel that his future success is assured and that he can "take it easy."

Our model would lead us to predict no necessary effect of either success or failure on level of performance. If the person desires to be successful, it follows from the argument presented in the previous chapter that the amount of effort that he expends in a task should be directly related to the amount of difference between the strength of his expectancies that higher and lower amounts of effort will be followed by success. It is not clear what effects a particular success or failure would have on the amount of this difference. Either may increase or decrease the difference between subjective probabilities of success following different amounts of effort. The specific effects would be predicted to depend on the amount of effort the subject was exerting prior to the success or failure, the persistence of the success or failure, and the strength of preexistent expectancies regarding the instrumentality of effort for success.

Wages

Wages represent an almost universal form of inducement for individuals to perform work. Most workers receive some kind of economic remuneration for working, and formal organizations develop complex systems for determining the amount of the remuneration to be given to an individual worker. The size of a worker's weekly or monthly paycheck is typically a complex resultant of a large number of factors including the intrinsic content of his job, the relative supply and demand of labor for that job, the worker's seniority, and his level of performance. If the worker is a member of a labor union, the wage determination process is further influenced by negotiations between union and management, which often exercise a decisive influence on both absolute and relative wage levels.

Our interest here is in the effects of wages on workers' motivation to perform their jobs effectively. The question that we will seek to answer through an examination of the results of research concerns the ways in which the wages that workers receive affect the level of their performance on their jobs.

One possibility is that the strength of a worker's motivation to perform effectively is directly related to the amount of his wages.

The more wages he receives the higher his motivation to do an effective job. There is little evidence in support of such a relationship. To this writer's knowledge there is no reliable data indicating that increases in wages increase level of performance or that decreases in wages decrease level of performance. In part this may be due to the fact that marked changes in wages usually accompany job changes, making the determination of increases or decreases in performance impossible. This problem does not exist, however, for most negotiated wage increases or those resulting from an increased cost of living where the nature of the job remains unchanged; yet it is far from clear that these wage changes have significant effects on performance.

Adams's theory of equity (1963), which was described in Chapter Five, has implications for the effects of amount of wages on worker productivity. According to this theory, workers strive to attain an equitable relationship between their job inputs and outcomes and those of others. If a worker believes that he is overpaid relative to others with the same inputs, he is predicted to experience feelings of inequity and tension, which he will try to reduce. One means of doing this is to increase his inputs to his job, which may include increasing his level of performance. Similarly, if he believes that he is being underpaid relative to others with the same inputs, he is predicted to experience feelings of inequity and tension, which could be reduced by decreasing his level of performance. It should be noted that this theory does not predict that increases in wages will necessarily result in increased productivity or that decreased wages will necessarily result in decreased productivity. Productivity changes would be expected only when changes in wages affect workers' feelings regarding the equity of their wages in relation to those of others.

Existing evidence provides some support for these predictions. In one experiment, Adams and Rosenbaum (1962) attempted to make one group of subjects believe that they were being overcompensated relative to others, and to make a second group of subjects believe that they were being equitably compensated. There were eleven subjects in each group, all of whom were male university students. Each subject was hired for temporary work as an interviewer. He was told that the rate of pay would be $3.50 per hour and that his job would be to conduct a standard interview with adult members of the general public. He was further led to believe that he was being hired for a real task and that his employment would continue for several months.

During the hiring interview, the "overcompensated" group of subjects were told that they were being hired at the $3.50 per hour rate despite their lack of training and experience for the job. In contrast, the "equitably compensated" group were told that they were fully qualified by virtue of their superior education and intelligence to earn this rate. It was predicted that the "overcompensated" group would be more highly motivated to perform the task effectively than the "equitably compensated" group since effective performance was, for them, a means of decreasing the inequity in their wages. The results support this prediction. During the two and one-half hours in which they worked, the "overcompensated" group collected significantly more interviews per unit time than did the "equitably compensated" group.

It is possible that the results of this experiment reflect the fact that the "overcompensated" subjects were working harder in order to protect their jobs. To test this possibility, Arrowood conducted a similar experiment (reported in Adams, 1963) in which subjects who were either "overcompensated" or "equitably compensated" performed the same work under either "public" or "private" conditions. In the public condition, the subjects submitted their interviews directly to the employer, whereas, in the private condition, they mailed them to another city and were under the impression that the employer would never see their work. The results show superior performance of overpaid subjects under both public and private conditions.

Adams (1963) argues that subjects can only reduce inequity associated with overcompensation by increasing productivity if they are paid in accordance with the amount of time worked. If "overcompensated" workers are paid on a piecework basis, an increase in their productivity should increase inequity—the more they produce the greater the inequity. Only by restricting productivity can inequity be minimized. Consequently, "overcompensated" workers are predicted to perform less effectively than those who are "equitably compensated" when they are being paid on a piece-rate basis and to perform more effectively when they are being paid on an hourly basis.

In order to test this derivation, Adams and Rosenbaum (1962) carried out a second experiment. The subjects, procedure, and task were similar to that used in the first experiment. However, four groups of subjects were used instead of two: (1) an "overcompensated" group, which was paid by the hour, (2) an "equitably compensated" group, which was paid by the hour, (3) an "overcompensated" group, which was paid by the interview, and (4) an "equitably compensated" group, which was paid by the interview. The results are consistent with the predictions. The number of interviews per unit time of the "overcompensated" hourly group was greater than that of the "equitably compensated" hourly group; and the number of interviews per unit time of the "equitably compensated," piece-rate group was greater than that of the "over compensated," piece-rate group. Although these differences did not reach customary levels of statistical significance, the interaction between method and equity of compensation was found to be significant at the .01 level of confidence.

Although a person on piecework who believes he is being overcompensated cannot reduce his feeling of inequity by increasing the quantity of his performance, he can accomplish the same effect by improving the quality of his work. Adams and Jacobsen (1963) have recently investigated this possibility. The subjects were hired for a job that consisted of proofreading a manuscript. They had previously been told that the pay for the job was 30 cents per page. As in the previous experiment, subjects induced to believe that they were unqualified to earn 30 cents per page, but who were nonetheless hired at that rate of pay, turned out a significantly lower quantity of work, that is, completed a smaller number of pages in the hour they were given, than did those who were induced to believe that they were qualified for the task. However, these "overcompensated" subjects exhibited significantly higher quality of work, that is, detected a larger number of errors per page, than did the "equitably compensated" subjects. A third group of subjects, who were told that they were unqualified to earn 30 cents per page and were hired at a lower rate of 20 cents per page, performed (from the point of view of both quantity and quality) in a manner comparable to that of the "equitably compensated" subjects.

The results presented have been interpreted as reflecting the fact that workers strive to maximize *the equity of their wages* and attempt to perform at a level that is most consistent with their conceptions of the relative wages and qualifications of themselves and their co-workers. It is also possible that workers strive to maximize *the amount of their wages* and, all other things being equal, attempt to perform at a level that brings them the greatest economic return. If this proposition is correct we should find that, when workers' wages are related to the level of their performance, they will perform at a higher level than if their wages are not contingent on their performance.

There are many different kinds of evidence supporting this proposition. Several experiments conducted in the laboratory (Atkinson and Reitman, 1956; Kaufmann, 1962) have shown that subjects achieve higher levels of task performance when they are told they will receive financial rewards for good performance. Atkinson (1958b) has shown further that, under such conditions, level of performance is related to the amount of the promised economic reward and to the indicated probability that the subject would receive it.

Further evidence for the effectiveness of linking wages to the amount of work performed was obtained in a field experiment carried out by Wyatt (1934). The subjects were ten female workers in a British candy factory. During the period of the investigation each of the subjects performed five different jobs: (1) unwrapping, (2) wrapping, (3) packaging, (4) weighing, and (5) weighing and wrapping. Rotation from one job to another was on a daily basis. For the first nine weeks, the workers were paid a fixed weekly wage. This method of payment was followed by the introduction of a competitive bonus system, which remained in operation for fifteen weeks. During this period the workers were ranked each week according to output, the slowest worker receiving the same weekly wage as before, the second slowest receiving an additional sixpence, the third slowest an additional shilling, and so on throughout the group. The immediate effect of the introduction of the bonus system was an increase in production of 46 percent, which was maintained throughout the fifteen-week period. A flat piece rate was then introduced, which resulted in a further increase in output of 30 percent, which was maintained throughout the remaining twelve weeks of observation.

Although increasing the degree of relationship between individual performance and wages resulted in a marked increase in level of performance, there were substantial differences in its effects on the five different jobs. On the wrapping job, there were marked increases in output following the changes in method of payment. The total increase from the first week under the weekly rate to the first week under the piece rate was over 200 percent. In contrast, in the unwrapping job, there was practically no change in output following the introduction of the different methods of payment. From interviews with the girls, Wyatt obtained information concerning their preferences among the five jobs and observed a strong positive relationship between workers' liking for a task and the amount of improvement in output resulting from the introduction of wage incentives. Changes from hourly to bonus payment and from bonus to piece-rate payment increased level of performance on the most preferred jobs to a much greater extent than it did on the least preferred jobs. The explanation of this finding is not immediately clear.

Most surveys of companies' experience with wage incentive plans indicate that substantial increases in productivity have followed their installation. Viteles (1953), who reviews this evidence in detail, suggests that wage incentives do contribute to greater productivity but cautions that the specific effects of such plans are often difficult to isolate. He points out that

> In practice, the installation of a wage-incentive plan is generally accompanied by other changes in working conditions, personnel policies, and practices which are frequently major in character. . . . As a result, management and industrial engineers have frequently been unable to present clear-cut and unequivocal evidence as to the specific effects of wage incentives (pp. 29–30).

Wages may be related to either individual or group performance. Under group incentive plans, the wages of individual group members are based on the total productivity of the work group. There is little reliable evidence concerning the differences in workers' level of performance when they are paid in accordance with the amount of time that they have worked and when they are paid in accordance with the level of productivity of their work group. Many writers have, however, commented favorably on company experience with group incentive payment. For example, Balderston (1930), after reviewing industrial experience with group incentive plans, concludes that "the employers who have substituted group payment for day work have universally experienced a reduction in direct labor cost" (p. 10).

Although all piece-rate or bonus-payment plans enable the individual to acquire greater wages through higher performance, this opportunity is greater in individual than in group incentive plans. In group plans the relationship between the level of performance of any single worker and his wages is lower than in individual plans. Furthermore, the amount of this relationship decreases as the size of the group increases. On the basis of such economic considerations we might expect to find group incentive plans more successful in motivating workers to perform effectively on their jobs when the size of the group is small than when it is large. Marriott (1949) obtained some results bearing on this point. He studied the relationship between the size of work group and output of male production workers on group incentive plans in two British factories. In factory *A*, the workers were paid on a group bonus plan while in factory *B* they were paid on a group piecework plan. Table 8.4 shows the relative output of groups of different sizes during the period in which they were studied.

It can be seen that the mean level of individual performance decreases as group size increases in both factories. This trend is consistent with the exception of groups of fifty and over where performance increases slightly. Marriott also found that workers in factory *B*, who were paid individually, had higher mean output per man than was found in even the smallest groups.

It should not be concluded that individual incentive plans are always more effective than group incentive plans. The latter have been most frequently used for jobs that are highly interdependent and where it is impossible to obtain comprehensive and mean-

Table 8.4. Size of Group and Output.

	Factory A		Factory B	
Size of Group	Number of Groups	Average Efficiency Percentage	Average[a] Number of Groups	Average[a] Piecework Earnings
Under 10	20	133.8	61.5	36.4
10-19	41	132.2	9.8	35.4
20-29	35	129.5	6.3	33.5
30-39	24	128.8	1.8	31.2
40-49	13	126.1	2.0	31.0
50 and over	20	127.1	6.0	31.7

[a]Data for Factory B are based on four work periods. Since the size of some groups changed between these work periods, the figures shown are mean numbers of group of each size for the four work periods combined and the mean piecework earnings of groups of each size for combined work periods.

Source: From Marriott, 1949, pp. 50–51.

ingful measures of individual performance. Babchuk and Goode (1951) have described the results of the introduction of individual incentive payment into a small selling unit of a department store. Even though total sales increased, there was considerable "sales grabbing" and "tying up the trade," as well as a general neglect of such unrewarded, but nonetheless necessary, functions as stock work and arranging merchandise for displays. Morale declined and the group informally replaced the competitive incentive system with a cooperative system of pooling. Stock work was equally distributed, quotas were set, and sales shared among group members so that each person received an equal paycheck at the end of the week regardless of individual cash register readings.

Although the experimental and correlational evidence generally supports the assumption that workers will perform more effectively if their wages are related to their performance, there is evidence from case studies that, in some instances, wage incentive plans may encourage restriction of output. Mathewson (1931) first drew attention to this problem in an early study of nonunionized workers. His work was followed by Roethlisberger and Dickson's (1939) investigation of restriction of output in the Bank Wiring Room and by more recent studies by Collins, Dalton, and Roy

(1946), Roy (1952), Whyte (1955), and Hickson (1961). This research has demonstrated that workers on wage incentive plans may be pressured by their co-workers to hold down production. Individuals whose production exceeds some informal group standard of production are subject to persistent influence attempts and, if these are unsuccessful, they tend to be rejected by their co-workers.

Group standards and social pressure represent, at best, a partial explanation of the origins of restriction of output under wage incentive plans. We must also inquire into the origin of the group standards. Why do workers attempt to influence their co-workers to perform at a low level? Among their frequently cited causes are a fear that a high level of performance will result in a tightening of rates (Whyte, 1955; Hickson, 1961) and fear of unemployment (Roethlisberger and Dickson, 1939; Mathewson, 1931).

These observations in no way invalidate the proposition that a person's motivation to perform effectively on his job is directly related to the extent to which his wages are contingent on his performance. It does, however, suggest that changes in the immediate economic consequences of performance in industry may be accompanied by changes in other expected consequences of performance. The introduction of wage incentive plans may alter not only the expected consequences of performance for wages but also its expected consequences for cutting of rates and unemployment.

A field study by Georgopoulos, Mahoney, and Jones (1957) sheds some light on individual differences in the performance of workers on an individual wage incentive plan. They found a larger proportion of "high producers" among workers who reported that productivity would result in their receiving "more money in the long run," than among those who reported that productivity was either irrelevant to, or hindered the attainment of, money. They also found a larger proportion of "high producers" among workers who reported that productivity would result in greater acceptance by their co-workers than among those who reported that it was irrelevant to, or would hinder, acceptance. The relationship between performance and workers' expectations concerning its long-term economic consequences was greatest among workers who ranked money relatively high in importance, whereas the relationship between performance and workers' expectations concerning its social consequences was greatest for those who ranked acceptance by co-workers relatively high.

Further evidence concerning individual differences in performance under wage incentive plans was obtained in a case study of "restrictors" and "rate-busters" carried out by Dalton (reported in Whyte, 1955). Dalton studied the personal characteristics of eighty-four production workers working on an individual bonus system. Each of the workers had been working in the same department for at least seven years. For purposes of the study, nine out of the eighty-four were classified as "rate-busters" because their production exceeded the informal "ceiling" of 150 percent of standard. Twenty-five of the remainder were classified as "restrictors" because their production was below 100 percent of standard. Dalton found marked differences between these two groups. Twenty-two of the twenty-five "restrictors" were Democrats. They were generally sons of unskilled industrial workers and had grown up in large cities where they had been active in boys' gangs. In contrast, eight of the nine "rate-busters" were Republicans and most had grown up either on farms or in urban, lower middle-class families. The "restrictors" led an active social life both during and outside the work situation and were described as "living in the present," spending money on themselves or on others while carrying out their social activities. In contrast, the "rate-busters" tended to be "social isolates" both within and outside the work situation. They were described as shunning activities that cost money, seeking instead to build up their savings or to invest in property of recognized market value.

The findings that have been described are generally consistent with our model. On the assumption that money is positively valent, we would predict that the valence of effective performance on a job would be directly related to the instrumentality of performance for its attainment (Proposition 1). Supporting this prediction are a large number of investigations indicating that level of performance increases as the expected relationship between performance and wages increases. It is also supported by the finding that this effect is greatest for workers who report that money is relatively important to them.

Evidence from case studies of restriction of output among

workers on wage incentives can be explained, in ad hoc fashion, if one postulates that the introduction of an incentive system alters the expected relationship of performance to other outcomes. This assumption has, in fact, been the traditional interpretation of such observations. Workers who restricted output are described as fearing social pressure, unemployment, or changes in rates.

The experiments of Adams and Rosenbaum (1962) and Arrowood (reported in Adams, 1963) suggest that the valence of a given level of wages to a worker is dependent not only on its amount but also on the extent to which it is believed to be deserved. Explaining their findings in terms of the model requires the additional assumption that workers prefer equitable to unequitable payment and tend to perform at a level that maximizes the equity of their wages.

Promotional Opportunities

As a result of expansion, retirement, or resignation, organizations acquire vacancies in higher level positions. Although they sometimes look outside the organization to fill the vacancies, more frequently an existing member of the organization is promoted to the position. The criteria used in awarding promotions are usually dependent on the position being filled as well as on the policies of the organization in which the position is located. March and Simon (1958) have hypothesized that organizations in which promotion is contingent on performance will be more productive than those "that promote on the basis of family relationships, internal policies, or old school tie" (p. 61). The implicit assumption is that promotions are desired and that workers will strive to perform effectively in their jobs if they expect that by doing so they will increase their chances of receiving a promotion.

Our society has often been described as one in which great importance is attached to promotion and advancement. Studies of managers and executives (Henry, 1949; Dill, Hilton, and Reitman, 1962) suggest that a strong desire to move continually upward is particularly characteristic of members of this occupational group. There have also been a number of studies of the criteria used in awarding promotions (Newcomer, 1955; Benge, 1956; Coates and

Pellegrin, 1957; Brooks, 1958; Dalton, 1959). Surprisingly, there is little quantitative evidence concerning the joint effects of promotional systems and promotional desires on behavior. The only study of this type that we were able to find was conducted on hourly workers. In a study of over six hundred workers in a household appliances factory, Georgopoulos, Mahoney, and Jones (1957) found a higher proportion of "high producers" among workers who reported on a questionnaire that low productivity would hurt their chances for promotion than among those who stated that productivity was irrelevant to promotion. This difference was found to be statistically significant only for workers who reported that receiving a promotion was relatively important to them and who were free to set their own pace of work.

This finding suggests that the level of performance of individual workers is related to the extent to which they believe that their chances of receiving a promotion are related to their level of performance on their job and to the valence of the promotion. If workers are indifferent to receiving a promotion, *or* if they expect that their chances of receiving it are independent of their level of performance, they will perform less effectively than if they desire a promotion and believe that their chances of receiving it are directly related to their level of performance.

Some Theoretical Issues

Thus far we have considered a large number of specific research investigations bearing on conditions affecting the extent to which workers perform effectively on jobs or tasks. We have looked, in turn, at evidence regarding the effects on performance of supervision, the work group, job content, wages, and promotional opportunities, conditions that are usually assumed to influence the motivation of workers to carry out their jobs effectively. In the remainder of this chapter, we will use this evidence in an examination of some problems of a more basic theoretical nature concerning the motivational determinants of performance.

Satisfaction and Performance. The extent to which a worker is satisfied with his work role and the extent to which he is motivated to perform effectively in it can be defined independently of one another, conceptually and operationally. This enables us not only to assess the relationship between these two variables but also to find out if they are the result of similar conditions. If one compares the evidence concerning the determinants of job satisfaction presented in Chapter Five with the evidence concerning the determinants of motivation for effective performance presented in this chapter, both similarities and differences become apparent.

The major similarity involves the limited usefulness of explanations using only situational or personality variables. It was concluded in Chapter Five that explanations of job satisfaction based exclusively on either the objective properties of the work role or on the personality of the worker were inadequate. A similar conclusion seems to be indicated with respect to motivation. The extent to which a worker strives to perform effectively in a job is not solely a function of his personality or of the nature of his work role but a complex resultant of both types of variables. This does not mean, in the language of analysis of variance, that there are no "main effects" of either situational or personality variables but rather that there are, in addition, important interactions between these two types of variables. Interactions of this type have been found in no less than ten of the research investigations reported thus far in this chapter (Hurlock, 1924; Anderson, 1928; Forlano and Axelrod, 1937; Abel, 1938; Thompson and Hunnicutt, 1944; French, 1955; Bernadin and Jessor, 1957; Georgopoulos, Mahoney, and Jones, 1957; French, 1958; Vroom, 1959a).

The argument that worker satisfaction and motivation should be viewed as a joint function of situational and personality variables by no means implies that their determinants are identical. In fact, there is considerable evidence that this is not the case. Such a conclusion is indicated by the absence of any appreciable correlation between job satisfaction and job performance (see Chapter Six) and also by a consideration of the results of investigations of the role of such variables as wages, promotional opportunities, and the work group in determining both worker satisfaction and performance.

Our model led us to predict that differences in job satisfaction could, in large part, be explained in terms of the amount of different outcomes provided by the work role and by the valence of these outcomes for the worker. Thus, to the extent to which a worker desires an outcome, his job satisfaction will be increased by increases in the amount of the outcome he receives from his job. To the extent to which he dislikes an outcome, increases in the extent to which he receives it from his job will decrease his job satisfaction. In Chapter Five we found considerable evidence in support of these predictions. However, our review of the literature in this chapter indicates that the same variables cannot account for differences in job performance. There is little or no evidence, for example, that increases in such generally desired outcomes as wages, promotional opportunities, or acceptance by co-workers result in increases in workers' level of performance. This does not mean that wages, promotional opportunities, or co-workers have no effects on performance but rather that their effects on performance are different than on satisfaction.

The basis for predicting effects of motivational variables on performance from the model was specified in Chapter Seven. To recapitulate, we defined a person's motivation to perform a task or job effectively in terms of the relative strength of forces acting on him to exert different levels of effort. From Proposition 2 it follows that these forces will depend on (1) the strength of his preference for effective performance over ineffective performance, and (2) his expectancies regarding the consequences of different levels of effort on the attainment of effective and ineffective performance.

The findings reported in this chapter bear most directly on the first of these variables—the strength of the worker's preference for effective over ineffective performance. Other things being equal, we would expect the performance of workers to increase as the valence of effective performance increases. In other words, level of performance should be a function of the valence of effective performance on the job rather than of the valence of the job itself, that is, job satisfaction. The valence of effective performance should in turn be explainable, at least in part, in terms of its instrumental relationship to other outcomes. If effective performance leads to the attainment of positively valent outcomes or prevents the attainment of negatively valent outcomes, then it should be positively valent; if it is irrelevant to the attainment of either positively or negatively valent outcomes, it should have a valence of zero; and if it leads to the attainment of negatively valent outcomes and prevents the attainment of positively valent outcomes, it should be negatively valent (Proposition 1).

Many of the findings presented in this chapter support these predictions. The level of performance of workers has been demonstrated to vary with three different indicators of the expected consequences of performance. Performance has been shown to be directly related to workers' *reports concerning its instrumentality* for the attainment of money, acceptance by co-workers, and promotions; to its *actual instrumentality* for the attainment of wages; and to *communicated instrumentality* for the attainment of money and acceptance by co-workers. Furthermore, the magnitude of these relationships has been shown to vary with measures of the valence of each of these outcomes in the manner predicted by the model.

Returning to the question of the differences between the determinants of job satisfaction and job performance, it seems fair to conclude that job satisfaction is closely affected by the amount of rewards that people derive from their jobs and that level of performance is closely affected by the basis for attainment of rewards. Individuals are satisfied with their jobs to the extent to which their jobs provide them with what they desire, and they perform effectively in them to the extent that effective performance leads to the attainment of what they desire.

The Problem of Ego Involvement. Some findings presented in this chapter are not so easily explained in terms of the idea that people perform effectively only to the degree to which performance leads to some other reward. For example, we observed that people perform at a higher level when they are given increased knowledge of results, even though they have overlearned the task and the cue properties of these results are minimized. Such results suggest that, under certain conditions, effective performance may be its own reward.[5] People may derive satisfaction from a high level of perfor-

---

[5]The reader will note that in Chapter Two we postulated that the valence of an outcome was a *function* of the valence of its expected consequences for other outcomes, not that it was *equal* to the valence of these consequences. This formulation allows for the possibility that outcomes may

mance on a task even though no externally mediated reward is forthcoming, and they may experience dissatisfaction from a low level of performance even though no punishment is administered. A number of different terms have been used to describe this phenomenon including pride in work, ego involvement, and internalized motivation. But as Maier (1960) has pointed out, giving a phenomenon a name does not explain it. We must also determine the conditions under which it occurs. In this case, the crucial problem is to ascertain the conditions under which workers derive satisfaction from effectively performing tasks and dissatisfaction from ineffectively performing them.

One approach to this problem is provided by McClelland, Atkinson, Clark, and Lowell (1953) and by Atkinson (1958b). They developed a method of measuring the strength of individuals' need for achievement, which they defined as a predisposition to derive satisfaction from "success in competition with some standard of excellence." The amount of satisfaction derived by a person from successful performance on a task is assumed to be directly related to the difficulty (1 - probability of success) of the task and to the strength of his need for achievement (Atkinson, 1958b).

Lending some support to this hypothesis is evidence that persons high in need achievement tend to perform more effectively on terms than those low in need achievement (Lowell, 1952; French, 1955; Wendt, 1955; Atkinson and Raphelson, 1956). Furthermore, this difference is most consistently found when the person is given achievement-orienting instructions (French, 1955), when other motives are not aroused (Atkinson and Reitman, 1956) and when his subjective probability of success on the task is low (Atkinson, 1958b).

Alternative approaches to this problem are suggested by the theoretical work of Vroom (1961) and Adams (1963). These investigators took as their point of departure the assumption of cognitive dissonance theory (Festinger, 1957), that is, consistency among

---

have terminal as well as instrumental value and eliminates the logical difficulties of an infinite regress.

cognitions is pleasant and inconsistency unpleasant. Consequently, they assumed that a person will be motivated to perform effectively when effective performance is more consistent with his other beliefs and opinions than ineffective performance. Adams and Vroom differed, however, in the kinds of consistency with which they dealt. Adams emphasized the consistency between a person's inputs (including his level of performance) and his outcomes (including his wages) and those of other persons. A person is motivated to perform effectively on a task or job when effective performance serves to reduce feelings of inequity. Vroom, in contrast, emphasized consistency between a person's performance and his self-concept. A person is assumed to be motivated to perform effectively when effective performance is consistent with his conception of his abilities. These two theories and the empirical work based on them have been described elsewhere in this book. It is sufficient to state here that both are consistent with some experimental evidence and open promising avenues for further research.

The problem of achieving an understanding of the sources of satisfaction and dissatisfaction that are intrinsic to the performance of tasks or jobs is one of the most important but least studied aspects of industrial psychology. Its importance is just beginning to be realized as the psychologist extends his purview beyond the rank and file worker to include the scientist, the engineer, the entrepreneur, and the manager.

A large number of questions of both practical and theoretical importance remain to be answered. For example, we know little about the relative amounts of task motivation that can be produced by externally and internally mediated incentives, about the functional relationships between motivation from these two sources, or about the conditions under which each is more valuable. Preliminary evidence on this last point from field studies (Vroom, 1962; Pelz, 1961) and laboratory experimentation (Wendt, 1955) suggests that the strength of motivation from the use of internally mediated incentives is more highly related to performance when the worker is relatively free to set his own pace of work.

The apparent complexity of the problem as revealed in existing research results belies the oversimplified generalizations so frequently found in writings on human relations and management.

The evidence suggests that there is no single "answer" to this problem. On the contrary, there seem to be a multiplicity of different sources of satisfaction and dissatisfaction intrinsic to job performance each of which is a function of both characteristics of the task and characteristics of the person performing it.

Summary

In this chapter we attempted to shed some light on the conditions affecting the strength of a worker's motivation to perform his job effectively. We examined evidence from research conducted in both laboratory and field situations dealing with the effects of supervision, the work group, job content, wages, and promotional opportunities on job performance.

Many of the findings that we discussed are consistent with the view that workers perform most effectively when performance is a means of attaining goals that are extrinsic to the content of the work. We observed that the level of performance of workers is related to the extent to which performance is instrumental to the attainment of higher wages, promotions, and acceptance by coworkers. In each case this relationship is strongest for workers who most strongly value each of these outcomes.

We have also seen that the performance of workers varies with conditions that appear to be motivational in nature but are not obviously related to the responses of either the formal or the informal organization to different levels of performance. This suggests that performance may be an end as well as a means to the attainment of an end, that is, that individuals may derive satisfaction from effective performance and dissatisfaction from ineffective performance regardless of the externally mediated consequences of performance. Among the most relevant findings are the following: (1) level of performance varies directly with the strength of individuals' need for achievement, particularly when the task is represented as difficult and challenging; (2) workers paid on an hourly basis perform at a higher level if they are led to believe that they are being "overcompensated" for their job; (3) individuals perform at a higher level if they are led to believe that the task requires abilities that they value or believe themselves to possess; (4) workers who have overlearned a task perform at a higher level when they are given feed-back concerning their level of performance; and (5) persons who are given an opportunity to participate in making decisions that have future effects on them perform at a higher level than those who are not given such an opportunity.

No single theory can encompass all of these observations. Much more data are needed before we can claim to understand adequately these determinants of performance. It appears that a person's desire to perform effectively on a task cannot be completely understood through an examination of the social reward and punishment systems used to control behavior. Effective and ineffective performance may have affective consequences per se; the magnitude of these consequences is a function of the nature of the task, the "personality" of the worker, and their interrelation.

Part Five

Conclusion

9

Concluding Observations on
Method and Theory

In this book we examined various aspects of the relationship between the motivations of people and the work they perform. Existing data and theories were scrutinized in an effort to shed some light
on such matters as the choices that persons make among alternative
forms of work, the extent of their satisfaction with the work they
select, and the effectiveness of their work performance. In this chapter we consider some implications for problems of method and
theory.

Method

Well over five hundred research investigations were cited in the
preceding pages. There are many ways of classifying the methods
used in these investigations; we found it helpful to distinguish three
broad classes of methods: (1) correlational studies,[1] (2) laboratory
experiments, and (3) field experiments.

   In *correlational studies,* observations relevant to two or more
variables are made of each of a sample of persons or groups. The
degree and direction of relationship among these observations is

---

[1]The writer used the terms field study and correlational study interchangeably. The former term is traditionally used in a somewhat broader sense to
include intensive nonquantitative studies of single cases as well as statistical
analyses of relationships among variables in a larger number of cases.

then determined by the use of statistical methods. There is no attempt on the part of the investigator to manipulate variables. Instead of creating conditions and determining their effects, he observes naturally occurring phenomena and relates these observations to one another.

The correlational method is widely used in the investigations reported in this book. Examples include McClelland's investigation (1955) of the association between the need for achievement and preference for business occupations, Walker and Guest's exploration (1952) of the relationship between the number of operations involved in the jobs of assembly line workers and their satisfaction with their jobs, and Marriott's study (1949) of the relationship between the size of work groups and the mean level of performance of group members.

In carrying out a *laboratory experiment,* an investigator creates conditions in the laboratory and studies their effects on the behavior of people exposed to them. Subjects are recruited for the experiment and are allocated to conditions in such a way as to minimize or eliminate any "confounding" of subject characteristics with conditions.

An exceedingly wide range of conditions can be created in laboratory experiments and many of them are of interest to the applied psychologist because they represent "simulations" of real-life conditions. Accordingly, we deemed it appropriate to include a number of laboratory experiments in this book. For example, we described Rosen's experiment (1961) on the effects of contrived information concerning the probability of a person being able to enter an occupation, Jones and Vroom's experiment (1964) on the affective consequences of competitive and cooperative social situations, and Arps' experiment (1920) on the motivational effects of knowledge of results.

A *field experiment* is similar to one conducted in the laboratory in that the experimenter is studying the effects of specially created conditions. However, the field experiment is carried out in a real-life setting. The subjects may be workers in a factory, students in a classroom, members of a club, or participants in any ongoing social organization. Their conception of their role as subjects in an experiment is minimized and in many field experiments the subjects are not aware that an experiment is being conducted.

Among the field experiments described in this book are Lieberman's investigation (1956) of the effects of promotion to foreman and election to shop steward on the attitudes of workers toward the company and union, Morse and Reimer's experiment (1956) on the effects of changing the locus of decision making in an organization, and Coch and French's experiment (1948) on the effects of worker participation in decision making regarding changes in work methods.

We described investigations employing each of these three methods,[2] but the largest proportion of investigations cited were correlational studies, followed by laboratory experiments and field experiments in that order. A rough classification of the methods used in investigations cited in Parts Two, Three, and Four shows that 65 percent of these were correlational studies, 25 percent were laboratory experiments, and 10 percent were field experiments.

Although correlational studies seem to dominate the empirical field, they are used more frequently on some topics than on others. The investigations of the determinants of occupational choice are almost exclusively correlational in nature. Use of field or laboratory experiments is rare. The situation is similar in investigations of the determinants of job satisfaction, although experimentation is slightly more common than in occupational choice. The most significant departure from this pattern is found in investigations of performance. By far the greatest application of experimental methods to date has occurred in work on the motivational determinants of job performance. Both laboratory and field experiments on this problem are relatively common.[3]

Which method shows the greatest promise for increasing our knowledge concerning the problems discussed in this book? Should

[2]For a more extensive discussion of these three methods, see Festinger and Katz (1953).

[3]The differences in relative use of these methods can be seen in the percentages of references in various chapters of this book to investigations of each type. In Part Two, on choice of work role, 93 percent of the references were to correlational studies, 5 percent to field experiments, and 2 percent to laboratory experiments. In Part Three, on satisfaction with work roles, 75 percent of the references were to correlational studies, 6 percent to field experiments, and 19 percent to laboratory experiments. Finally, in Part

there be more field or laboratory experiments in occupational choice? Should there be a greater use of correlational studies in investigations of performance? These are questions that are difficult to answer in any objective manner. In this writer's opinion, each method serves a useful function. Correlational studies are particularly valuable in initial exploration of a problem area. A large number of variables can be studied simultaneously and, with new data-processing methods, extremely complex statistical analyses can be performed quickly and economically. Many variables that would be difficult or impossible to manipulate experimentally can be measured and related statistically to hypothetical determinants or consequences.

The biggest disadvantage of the correlational method stems from the fact that it does not permit conclusive inferences regarding causal relations among variables. It is seldom possible to determine conclusively from correlational studies whether a statistical association between two variables, A and B, is attributable to the fact that A causes B, that B causes A, or that A and B are caused by some third variable, C. The associations obtained in correlational studies may be a useful source of causal hypotheses, but a rigorous testing of such hypotheses requires the use of other methods.

Laboratory experiments are particularly suited to a determination of causality. They permit a high degree of control with relatively low cost. Although this feature has made the laboratory experiment the method "par excellence" of scientists in a variety of disciplines, it is not without its disadvantages for research on human subjects. One of these disadvantages is a result of its artificiality. Even though the experimenter takes steps to disguise the purpose of the experiment, it is seldom possible for him to conceal from the subjects the fact that they are participating in an exper-

---

Four on performance in work roles, only 31 percent of the references were to correlational studies, while 19 percent were to field experiments, and 50 percent to laboratory experiments. Caution must be exercised in drawing strict inferences from these figures for we do not claim to have included every investigation that is relevant to each of these problems and some readers might disagree with our interpretation of the relevance of investigations that have been cited.

iment. This awareness of their role as subject may have a substantial effect on the behavior they exhibit. Orne (1962) has suggested that the psychological experiment be viewed as a very special form of social interaction. He argues that human subjects in laboratory experiments usually strive to ascertain the true purpose of the experiment and attempt to respond in a manner that will support the hypothesis being tested. Thus, the experimental results may reflect effects not only of the conditions created by the experimenter but also of the subject's conception of the desired results.

Laboratory experiments are also limited in the length of time that subjects can be observed. In most experiments, the subjects' encounter with the experimental conditions is short in duration. It is virtually impossible to approximate the length of exposure to conditions that are characteristic of most "real-life" work settings. As a result, the behaviors observed are, at best, short-term effects of the conditions and may not accurately reflect longer-term effects of the same conditions.

Field experiments are seldom subject to the difficulties of artificiality and short duration that we have noted in connection with those conducted in the laboratory. They are, however, quite costly to execute and often provide much less control over possible confounding variables.

Undoubtedly, each of these three types of methods will continue to be useful in research on work and motivation. In this writer's view, experimentation, both in the laboratory and in the field, will play an increasingly important role in years to come. Many of the most important unresolved questions involve matters of causality, and answers to them are most likely to be found through controlled experimentation. Fortunately, it would appear that social scientists are in a better position to undertake research of this kind than ever before. There has been considerable progress within the last decade in the development of new methods of manipulating variables in the laboratory, and there are signs of a greater willingness on the part of industrial organizations to undertake controlled experiments on their operations.

With continued success in extending the frontiers of our knowledge, it will be necessary to undertake more and more elaborate research designs. We must turn our attention from a search for simple cause-effect relations between variables to interactions among variables and to mediating processes. For example, instead of asking whether participation in decision making increases productivity or whether the repetitiveness of the job affects job satisfaction, we need to ask under what conditions these effects are maximized or minimized.

No discussion of methods would be complete without some mention of techniques for measuring variables. The research discussed in this book has relied very heavily on verbal reports of individuals for the measurement of motivational variables. Measures of occupational preferences, job satisfaction, group cohesiveness, and worker motives or needs are usually based on the responses by persons to direct questions concerning their likes and dislikes. It is assumed that persons' reports of the attractiveness of objects and events mirror the "real attractiveness" of these objects or events. Such measures are popular because their reliability is relatively high and they are easy to construct and score. Methods based on other assumptions are seldom readily available and require a heavier investment in methodological research.

However, we cannot overlook the evidence that self-report measures of motivational variables are far from perfect predictors of choices that would, on a theoretical basis, be expected to follow from them. The literature of social psychology includes many investigations showing negligible relationships between the attitudes of persons, based on self-reports, and overt behavior toward the objects of these attitudes. Similarly, the literature in the field of personality further illustrates the tenuous connection between persons' actions and their reports of their desires. McClelland (1958a) concludes an excellent summary of the literature on the usefulness of self-report measures of motivational variables with the following observation:

> On balance, self-descriptive or choice measures of motivation do not appear very promising. They fail to measure up to the criteria of a good measure at a number of points. But, perhaps, the argument from history is the most persuasive of all: if they had been good measures of motivation, why has the psychology

of motivation been so slow in developing as compared, for instance, with the psychology of learning, especially when such measures have been in use for a long time? Why has a whole psychoanalytic view of unconscious motivation developed entirely independently of such measures if they were really adequate? (pp. 25–26).

It would be foolish to exclude self-reports of motivational states from the domain of behavior to be studied by psychologists. They do, after all, constitute a form of behavior that will require explanation like any other. However, it would also seem to be foolish, in the light of present evidence, to rely exclusively on such behaviors for the measurement of motivational variables. Instead of putting all our eggs in one methodological basket, we should be directing more of our resources toward the development of new methods[4] and the study of the relationship between methods based on different assumptions. A broader-based approach to the measurement problem will avoid the risks associated with a premature commitment to a single method.

Theory

We started this book with certain preconceptions about the kinds of variables that might prove useful in explanations of behavior. In Chapter Two we attempted to make these preconceptions explicit by introducing a conceptual model, and we referred to this model in much of our later discussion. The model asserts that the probability of a person performing an act is a direct function of the algebraic sum of the products of the valence of outcomes and expectancies that they will occur given the act. From our point of view, the specific mathematical properties of the model are not too important. They are more easily tested in situations that permit a much higher degree of control than that which is possible to achieve in studying the complex problems to which we have addressed our-

[4]See, for example, the work by Libo (1953) on a projective measure of group cohesiveness.

selves. The important feature of the model, as far as we are concerned, is its view of behavior as subjectively rational and as directed toward the attainment of desired outcomes and away from aversive outcomes.

The model forced us to be rather parsimonious in our use of concepts. We have sought to relate the large number of concepts, found in the literature of applied psychology, to the basic concepts in the model. In some cases the "fit" has been an easy one. Terms such as occupational preference, morale, need achievement, group cohesiveness, job satisfaction, and the motivation for effective performance have been relatively easy to translate into the more basic concepts of the model. Their conceptual properties were similar to those of the more basic concepts, and the operations used in their measurement corresponded to one or more of the "admissible" operations of the basic concepts. In other cases, the "fit" has been much more difficult. The relationship between such terms as participation in decision making, repetitiveness of the job, and supervisory consideration and the concepts in the model is far from clear and is probably complex.

There are some advantages to be gained by the use of a relatively simple and basic set of concepts to describe and analyze the complex phenomena of interest to the applied psychologist. Applied psychologists have rarely been precise or systematic in their language. It is not uncommon to find almost as many terms for a referent as there are investigators concerned with it. These terms are usually borrowed from "everyday" language and are seldom adequately defined or systematically related to other concepts. As a result, the relationship between the work of different investigators is often obscured and the lines of progress are difficult to discern.

Consistent use of a unitary conceptual model makes it easier to see the relationship between the research of different investigators dealing with the same basic problem. Superficial differences in language are ignored in the presence of basic similarities in conceptual properties and in operational definitions. For example, we can forget the fact that one researcher describes his study as an investigation of the determinants of morale, a second as an investigation of the determinants of job satisfaction, and a third as an investigation of the determinants of attitudes toward the job, if all are seeking to ascertain the conditions affecting the attractiveness of a job to its occupant and attempting to measure this attractiveness through verbal report.

It also becomes easier to see the relevance of research on one problem for research on other problems. We have argued that researchers interested in the occupational choice process and those studying the determinants of job satisfaction are, at least partly, dealing with the same problem—the conditions affecting the valence of a job to a person. This similarity of interest has been obscured by the fact that those investigating these two problems have couched their research in very different terms. There has, in fact, been remarkably little exchange between investigators concerned with these two dependent variables and, as has been pointed out, the study of each has taken quite different directions. Those interested in occupational choice have most frequently looked at individual differences in personality, while those interested in job satisfaction have sought their explanations in terms of differences in work roles.

To be of scientific value, a model must do more than provide a means of describing phenomena. It must provide explanations that are potentially verifiable. The model outlined in Chapter Two sets forth a complex network of relations among different measures of behavior, and between both past and present situational conditions and behavior. Perhaps the best tests of the various components of this model are to be found in basic experimentation not described in this book. However, our concern at this point is with the extent to which it helps us make "sense" out of the literature on work and motivation.

At various places in the book we have attempted to compare the evidence with predictions from the model, but this has not been done in any formal or systematic fashion. In an effort to be a little more systematic about the relationship between the model and existing data, let us restate the two major propositions in the model. From each of these propositions we will formally derive hypotheses concerning persons' occupational choices, their job satisfaction, and their job performance. Following the statement of each hypothesis we will briefly summarize the relevant evidence.

Proposition 1: The valence of an outcome to a person is a monotonically increasing function of the algebraic sum of

the products of the valences of all other outcomes and his
conceptions of its instrumentality for the attainment of
these other outcomes.

Hypothesis 1a (Occupational Choice): The valence of an
occupation to a person is a monotonically increasing function of the algebraic sum of the products of the valences of
all other outcomes and his conceptions of the instrumentality of the occupation for the attainment of these other
outcomes.

Most of the evidence supporting this hypothesis is correlational. Investigators have measured the valence of occupations to
persons and related them to measures of their motives (that is, the
valence of other outcomes) and to measures of their beliefs regarding the occupation (that is, conceptions of the instrumentality of
the occupation for the attainment of outcomes). Judging from the
reported literature, the model is reasonably consistent with existing
data. There is considerable evidence that people's *stated preferences*
among occupations are logically consistent with their reported
values or motives (Stone, 1933; Astin, 1958), and further evidence
that they are consistent with their motives as revealed in an analysis
of their fantasy (McClelland, 1955). People tend to describe as attractive the occupations that actually provide outcomes they desire to
attain.

There are also data indicating that persons' *choices* among
occupations can be predicted from measures of the strength of their
values or motives. There are a large number of investigations showing a logical consistency between people's occupational choices and
their reported motives (Vernon and Allport, 1931; Pintner, 1933;
Cantril and Allport, 1933; Duffy and Crissey, 1940; Traxler and
McCall, 1941; Yum, 1942; Marzolf, 1946; Kuder, 1946; Seashore,
1947; Allport, Vernon, and Lindzey, 1951; Rosenberg, 1957; Conrad
and Jaffe, 1960), and other investigations showing such a consistency between choices of tasks in laboratory situations and motives
revealed in an analysis of fantasy (Atkinson and Litwin, 1960; Atkinson, Bastian, Earl, and Litwin, 1960).

The most direct test of the hypothesis is found in a study by
Englander (1960) and in an unpublished study by Vroom. In both

investigations, index scores obtained by combining data on the valence of outcomes and data on the instrumentality of occupations for their attainment in the manner specified in the hypothesis were found to be highly related to occupational preferences and choices.

Hypothesis 1b (Job Satisfaction): The valence of a job to a person performing it is a monotonically increasing function of the algebraic sum of the products of the valences of all other outcomes and his conceptions of the instrumentality of the job for the attainment of these other outcomes.

There are considerable data indicating that persons' reports of the attractiveness of their jobs (that is, the extent of their job satisfaction) are directly related to the extent to which their jobs are instrumental to the attainment of outcomes that might be assumed to be generally attractive to persons. Thus we find evidence that the amount of satisfaction with their jobs reported by persons is directly related to the amount of pay they receive (Thompson, 1939; Miller, 1941; Barnett, Handelsman, Stewart, and Super, 1952), to the amount of consideration that they report receiving from their supervisors (Fleishman, Harris, and Burtt, 1955; Halpin and Winer, 1957; Seeman, 1957; Likert, 1961), to their reports concerning the probability of their promotion (Morse, 1953; Sirota, 1959), to the extent to which they can interact with their co-workers (Sawatsky, 1951; Richards and Dobryns, 1957), to the amount of their acceptance by co-workers (Van Zelst, 1951; Zaleznik, Christensen, and Roethlisberger, 1958), to the number of different operations that they perform (Wyatt, Fraser, and Stock, 1929; Walker, 1950; Walker and Guest, 1952; Elliott, 1953; Guest, 1957), to the extent to which they have control over their pace of work (Walker and Marriott, 1951; Marriott and Denerley, 1955), and to the extent to which they can influence decisions that have future effects on them (Jacobson, 1951; Baumgartel, 1956; Morse and Reimer, 1956; French, Israel, and Ås, 1960; Vroom, 1960a).

Some of these variables have been found to be related to absences and turnover. Wickert (1951) and Ross and Zander (1957) found that people who remained on the job more frequently reported that they had a chance to make decisions than those who resigned; Kerr, Koppelmeir, and Sullivan (1951) found the highest turnover among persons with the least opportunity for informal interaction; Baldamus (1951) found a positive correlation between the repetitiveness of jobs and the rate of turnover among their occupants; Fleishman, Harris, and Burtt (1955) found a negative relationship between supervisory consideration and absenteeism; and Fleishman and Harris (1962) found a negative relationship between consideration and turnover.

Insofar as people differ in their desires and aversions, the effects of work role variables on job satisfaction would be expected to differ from one person to another. Some specific predictions of this type may be derived from the hypothesis. If an outcome is negatively valent to a person, an increase in the perceived instrumentality of his job with respect to that outcome would decrease the valence of his job; if he were indifferent to the outcome, such an increase in instrumentality would have no effect on the valence of his job; and if the outcome were positively valent, such an increase would increase the valence of his job. Support for this type of interaction between work role variables and individual differences in motives has been obtained in correlational studies (Schaffer, 1953; Vroom, 1959a, 1960a) and in a field experiment (Tannenbaum and Allport, 1956).

Hypothesis 1c (Job Performance): The valence of effective performance on a task or job is a monotonically increasing function of the algebraic sum of the products of the valences of all other outcomes and the worker's conceptions of the instrumentality of effective performance for the attainment of these outcomes.

The principal evidence relevant to this hypothesis is based on observations of the conditions under which persons actually perform effectively on tasks or jobs. Most of the findings are experimental, although some correlational studies have been conducted.

If we assume that the valence of money is positive, it follows from the hypothesis that the valence of effective performance will increase as the instrumentality of effective performance for the attainment of money increases. There is considerable evidence in support of this prediction. Wyatt (1934) found that workers in a candy factory increased their level of performance when shifted from payment on a time basis to payment on a bonus system. There was a further increase when the payment was shifted to a straight piece rate. Atkinson and Reitman (1956), Atkinson (1958b), and Kaufmann (1962) observed a higher level of performance on the part of subjects performing tasks in laboratory settings who were told that the amount of money they would earn would be dependent on the effectiveness of their performance. Georgopoulos, Mahoney, and Jones (1957) found that workers who report that effective performance is instrumental to higher wages perform more effectively than those who report that effective performance is irrelevant to or will hinder the attainment of wages. Because, for workers on a group incentive system, the instrumentality of effective performance for the attainment of money is greater in small than in large groups, Marriott's finding (1949) that the mean level of individual performance for workers on group incentives is negatively related to group size may also be interpreted as supporting this prediction.

If we assume that the valence of acceptance by co-workers is positive, it follows that the valence of effective performance will increase as the instrumentality of effective performance for the attainment of such acceptance increases. Supporting this hypothesis is evidence from laboratory experiments (Schachter, Ellertson, McBride, and Gregory, 1951; Berkowitz, 1954) that subjects tend to conform to influence attempts from co-workers to raise or lower their level of productivity. It is also supported by the finding of Georgopoulos, Mahoney, and Jones (1957) that workers who report that effective performance increases their acceptance by their co-workers tend to perform more effectively than those who report that effective performance is unrelated to or will hinder acceptance by co-workers.

It also follows from the hypothesis that the effects on performance of changes in its instrumentality for the attainment of an outcome will vary with the valence of that outcome. If the outcome is strongly desired, then an increase in the instrumentality of effective performance for its attainment will result in a greater increase in the valence of effective performance than if the outcome is less strongly desired. The results of several investigations are consistent with this prediction. Georgopoulos, Mahoney, and Jones (1957) found that the relationship between performance and workers' reports concerning its instrumentality for the attainment of wages was more positive for those who rated money relatively high in importance. The same investigators also obtained evidence for an interaction between instrumentality of performance for the attainment of acceptance by co-workers and promotions and the valence of these outcomes.

Also relevant to this interaction are the findings of Schachter, Ellertson, McBride, and Gregory (1951) and Berkowitz (1954). They found that experimentally created group norms regarding production had greater effect on the level of performance of high cohesiveness groups, where acceptance by other group members might be presumed to be relatively important, than on the level of performance of low cohesiveness groups, where acceptance by other group members might be presumed to be relatively unimportant. These results are, in turn, consistent with Seashore's finding (1954) that workers in high cohesiveness groups are more likely to perform at the same level as their co-workers than workers in low cohesiveness groups.

Proposition 2: The force on a person to perform an act is a monotonically increasing function of the algebraic sum of the products of the valences of all outcomes and the strength of his expectancies that the act will be followed by the attainment of these outcomes.

Hypothesis 2a (Occupational Choice): The force on a person to attempt to enter an occupation is a monotonically increasing function of the product of the valence of the occupation and of his expectancy that his attempt will be successful.

There is relatively little evidence bearing directly on this hypothesis. It is clear that individuals' reports concerning their preferences among occupations disproportionately favor higher status occupations (Kroger and Louttit, 1935; Sisson, 1938; Livesay, 1941) and do not always coincide with the choices that they make among them (Williamson, 1939; Rosenberg, 1957; Walster, 1963). Strong (1943) has listed a number of factors that might be responsible for the differences between actual choices and reported preferences, but there has been little attempt to measure them or to systematically relate them to models of the occupational choice process.

The investigation having the most direct bearing on this hypothesis is the experiment conducted by Rosen (1961). He found that the probability of a person making responses that were relevant to the attainment of an occupation was positively related to his previous report of the attractiveness of the occupation and to the indicated probability that he will be successful in entering it. There was, however, no evidence of an interaction between valence and expectancy, such as would be predicted by the hypothesis.

Hypothesis 2b (Job Satisfaction): The force on a person to remain in a job in which he is presently working is a mono-tonically increasing function of the product of the valence of that job and the strength of his expectancy that he will be able to remain in it.

There is considerable evidence bearing on the relationship between the measured or experimentally manipulated valence of a job or group to the probability of a person permanently or temporarily leaving the job or group. Some investigators have shown that the probability that a worker will resign from a job is inversely related to the extent of his reported satisfaction with it (Weitz and Nuckols, 1953; Webb and Hollander, 1956), and others have found that the probability of a person withdrawing from a group is inversely related to the strength of attraction he reports for it (Sagi, Olmstead, and Atelsek, 1955; Libo, 1953). In addition, there is evidence of a negative correlation between the turnover rates of groups and the level of their morale or job satisfaction (Giese and Ruter, 1949; Fleishman, Harris, and Burtt, 1955).

In a laboratory experiment dealing with this relationship, Libo (1953) found that a smaller proportion of members chose to withdraw from groups in which a high level of attraction to the group was experimentally created than from groups in which a low level of attraction to the group was created. He also found a marked positive relationship between subjects' scores on a projective measure of attraction to the group and the likelihood that they would decide to remain in the group.

It follows from our model that the outcome of a person's

decision to remain in or to leave his job is dependent on the relative strength of the forces to remain and to leave. One rough indicator of the strength of the latter force might be the state of the labor market. If jobs are scarce the force to leave should be weaker than if jobs are abundant. Supporting this prediction are the results of several studies (Brissenden and Frankel, 1922; Woytinsky, 1942; Behrend, 1953) indicating that voluntary turnover rates are higher in periods of full employment than in periods of considerable unemployment.

A significant negative relationship has also been reported between measures of job satisfaction and absence rates (Kornhauser and Sharp, 1932; Van Zelst and Kerr, 1953; Metzner and Mann, 1953; Fleishman, Harris, and Burtt, 1955). However, the size and even the direction of this relationship appears to depend somewhat on the kind of absence measure used (Kerr, Koppelmeir, and Sullivan, 1951; Metzner and Mann, 1953) and on the population studied (Metzner and Mann, 1953).

> **Hypothesis 2c (Job Performance):** The force on a person to exert a given amount of effort in performance of his job is a monotonically increasing function of the algebraic sum of the products of the valences of different levels of performance and his expectancies that this amount of effort will be followed by their attainment.

If we assume that people usually expect increased effort to increase their level of performance, it follows from this hypothesis that increases in the valence of effective performance will increase level of performance. There is a great deal of evidence bearing on this relationship. Some of this evidence has already been summarized in this chapter in connection with the hypothesis dealing with the functional relations between the valence of effective performance and the valence of other outcomes to which it is instrumental. We have also argued that there are affective consequences associated with different levels of performance that are independent of their externally mediated consequences. Effective performance may constitute a reward as well as a means to the attainment of rewards. The most direct evidence of this fact is the association between task performance and need for achievement as measured by an analysis of fantasy (Lowell, 1952; French, 1955; Wendt, 1955; Atkinson and Raphelson, 1956).

It seems likely that the evidence regarding the effects on performance of participation in decision making (Lewin, Lippitt, and White, 1939; Coch and French, 1948; Bavelas, 1950; Lawrence and Smith, 1955; Morse and Reimer, 1956; Vroom, 1959a, 1960a) and of knowledge of results (Arps, 1920; Johanson, 1922; Bingham, 1932; Manzer, 1935; Smode, 1958) can be attributed, at least in part, to a tendency for persons to derive satisfaction from successfully executing decisions that they have helped to make and to derive satisfaction from improving upon their previous level of performance. However, we have noted that there may be a number of psychological bases for the effects of both of these variables and that the specific role of each has not been clearly determined.

If effective performance is preferred to ineffective performance, it follows from the hypothesis that performance should increase as the expected relationship between level of effort and level of performance increases. There are little data in the literature that are relevant to this prediction. Investigations of the consequences of experimentally manipulated success and failure on effort and performance are not unequivocal tests of this prediction and have produced conflicting results. We speculated that the effects of success and failure might be dependent on the level of effort exerted by the subject prior to succeeding or failing, the persistence of the success or failure, and previously established beliefs concerning the probability of success under different levels of effort.

It can be seen that there is considerable correspondence between the derivations from our basic propositions and evidence that is presently available concerning the determinants of occupational choice, job satisfaction, and job performance. This evidence in no sense "proves" the propositions, but it does suggest that they constitute a fruitful point of departure in our efforts to find principles and generalizations concerning work and motivation.

Our stress in this chapter on the consistency between predicted and observed relations does not mean that our model can account for all of the findings reported in this book. Many of the studies we described are irrelevant to it. For example, we had no firm basis for predicting or accounting for the influence of sex or of father's occupation on occupational choice. The variables of sex and of father's occupation do not correspond to any of the operational definitions of the concepts in the model that were presented in Chapter Two. Needless to say, we can always speculate concerning their psychological basis. However, these speculations would clearly be "ad hoc" and not subject to verification from data presently in hand.

Some of the findings not explicitly predicted in advance become interpretable in terms of the model if it is assumed that all people share a particular system of preferences. One set of data that can be explained in this way concerns the influence of the self-concept on occupational choice, job satisfaction, and job performance. Let us briefly summarize this evidence and then present the assumptions about motivation needed to account for them.

In Chapter Four we noted a relationship between people's reports of their preferences among activities and their estimates of their ability to perform them (Thorndike, 1917; King and Adelstein, 1917; Fryer, 1927). We also observed that occupational preferences and choices were predictable from the degree of congruence between peoples' ratings of their abilities and of occupational requirements (Vroom, unpublished study) and that occupational preferences could be systematically altered by providing people with false information about their ability to perform them (Rosen, 1961). In Chapter Five, we found that a person's job satisfaction was correlated with the extent to which he viewed the job as requiring his abilities (Brophy, 1959; Vroom, 1962; Kornhauser, 1965) and that failure on a task had more negative effects on the satisfaction of persons who believed that the task required abilities that they had been induced to value (Kaufmann, 1962). Finally, in Chapter Eight, we discovered that level of performance could be increased by instructions to the effect that the task required valued abilities (Kaustler, 1951; Atkinson, reported in McClelland, Atkinson, Clark, and Lowell, 1953; French, 1955) or abilities that they thought they possessed (Kaufmann, 1962). We also described one experiment that indicates that people strive to perform at a level that is consistent with their conceptions of their abilities (Aronson and Carlsmith, 1962).

Interpretation of these findings in terms of our model appears to require three assumptions about motivation: (1) people prefer tasks and jobs that they believe require the use of their abilities; (2) people prefer consistent information about their abilities to inconsistent information; and (3) people prefer receiving information to the effect that they possess valued abilities to information that they do not possess valued abilities.

None of these assumptions about motivation is implausible but they are not derivable from one another. Although further research will undoubtedly indicate individual differences in the strength of these motives and lead to the identification of the conditions affecting their strength, these crude assumptions appear to hold considerable promise for increasing our understanding of occupational choice, job satisfaction, and job performance.

Of equal or greater significance in evaluating the usefulness of our assumptions about motivation is the extent to which they help to identify gaps in the existing literature and point to new areas for research. If our conceptual framework helps to identify overlooked variables or processes, then it will have been fruitful, even though details of the model may later be shown to be incorrect.

At various places in the book we suggested problems for future research. Many of these problems were stimulated by a comparison of the model with the existing literature. No attempt will be made to summarize these suggestions here. We will merely note one of the most general implications of the model—that occupational choice, job satisfaction, and job performance should be regarded as joint functions of individual differences in motives and cognized or actual properties of work roles. We should not expect to be able to account for these phenomena solely in terms of individual differences in desires and aversions or solely in terms of beliefs about or actual properties of work roles. Both sets of variables are involved, and there are important interactions between them.

Theories that do not lead to the systematic collection of data to test them are of limited value. Similarly, data collection in the absence of the construction of models or theory to explain the data can be wasted effort. The construction of theory and accumulation of empirical observations must work hand in hand, with each providing the necessary corrective adjustments in the other. Traditionally, industrial and occupational psychologists have focused on the accumulation of empirical observations and neglected the contribution of theory. It is frequently argued that the problems are too complex or that present knowledge is too scanty to permit theoretical development. Although these arguments seem persuasive, it is hard to be impressed by the results of adherence to this position of "raw empiricism." Principles are either nonexistent or few and far between. Instead of contributing to the construction of a permanent edifice of knowledge, most additions to the morass of existing data only serve to increase our respect for the complexity of human behavior and to emphasize our inability to achieve any lasting understanding of it.

Although greater attention to matters of theory and the psychological processes underlying the problems studied by the applied psychologist in no sense represents a panacea, it can prove extremely useful. We found that our model of the motivation process served three important functions: (1) it provided us with a general language for conceptualizing diverse problems; (2) it permitted us to derive hypotheses that are reasonably consistent with existing evidence; and (3) it suggested new approaches to old problems, that is, variables that the model would suggest to be important have customarily been overlooked in existing research.

The model of motivation that we utilized throughout this book is offered merely as a point of departure. Undoubtedly it will have to be modified and expanded to better approximate the complexities of human behavior. We hope that its presentation here will stimulate other investigators' attempts to identify its weaknesses and replace it with more useful models.

Our focus on motivation does not mean that we believe it to be the only psychological process relevant to an understanding of the behavior of persons at work. It would have been equally meaningful to have written a book entitled *Work and Learning, Work and Perception,* or *Work and Problem Solving.* The guiding models would have been different, as would the problems and empirical investigations that we would have chosen to discuss. The common element would have been the conviction, which we hope was represented in these pages, that the explanation of the behavior of people in work situations has to be sought in an examination of basic psychological processes.

Conclusion

This was not a book on "how to do it." Our emphasis was on scientific or empirical questions rather than on technological ones. We sought to describe what is known about certain aspects of the relationship between people and their work and said little about available techniques for influencing this relationship. The methods of vocational guidance, time and motion study, sensitivity training, and employee counseling, to name just a few, received only casual mention, if they were discussed at all.

This emphasis should not be construed as reflecting indifference to the application of knowledge. It merely represents the conviction that existing technologies in the behavioral sciences are seldom adequate to handle the complexities of the phenomena with which they purport to deal and that improvements in these technologies are likely to come about through advances in scientific knowledge.

The relationship between science and technology is much closer in the physical and biological sciences than it is in the behavioral sciences. In the former fields, professional practice rests on a rather firm foundation of scientific knowledge in the underlying disciplines; in the behavioral sciences this gap is much larger. The methods and procedures of the professional, whether his field is psychotherapy or management development, labor arbitration or advertising, are rooted in his own experience and the experience of those who have gone before him, and have a most tenuous relationship to data accumulated from the use of the scientific method.

We cannot lay the blame for this unfortunate state of affairs at the feet of the professional. The results of scientific investigations are seldom written in a language that he can understand and are typically concerned with problems that he views as irrelevant to his work. Nor can we criticize the behavioral scientist, who chooses to focus on simple and easily researchable matters and prefers to leave more complex problems to a later stage in the development of his discipline. Research on the behavior of the white rat in a T-maze can be carried out with much greater precision and control than research on the behavior of the consumer in the marketplace, the patient on the couch, or the worker on his job.

This book has been directed toward filling in part of the middle ground between the science of psychology and technologies for influencing human behavior. We have attempted to treat the ever-growing empirical literature on people and their jobs as special cases of more basic psychological laws, on the assumption that in such literature may be found the needed foundation for the technologies of tomorrow. Although there are undoubtedly many unsolved questions, we hope that the preceding pages have helped to bring these to light and that, in the future, research may be carried out to obtain the needed answers.

References

Abel, T. M. The influence of social facilitation on motor performance at different levels of intelligence. *Amer. J. Psychol.*, 1938, *51*, 379-389.

Adams, J. S. Toward an understanding of inequity. *J. abnorm. soc. Psychol.*, 1963, *67*, 422-436.

Adams, J. S., and Jacobsen, P. R. *The behavioral manifestation of cognitive dissonance reduction in a work situation.* New York: General Electric Co. Behavioral Research Service, 1963 (Mimeo).

Adams, J. S., and Rosenbaum, W. B. The relationship of worker productivity to cognitive dissonance about wage inequities. *J. appl. Psychol.*, 1962, *46*, 161-164.

Adkins, D. C., and Kuder, G. F. The relation of primary mental abilities to activity preference. *Psychometrika*, 1940, *5*, 251-262.

Adorno, T. W., Frenkel-Brunswik, E., Levinson, D. J., and Sanford, R. N. *The authoritarian personality.* New York: HarperCollins, 1950.

Allport, F. H. The influence of the group upon association and thought. *J. exp. Psychol.*, 1920, *3*, 159-182.

Allport, G. The historical background of modern social psychology. In Lindzey, G. (ed.) *Handbook of social psychology.* Cambridge, Mass.: Addison-Wesley, 1954, pp. 3-56.

Allport, G. W., Vernon, P. E., and Lindzey, G. *Study of values.* (Revised edition.) Boston: Houghton Mifflin, 1951.

Alper, T. G. Memory for completed and incomplete tasks as a

function of personality: An analysis of group data. *J. abnorm. soc. Psychol.*, 1946a, *41*, 403-421.

Alper, T. G. Task-orientation vs. ego-orientation in learning and retention. *Amer. J. Psychol.*, 1946b, *59*, 236-248.

Alper, T. G. Task-orientation and ego-orientation as factors in reminiscence. *J. exp. Psychol.*, 1948, *38*, 224-238.

Alpert, R. Anxiety in academic achievement situations: Its measurement and relation to aptitude. Unpublished doctoral dissertation. Stanford, Calif.: Stanford University, 1957.

Ammons, R. B. Effects of knowledge of performance: A survey and tentative theoretical formulation. *J. gen. Psychol.*, 1956, *54*, 279-299.

Anderson, C. A. An experimental study of "social facilitation" as affected by intelligence. *Amer. J. Sociol.*, 1928, *34*, 874-881.

Anderson, H. D., and Davidson, P. E. *Recent occupational trends in the American labor market.* Stanford, Calif.: Stanford University Press, 1945.

Annett, J., and Kay, H. Knowledge of results and skilled performance. *Occup. Psychol.*, 1957, *31*, 69-79.

Argyle, M., Gardner, G., and Cioffi, F. Supervisory methods related to productivity, absenteeism, and labour turnover. *Hum. Relat.*, 1958, *11*, 23-40.

Argyris, C. *Interpersonal competence and organizational effectiveness.* Homewood, Ill.: Irwin, 1962.

Aronson, E. The effect of effort on the attractiveness of rewarded and unrewarded stimuli. *J. abnorm. soc. Psychol.*, 1961, *63*, 373-380.

Aronson, E., and Carlsmith, J. M. Performance expectancy as a determinant of actual performance. *J. abnorm. soc. Psychol.*, 1962, *65*, 178-182.

Arps, G. F. Work with knowledge of results versus work without knowledge of results. *Psychol. Monogr.*, 1920, *28*, No. 3 (entire issue 125).

Ash, P. The S R A employee inventory—a statistical analysis. *Personnel Psychol.*, 1954, *7*, 337-364.

Astin, A. W. Dimensions of work satisfaction in the occupational choices of college freshmen. *J. appl. Psychol.*, 1958, *42*, 187-190.

Atkinson, J. W. Motivational determinants of risk-taking behavior. *Psychol. Rev.*, 1957, *64*, 359-372.

Atkinson, J. W. (ed.) *Motives in fantasy, action, and society.* New York: Van Nostrand Reinhold, 1958a.

Atkinson, J. W. Towards experimental analysis of human motivation in terms of motives, expectancies, and incentives. In Atkinson, J. W. (ed.) *Motives in fantasy, action, and society.* New York: Van Nostrand Reinhold, 1958b, pp. 288-305.

Atkinson, J. W., Bastian, J. R., Earl, R. W., and Litwin, G. H. The achievement motive, goal setting, and probability preferences. *J. abnorm. soc. Psychol.*, 1960, *60*, 27-36.

Atkinson, J. W., and Litwin, G. H. Achievement motive and test anxiety conceived as motive to approach success and motive to avoid failure. *J. abnorm. soc. Psychol.*, 1960, *60*, 52-63.

Atkinson, J. W., and Raphelson, A. C. Individual differences in motivation and behavior in particular situations. *J. Pers.*, 1956, *24*, 349-363.

Atkinson, J. W., and Reitman, W. R. Performance as a function of motive strength and expectancy of goal attainment. *J. abnorm. soc. Psychol.*, 1956, *53*, 361-366.

Babchuk, N., and Goode, W. J. Work incentives in a self-determined group. *Amer. soc. Rev.*, 1951, *16*, 679-687.

Bachman, J. G. Some motivated effects of control in a task situation as a function of ability. [Unpublished doctoral dissertation.] Philadelphia: University of Pennsylvania, 1962.

Back, K. W. Influence through social communication. *J. abnorm. soc. Psychol.*, 1951, *46*, 9-23.

Baehr, M. E. A factorial study of the S R A employee inventory. *Personnel Psychol.*, 1954, *7*, 319-336.

Bakke, E. W. *Citizens without work.* New Haven: Yale University Press, 1940a.

Bakke, E. W. *The employed worker.* New Haven: Yale University Press, 1940b.

Baldamus, W. Type of work and motivation. *Brit. J. Sociol.*, 1951, *2*, 44-58.

Balderston, C. C. *Group incentives.* Philadelphia: University of Pennsylvania Press, 1930.

Baldwin, A. L. The role of an "ability" construct in a theory of behavior. In McClelland, D. C., Baldwin, A. L., Bronfenbrenner, U., and Strodtbeck, F. L. (eds.) *Talent and society*. New York: Van Nostrand Reinhold, 1958, pp. 195-232.

Bancroft, G. *The American labor force*. New York: Wiley, 1958.

Barnett, G. J., Handelsman, I., Stewart, L. H., and Super, D. E. The occupational level scale as a measure of drive. *Psychol. Monogr.*, 1952, *66*, No. 10 (entire issue 342).

Bass, B. M. Leadership opinions as forecasts of supervisory success. *J. appl. Psychol.*, 1956, *40*, 345-346.

Bass, B. M. Leadership opinions as forecasts of supervisory success: A replication. *Personnel Psychol.*, 1958, *11*, 515-518.

Bass, B. M. *Leadership, psychology, and organizational behavior*. New York: HarperCollins, 1960.

Baumgartel, H. Leadership, motivations, and attitudes in research laboratories. *J. soc. Issues*, 1956, *12*(2), 24-31.

Bavelas, A. Communication patterns in task-oriented groups. *J. acoust. Soc. Amer.*, 1950, *22*, 725-730.

Behling, O., and Starke, F. A. The postulates of expectancy theory. *Acad. Mgt. J.*, 1973, *16*, 376-381.

Behrend, H. Absence and labour turnover in a changing economic climate. *Occup. Psychol.*, 1953, *27*, 69-79.

Bell, G. B., and French, R. L. Consistency of individual leadership position in small groups of varying membership. *J. abnorm. soc. Psychol.*, 1950, *45*, 764-767.

Bellows, R. M. *Psychology of personnel in business and industry*. Englewood Cliffs, N.J.: Prentice-Hall, 1949.

Bendix, R., Lipset, S. M., and Malm, F. T. Social origins and occupational career patterns. *Industr. lab. relat. Rev.*, 1954, *7*, 246-261.

Benge, E. J. Promotional Practices for Technical Men. *Advanc. Mgmt.*, Mar. 1956, *21*, 10-12.

Bennett, E. B. Discussion, decision, commitment, and consensus in "group decision." *Hum. Relat.*, 1955, *8*, 251-273.

Bennett, G. K., Seashore, H. G., and Wesman, A. G. Aptitude testing: Does it "prove out" in counseling practice? *Occupations*, 1952, *30*, 584-593.

Berdie, R. F. Factors related to vocational interests. Unpublished doctoral dissertation. Minneapolis: University of Minnesota, 1942.

Berkowitz, L. Group standards, cohesiveness, and productivity. *Hum. Relat.*, 1954, *7*, 509-519.

Berlyne, D. E. *Conflict arousal and curiosity.* New York: McGraw-Hill, 1960.

Bernadin, A. C., and Jessor, R. A construct validation of the Edwards Personal Preference Schedule with respect to dependency. *J. consult. Psychol.*, 1957, *21*, 63-67.

Bernberg, R. E. Socio-psychological factors in industrial morale: I. The prediction of specific indicators. *J. soc. Psychol.*, 1952, *36*, 73-82.

Besco, R. O., and Lawshe, C. H. Foreman leadership as perceived by superiors and subordinates. *Personnel Psychol.*, 1959, *12*, 573-582.

Bevan, W., and Adamson, R. Reinforcers and reinforcement: Their relation to maze performance. *J. exp. Psychol.*, 1960, *59*, 226-232.

Bexton, W. H., Heron, W., and Scott, T. H. Effects of decreased variation in the sensory environment. *Canad. J. Psychol.*, 1954, *8*, 70-76.

Bills, Marian A. Relation of mental alertness test scores to positions and permanency in company. *J. appl. Psychol.*, 1923, *7*, 154-156.

Bilodeau, E. A., Bilodeau, I. McD., and Schumsky, D. A. Some effects of introducing and withdrawing knowledge of results early and late in practice. *J. exp. Psychol.*, 1959, *58*, 142-144.

Bilodeau, E. A., and Bilodeau, I. McD. Motor-skills learning. In *Annual review of psychology.* Vol. 12. Palo Alto, Calif.: Annual Reviews, 1961, pp. 243-280.

Bingham, W. V. Making work worthwhile. In Bingham, W. V. (ed.) *Psychology today.* Chicago: University of Chicago Press, 1932, pp. 262-271.

Birch, H. G. The role of motivational factors in insightful problem-solving. *J. comp. Psychol.*, 1945, *38*, 295-317.

Black, R., Adamson, R., and Bevan, W. Runway behavior as a function of apparent intensity of shock. *J. comp. physiol. Psychol.*, 1961, *54*, 270-274.

Blakelock, E. Study of work and life satisfaction: III: Satisfaction with shift work. Ann Arbor: University of Michigan, Institute for Social Research, 1959 (Mimeo).

Blakelock, E. A new look at the new leisure. *Admin. Sci. Quart.*, 1960, *4*, 446-467.

Blocher, D. H., and Schutz, R. A. Relationships among self-descriptions, occupational stereotypes, and vocational preferences. *J. counsel. Psychol.*, 1961, *8*, 314-317.

Bowers, D. G. Self-esteem and the diffusion of leadership style. *J. appl. Psychol.*, 1963, *47*, 135-140.

Brayfield, A. H., and Crockett, W. H. Employee attitudes and employee performance. *Psychol. Bull.*, 1955, *52*, 396-424.

Brayfield, A. H., and Rothe, H. F. An index of job satisfaction. *J. appl. Psychol.*, 1951, *35*, 307-311.

Brayfield, A. H., Wells, R. V., and Strate, N. W. Interrelationships among measures of job satisfaction and general satisfaction. *J. appl. Psychol.*, 1957, *41*, 201-205.

Brenner, B. Effects of immediate and delayed praise and blame upon learning and recall. *Teach. Coll. Contr. Educ.*, 1934, No. 620.

Bridges, J. W., and Dollinger, V. M. The correlation between interests and abilities in college courses. *Psychol. Rev.*, 1920, *27*, 308-314.

Brill, A. A. *Basic principles of psychoanalysis.* New York: Doubleday, 1949.

Brissenden, P. F., and Frankel, E. *Labor turnover in industry.* New York: Macmillan, 1922.

Brody, M. The relationship between efficiency and job satisfaction. Unpublished master's thesis. New York: New York University, 1945.

Brogden, H. E., and Taylor, E. K. The dollar criterion—applying the cost accounting concept to criterion construction. *Personnel Psychol.*, 1950, *3*, 133-154.

Brooks, T. Promotion practices. *State of New York Industr. Bull.*, Aug. 1958, pp. 3-7.

Brophy, A. L. Self, role, and satisfaction. *Genet. Psychol. Monogr.*, 1959, *59*, 263-308.

Brown, C. W., and Ghiselli, E. E. The prediction of labor turnover by aptitude tests. *J. appl. Psychol.*, 1953, *37*, 9-12.

Brown, J. A. C. *The social psychology of industry.* Baltimore: Penguin Books, 1954.

Bruner, J. S., Matter, J., and Papanek, M. L. Breadth of learning as a function of drive level and mechanization. *Psychol. Rev.,* 1955, *62,* 1-10.

Burnstein, E. Fear of failure, achievement motivation, and aspiring to prestigeful occupations. *J. abnorm. soc. Psychol.,* 1963, *67,* 189-193.

Butler, R. A. Discrimination learning by rhesus monkeys to visual-exploration motivation. *J. comp. physiol. Psychol.,* 1953, *46,* 95-98.

Butler, R. A., and Harlow, H. F. Discrimination learning and learning sets to visual exploration incentives. *J. gen. Psychol.,* 1957, *57,* 257-264.

Byrns, R. Relation of vocational choice to mental ability and occupational opportunity. *School Rev.,* 1939, *47,* 101-109.

Cantril, H., and Allport, G. W. Recent applications of the Study of Values. *J. abnorm. soc. Psychol.,* 1933, *28,* 259-273.

Caplow, T. *The sociology of work.* Minneapolis: University of Minnesota Press, 1954.

Carey, H. H. Consultative supervision and management. *Personnel,* 1942, *18,* 286-295.

Carlson, E. R. Attitude change through modification of attitude structure. *J. abnorm. soc. Psychol.,* 1956, *52,* 256-261.

Carter, H. D., Taylor, K. vonF., and Canning, L. B. Vocational choices and interest test scores of high school students. *J. Psychol.,* 1941, *11,* 297-306.

Cartwright, D. Decision-time in relation to the differentiation of the phenomenal field. *Psychol. Rev.,* 1941, *48,* 425-442.

Cartwright, D. The effect of interruption, completion, and failure upon the attractiveness of activities. *J. exp. Psychol.,* 1942, *31,* 1-16.

Cartwright, D. Lewinian theory as a contemporary systematic framework. In Koch, S. (ed.) *Psychology: A study of a science.* Vol. 2. New York: McGraw-Hill, 1959, pp. 7-91.

Cartwright, D., and Zander, A. *Group dynamics.* (2nd ed.) Evanston, Ill.: Row, Peterson, 1960.

Castaneda, A., and Palermo, D. S. Psychomotor performance as a function of amount of training and stress. *J. exp. Psychol.*, 1955, *50*, 175-179.

Cattell, R. B., Saunders, D. R., and Stice, G. F. The dimensions of syntality in small groups. *Hum. Relat.*, 1953, *6*, 331-356.

Centers, R. Attitude and belief in relation to occupational stratification. *J. soc. Psychol.*, 1948a, *27*, 159-185.

Centers, R. Motivational aspects of occupational stratification. *J. soc. Psychol.*, 1948b, *28*, 187-217.

Centers, R., and Cantril, H. Income satisfaction and income aspiration. *J. abnorm. soc. Psychol.*, 1946, *41*, 64-69.

Chaiken, S. Heuristic versus systematic information processing and the use of source versus message cues in persuasion. 1980, *J. Pers. Soc. Psychol.*, *39*, 752-766.

Child, I. L. Children's preferences for goals easy or difficult to obtain. *Psychol. Monogr.*, 1946, *60*, No. 4 (entire issue 280).

Child, I. L., and Adelsheim, E. The motivational value of barriers for young children. *J. genet. Psychol.*, 1944, *65*, 97-111.

Clarke, A. V., and Grant, D. L. Application of a factorial method in selecting questions for an employee attitude survey. *Personnel Psychol.*, 1961, *14*, 131-139.

Coates, C. H., and Pellegrin, R. J. Executives and supervisors: Informal factors in differential bureaucratic promotion. *Admin. Sci. Quart.*, 1957, *2*, 200-215.

Coch, L., and French, J. R. P., Jr. Overcoming resistance to change. *Hum. Relat.*, 1948, *1*, 512-532.

Cohen, J. An aid in the computation of correlations based on Q-sorts. *Psychol. Bull.*, 1957, *54*, 138-9.

Collier, G., and Marx, M. H. Changes in performance as a function of shifts in magnitude of reinforcement. *J. exp. Psychol.*, 1959, *57*, 305-309.

Collins, O., Dalton, M., and Roy, D. Restriction of output and social cleavage in industry. *Appl. Anthrop.*, 1946, *5*(3), 1-14.

Conrad, R., and Jaffe, H. Occupational choice and values in a mass society. Paper read at meeting of the American Sociological Association, New York, August 28-31, 1960.

Cowdery, K. M. Measurement of professional attitudes: Differences between lawyers, physicians and engineers. *J. Personnel Res.*, 1926, *5*, 131-141.

Crespi, L. P. Quantitative variation of incentive and performance in the white rat. *Amer. J. Psychol.*, 1942, *55*, 467-517.

Crockett, H. J., Jr. Achievement motivation and occupational mobility in the United States. Unpublished doctoral dissertation. Ann Arbor: University of Michigan, 1961.

Cronbach, L. J. The two disciplines of scientific psychology. *Amer. Psych.*, 1957, *12*, 671-684.

Cronbach, L. J. *Essentials of psychological testing.* (2nd ed.) New York: HarperCollins, 1960.

Cronbach, L. J., and Gleser, G. C. *Psychological tests and personnel decisions.* Urbana: University of Illinois Press, 1957.

Crowne, D. P., and Marlowe, D. A new scale of social desirability independent of psychopathology. *J. consult. Psychol.*, 1960, *24*, 349-354.

Cyert, R. M., and March, J. G. *A behavioral theory of the firm.* Englewood Cliffs, N.J.: Prentice-Hall, 1963.

Dabas, Z. S. The dimensions of morale: An item factorization of the S R A employee inventory. *Personnel Psychol.*, 1958, *11*, 217-234.

Dalton, M. *Men who manage: Fusions of feeling and theory in administration.* New York: Wiley, 1959.

Darley, J. G. Relationships among the Primary Mental Abilities Tests, selected achievement measures, personality tests, and tests of vocational interests. *University of Minnesota studies in higher education*, 1941, pp. 192-200.

Dashiell, J. F. Experimental studies of the influence of social situations on the behavior of individual human adults. In Murchison, C. (ed.) *A handbook of social psychology.* Worcester, Mass.: Clark University Press, 1935.

Davidson, D., Suppes, P., and Siegel, S. *Decision making: An experimental approach.* Stanford, Calif.: Stanford University Press, 1957.

Davidson, P. E., and Anderson, H. D. *Occupational mobility in an American community.* Stanford, Calif.: Stanford University Press, 1937.

Davis, A. The motivation of the underprivileged worker. In Whyte, W. F. (ed.) *Industry and society.* New York: McGraw-Hill, 1946, pp. 84-106.

Davis, B. Eminence and level of social origin. *Amer. J. Sociol.*, 1953, *59*, 11–18.

Davis, K. *Human relations at work.* New York: McGraw-Hill, 1962.

Davis, L. E. Job design and productivity: A new approach. *Personnel*, 1957, *33*, 418–430.

Davitz, J. R. Social perception and sociometric choice of children. *J. abnorm. soc. Psychol.*, 1955, *50*, 173–176.

Deci, E. L., and Ryan, R. M. *Intrinsic motivation and self-determination in human behavior.* New York: Plenum, 1985.

DeMan, H. *Joy in work.* (Paul, C., trans.) Troy, Mo.: Holt, Rinehart & Winston, 1927.

Deutsch, M. An experimental study of the effects of co-operation and competition upon group process. *Hum. Relat.*, 1949, *2*, 199–231.

Diggory, J. C., Klein, S. J., and Cohen, M. Muscle action potentials and estimated probability of success. Paper read at meeting of the American Psychological Association, St. Louis, Mo., Sept. 3, 1962.

Diggory, J. C., and Loeb, A. Level of aspiration, probability of success, and actual performance in chronic schizophrenic patients. Paper read at meeting of the Eastern Psychological Association, Atlantic City, N.J., Apr. 27, 1962.

Diggory, J. C., and Magaziner, D. E. Self-evaluation as a function of instrumentally relevant capacities. *Bull. de l'Ass. int. de Psychol. appl.*, 1959, *8*, 3–19.

Diggory, J. C., and Ostroff, B. Estimated probability of success as a function of variability in performance. *Amer. J. Psychol.*, 1962, *75*, 94–101.

Diggory, J. C., Riley, E. J., and Blumenfeld, R. Estimated probability of success for a fixed goal. *Amer. J. Psychol.*, 1960, *73*, 41–55.

Dill, W. R., Hilton, T. L., and Reitman, W. R. *The new managers: Patterns of behavior and development.* Englewood Cliffs, N.J.: Prentice-Hall, 1962.

Dittes, J. E. Attractiveness of group as function of self-esteem and acceptance by group. *J. abnorm. soc. Psychol.*, 1959, *59*, 77–82.

Dittes, J. E., and Kelley, H. H. Effects of different conditions of acceptance upon conformity to group norms. *J. abnorm. soc. Psychol.*, 1956, *53*, 100-107.

Duffy, E., and Crissy, W. J. E. Evaluative attitudes as related to vocational interests and academic achievement. *J. abnorm. soc. Psychol.*, 1940, *35*, 226-245.

Dunnette, M. D. *Handbook of industrial and organizational psychology*. Skokie, Ill.: Rand McNally, 1976.

Dunnette, M. D., and Hough, L. M. (eds.) *Handbook of industrial and organizational psychology*, Vol. I. Palo Alto, Calif.: Consulting Psychologists Press, 1990.

Dvorak, B. J. Adjustment of premedical freshmen to the university. Unpublished master's thesis. Minneapolis: University of Minnesota, 1930.

Dvorak, B. J. The new U.S.E.S. general aptitude test battery. *Occupations*, 1947, *26*, 42-44.

Edwards, A. L. *The social desirability variable in personality assessment and research*. New York: Dryden, 1957.

Edwards, W. The theory of decision making. *Psychol. Bull.*, 1954, *51*, 380-417.

Elliott, J. D. Increasing office productivity through job enlargement. In *The human side of the office manager's job*. New York: American Management Association, 1953, Office Management Series, No. 134, pp. 3-15.

Elwell, J. L., and Grindley, G. C. The effect of knowledge of results on learning and performance I: A coordinated movement of the two hands. *Brit. J. Psychol.*, 1938, *29*, 39-53.

Englander, M. E. A psychological analysis of vocational choice: teaching. *J. counsel. Psychol.*, 1960, *7*, 257-264.

Ericksen, C. W. Individual differences in defensive forgetting. *J. exp. Psychol.*, 1952, *44*, 442-446.

Estes, W. K. Stimulus-response theory of drive. In Jones, M. R. (ed.) *Nebraska symposium on motivation*. Lincoln: University of Nebraska Press, 1958, pp. 35-69.

Farber, B. An index of marital integration. *Sociometry*, 1957, *20*, 117-134.

Farber, I. E., and Spence, K. W. Complex learning and conditioning as a function of anxiety. *J. exp. Psychol.*, 1953, *45*, 120-125.

Feldman, H. *Problems in labor relations.* New York: Macmillan, 1937.

Festinger, L. *A theory of cognitive dissonance.* Evanston, Ill.: Row, Peterson, 1957.

Festinger, L. The psychological effects of insufficient rewards. *Amer. Psychologist,* 1961, *16,* 1–11.

Festinger, L., and Aronson, E. The arousal and reduction of dissonance in social contexts. In Cartwright, D., and Zander, A. (eds.) *Group Dynamics.* (2nd ed.) Evanston, Ill.: Row, Peterson, 1960, pp. 214–231.

Festinger, L., and Katz, D. (eds.) *Research methods in the behavioral sciences.* New York: Dryden, 1953.

Festinger, L., Schachter, S., and Back, K. *Social pressures in informal groups.* New York: HarperCollins, 1950.

Fiedler, F. E. Assumed similarity measures as predictors of team effectiveness. *J. abnorm. soc. Psychol.,* 1954, *49,* 381–388.

Fiedler, F. E. *Leader attitudes and group effectiveness.* Urbana: University of Illinois Press, 1958.

Fiedler, F. E., Warrington, W. G., and Blaisdell, F. J. Unconscious attitudes as correlates of sociometric choice in a social group. *J. abnorm. soc. Psychol.,* 1952, *47,* 790–796.

Fleishman, E. A. Leadership climate, human relations, training, and supervisory behavior. *Personnel Psychol.,* 1953, *6,* 205–222.

Fleishman, E. A. A leader behavior description for industry. In Stogdill, R. M., and Coons, A. E. (eds.) *Leader behavior: Its description and measurement.* Columbus: Ohio State University, Bureau of Business Research, Res. Monogr. No. 88, 1957a, pp. 103–119.

Fleishman, E. A. The leadership opinion questionnaire. In Stogdill, R. M., and Coons, A. E. (eds.) *Leader behavior: Its description and measurement.* Columbus: Ohio State University, Bureau of Business Research, Res. Monogr. No. 88, 1957b, pp. 120–133.

Fleishman, E. A. A relationship between incentive motivation and ability level in psychomotor performance. *J. exp. Psychol.,* 1958, *56,* 78–81.

Fleishman, E. A. *Manual for leadership opinion questionnaire.* Chicago: Science Research Associates, 1960.

Fleishman, E. A., and Harris, E. F. Patterns of leadership behavior related to employee grievances and turnover. *Personnel Psychol.*, 1962, *15*, 43–56.

Fleishman, E. A., Harris, E. F., and Burtt, H. E. *Leadership and supervision in industry*. Columbus: Ohio State University, Bureau of Educational Research, 1955.

Forer, B. R. Personality factors in occupational choice. *Educ. psychol. Measmt.*, 1953, *13*, 361–366.

Forlano, G., and Axelrod, H. C. The effect of repeated praise or blame on the performance of introverts and extroverts. *J. educ. Psychol.*, 1937, *28*, 92–100.

Forster, M. C. A study of father-son resemblance in vocational interest patterns. Unpublished master's thesis. Minneapolis: University of Minnesota, 1931.

Frank, J. D. The influence of level of performance in one task on the level of aspiration in another. *J. exp. Psychol.*, 1935, *18*, 159–171.

French, E. G. Some characteristics of achievement motivation. *J. exp. Psychol.*, 1955, *50*, 232–236.

French, E. G. Effects of interaction of achievement, motivation, and intelligence on problem solving success. *Amer. Psychologist*, 1957, *12*, 399–400 (abstract).

French, E. G. Effects of the interaction of motivation and feedback on task performance. In Atkinson, J. W. (ed.) *Motives in fantasy, action, and society*. New York: Van Nostrand Reinhold, 1958, pp. 400–408.

French, J. R. P., Jr. Field experiments: Changing group productivity. In Miller, J. G. (ed.) *Experiments in social process: A symposium on social psychology*. New York: McGraw-Hill, 1950.

French, J. R. P., Jr., Israel, J., and Ås, D. An experiment on participation in a Norwegian factory. *Hum. Relat.*, 1960, *13*, 3–19.

French, R. L. Sociometric measures in relation to individual adjustment and group performance among naval recruits. *Amer. Psychologist*, 1949, *4*, 262 (abstract).

Freud, S. *Civilization and its discontents*. London: Hogarth Press, 1930.

Freyd, M. The personalities of the socially and the mechanically inclined. *Psychol. Monogr.*, 1924, *33*, No. 4 (entire issue 151).

Friedmann, E. A., and Havighurst, R. J. *The meaning of work and retirement.* Chicago: University of Chicago Press, 1954.

Fryer, D. Significance of interest for vocational prognosis. *Ment. Hyg., N.Y.,* 1924, *8,* 466-505.

Fryer, D. Interest and ability in educational guidance. *J. educ. Research,* 1927, *16,* 27-39.

Fryer, D. *The measurement of interests in relation to human adjustment.* Troy, Mo.: Holt, Rinehart & Winston, 1931.

Gadel, M. S., and Kriedt, P. H. Relationship of aptitude, interest, performance, and job satisfaction of IBM operators. *Personnel Psychol.,* 1952, *5,* 207-212.

Gagné, R. M., and Fleishman, E. A. *Psychology and human performance.* Troy, Mo.: Holt, Rinehart & Winston, 1959.

Galinsky, M. D. Personality development and vocational choice of clinical psychologists and physicists. *J. counsel. Psychol.,* 1962, *9,* 299-305.

Gebhard, M. E. The effect of success and failure on the attractiveness of activities as a function of experience, expectation, and need. *J. exp. Psychol.,* 1948, *38,* 371-388.

Gengerelli, J. A. The principle of maxima and minima in animal learning. *J. comp. Psychol.,* 1931, *11,* 193-236.

Georgopoulos, B. S., Mahoney, G. M., and Jones, N. W. A path-goal approach to productivity. *J. appl. Psychol.* 1957, *41,* 345-353.

Gewirtz, H. B. Generalization of children's preferences as a function of reinforcement and task similarity. *J. abnorm. soc. Psychol.,* 1959, *58,* 111-118.

Gibb, C. A. Leadership. In Lindzey, G. (ed.) *Handbook of social psychology.* Vol. II. Reading, Mass.: Addison-Wesley, 1954, pp. 877-920.

Gibb, J. R. The effects of group size and of threat reduction upon creativity in a problem-solving situation. *Amer. Psychologist,* 1951, *6,* 324 (abstract).

Giese, W. J., and Ruter, H. W. An objective analysis of morale. *J. appl. Psychol.,* 1949, *33,* 421-427.

Gilbreth, F. B., and Gilbreth, L. M. *Fatigue study.* New York: Macmillan, 1919.

Gilchrist, E. P. The extent to which praise and reproof affect a pupil's work. *Sch. and Soc.*, 1916, *4*, 872-874.

Ginzberg, E., Ginsburg, S. W., Axelrod, S., and Herma, J. L. *Occupational choice.* New York: Columbia University Press, 1951.

Goldstein, K. *Human nature in the light of psychopathology.* Cambridge, Mass.: Harvard University Press, 1940.

Gouldner, A. W. Cosmopolitans and locals: Toward an analysis of latent social roles—I. *Admin. Sci. Quart.*, 1957, *2*, 281-306.

Gross, C. R. An observational analysis of supervisory behavior. Unpublished master's thesis. East Lansing: Michigan State University, 1956.

Guest, R. H. Job enlargement: a revolution in job design. *Personnel Admin.*, 1957, *20*(2), 9-16.

Guion, R. M. Industrial morale (A symposium) 1. The problem of terminology. *Personnel Psychol.*, 1958, *11*, 59-64.

Gurin, G., Veroff, J., and Feld, S. *Americans view their mental health.* New York: Basic Books, 1960.

Gustad, J. W. Vocational interests and Q-L scores on the A. C. E. *J. appl. Psychol.*, 1951, *35*, 164-168.

Hackman, J. R., and Oldham, G. R. *Work redesign.* Reading, Mass.: Addison-Wesley, 1980.

Haire, M. Industrial social psychology. In Lindzey, G. (ed.) *Handbook of social psychology.* Reading, Mass.: Addison-Wesley, 1954, pp. 1104-1123.

Hall, O. M. Attitudes and unemployment: A comparison of the opinions and attitudes of employed and unemployed men. *Arch. Psychol.*, 1934, *25*, No. 165.

Halpin, A. W. The leader behavior and effectiveness of aircraft commanders. In Stogdill, R. M., and Coons, A. E. (eds.) *Leader behavior: Its description and measurement.* Columbus: Ohio State University, Bureau of Business Research, Res. Monogr. No. 88, 1957, pp. 52-64.

Halpin, A. W., and Winer, B. J. A factorial study of the leader behavior descriptions. In Stogdill, R. M., and Coons, A. E. (eds.) *Leader behavior: Its description and measurement.* Columbus: Ohio State University, Bureau of Business Research, Res. Monogr. No. 88, 1957, pp. 39-51.

Hamid ud-Din, M. The relationship between job performance and job satisfaction. *Dissert. Abstr.*, 1953, *13*, 343-435 (Abstract).

Harding, F. D., and Bottenberg, R. A. Effect of personal characteristics on relationships between attitudes and job performance. *J. appl. Psychol.*, 1961, *45*, 428-430.

Hariton, T. Conditions influencing the effects of training foremen in human relations principles. Unpublished doctoral dissertation. Ann Arbor: University of Michigan, 1951.

Harlow, H. F. Mice, monkeys, men, and motives. *Psychol. Rev.*, 1953, *60*, 23-32.

Harlow, H. F., Harlow, M. K., and Meyer, D. R. Learning motivated by a manipulation drive. *J. exp. Psychol.*, 1950, *40*, 228-234.

Harrell, T. W., and Harrell, M. S. Army General Classification Test scores for civilian occupations. *Educ. psychol. Measmt.*, 1945, *5*, 229-239.

Harrison, R. Cumulative communality cluster analysis of workers' job attitudes. *J. appl. Psychol.*, 1961, *45*, 123-125.

Hartman, R., and Dashiell, J. F. An experiment to determine the relation of interests to abilities. *Psychol. Bull.*, 1919, *16*, 259-262.

Havemann, E., and West, P. S. *They went to college: The college graduate in America today.* Orlando, Fla.: Harcourt Brace Jovanovich, 1952.

Hebb, D. O. *The organization of behavior.* New York: Wiley, 1949.

Heider, F. Attitudes and cognitive organization. *J. Psychol.*, 1946, *21*, 107-112.

Heider, F. *The psychology of interpersonal relations.* New York: Wiley, 1958.

Helson, H. Adaptation-level as frame of reference for prediction of psychophysical data. *Amer. J. Psychol.*, 1947, *60*, 1-29.

Hemphill, J. K. *Group dimensions: A manual for their measurement.* Columbus: Ohio State University, Bureau of Business Research, Res. Monogr. No. 87, 1956.

Hemphill, J. K., and Coons, A. E. Development of the leader behavior description questionnaire. In Stogdill, R. M., and Coons, A. E. (eds.) *Leader behavior: Its description and measurement.* Columbus: Ohio State University, Bureau of Business Research, Res. Monogr. No. 88, 1957, pp. 6-38.

Henderson, H. L. The relationship between interests of fathers and sons and sons' identification with fathers. Unpublished doctoral dissertation. New York: Columbia University, Teachers' College, 1958.

Hendrick, I. Work and the pleasure principle. *Psychoanalytic Quart.*, 1943, *12*, 311–329.

Henry, W. E. The business executive: the psychodynamics of a social role. *Amer. J. Sociol.*, 1949, *54*, 286–291.

Heron, A. R. *Why men work.* Stanford, Calif.: Stanford University Press, 1948.

Heron, A. A psychological study of occupational adjustment. *J. appl. Psychol.*, 1952, *36*, 385–387.

Heron, A. Satisfaction and satisfactoriness: Complementary aspects of occupational adjustment. *Occup. Psychol.*, 1954, *28*, 140–153.

Heron, A. Personality and occupational adjustment: A cross-validation study. *Canad. J. Psychol.*, 1955, *9*, 15–20.

Herzberg, F., Mausner, B., Peterson, R. O., and Capwell, D. F. *Job attitudes: Review of research and opinion.* Pittsburgh, Penn.: Psychological Service of Pittsburgh, 1957.

Herzberg, F., Mausner, B., and Snyderman, B. *The motivation to work.* (2nd ed.) New York: Wiley, 1959.

Hewitt, D., and Parfit, J. A note on working morale and size of group. *Occup. Psychol.*, 1953, *27*, 38–42.

Hickson, D. J. Motives of workpeople who restrict their output. *Occup. Psychol.*, 1961, *35*, 110–121.

Hill, J. M. M., and Trist, E. L. A consideration of industrial accidents as a means of withdrawal from the work situation. *Hum. Relat.*, 1953, *6*, 357–380.

Hill, W. F. Activity as an autonomous drive. *J. comp. physiol. Psychol.*, 1956, *49*, 15–19.

Hoffman, L. R. Similarity of personality: A basis for interpersonal attraction? *Sociometry*, 1958, *21*, 300–308.

Hoffman, L. R. Homogeneity of member personality and its effect on group problem-solving. *J. abnorm. soc. Psychol.*, 1959, *58*, 27–32.

Homans, G. C. *The human group.* Orlando, Fla.: Harcourt Brace Jovanovich, 1950.

Homans, G. C. *Social behavior: Its elementary forms*. Orlando, Fla.: Harcourt Brace Jovanovich and New York: World, 1961.

Hoppe, F. Erfolg und Misserfolg. *Psychol. Forsch.*, 1930, *14*, 1-62.

Hoppock, R. *Job satisfaction*. New York: HarperCollins, 1935.

Hsee, K. Elastic justification: Affective influences on monetary decision making. Unpublished doctoral dissertation, Yale University, 1993.

Hull, C. L. *Principles of behavior*. New York: Appleton-Century, 1943.

Hull, C. L. *Essentials of behavior*. New Haven: Yale University Press, 1951.

Hurlock, E. B. The value of praise and reproof as incentives for children. *Arch. Psychol.*, 1924, *11*, No. 71.

Hurlock, E. B. An evaluation of certain incentives used in school work. *J. educ. Psychol.*, 1925, *16*, 145-159.

Hurlock, E. B. The use of group rivalry as an incentive. *J. abnorm. soc. Psychol.*, 1927, *22*, 278-290.

Isen, A. M. Positive affect, cognitive processes, and social behavior. In Berkowitz, L. (ed.) *Advances in experimental social psychology*, 20, San Diego, Calif.: Academic Press, 1987.

Israeli, N. Distress in the outlook of Lancashire and Scottish unemployed. *J. appl. Psychol.*, 1935, *19*, 67-69.

Jackson, D. N., and Messick, S. Content and style in personality assessment. *Psychol. Bull.*, 1958, *55*, 243-252.

Jackson, J. M. The effect of changing the leadership of small work groups. *Hum. Relat.*, 1953, *6*, 25-44.

Jackson, J. M. Reference group processes in a formal organization. *Sociometry*, 1959, *22*, 307-327.

Jacobson, E. Foreman-steward participation practices and worker attitudes in a unionized factory. Unpublished doctoral dissertation. Ann Arbor: University of Michigan, 1951.

James, W. *The principles of psychology*. Troy, Mo.: Holt, Rinehart & Winston, 1890.

Jaques, E. *Measurement of responsibility: A study of work, payment, and individual capacity*. Cambridge, Mass.: Harvard University Press, 1956.

Jaques, E. *Equitable payment*. New York: Wiley, 1961.

Jenkins, W. O. A review of leadership studies with particular reference to military problems. *Psychol. Bull.*, 1947, *44*, 54-79.

Jenson, P. G., and Kirchner, W. K. A rational answer to the question, "Do sons follow their fathers' occupations?" *J. appl. Psychol.*, 1955, *39*, 419-421.

Johanson, A. M. The influence of incentive and punishment upon reaction-time. *Arch. Psychol.*, 1922, *8*, No. 54.

Johnson, E. E. The role of motivational strength in latent learning. *J. comp. physiol. Psychol.*, 1952, *45*, 526-530.

Jones, S. C., and Vroom, V. H. Division of labor and performance under cooperative and competitive conditions. *J. abnorm. soc. Psychol.*, 1964, *68*, 313-320.

Jucknat, M. Leistung, Anspruchsniveau and Selbstbewusstsein. *Psychol. Forsch.*, 1937, *22*, 89-179.

Jurgenson, C. E. What do job applicants want? *Personnel*, 1949, *25*, 352-355.

Kagan, J., and Berkun, M. The reward value of running activity. *J. comp. physiol. Psychol.*, 1954, *47*, 108.

Kahn, R. L. Human relations on the shop floor. In Hugh-Jones, E. M. (ed.) *Human relations and modern management.* Amsterdam: North-Holland, 1958.

Kahn, R. L. Productivity and job satisfaction. *Personnel Psychol.*, 1960, *13*, 275-287.

Kahn, R. L., and Katz, D. Leadership practices in relation to productivity and morale. In Cartwright, D., and Zander, A. (eds.) *Group Dynamics.* (2nd ed.) Evanston, Ill.: Row, Peterson, 1960, pp. 554-570.

Kahneman, D., Slovic, P., and Tversky, A. (eds.) *Judgment under uncertainty: Heuristics and biases.* New York: Cambridge University Press, 1982.

Kanfer, R. *Motivation theory and industrial and organizational psychology.* In Dunnette, M. D., and Hough L. M. (eds.) *Handbook of industrial and organizational psychology.* Vol. 1. Palo Alto, Calif.: Consulting Psychologists Press, 1990, pp. 75-170.

Karsten, A. Psychische Sättigung. *Psychol. Forsch.*, 1928, *10*, 142-254.

Kates, S. L. Rorschach responses related to vocational interests and job satisfaction. *Psychol. Monogr.*, 1950, *64*, No. 3 (entire issue 309).

Katz, D. Morale and motivation in industry. In Dennis, W. (ed.) *Current trends in industrial psychology.* Pittsburgh, Penn.: University of Pittsburgh Press, 1949, pp. 145-171.

Katz, D. Satisfactions and deprivations in industrial life. In Kornhauser, A., Dubin, R., and Ross, A. M. (eds.) *Industrial conflict.* New York: McGraw-Hill, 1954, pp. 86-106.

Katz, D., and Braly, K. Racial stereotypes of 100 college students. *J. abnorm. soc. Psychol.*, 1933, *28*, 280-290.

Katz, D., and Kahn, R. L. *The social psychology of organizations.* New York: Wiley, 1966.

Katz, D., Maccoby, N., Gurin, G., and Floor, L. G. *Productivity, supervision, and morale among railroad workers.* Ann Arbor: University of Michigan, Survey Research Center, Institute for Social Research, 1951.

Katz, D., Maccoby, N., and Morse, N. C. *Productivity, supervision, and morale in an office situation.* Ann Arbor: University of Michigan, Institute for Social Research, 1950.

Katzell, R. A. Industrial psychology. In *Annual review of psychology.* Vol. 8. Palo Alto, Calif.: Annual Reviews, 1957, pp. 237-268.

Katzell, R. A., Barrett, R. S., and Parker, T. C. Job satisfaction, job performance, and situational characteristics. *J. appl. Psychol.*, 1961, *45*, 65-72.

Kaufmann, H. Task performance, expected performance, and responses to failure as functions of imbalance in the self-concept. Unpublished doctoral dissertation. Philadelphia: University of Pennsylvania, 1962.

Kaustler, D. H. A study of the relationship between ego-involvement and learning. *J. Psychol.*, 1951, *32*, 225-230.

Kay, E., French, J. R. P., Jr., and Meyer, H. H. *A study of the performance appraisal interview.* New York: General Electric Co., 1962.

Keller, F. S. Studies in International Morse Code I. A new method of teaching code reception. *J. appl. Psychol.*, 1943, *27*, 407-415.

Kelley, H. H., and Shapiro, M. M. An experiment on conformity to group norms where conformity is detrimental to group achievement. *Amer. soc. Rev.*, 1954, *19*, 667-677.

Kelly, E. L., and Fiske, D. W. The prediction of success in the VA training program in clinical psychology. *Amer. Psychologist,* 1950, *5,* 395-406.

Kennedy, J. E., and O'Neill, H. E. Job content and workers' opinions. *J. appl. Psychol.,* 1958, *42,* 372-375.

Kephart, N. C. Visual skills and labor turnover. *J. appl. Psychol.,* 1948, *32,* 51-55.

Kerr, W. A. On the validity and reliability of the job satisfaction tear ballot. *J. appl. Psychol.,* 1948, *32,* 275-281.

Kerr, W. A., Koppelmeir, G., and Sullivan, J. J. Absenteeism, turnover, and morale in a metals fabrication factory. *Occup. Psychol.,* 1951, *25,* 50-55.

King, I., and Adelstein, M. The permanence of interests and their relation to abilities. *Sch. and Soc.,* 1917, *6,* 359-360.

Kipnis, D. McB. Interaction between members of bomber crews as a determinant of sociometric choice. *Hum. Relat.,* 1957, *10,* 263-270.

Kitson, H. D. Investigation of vocational interest among workers. *Psychol. Clinic,* 1930, *19,* 48-52.

Knapp, R. H., and Goodrich, H. B. *The origins of American scientists.* Chicago: University of Chicago Press, 1952.

Komarovsky, M. *The unemployed man and his family: The effect of unemployment upon the status of the man in fifty-nine families.* New York: The Dryden Press, 1940.

Kornhauser, A. W. Some business applications of a mental alertness test. *J. Personnel Res.,* 1922, *1,* 103-121.

Kornhauser, A. W. *Mental health of the industrial worker: A Detroit study.* New York: Wiley, 1965.

Kornhauser, A. W., and Sharp, A. A. Employee attitudes: suggestions from a study in a factory. *Personnel J.,* 1932, *10,* 393-404.

Krech, D., and Crutchfield, R. S. *Theory and problems of social psychology.* New York: McGraw-Hill, 1948.

Kriedt, P. H., and Gadel, M. S. Prediction of turnover among clerical workers. *J. appl. Psychol.,* 1953, *37,* 338-340.

Kroger, R., and Louttit, C. M. The influence of father's occupation on the vocational choices of high school boys. *J. appl. Psychol.,* 1935, *19,* 203-212.

Kuder, G. F. *Kuder preference record—occupational.* Chicago: Science Research Associates, 1959.

Kuder, G. F. *Revised manual for the Kuder Preference Record.* Chicago: Science Research Associates, 1946.

Kuhlen, R. G. Needs, perceived need satisfaction opportunities, and satisfaction with occupation. *J. appl. Psychol.,* 1963, *47,* 56–64.

Kuo, Z. Y. The nature of unsuccessful acts and their order of elimination in animal learning. *J. comp. Psychol.,* 1922, *2,* 1–27.

Lantz, B. Some dynamic aspects of success and failure. *Psychol. Monogr.,* 1945, *59,* No. 1 (entire issue 271).

Lasswell, H. D. Morale. In Seligman, E. R. A., and Johnson, A. (eds.) *Encyclopedia of the social sciences.* Vol. 10. New York: Macmillan, 1948, pp. 640–642.

Latham, G. P., and Locke, E. A. Goal setting: A motivational technique that works. *Org. Dyn.,* 1979, *8,* 68–80.

Lawler, E. E. III. *Motivation in work organizations.* Pacific Grove, CA: Brooks/Cole, 1973.

Lawler, E. E., and Porter, L. W. Perceptions regarding management compensation. *Industr. Relat.,* 1963, *3,* 41–49.

Lawrence, L. C., and Smith, P. C. Group decision and employee participation. *J. appl. Psychol.,* 1955, *39,* 334–337.

Lawshe, C. H., and Nagle, B. F. Productivity and attitude toward supervision. *J. appl. Psychol.,* 1953, *37,* 159–162.

Lazarsfeld, P. An unemployed village. *Charact. and Personal.,* 1932, *1,* 147–151.

Lazarus, R. S., and Eriksen, C. W. Effects of failure stress upon skilled performance. *J. exp. Psychol.,* 1952, *43,* 100–105.

Leavitt, H. J. Some effects of certain communication patterns on group performance. *J. abnorm. soc. Psychol.,* 1951, *46,* 38–50.

Lecky, P. *Self-consistency: A theory of personality.* New York: Island, 1945.

Lehman, H. C., and Witty, P. A. Sex differences in vocational attitudes. *J. appl. Psychol.,* 1936, *20,* 576–585.

Lewin, K. *A dynamic theory of personality.* New York: McGraw-Hill, 1935.

Lewin, K. *Principles of topological psychology.* New York: McGraw-Hill, 1936.

Lewin, K. The conceptual representation and the measurement of psychological forces. *Contr. psychol. Theory.* Durham, N.C.: Duke University Press, 1938, *1*, No. 4.

Lewin, K. Group decision and social change. In Newcomb, T. M., and Hartley, E. L. (eds.) *Readings in social psychology.* Troy, Mo.: Holt, Rinehart & Winston, 1947, pp. 330–344.

Lewin, K. *Field theory in social science.* (D. Cartwright, ed.) New York: HarperCollins, 1951.

Lewin, K., Dembo, T., Festinger, L., and Sears, P. S. Level of aspiration. In Hunt, J. McV. (ed.) *Personality and the behavior disorders.* Vol. I. New York: Ronald, 1944, pp. 333–378.

Lewin, K., Lippitt, R., and White, R. K. Patterns of aggressive behavior in experimentally created social climates. *J. soc. Psychol.,* 1939, *10*, 271–299.

Lewis, H. B., and Franklin, M. An experimental study of the role of the ego in work. II. The significance of task-orientation in work. *J. exp. Psychol.,* 1944, *34*, 195–215.

Lewis, M., and Cairns, R. B. Some non-decremental effects of effort. Unpublished manuscript. Philadelphia: University of Pennsylvania, Department of Psychology, 1961.

Libo, L. M. *Measuring group cohesiveness.* Ann Arbor: University of Michigan, Research Center for Group Dynamics, Institute for Social Research, 1953.

Lieberman, S. The effects of changes in roles on the attitudes of role occupants. *Hum. Relat.,* 1956, *9*, 385–402.

Likert, R. Effective supervision: An adaptive and relative process. *Personnel Psychol.,* 1958a, *11*, 317–332.

Likert, R. Measuring organizational performance. *Harvard Business Rev.,* 1958b, *36*, 41–50.

Likert, R. Motivational approach to management development. *Harvard Business Rev.,* 1959a, *37*, 75–82.

Likert, R. A motivational approach to a modified theory of organization and management. In Haire, M. (ed.) *Modern organizational theory: A symposium of the foundation for research on human behavior.* New York: Wiley, 1959b, pp. 184–217.

Likert, R. *New patterns of management.* New York: McGraw-Hill, 1961.

Likert, R., and Willits, J. M. *Morale and agency management.*

Vol. 1. *Morale—the mainspring of management.* Hartford: Life Insurance Sales Research Bureau, 1940.

Livesay, T. M. Test intelligence and future vocation of high school seniors in Hawaii. *J. appl. Psychol.*, 1941, *25*, 679-686.

Logan, F. A. A micromolar approach to behavior theory. *Psychol. Rev.*, 1956, *63*, 63-73.

Lopez, F. M. A psychological analysis of the relationship of role consensus and personality consensus to job satisfaction and job performance. Unpublished doctoral dissertation. New York: Columbia University, 1962.

Lott, A. J., Schopler, J. H., and Gibb, J. R. Effects of feeling-oriented and task-oriented feedback upon defensive behavior in small problem-solving groups. *Amer. Psychologist*, 1955, *10*, 335-336 (abstract).

Lowell, E. L. The effect of need for achievement on learning and speed of performance. *J. Psychol.*, 1952, *33*, 31-40.

Luce, R. D. Psychological studies of risky decision making. In Strother, G. B. (ed.) *Social science approaches to business behavior.* Belmont, Calif.: Dorsey Press, 1962, 141-161.

Lyman, E. L. Occupational differences in the value attached to work. *Amer. J. Sociol.*, 1955, *61*, 138-144.

McArthur, C., and Stevens, L. B. The validation of expressed interests as compared with inventoried interests: A fourteen-year follow-up. *J. appl. Psychol.*, 1955, *39*, 184-189.

McClelland, D. C. *Personality.* New York: Sloane, 1951.

McClelland, D. C. Some social consequences of achievement motivation. In Jones, M. R. (ed.) *Nebraska symposium on motivation.* Lincoln: University of Nebraska Press, 1955, pp. 41-64.

McClelland, D. C. The calculated risk: An aspect of scientific performance. In Taylor, C. W. (ed.) *Research conference on the identification of creative scientific talent.* Salt Lake City: University of Utah Press, 1956, pp. 96-110.

McClelland, D. C. Methods of measuring human motivation. In Atkinson, J. W. (ed.) *Motives in fantasy, action, and society.* New York: Van Nostrand Reinhold, 1958a, pp. 7-42.

McClelland, D. C. Risk taking in children with high and low need for achievement. In Atkinson, J. W. (ed.) *Motives in fantasy, action, and society.* New York: Van Nostrand Reinhold, 1958b, pp. 306-321.

McClelland, D. C. *The achieving society.* New York: Van Nostrand Reinhold, 1961.

McClelland, D. C. On the psychodynamics of creative physical scientists. In Gruber, H. E., Terrell, G., and Wertheimer, M. (eds.) *Contemporary approaches to creative thinking; a symposium held at the University of Colorado.* New York: Atherton Press, 1962.

McClelland, D. C., and Apicella, F. S. Reminiscence following experimentally induced failure. *J. exp. Psychol.,* 1947, *37,* 159-169.

McClelland, D. C., Atkinson, J. W., Clark, R. A., and Lowell, E. L. *The achievement motive.* New York: Appleton-Century-Crofts, 1953.

McClelland, D. C., Rindlisbacher, A., and deCharms, R. Religious and other sources of parental attitudes toward independence training. In McClelland, D. C. (ed.) *Studies in motivation.* New York: Appleton-Century-Crofts, 1955, pp. 389-397.

McDougall, W. *Outline of psychology.* New York: Charles Scribner's Sons, 1923.

McGee, R. K. Response style as a personality variable: By what criterion. *Psychol. Bull.,* 1962, *59,* 284-295.

McGehee, W., and Thayer, P. W. *Training in business and industry.* New York: Wiley, 1961.

McGregor, D. Getting effective leadership in the industrial organization. *Advanc. Mgmt,* 1944, *9,* 148-153.

McGregor, D. *The human side of enterprise.* New York: McGraw-Hill, 1960.

McKinney, F. Certain emotional factors in learning and efficiency. *J. gen. Psychol.,* 1933, *9,* 101-116.

McNulty, J. E. Some economic aspects of business bureaucracy. Unpublished manuscript. Philadelphia: University of Pennsylvania, Wharton School of Finance and Commerce, 1962.

MacPherson, S. J., Dees, V., and Grindley, G. C. The effect of knowledge of results on learning and performance. II. Some characteristics of very simple skills. *Quart. J. exp. Psychol.,* 1948, *1,* 68-78.

Mace, C. A. Incentives: Some experimental studies. *Indust. Health Res. Bd. Report No. 72.* London: H. M. Stationery Office, 1935.

Mahone, C. H. Fear of failure and unrealistic vocational aspiration. *J. abnorm. soc. psychol.*, 1960, *60*, 253–261.

Mahoney, G. M. The psychological components of morale in an industrial situation. Unpublished doctoral dissertation. Montreal: McGill University, 1949.

Maier, N. R. F. *Frustration: The study of behavior without a goal.* New York: McGraw-Hill, 1949.

Maier, N. R. F. The quality of group decisions as influenced by the discussion leader. *Hum. Relat.*, 1950, *3*, 155–174.

Maier, N. R. F. *Principles of human relations: Applications to management.* New York: Wiley, 1952.

Maier, N. R. F. An experimental test of the effect of training on discussion leadership. *Human Relat.*, 1953, *6*, 161–173.

Maier, N. R. F. *Psychology in industry.* (2nd ed.) Boston: Houghton Mifflin, 1955.

Maier, N. R. F. Frustration theory: Restatement and extension. *Psychol. Rev.*, 1956, *63*, 370–388.

Maier, N. R. F. Maier's law. *Amer. Psychologist*, 1960, *15*, 208–212.

Maier, N. R. F. *Problem-solving discussions and conferences: Leadership methods and skills.* New York: McGraw-Hill, 1963.

Maier, N. R. F., Glaser, N. M., and Klee, J. B. Studies of abnormal behavior in the rat. III. The development of behavior fixations through frustration. *J. exp. Psychol.*, 1940, *26*, 521–546.

Maier, N. R. F., and Hayes, J. J. *Creative management.* New York: Wiley, 1962.

Maier, N. R. F., and Hoffman, L. R. Using trained "developmental" discussion leaders to improve further the quality of group decisions. *J. appl. Psychol.*, 1960, *44*, 247–251.

Maier, N. R. F., and Hoffman, L. R. Group decision in England and the United States. *Personnel Psychol.*, 1962, *15*, 75–87.

Maier, N. R. F., and Klee, J. B. Studies of abnormal behavior in the rat. VII. The permanent nature of abnormal fixations and their relation to convulsive tendencies. *J. exp. Psychol.*, 1941, *29*, 380–389.

Maier, N. R. F., and Klee, J. B. Studies of abnormal behavior in the rat: XVII. Guidance versus trial and error in the alteration of habits and fixations. *J. Psychol.*, 1945, *19*, 133-163.

Maller, J. B. Cooperation and competition. *Teach. Coll. Contr. Educ.*, 1929, No. 384.

Mann, F. C. A study of work satisfactions as a function of the discrepancy between inferred aspirations and achievement. Unpublished doctoral dissertation. Ann Arbor: University of Michigan, 1953.

Mann, F. C. Studying and creating change: A means to understanding social organization. In Arensberg, C. M. and others (eds.) *Research in industrial human relations.* New York: HarperCollins, 1957, pp. 146-147.

Mann, F. C., and Hoffman, L. R. *Automation and the worker.* Troy, Mo.: Holt, Rinehart & Winston, 1960.

Mann, F. C., Indik, B. P., and Vroom, V. H. *The productivity of work groups.* Ann Arbor: University of Michigan, Institute for Social Research, Survey Research Center, 1963.

Mann, R. D. A review of the relationship between personality and performance in small groups. *Psychol. Bull.*, 1959, *56*, 241-270.

Manzer, C. W. The effect of knowledge of output on muscular work. *J. exp. Psychol.*, 1935, *18*, 80-90.

March, J. G., and Simon, H. A. *Organizations.* New York: Wiley, 1958.

Marriott, R. Size of working group and output. *Occup. Psychol.*, 1949, *23*, 47-57.

Marriott, R., and Denerley, R. A. A method of interviewing used in studies of workers' attitudes: II. Validity of the method and discussion of the results. *Occup. Psychol.*, 1955, *29*, 69-81.

Marrow, A. J. Goal tensions and recall (I and II). *J. gen. Psychol.*, 1938, *19*, 3-35, 37-64.

Marschak, T. Centralization and decentralization in economic organizations. *Econometrica*, 1959, *27*, 399-430.

Marvick, D. *Career perspectives in a bureaucratic setting.* Ann Arbor: University of Michigan Press, 1954.

Marzolf, S. S. Interests and choice of teaching field. *Illinois Acad. Sci. Trans.*, 1946, *39*, 107-113.

Maslow, A. H. A theory of human motivation. *Psychol. Rev.*, 1943, *50*, 370-396.

Maslow, A. H. *Motivation and personality*. New York: Harper-Collins, 1954.

Maslow, A. H. Deficiency motivation and growth motivation. In Jones, M. R. (ed.) *Nebraska symposium on motivation*. Lincoln: University of Nebraska Press, 1955, pp. 1-30.

Mathewson, S. B. *Restriction of output among unorganized workers*. New York: Viking Penguin, 1931.

Mayo, E. *The social problems of an industrial civilization*. Boston: Harvard University, Graduate School of Business Administration, 1945.

Merrihue, W. V., and Katzell, R. A. ERI—Yardstick of employee relations. *Harvard Business Rev.*, 1955, *33*, 91-99 (Nov.-Dec.).

Merton, R. K. The machine, the worker, and the engineer. *Science*, 1947, *105*, 79-84.

Metzner, H., and Mann, F. Employee attitudes and absences. *Personnel Psychol.*, 1953, *6*, 467-485.

Meyer, H. H., Walker, W. B., and Litwin, G. H. Motive patterns and risk preferences associated with entrepreneurship. *J. abnormal soc. Psychol.*, 1961, *63*, 570-574.

Miller, D. C. Economic factors in the morale of college-trained adults. *Amer. J Sociol.*, 1941, *47*, 139-156.

Miller, D. C., and Form, W. H. *Industrial sociology*. New York: HarperCollins, 1951.

Miller, N. E., and Dollard, J. *Social learning and imitation*. New Haven: Yale University Press, 1941.

Misumi, J. Experimental studies on "group dynamics" in Japan. *Psychologia*, 1959, *2*, 229-235.

Montague, E. K. The role of anxiety in serial rote learning. *J. exp. Psychol.*, 1953, *45*, 91-96.

Montgomery, K. C. The role of the exploratory drive in learning. *J. comp. physiol. Psychol.*, 1954, *47*, 60-64.

Morrison, R. L. Self-concept implementation in occupational choices. *J. counsel. Psychol.*, 1962, *9*, 255-260.

Morse, N. C. *Satisfactions in the white-collar job*. Ann Arbor: University of Michigan, Institute for Social Research, Survey Research Center, 1953.

Morse, N. C., and Reimer, E. The experimental change of a major organizational variable. *J. abnorm. soc. Psychol.*, 1956, *52*, 120-129.

Morse, N. C., and Weiss, R. S. The function and meaning of work and the job. *Amer. sociol. Rev.*, 1955, *20*, 191-198.

Mossin, A. C. *Selling performance and contentment in relation to school background.* New York: Columbia University, Teachers' College, Bureau of Publications, 1949.

Mosteller, F., and Nogee, P. An experimental measurement of utility. *J. pol. Econ.*, 1951, *59*, 371-404.

Mowrer, O. H. A stimulus-response analysis of anxiety and its role as a reinforcing agent. *Psychol. Rev.*, 1939, *46*, 553-565.

Mulder, M. Communication structure, decision structure, and group performance. *Sociometry*, 1960, *23*, 1-14.

Murray, H. A. *Explorations in personality.* New York: Oxford University Press, 1938.

Nachmann, Barbara. Childhood experience and vocational choice in law, dentistry, and social work. *J. counsel. Psychol.*, 1960, *7*, 243-250.

Naylor, J. C., Pritchard, R. D., and Ilgen, D. R. *A theory of behavior in organizations.* New York: Academic Press, 1980.

Nelson, E. Fathers' occupations and student vocational choices. *Sch. and Soc.*, 1939, *50*, 572-576.

Newcomb, T. M. Motivation in social behavior. In *Current theory and research in motivation.* Lincoln: University of Nebraska Press, 1953.

Newcomb, T. M. The prediction of interpersonal attraction. *Amer. Psychologist*, 1956, *11*, 575-586.

Newcomb, T. M. *The acquaintance process.* Troy, Mo.: Holt, Rinehart & Winston, 1961.

Newcomer, Mabel. *The big business executive: The factors that made him, 1900-1950.* New York: Columbia University Press, 1955.

Nietzsche, F. *Der Wille zur Macht.* Leipzig: C. G. Naumann, 1901.

Olds, J. The influence of practice on the strength of secondary approach drives. *J. exp. Psychol.*, 1953, *46*, 232-236.

Orne, M. T. On the social psychology of the psychological experiment: with particular reference to demand characteristics and their implications. *Amer. Psychologist*, 1962, *17*, 776-783.

Ovsiankina, M. Die Wiederaufnahme unterbrochener Handlungen. *Psychol. Forsch.*, 1928, *11*, 302–379.

Patchen, M. Absence and employee feelings about fair treatment. *Personnel Psychol.*, 1960, *13*, 349–360.

Patchen, M. *The choice of wage comparisons.* Englewood Cliffs, N.J.: Prentice-Hall, 1961.

Paterson, D. G., and Darley, J. G. *Men, women, and jobs.* Minneapolis: University of Minnesota Press, 1936.

Paterson, D. G., and Stone, C. H. Dissatisfaction with life work among adult workers. *Occupations*, 1942, *21*, 219–221.

Patrick, J. R. Studies in rational behavior and emotional excitement. II. The effect of emotional excitement on rational behavior in human subjects. *J. comp. Psychol.*, 1934, *18*, 153–195.

Payne, R. B., and Hauty, G. T. Effect of psychological feedback upon work decrement. *J. exp. Psychol.*, 1955, *50*, 343–351.

Peak, H. Attitude and motivation. In Jones, M. R. (ed.) *Nebraska symposium on motivation.* Lincoln: University of Nebraska Press, 1955, pp. 149–188.

Peak, H. The effect of aroused motivation on attitudes. *J. abnorm. soc. Psychol.*, 1960, *61*, 463–468.

Pellegrin, R. J., and Coates, C. H. Executives and supervisors: Contrasting definitions of career success. *Admin. Sci. Quart.*, 1957, *1*, 506–517.

Pelz, D. C. Leadership within a hierarchical organization. *J. soc. Issues*, 1951, *7*(3), 49–55.

Pelz, D. C. Some social factors related to performance in a research organization. *Admin. Sci. Quart.*, 1956, *1*, 310–325.

Pelz, D. C. Self-determination and self-motivation in relation to performance: A study of interaction effects. Unpublished manuscript. Ann Arbor: University of Michigan, Institute for Social Research, 1961.

Perrow, C. Pfeffer slips. Letter to the editor, *Acad. of Mgt. Rev., 19*, forthcoming.

Petty, R. E., and Caccioppo, J. T. *Communication and persuasion: Central and peripheral routes to attitude change.* New York: Springer-Verlag, 1986.

Pfeffer, J. Barrier to the advance of organizational science: Paradigm development as a dependent variable. *Acad. of Mgt. Rev.*, 1993, *18*, 599-620.

Pintner, R. A comparison of interests, abilities and attitudes. *J. abnorm. soc. Psychol.*, 1933, *27*, 351-357.

Porter, L. W. Job attitudes in management: I. Perceived deficiencies in need fulfillment as a function of job level. *J. appl. Psychol.*, 1962, *46*, 375-384.

Porter, L. W. Job attitudes in management: II. Perceived importance of needs as a function of job level. *J. appl. Psychol.*, 1963, *47*, 141-148.

Porter, L. W., and Lawler, E. E. III. *Managerial attitudes and performance.* Belmont, Calif.: Dorsey Press, 1968.

Postman, L. The history and present status of the law of effect. *Psychol. Bull.*, 1947, *44*, 489-563.

Preston, M. G., and Baratta, P. An experimental study of the auction-value of an uncertain outcome. *Amer. J. Psychol.*, 1948, *61*, 183-193.

Preston, M. G., Peltz, W. L., Mudd, E. H., and Froscher, H. B. Impressions of personality as a function of marital conflict. *J. abnorm. soc. Psychol.*, 1952, *47*, 326-336.

Pryer, M. W., and Bass, B. M. Some effects of feedback on behavior in groups. *Sociometry*, 1959, *22*, 56-63.

Putnam, M. L. Improving employee relations. *Personnel J.*, 1930, *8*, 314-325.

Rambo, W. W. The construction and analysis of a leadership behavior rating form. *J. appl. Psychol.*, 1958, *42*, 409-415.

Raymond, C. K. Anxiety and task as determiners of verbal performance. *J. exp. Psychol.*, 1953, *46*, 120-124.

Recktenwald, L. N. Attitudes toward occupations before and after vocational information. *Occupations*, 1946, *24*, 220-223.

Reiss, A. J. (with Duncan, O. D., Hatt, P. K., and North, C. C.) *Occupations and social status.* New York: Free Press of Glencoe, 1961.

Reynolds, L. G. *The structure of labor markets.* New York: Harper-Collins, 1951.

Richards, C. B., and Dobryns, H. F. Topography and culture: The case of the changing cage. *Hum. Org.*, Spring 1957, *16*, 16-20.

Riesman, D. *The lonely crowd.* New Haven: Yale University Press, 1950.

Roach, D. E. Dimensions of employee morale. *Personnel Psychol.,* 1958, *11,* 419–431.

Roe, A. A Rorschach study of a group of scientists and technicians. *J. consult. Psychol.,* 1946, *10,* 317–327.

Roe, A. Analysis of group Rorschachs of biologists. *J. proj. Tech.,* 1949, *13,* 25–43.

Roe, A. Analysis of group Rorschachs of physical scientists. *J. proj. Tech.,* 1950, *14,* 385–398.

Roe, A. A psychological study of eminent physical scientists. *Genet. Psychol. Monogr.,* 1951a, *43,* 121–235.

Roe, A. A psychological study of eminent biologists. *Psychol. Monogr.,* 1951b, *65,* No. 14 (entire issue 331).

Roe, A. A study of imagery in research scientists. *J. Pers.,* 1951c, *19,* 459–470.

Roe, A. *The making of a scientist.* New York: Dodd, Mead, 1953a.

Roe, A. A psychological study of eminent psychologists and anthropologists, and a comparison with biological and physical scientists. *Psychol. Monogr.,* 1953b, *67,* No. 2 (entire issue 352).

Roe, A. *The psychology of occupations.* New York: Wiley, 1956.

Roethlisberger, F. J., and Dickson, W. J. *Management and the worker.* Cambridge, Mass.: Harvard University Press, 1939.

Roff, M. Intra-family resemblances in personality characteristics. *J. Psychol.,* 1950, *30,* 199–227.

Rosen, M. Valence, expectancy, and dissonance reduction in the prediction of goal striving. Paper presented at the meeting of the Eastern Psychological Association, Philadelphia, Apr. 7, 1961.

Rosenberg, M. J. Cognitive structure and attitudinal affect. *J. abnorm. soc. Psychol.,* 1956, *53,* 367–372.

Rosenberg, M. *Occupations and values.* Glencoe, Ill.: The Free Press, 1957.

Rosenzweig, S. An experimental study of "repression" with special reference to need-persistive and ego-defensive reactions to frustration. *J. exp. Psychol.,* 1943, *32,* 64–74.

Ross, I. C., and Zander, A. Need satisfactions and employee turnover. *Personnel Psychol.,* 1957, *10,* 327–338.

Rotter, J. B. The role of the psychological situation in determining the direction of human behavior. In Jones, M. R. (ed.) *Nebraska symposium on motivation.* Lincoln: University of Nebraska Press, 1955, pp. 245-268.

Rotter, J. B., Fitzgerald, B. J., and Joyce, J. N. A comparison of some objective measures of expectancy. *J. abnorm. soc. Psychol.,* 1954, *49,* 111-114.

Roy, D. Quota restriction and gold bricking in a machine shop. *Amer. J. Sociol.,* 1952, *57,* 427-442.

Rundquist, E. A., and Sletto, R. F. *Personality in the depression: A study in the measurement of attitudes.* Minneapolis: University of Minnesota Press, 1936.

Russell, W. A. Retention of verbal material as a function of motivating instructions and experimentally-induced failure. *J. exp. Psychol.,* 1952, *43,* 207-216.

Sagi, P. C., Olmstead, D. W., and Atelsek, F. Predicting maintenance of membership in small groups. *J. abnorm. soc. Psychol.,* 1955, *51,* 308-311.

Sanford, F. H. *Authoritarianism and leadership.* Philadelphia: Institute for Research in Human Relations, 1950.

Sawatsky, J. C. Psychological factors in industrial organization affecting employee stability. *Canad. J. Psychol.,* 1951, *5,* 29-38.

Schachter, S., Ellertson, N., McBride, D., and Gregory, D. An experimental study of cohesiveness and productivity. *Hum. Relat.,* 1951, *4,* 229-238.

Schachter, S., Willerman, B., Festinger, L., and Hyman, R. Emotional disruption and industrial productivity. *J. appl. Psychol.,* 1961, *45,* 201-213.

Schaffer, R. H. Job satisfaction as related to need satisfaction in work. *Psychol. Monogr.,* 1953, *67,* No. 14 (entire issue 364).

Schultz, M. K., and Angoff, W. H. The development of new scales for the aptitude and advanced tests of the Graduate Record Examinations. *J. educ. Psychol.,* 1956, *47,* 285-294.

Schutz, W. C. What makes groups productive? *Hum. Relat.,* 1955, *8,* 429-465.

Schutz, W. C. *FIRO: A three-dimensional theory of interpersonal behavior.* Troy, Mo.: Holt, Rinehart & Winston, 1958.

Schwartz, M. M., Jenusaitis, E., and Stark, H. Motivational factors among supervisors in the utility industry. *Personnel Psychol.*, 1963, *16*, 45–53.

Scodel, A., Ratoosh, P., and Minas, J. S. Some personality correlates of decision-making under conditions of risk. *Behav. Sci.*, 1959, *4*, 19–28.

Scott, W. G. *Human relations in management: A behavioral science approach.* Homewood, Ill.: Irwin, 1962.

Sears, R. R. Initiation of the repression sequence by experienced failure. *J. exp. Psychol.*, 1937, *20*, 570–580.

Seashore, H. G. Validation of the Study of Values for two vocational groups at the college level. *Educ. psychol. Measmt.*, 1947, *7*, 757–763.

Seashore, S. *Group cohesiveness in the industrial work group.* Ann Arbor: University of Michigan, Institute for Social Research, Survey Research Center, 1954.

Seeman, M. A comparison of general and specific leader behavior descriptions. In Stogdill, R. M., and Coons, A. E. (eds.) *Leader behavior: Its description and measurement.* Columbus: Ohio State University, Bureau of Business Research, Res. Monogr. No. 88, 1957, pp. 86–102.

Shaw, M. E. Some effects of problem complexity upon problem solution efficiency in different communication nets. *J. exp. Psychol.*, 1954, *48*, 211–217.

Sirota, D. Job performance as related to attitudes, motivation and understanding. Unpublished research report. Ann Arbor: University of Michigan, Institute for Social Research, 1958 (Mimeo).

Sirota, D. Some effects of promotional frustration on employees' understanding of, and attitudes toward, management. *Sociometry*, 1959, *22*, 273–278.

Sisson, E. D. An analysis of the occupational aims of college students. *Occupations*, 1938, *17*, 211–215.

Slater, Carol W. Some factors associated with internalization of motivation towards occupational role performance. Unpublished doctoral dissertation. Ann Arbor: University of Michigan, 1959.

Small, L. Personality determinants of vocational choice. *Psychol. Monogr.*, 1953, *67*, No. 1 (entire issue 351).

Smith, A. *An inquiry into the nature and causes of the wealth of nations.* London: Printed for W. Strahan and T. Cadell, 1776.

Smith, M. The temperamental factor in industry. *Human Factor,* London, 1936, *10,* 301-314.

Smith, P. C. The prediction of individual differences in susceptibility to industrial monotony. *J. appl. Psychol.,* 1955, *39,* 322-329.

Smith, P. C., Kendall, L. M., and Hulin, C. L. *The measurement of satisfaction in work and retirement.* Chicago: Rand McNally, 1969.

Smith, P. C., and Lem, C. Positive aspects of motivation in repetitive work: Effects of lot size upon spacing of voluntary work stoppages. *J. appl. Psychol.,* 1955, *39,* 330-333.

Smode, A. F. Learning and performance in a tracking task under two levels of achievement information feedback. *J. exp. Psychol.,* 1958, *56,* 297-304.

Solomon, R. L. The influence of work on behavior. *Psychol. Bull.,* 1948, *45,* 1-40.

Spector, A. J. Expectations, fulfillment, and morale. *J. abnorm. soc. Psychol.,* 1956, *52,* 51-56.

Speer, G. S., and Jasker, L. The influence of occupational information on occupational goals. *Occupations,* 1949, *28,* 15-17.

Spence, K. W., and Farber, I. E. Conditioning and extinction as a function of anxiety. *J. exp. Psychol.,* 1953, *45,* 116-119.

Spence, K. W., and Farber, I. E. The relation of anxiety to differential eyelid conditioning. *J. exp. Psychol.,* 1954, *47,* 127-134.

Spence, K. W., and Taylor, J. Anxiety and strength of the UCS as determiners of the amount of eyelid conditioning. *J. exp Psychol.,* 1951, *42,* 183-188.

Stagner, R., Flebbe, D. R., and Wood, E. F. Working on the railroad: A study of job satisfaction. *Personnel Psychol.,* 1952, *5,* 293-306.

Staw, B. M., and Barsade, S. G. Affect and managerial performance: A test of the sadder-but-wiser vs. happier-and-smarter hypotheses. *Admin. Sci. Quart.,* 1993, *38,* 304-331.

Staw, B. M., Bell, N. E., and Clausen, J. A. The dispositional approach to job attitudes: A lifetime longitudinal test. *Admin. Sci. Quart.,* 1986, *31,* 56-77.

Stephenson, W. *The study of behavior: Q-technique and its methodology.* Chicago: University of Chicago Press, 1953.

Stewart, N. AGCT scores of army personnel grouped by occupation. *Occupations,* 1947, *26,* 5-41.

Stogdill, R. M. Personal factors associated with leadership: A survey of the literature. *J. Psychol.,* 1948, *25,* 35-71.

Stone, C. H. The personality factor in vocational guidance. *J. abnorm. soc. Psychol.,* 1933, *28,* 274-275.

Stotland, E., and others. The effects of group expectations and self-esteem upon self-evaluation. *J. abnorm. soc. Psychol.,* 1957, *54,* 55-63.

Stotland, E., and Zander, A. Effects of public and private failure on self-evaluation. *J. abnorm. soc. Psychol.,* 1958, *56,* 223-229.

Stouffer, S. A., and Lazarsfeld, P. F. *Research memorandum on the family in the depression.* New York: Social Science Research Council, 1937.

Stouffer, S. A., and others. *The American soldier: Adjustment during army life.* Vol. 1. Princeton: Princeton University Press, 1949.

Strodtbeck, F. L. Family interaction, values, and achievement. In McClelland, D. C., Baldwin, A. L., Bronfenbrenner, U., and Strodtbeck, F. L. (eds.) *Talent and society.* New York: Van Nostrand Reinhold, 1958, pp. 195-232.

Strodtbeck, F. L., and Hook, L. H. The social dimensions of a twelve man jury table. *Sociometry,* 1961, *24,* 397-415.

Strong, E. K., Jr. A vocational interest test. *Educ. Rec.,* 1929, *10,* 59-68.

Strong, E. K., Jr. *Vocational interests of men and women.* Stanford, Calif.: Stanford University Press, 1943.

Strong, E. K., Jr. Satisfactions and interests. *Amer. Psychologist,* 1958, *13,* 449-456.

Super, D. E. Occupational level and job satisfaction. *J. appl. Psychol.,* 1939, *23,* 547-564.

Super, D. E. Vocational adjustment: Implementing a self-concept. *Occupations,* 1951, *30,* 88-92.

Super, D. E. A theory of vocational development. *Amer. Psychol.,* 1953, *8,* 185-190.

Super, D. E. *The psychology of careers.* New York: HarperCollins, 1957.

Super, D. E. Some unresolved issues in vocational development research. *Personnel Guid. J.*, 1961, pp. 11-15.

Super, D. E., and others. *Vocational development: A framework for research*. New York: Columbia University, Teachers' College, Bureau of Publications, 1957.

Tageson, C. F. *The relationship of self-perceptions to realism of vocational preference*. Washington, D.C.: Catholic University of America Press, 1960.

Tannenbaum, A. S., and Allport, F. H. Personality structure and group structure: An interpretive study of their relationship through an event-structure hypothesis. *J. abnorm. soc. Psychol.*, 1956, *53*, 272-280.

Taylor, F. W. *The principles of scientific management*. New York: HarperCollins, 1911.

Taylor, J. A. The relationship of anxiety to the conditioned eyelid response. *J. exp. Psychol.*, 1951, *41*, 81-92.

Taylor, J. A. A personality scale of manifest anxiety. *J. abnorm. soc. Psychol.*, 1953, *48*, 285-290.

Taylor, J. A., and Spence, K. W. The relationship of anxiety level to performance in serial learning. *J. exp. Psychol.*, 1952, *44*, 61-64.

Terman, L. M. Scientists and non-scientists in a group of 800 gifted men. *Psychol. Monogr.*, 1954, *68*, No. 7, 1-44.

Terman, L. M., and Oden, M. H. *The gifted group at mid-life: Thirty-five years' follow-up of the superior child*. Stanford, Calif.: Stanford University Press, 1959.

Terman, L. M. and others. *Genetic studies of genius, Vol. I: Mental and physical traits of a thousand gifted children*. Stanford, Calif.: Stanford University Press, 1925.

Thompson, G. G., and Hunnicutt, C. W. The effect of repeated praise or blame on the work achievement of "introverts" and "extroverts." *J. educ. Psychol.*, 1944, *35*, 257-266.

Thompson, M. E. An experimental investigation of the gradient of reinforcement in maze learning. *J. exp. Psychol.*, 1944, *34*, 390-403.

Thompson, W. A. Eleven years after graduation. *Occupations*, 1939, *17*, 709-714.

Thorndike, E. L. *Animal intelligence: experimental studies.* New York: Macmillan, 1911.

Thorndike, E. L. Early interests: Their permanence and relation to abilities. *Sch. and Soc.,* 1917, *5,* 178-179.

Thorndike, E. L. The law of effect. *Amer. J. Psychol.,* 1927, *39,* 212-222.

Thorndike, E. L. Workers' satisfactions. *Occupations,* 1935, *13,* 704-706.

Thorndike, R. L., and Hagen, E. *Ten thousand careers.* New York: Wiley, 1959.

Thrall, R. M., Coombs, C. H., and Davis, R. L. (eds.) *Decision processes.* New York: Wiley, 1954.

Tilgher, A. *Work, what it has meant to men through the ages.* Orlando, Fla.: Harcourt Brace Jovanovich, 1930.

Tolman, E. C. *Purposive behavior in animals and men.* New York: Century, 1932.

Tolman, E. C. Cognitive maps in rats and men. *Psychol. Rev.,* 1948, *55,* 189-208.

Tolman, E. C. Principles of purposive behavior. In Koch, S. (ed.) *Psychology: A study of a science.* Vol. 2. New York: McGraw-Hill, 1959, pp. 92-157.

Traxler, A. E., and McCall, W. C. Some data on the Kuder Preference Record. *Educ. psychol. Measmt.,* 1941, *1,* 253-268.

Trist, E. L., and Bamforth, K. W. Some social psychological consequences of the longwall method of coal-getting. *Hum. Relat.,* 1951, *4,* 3-38.

Troland, L. T. *The fundamentals of human motivation.* New York: Van Nostrand Reinhold, 1928.

Trow, D. B. Autonomy and job satisfaction in task-oriented groups. *J. abnorm. soc. Psychol.,* 1957, *54,* 204-209.

Tsai, L. S. The laws of minimum effort and maximum satisfaction in animal behavior. *Psychol. Abstr.,* 1932, *6,* No. 4329 (abstract).

Turner, A. N., and Miclette, A. L. Sources of satisfaction in repetitive work. *Occup. Psychol.,* 1962, *36,* 215-231.

Twery, R., Schmid, J., Jr., and Wrigley, C. Some factors in job satisfaction: A comparison of three methods of analysis. *Educ. psychol. Measmt.,* 1958, *18,* 189-202.

Tyler, L. E. The relationship of interests to abilities and reputation among first grade children. *Educ. psychol. Measmt.*, 1951, *11*, 255–264.

Uhrbrock, R. S. Interest as an indication of ability. *J. appl. Psychol.*, 1926, *10*, 487–501.

Uhrbrock, R. S. Attitudes of 4,430 employees. *J. soc. Psychol.*, 1934, *5*, 365–377.

Van Zelst, R. H. Worker popularity and job satisfaction. *Personnel Psychol.*, 1951, *4*, 405–412.

Van Zelst, R. H. Sociometrically selected work teams increase production. *Personnel Psychol.*, 1952, *5*, 175–185.

Van Zelst, R. H., and Kerr, W. A. Workers' attitudes toward merit rating. *Personnel Psychol.*, 1953, *6*, 159–172.

Veblen, T. *The theory of the leisure class.* New York: Viking Penguin, 1935.

Vernon, H. M., and Wyatt, S. *On the extent and effects of variety in repetitive work.* Industrial Fatigue Research Board Report No. 26. London: H. M. Stationery Office, 1924.

Vernon, P. E., and Allport, G. W. A test for personal values. *J. abnorm. soc. Psychol.*, 1931, *26*, 231–248.

Veroff, J., Atkinson, J. W., Feld, S. C., and Gurin, C. The use of thematic apperception to assess motivation in a nationwide interview study. *Psychol. Monogr.*, 1960, *74*, No. 12 (entire issue 499).

Viteles, M. S. Selecting cashiers and predicting length of service. *J. Personnel Res.*, 1924, *2*, 467–473.

Viteles, M. S. *Industrial psychology.* New York: W.W. Norton, 1932.

Viteles, M. S. *Motivation and morale in industry.* New York: W.W. Norton, 1953.

Von Neumann, J., and Morgenstern, O. *Theory of games and economic behavior.* (2nd ed.) Princeton: Princeton University Press, 1947.

Vroom, V. H. Some personality determinants of the effects of participation. *J. abnorm. soc. Psychol.*, 1959a, *59*, 322–327.

Vroom, V. H. Projection, negation, and the self concept. *Hum. Relat.*, 1959b, *12*, 335–344.

Vroom, V. H. *Some personality determinants of the effects of participation.* Englewood Cliffs, N.J.: Prentice-Hall, 1960a.

Vroom, V. H. The effects of attitudes on perception of organizational goals. *Hum. Relat.*, 1960b, *13*, 229-240.

Vroom, V. H. The self-concept—a balance-theoretical treatment. Unpublished manuscript. Philadelphia: University of Pennsylvania, 1961.

Vroom, V. H. Ego-involvement, job satisfaction, and job performance. *Personnel Psychol.*, 1962, *15*, 159-177.

Vroom, V. H. Improvising and muddling through. In Bedeian, A. (ed.) *Management laureates*. Vol. 3. 1993, pp. 257-284.

Vroom, V. H., and Jago, A. G. *The new leadership: Managing participation in organizations.* Englewood Cliffs, N.J.: Prentice-Hall, 1988.

Vroom, V. H., and Maier, N. R. F. Industrial social psychology. In *Annual review of psychology.* Vol. 12. Palo Alto, Calif.: Annual Reviews, 1961, pp. 413-446.

Vroom, V. H., and Mann, F. C. Leader authoritarianism and employee attitudes. *Personnel Psychol.*, 1960, *13*, 125-140.

Vroom, V. H., and Yetton, P. W. *Leadership and decision making.* Pittsburgh, Penn.: University of Pittsburgh Press, 1973.

Walker, C. R. The problem of the repetitive job. *Harvard Business Rev.*, 1950, *28*(3), 54-58.

Walker, C. R. Work methods, working conditions, and morale. In Kornhauser, A., Dubin, R., and Ross, A. M. (eds.) *Industrial conflict.* New York: McGraw-Hill, 1954.

Walker, C. R., and Guest, R. H. *The man on the assembly line.* Cambridge, Mass.: Harvard University Press, 1952.

Walker, J., and Marriott, R. A study of some attitudes to factory work. *Occup. Psychol.*, 1951, *25*, 181-191.

Walker, K. F. A study of occupational stereotypes. *J. appl. Psychol.*, 1958, *42*, 122-124.

Wallin, P., and Clark, A. Marital satisfaction and husbands' and wives' perception of similarity in their preferred frequency of coitus. *J. abnorm. soc. Psychol.*, 1958, *57*, 370-373.

Walster, E. Post-decisional re-evaluation of alternatives: Regret and dissonance reduction. Unpublished doctoral dissertation. Stanford, Calif.: Stanford University, 1963.

Walton, R. E. From control to commitment in the workplace. *Harv. Bus. Rev.*, 1985, *63*, 77-84.

Warner, W. L., Meeker, M., and Eells, K. *Social class in America.* Chicago: Science Research Associates, 1949.

Waters, R. H. The principle of least effort in learning. *J. gen. Psychol.,* 1937, *16,* 3-20.

Webb, W. B., and Hollander, E. P. Comparison of three morale measures: A survey, pooled group judgments, and self-evaluations. *J. appl. Psychol.,* 1956, *40,* 17-20.

Weber, M. *The Protestant ethic and the spirit of capitalism.* (Parsons, T., trans.) New York: Charles Scribner's Sons, 1930.

Weitz, J., and Nuckols, R. C. The validity of direct and indirect questions in measuring job satisfaction. *Personnel Psychol.,* 1953, *6,* 487-494.

Wendt, H. W. Motivation, effort, and performance. In McClelland, D. C. (ed.) *Studies in motivation.* New York: Appleton-Century-Crofts, 1955, pp. 448-459.

Weschler, I. R., and Bernberg, R. E. Indirect methods of attitude measurement. *Int. J. Opin. Attitude Res.,* 1950, *4,* 209-228.

Weston, S. B., and English, H. B. The influence of the group on psychological test scores. *Amer. J. Psychol.,* 1926, *37,* 600-601.

Wherry, R. J. An orthogonal re-rotation of the Baehr and Ash studies of the S R A employee inventory. *Personnel Psychol.,* 1954, *7,* 365-380.

Wherry, R. J. Industrial morale (A symposium). 4. Factor analysis of morale data: Reliability and validity. *Personnel Psychol.,* 1958, *11,* 78-89.

White, R. W. Motivation reconsidered: The concept of competence. *Psychol. Rev.,* 1959, *66,* 297-333.

White, R. K., and Lippitt, R. *Autocracy and democracy: An experimental inquiry.* New York: HarperCollins, 1960.

Whyte, W. F. *Money and motivation: An analysis of incentives in industry.* New York: HarperCollins, 1955.

Whyte, W. H. *The organization man.* New York: Simon & Schuster, 1956.

Wickens, D. D. The effect of competition on the performance of tasks of differing degrees of difficulty. *Psychol. Bull.,* 1942, *39,* 595 (abstract).

Wickert, F. R. Turnover, and employees' feelings of ego-involvement in the day-to-day operations of a company. *Personnel Psychol.*, 1951, *4*, 185-197.

Williams, J. M. *Human aspects of unemployment and relief.* Chapel Hill: University of North Carolina Press, 1933.

Williams, M. An experimental study of intellectual control under stress and associated Rorschach factors. *J. consult. Psychol.*, 1947, *11*, 21-29.

Williamson, E. G. *How to counsel students.* New York: McGraw-Hill, 1939.

Winterbottom, M. R. The relation of need for achievement to learning experiences in independence and mastery. In Atkinson, J. W. (ed.) *Motives in fantasy, action, and society.* New York: Van Nostrand Reinhold, 1958, 453-478.

Wolfle, D., and Oxtoby, T. Distributions of ability of students specializing in different fields. *Science*, 1952, *116*, 311-314.

Worthy, J. C. Organizational structure and employee morale. *Amer. sociol. Rev.*, 1950, *15*, 169-179.

Woytinsky, W. S. *Three aspects of labor dynamics.* Washington, D.C.: Social Science Research Council, 1942.

Wright, H. F. The influence of barriers upon strength of motivation. *Contr. psychol. Theory.* Durham, N.C.: Duke University Press, 1937, *1*, No. 3.

Wyatt, S. (assisted by Frost, L., and Stock, F. G. L.) *Incentives in repetitive work: A practical experiment in a factory.* Industrial Health Research Board, Report No. 69. London: H. M. Stationery Office, 1934.

Wyatt, S., and Fraser, J. A. (assisted by Stock, F. G. L.) *The comparative effects of variety and uniformity in work.* Industrial Fatigue Research Board Report No. 52. London: H. M. Stationery Office, 1928.

Wyatt, S., Fraser, J. A., and Stock, F. G. L. *The effects of monotony in work.* Industrial Fatigue Research Board Report No. 56. London: H. M. Stationery Office, 1929.

Yerkes, R. M. (ed.) *Psychological examining in the U.S. Army.* Washington, D.C.: U.S. Government Printing Office, 1921.

Yerkes, R. M., and Dodson, J. D. The relation of strength of stimulus to rapidity of habit-formation. *J. comp. neurol. Psychol.*, 1908, *18*, 459-482.

Young, K. *Social psychology.* (2nd ed.) New York: Appleton-Century-Crofts, 1944.

Yum, K. S. Student preferences in divisional studies and their preferential activities. *J. Psychol.,* 1942, *13*, 193–200.

Zaleznik, A., Christensen, C. R., and Roethlisberger, F. J. *The motivation, productivity, and satisfaction of workers; a prediction study.* Boston: Harvard University, Graduate School of Business Administration, 1958.

Zander, A., and Cohen, A. R. Attributed social power and group acceptance: A classroom experimental demonstration. *J. abnorm. soc. Psychol.,* 1955, *51*, 490–492.

Zeaman, D. Response latency as a function of the amount of reinforcement. *J. exp. Psychol.,* 1949, *39*, 466–483.

Zeigarnik, B. Das Behalten erledigter und unerledigter Handlungen. *Psychol. Forsch.,* 1927, *9*, 1–85.

Zeleny, L. D. Sociometry of morale. *Amer. sociol. Rev.,* 1939, *4*, 799–808.

Name Index

Subject Index

A

Ability: as codeterminant of performance, 230-238; job satisfaction and use of, 164-168; measurement of, 3; occupational attainment and, 83-84; occupational choice and, 80, 82-83, 110-111; occupational preference and, 81-82; tasks requiring possessed, 289-290; tasks requiring valued, 285-289

Absenteeism: gender differences in, 210-211; job repetitiveness and, 156; job satisfaction and, 209-211, 218

Acceptance, 143-145

Accident rates, 211-212, 218

Achievement motive: analysis of, 25; economic growth and, 69; interaction of intelligence with, 234; occupational preferences and, 68-70, 107; occupational status and, 75

Activity, feelings of well-being and, 40-41

Affiliation motive: analysis of, 25; occupational status and, 75-76

Age, effects of effort on valence and, 43

Allport-Vernon-Lindzey Study of Values, 24; description of, 66, 67, 68; use of, 70-71

American Council on Education (ACE) scores, 81

Anxiety, performance impairment due to, 242-244

Aptitude: measurement of, 3; for various occupations, 84

Army General Classification Test, 82, 83

Arousal, assumptions about motive, 27-28

Assumed Similarity Between Opposites (ASO), 255-256

Attitudes: determinants of, 18-19; effect of change in work roles on, 79-80; gender differences in, 210-211; measurement of, 24, 118-119; role in decision making and subordinate, 134; supervisory consideration and subordinate, 131; work groups and similarity of, 142-143

Authoritarianism, supervisory, 125

Automation, 53. *See also* Specialization

Autonomy, job performance and, 261, 262